S0-BDP-240

$ 9.98

A Guide to the

ARCHITECTURE
OF LONDON

A Guide to the
ARCHITECTURE OF LONDON

Edward Jones &
Christopher Woodward

THAMES AND HUDSON

Pevsner

First published in Great Britain in 1983 by
George Weidenfeld and Nicolson Ltd
Second edition published in the United States
of America in 1992 by Thames and Hudson Inc.,
500 Fifth Avenue, New York, New York 10110

Library of Congress Catalog Card No. 91-65313

Original design by Tamasin Cole
Second edition layout by Martin Richards
and Lucy Allen

Filmset by Keyspools Ltd, Golborne, Lancashire
Printed in Italy.

Author's Acknowledgements

Our thanks are due first to Alexandra
Boyle who proposed that we write this
book, and who then guided it through its
earlier stages.

We are indebted to Sir Nikolaus Pevsner,
without whose *Buildings of England: London*, vols 1 and 2, this book would have
taken at least another decade to prepare,
and to Sir John Summerson, who lectured
us as students, and whose *Georgian London*
remains the most important and enjoyable work on eighteenth-century London.

We should like to thank the following
people who have offered valuable advice
and criticism: David Chipperfield, Dan
Cruickshank, Ray Head, Margaret Richardson Assistant Curator of the British
Architectural Library RIBA Drawings
Collection (and for her advice and help in
finding the illustrations for the historical
charts), Michael Robbins, Douglas Stephen, José Santos, John Winter and Bren-
dan Woods; and Hugh Chapman, Charlotte Harding, and Rosemary Weinstein of
the Museum of London.

We are especially grateful to Kenneth
Frampton for his generous encouragement and advice.

Credit and thanks are due to Margot
Griffin who made the drawings of the
plans.

Anthea Head, Anne Morley, Veronica
Pratt and Arabella Weir patiently typed
and retyped the manuscript, and Mary
Arnold Foster helped research the historical charts.

Finally we extend our warm thanks to our
editor, Barbara Mellor, who charmingly
directed the book through its final stages,
and whose advice was always correct, and
Emma Way for her support and enthusiasm in producing the second edition.

✕ See "Further Reading" on page 427

Contents

Authors' Introduction

The reasons for writing this book are both practical and theoretical. Despite a plethora of books about London, there has not hitherto been a convenient guide documenting the city's buildings chronologically. This was our first aim. Our second was to review London's architecture comparatively and comprehensively. In the 1970s, most planners and architects could not see beyond the horizon of Modern Architecture, then widely considered the only possible pattern for the future. Since then there has been a period of reassessment within architectural theory which has brought about a wider view, in which the architecture of previous centuries is once more available as a source of models for the buildings of the present. The comprehensive redevelopments of the 1950s and '60s now appear merely to have scarred London's skyline.

In selecting buildings for inclusion in this guide, we have broadly categorized London's architecture as follows: works of excellence judged by international standards, by architects such as Hawksmoor, Nash, Soane, Butterfield and Lutyens; lesser and early works by these masters; districts, streets and squares which constitute the matrix for these outstanding buildings; engineering works which because of their scale have transformed the city more drastically than single buildings could; architecturé which is the biggest, longest or most conspicuous of its kind; and buildings which show the development of a particular type – the artist's studio, the shopping arcade and the department store, for example.

London has expanded steadily since its Roman foundation, but has always resisted systematic reconstruction in any one period (unlike say Haussman's Paris or Cerda's Barcelona). The maps below demonstrate this: drawn to the same scale, 4km by 1km (3 miles by 0·6 mile), they show an area of London from Marble Arch to Kilburn; Paris from the Arc de Triomphe to the Louvre; Barcelona, with Cerda's rectangular grid grafted onto the city's historic core; and a section of Manhattan from 21st Street to 75th Street. London is notable for its looseness of structure, and mainly residential fabric. The streets and

ondon   Paris   Barcelona   Manhattan

squares of its housing form a background to its monumental and institutional buildings.

In visiting and revisiting the buildings catalogued here, we have been continually surprised and delighted by the amazing richness of London's domestic and monumental architectural past, and horrified by the crass mindlessness of much recent work. We hope that this guide will help the reader to enjoy and understand the first, and to avoid the second.

How to use this Guide

This guide contains about 1000 *entries*: buildings, streets or areas. These are arranged by *section*. London's administrative districts, the boroughs, are very large, each with a population of about 250,000, and do not form useful or visible subdivisions. The 30km square approximating to the old administrative area of the County of London has therefore been arbitrarily divided into nine squares. The middle one nets central London, defined as the area between Shepherd's Bush to the west, the Tower of London to the east, Hampstead Heath to the north and Battersea Park to the south. This central area has been further divided into sixteen squares. The inner squares have been lettered A to P, and the outer ones Q to X. These letters correspond to the book's *sections*. Coverage of outer London is not comprehensive; only exceptional buildings and those of interest nearby are included.

Each section is introduced by a large-scale map, with the *entries* shown in black, followed by a description of the area and its historical development. The pages following contain the *entries*, arranged chronologically.

To find an *entry*, look up its name in the general index: you will find it, together with its *reference*, a letter and a number. The letter tells you its *section*, the number shows you where it is in that *section*, and is marked on the section map. To help you find a number on the map, each *entry* in the text is followed by a map reference, and, in sections A to P, a lower case letter which corresponds to the subdivisions of the section map.

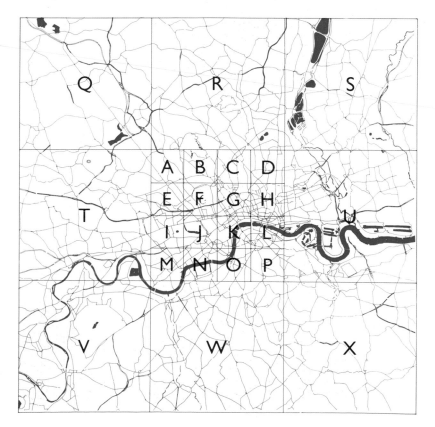

Roman and Anglo-Saxon London

Julius Caesar visited England in 54BC, but nearly a century passed before the Romans invaded in AD43, during the reign of Claudius. As a settlement London barely existed before the Roman invasion, and afterwards St Albans, Colchester, Lincoln, York and Gloucester were almost certainly more important administrative centres. But it was essential to the Romans to build roads to deploy their military strength in the new colony, and London's convenient position – at a point where the Thames could be bridged and at a navigable distance from the open sea – placed it at the centre of a monumental road system. By AD62, when the Britons of the eastern counties revolted under Boudicca, London had attained enough importance to warrant destruction, but the Roman town recovered and prospered as a centre of trade and administration. The Thames was bridged, as were the small Walbrook and Fleet rivers, and a small fort was built near Cripplegate. By 140 the town was circled by a defensive wall, which is now the main visible evidence of the Roman occupation of London. Archaeology has supplied the plan of the town, and the Museum of London H42 displays objects of everyday life.

The two centuries after Boudicca's rising were relatively peaceful, but by the end of the third century the town was menaced by Franks, Picts, Scots and Saxons. As the Roman Empire dwindled in the fourth century London declined. When the Romans withdrew in 410 the Saxons invaded, and there is no further record of London until 605, when Augustine was ordained London's first bishop.

The Anglo-Saxons were master craftsmen (see the treasures from the Sutton Hoo ship burial in the British Museum), but archaeological remains do not indicate that they were great builders. By 804, however, Bede could describe London as a flourishing trading town, and in 886 the walls were restored as a defence against repeated Danish invasions. But the next significant building was not until 1066, when Edward the Confessor's abbey at Westminster was completed, establishing London as the country's royal capital.

Roman wall at Trinity Square L2

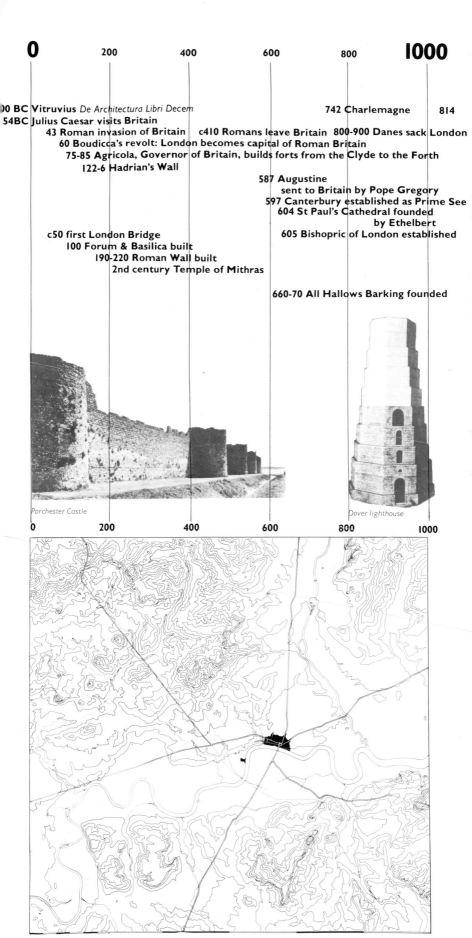

0   200   400   600   800   **1000**

00 BC **Vitruvius** *De Architectura Libri Decem*

54BC **Julius Caesar visits Britain**

43 **Roman invasion of Britain**   c410 **Romans leave Britain**   800-900 **Danes sack London**

60 **Boudicca's revolt: London becomes capital of Roman Britain**

75-85 **Agricola, Governor of Britain, builds forts from the Clyde to the Forth**

122-6 **Hadrian's Wall**

742 **Charlemagne**   814

587 **Augustine**
sent to Britain by Pope Gregory
597 **Canterbury established as Prime See**
604 **St Paul's Cathedral founded**
by Ethelbert
605 **Bishopric of London established**

c50 **first London Bridge**

100 **Forum & Basilica built**

190-220 **Roman Wall built**

2nd century Temple of Mithras

660-70 **All Hallows Barking founded**

Porchester Castle

Dover lighthouse

0   200   **400**   600   **800**   **1000**

Roman London

9

Medieval and Tudor London

The poles of late Saxon London were Westminster Abbey on marshy ground in the west, and a wooden St Paul's on Ludgate Hill in the east. In 1066 the Norman French invaded England, and their first building in London was the Tower. Started about 1078, and set on the bank of the Thames where the Roman wall met the river, it was built to awe the Saxon population, and to defend London from the east. The Normans brought a new architectural style – their heavy round-arched derivation of Romanesque – examples of which can be seen in St John's Chapel in the Tower L3, St Bartholomew the Great H3, and the much-restored old St Pancras Church G1. In 1097 William Rufus, William the Conqueror's successor, built the first Westminster Hall K5, continuing the functional separation of Westminster from the City of London (see the introduction to section K) started by Edward the Confessor. Westminster gradually became the focus of Court life, and the religious and administrative centre of the kingdom. The self-governing City, with its own cathedral, continued as a centre of trade and craft industry, as it had been under the Saxons. Retail trades and handicrafts were carried on in the small timber and plaster houses, and in the streets and markets (much as they are today in the small towns of North Africa). Transport was by boat, mule and foot.

In 1245, Henry III launched an ambitious building programme, of which the Gothic Westminster Abbey K2, and parts of the Tower remain. Earlier in the same century, royal charters had given the City of London considerable political and trading autonomy, similar to that of the contemporary free towns of France, Germany and Italy, vestiges of which remain today in the City's separate police force and the arcane rituals of its local government. The medieval guilds, the Livery Companies, exist still, with their Halls and their charitable and social activities. At the end of the fourteenth century, the establishment of the four Inns of Court, outside the City to its west, started the growing connection between Westminster and the City along the banks of the Thames.

Sixteenth-century England under the Tudors underwent sudden changes. Increased trade – the result of exploration and discovery abroad – and the burning of forests for fuel at home brought a surge of prosperity. The

Westminster Abbey K2

population of London grew fourfold, from about 50,000 in 1530 to 200,000 in 1600, while the proportion of that population living within the walls declined from two-thirds to less than half. The centre of trade remained on the banks of the Thames: the port, in the Pool of London below the bridge, was the largest in the country. Suburbs spread north from the City up Bishopsgate to Shoreditch, east towards Whitechapel and Wapping, west along the Strand, and south of the river on Bankside. Views of London, usually taken from the tower of St Mary Overie, Southwark, show it like a seaside town spreading from Westminster to the Tower along the Thames – its means of communication, drainage and water supply.

From 1509, the royal dockyards were established at Deptford and Woolwich to build men-of-war and to relieve the congestion of the medieval harbours and shipyards. Henry VIII made huge changes in the physical pattern of London: confiscated Church lands were made available for the building of royal and aristocratic palaces or the development of houses. Palaces were built or enlarged at Whitehall, Richmond, Windsor and Greenwich U2, and Wolsey's Hampton Court was confiscated. The royal hunting grounds of Hyde Park J2, Green Park J1 and St James's Park K9 were established, giving London its open, leafy centre. Between Whitehall and the City, a mile of palaces was built along the banks of the Thames: Northumberland House, the Palace of Savoy, Somerset House (from 1547), Arundel House, Essex House, Temple and Bridewell, and while none of the originals remains, their names are still in use. North of the Strand were more grand aristocratic houses, including that of the Bedford Estate on the Covent Garden. Lambeth existed at the beginning of the century, but by the end Southwark housed all the pastimes outlawed from the City: cock fighting, bear baiting, and the theatres – the Rose of 1587, the Swan, and the Globe in 1599.

The reign of Elizabeth was marked by little royal building, although the country and London rested on the continued prosperity produced by war and exploration. The culture of the Renaissance appeared first not in architecture but in the literature of Marlowe and Shakespeare. At the end of the century, Inigo Jones was twenty-seven.

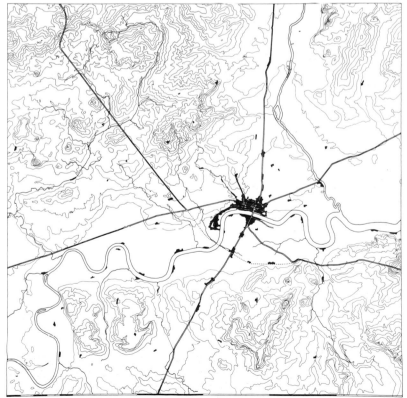

Medieval and Tudor London

11

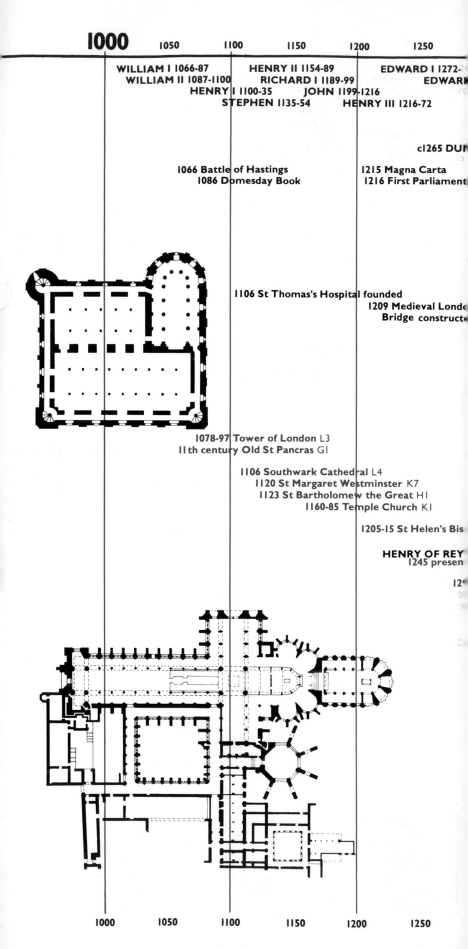

1000	1050	1100	1150	1200	1250

WILLIAM I 1066-87   HENRY II 1154-89   EDWARD I 1272-
    WILLIAM II 1087-1100   RICHARD I 1189-99   EDWARD
    HENRY I 1100-35   JOHN 1199-1216
    STEPHEN 1135-54   HENRY III 1216-72

c1265 DUN

1066 Battle of Hastings   1215 Magna Carta
    1086 Domesday Book   1216 First Parliament

1106 St Thomas's Hospital founded

1209 Medieval Lond
Bridge constructe

1078-97 Tower of London L3
11th century Old St Pancras GI

1106 Southwark Cathedral L4
1120 St Margaret Westminster K7
1123 St Bartholomew the Great HI
1160-85 Temple Church KI

1205-15 St Helen's Bis

HENRY OF REY
1245 presen

12

1000	1050	1100	1150	1200	1250

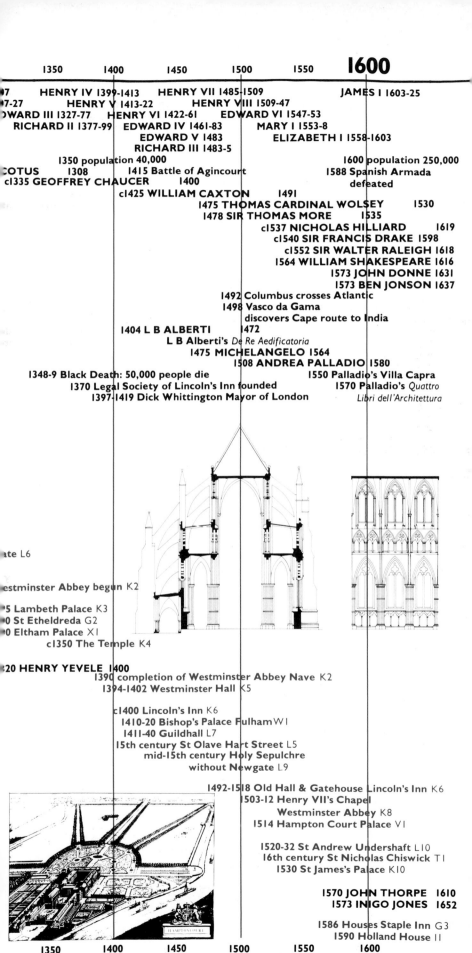

?7   **HENRY IV 1399-1413**   **HENRY VII 1485-1509**   **JAMES I 1603-25**

?7-27   **HENRY V 1413-22**   **HENRY VIII 1509-47**

DWARD III 1327-77   **HENRY VI 1422-61**   **EDWARD VI 1547-53**

RICHARD II 1377-99   **EDWARD IV 1461-83**   **MARY I 1553-8**

EDWARD V 1483   **ELIZABETH I 1558-1603**

RICHARD III 1483-5

1350 population 40,000   **1600 population 250,000**

COTUS   1308   **1415 Battle of Agincourt**   **1588 Spanish Armada**

c1335 GEOFFREY CHAUCER   1400   **defeated**

c1425 WILLIAM CAXTON   1491

1475 THOMAS CARDINAL WOLSEY   1530

1478 SIR THOMAS MORE   1535

c1537 NICHOLAS HILLIARD   1619

c1540 SIR FRANCIS DRAKE 1598

c1552 SIR WALTER RALEIGH 1618

1564 WILLIAM SHAKESPEARE 1616

1573 JOHN DONNE 1631

1573 BEN JONSON 1637

1492 Columbus crosses Atlantic

1498 Vasco da Gama

discovers Cape route to India

1404 L B ALBERTI   1472

L B Alberti's *De Re Aedificatoria*

1475 MICHELANGELO 1564

1508 ANDREA PALLADIO 1580

1348-9 Black Death: 50,000 people die   **1550 Palladio's Villa Capra**

1370 Legal Society of Lincoln's Inn founded   **1570 Palladio's** *Quattro*

1397-1419 Dick Whittington Mayor of London   *Libri dell'Architettura*

ate L6

estminster Abbey begun K2

?5 Lambeth Palace K3

?0 St Etheldreda G2

?0 Eltham Palace X1

c1350 The Temple K4

?20 HENRY YEVELE 1400

1390 completion of Westminster Abbey Nave K2

1394-1402 Westminster Hall K5

c1400 Lincoln's Inn K6

1410-20 Bishop's Palace Fulham W1

1411-40 Guildhall L7

15th century St Olave Hart Street L5

mid-15th century Holy Sepulchre

without Newgate L9

1492-1518 Old Hall & Gatehouse Lincoln's Inn K6

1503-12 Henry VII's Chapel

Westminster Abbey K8

1514 Hampton Court Palace V1

1520-32 St Andrew Undershaft L10

16th century St Nicholas Chiswick T1

1530 St James's Palace K10

1570 JOHN THORPE 1610

1573 INIGO JONES 1652

1586 Houses Staple Inn G3

1590 Holland House I1

Seventeenth-century London

By all accounts and by later standards Stuart London was not a beautiful city. It was a city of merchants, suspicious of the Crown, living mostly in ramshackle timber houses built on the medieval street pattern. With a few exceptions there was no great architecture, although master-craftsmen displayed their skill in such fine buildings as Cromwell House R4 and the College of Arms L21. Ten times larger than provincial cities like Bristol or Norwich, London was nevertheless small enough to walk across in a morning and more than adequately covered by sections K and L of this guide. The marshy land south of the river remained undeveloped except for Southwark, and London Bridge was the only permanent river crossing (and was to remain so until Westminster Bridge was built in 1738). Principal east-west transport was along the Thames, which contemporary prints show as a working river, busy with boats landing at wharfs and jetties on the north bank.

Terrible overcrowding and inadequate sanitary arrangements made the plague a constant threat. Open drains ran down the middle of most streets to issue where possible into the Thames, London's principal water supply. Royalty escaped the city's stench by retreating from the palace at Whitehall (destroyed by fire in 1698) to the many royal houses outside London – St James's Palace K10 and Hampton Court V1 to the west, and Greenwich U2, Richmond and Nonesuch to the south. Wealthy merchants withdrew to the country villages of Hampstead and Highgate. Meanwhile the theatre (the second Globe theatre was established on Bankside in 1616), bear baiting, cock fighting and public executions provided diversions for the average citizen.

The century's architecture was dominated by the work of two men, Inigo Jones and Christopher Wren. Important buildings had traditionally been produced by craftsmen in the service of State and Church. Now there was a new type of architect – men of flair or genius, who might be experts in almost anything but who were not master-craftsmen (although Jones had been apprenticed to a joiner). The diverse careers of both Jones and Wren anticipated the broad scope of learning and cultural interests in the Age of Enlightenment. Wren was a brilliant student of mathematics and law, who went on to become Professor of Astronomy at Oxford before designing his first building; Jones travelled extensively in Italy, designed masques and costumes for the theatre, and in 1601 annotated Palladio's *Quattro Libri dell'Architettura*.

Jones was the father of English Palladianism, whose few remaining buildings are mostly to be found in London. His Covent Garden Piazza K14 (1630) marked the birth of the London square, which increased in popularity as a residential type for the rest of the century. With the beginning of the Civil War in 1642 Jones's work was finished: the Commonwealth did not encourage architecture, apart from the extensive defensive earthworks surrounding London in 1643 – the last time the city was to be defended from the land.

Queen's House, Greenwich U2

The restoration of the monarchy in 1660 was followed by the Great Plague in 1665 and the Great Fire the following year. Most of the old city was destroyed, and the rebuilding presented an extraordinary opportunity for architecture and town planning. 13,200 houses, 87 churches and 44 halls of livery companies had been lost; the reoccupation of the burnt-out city was slow, the rich (apart from the aldermen) never returned, and as a result the city's westward expansion beyond the city walls was accelerated.

Many plans were made for rebuilding, mostly inspired by the avenues and *rond points* of continental examples. Wren's was the most ambitious, but none of them was realized, owing to the intricate patchwork of land ownership in the City, and the urgent need for new premises in which business could continue.

For the last forty years of the century Wren's output was prodigious. His rebuilding of the City churches and St Paul's Cathedral L27 was followed by other important buildings, and he became the dominant figure of a growing circle of classical architects. By the beginning of the following century other major talents were emerging. Wren's brilliant disciple Nicholas Hawksmoor, Sir John Vanbrugh, Thomas Archer, James Gibbs and William Kent were the chief architects of English classicism, a movement dependent on the initiative and works of Wren and Inigo Jones.

Events in this century dictated London's present form. After the Commonwealth the city was no longer threatened by invasion from the land and could therefore spread at will, and rebuilding after the Great Fire gave unprecedented opportunities for land speculation by private entrepreneurs. Speculative builders leased land from the Great Estates to build squares, the century's most significant urban innovation. Their semi-public gardens surrounded by simple brick houses combined elements of town and country in a revolutionary way, forming a strong contrast to the old city's dense and treeless network of alleys. The effects of such building were startling: by the end of the century London had been transformed from a timber-built medieval port into a classical and predominantly brick city.

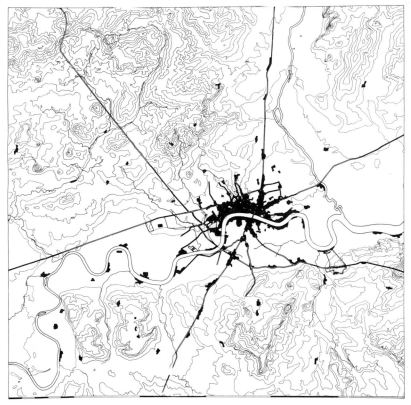

Seventeenth-century London

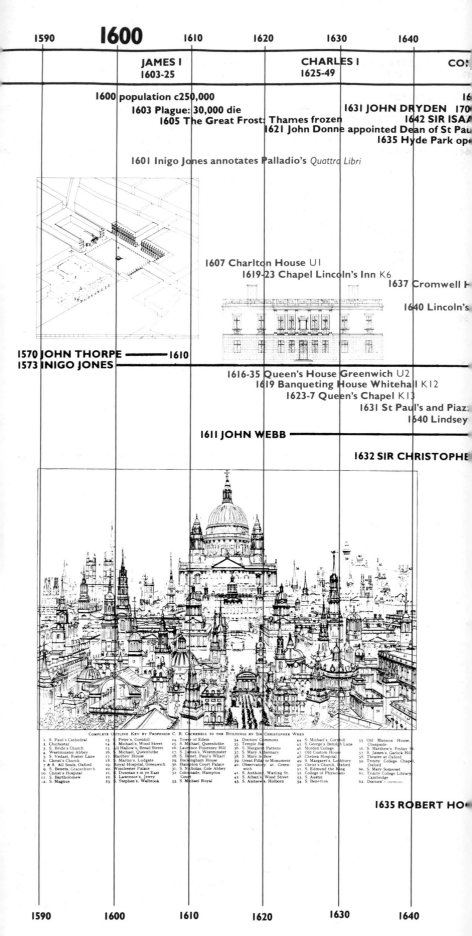

| 1590 | **1600** | 1610 | 1620 | 1630 | 1640 |

JAMES I
1603-25

CHARLES I
1625-49

CO:

1600 population c250,000

1603 Plague: 30,000 die

1605 The Great Frost: Thames frozen

1621 John Donne appointed Dean of St Pau

16

1631 JOHN DRYDEN 170

1642 SIR ISAA

1635 Hyde Park op

1601 Inigo Jones annotates Palladio's *Quattro Libri*

1607 Charlton House U1

1619-23 Chapel Lincoln's Inn K6

1637 Cromwell H

1640 Lincoln's

1570 JOHN THORPE ———— 1610
1573 INIGO JONES

1616-35 Queen's House Greenwich U2

1619 Banqueting House Whitehall K12

1623-7 Queen's Chapel K13

1631 St Paul's and Piaz

1640 Lindsey

1611 JOHN WEBB ————

1632 SIR CHRISTOPHE

COMPLETE OUTLINE KEY BY PROFESSOR C. R. COCKERELL to the Buildings by SIR CHRISTOPHER WREN

1. S. Paul's Cathedral
2. Chichester
3. S. Bride's Church
4. Westminster Abbey
5. S Vedast, Foster Lane
6. Christ's Church
7 & 8. All Souls, Oxford
9. S. Benets, Gracechurch
10. Christ's Hospital
11. S. Bartholomew
12. S. Magnus

13. S. Peter's, Cornhill
14. S. Michael's, Wood Street
15. All Hallow's, Bread Street
16. S. Michael, Queenhithe
17. Marlbro' House
18. S. Martin's, Ludgate
19. Royal Hospital, Greenwich
20. Winchester Palace
21. S. Dunstan's in ye East
22. S. Lawrence's, Jewry
23. S. Stephen's, Walbrook

24. Tower of Eden
25. S. Michael, Queenhithe
26. Laurence Pountney Hill
27. S. James's, Westminster
28. S. Benet, Paul's Wharf
29. Buckingham House
30. Hampton Court Palace
31. S. Nicholas, Cole Abbey
32. Colonnade, Hampton Court
33. S. Michael Royal

34. Doctors' Commons
35. Temple Bar
36. S. Margaret Pattens
37. S. Mary Aldermary
38. S. Mary le Bow
39. Great Pillar or Monument
40. Observatory at Greenwich
41. S. Anthony, Watling St.
42. S. Alban's, Wood Street
43. S. Andrew's, Holborn

44. S. Michael's, Cornhill
45. S. George's, Botolph Lane
46. Morden College
47. Old Custom House
48. Chelsea Hospital
49. S. Margaret's, Lothbury
50. Christ's Church, Oxford
51. S. Edmund the King
52. College of Physicians
53. S. Austin
54. S. Benet fink

55. Old Mansion House, Cheapside
56. S. Matthew's, Friday St.
57. S. James's, Garlick Hill
58. Theatre at Oxford
59. Trinity College Chapel, Oxford
60. S. Mary Somerset
61. Trinity College Library, Cambridge
62. Doctors' Commons

1635 ROBERT HO

| 1590 | 1600 | 1610 | 1620 | 1630 | 1640 |

NWEALTH **CHARLES II**   **JAMES II WILLIAM &**   **ANNE**
49-60   1660-85   **1685-88 MARY 1689-1702**   **1702-14**

pulation 350,000   1700 population c674,000
       1665 Great Plague   1680 Versailles begun   1694 Bank of England founded
EWTON   1727   1666 Great Fire: 13,200 houses burnt
650 Hampton Court, Richmond Greenwich and Windsor Palaces
to the public   1662 Royal Society founded   1698 Whitehall Palace destroyed:
648 **GRINLING GIBBONS**   1720   Court moved to St James's Palace

e R4

ields K6
50 Field Court, Gray's Inn G6
   1660 Bloomsbury Square
       1670 Leicester Square K19
       1673 Golden Square K20
          1678-88 Gray's Inn Square G6
          1680 Bedford Row G4
          1681 Soho Square K24
vent Garden K14 K15   1684 St James's Square K18
e K16   1690 Seven Dials K25
              1690 New Square K26

       1672
    1665-8 Greenwich Palace U3

REN   1723
1661-1702 Kensington Palace I2
      1670-2 St Michael Cornhill L8
      1670-3 St Vedast alias Foster L13
      1670-6 St Mary-at-Hill L14
      1670-87 St Lawrence Jewry L18
      1670-1703 St Bride Fleet Street L17
      1670-83 St Mary-le-Bow L16
      1671-1705 St Magnus L24
     1672-1717 St Stephen Walbrook L25
       1674-87 St James Garlickhithe L26
       1675-1711 St Paul's Cathedral L27
       1676-84 St James Piccadilly K21
       1677-80 St Anne and St Agnes L29
       1677-83 St Benet Paul's Wharf L30
       1677-87 Christ Church L31
       1677-87 St Martin Ludgate Hill L32
       1677-87 St Peter upon Cornhill L33
        1681-86 St Mary Abchurch L36
        1681-91 Royal Hospital Chelsea N2
        1682 St Mary Aldermary L37
         1683-7 St Clement Eastcheap L38
        1684-9 St Margaret Pattens L39
         1685-95 St Andrew by the Wardrobe L40
         1686-94 St Michael Paternoster Royal L42
         1686-90 St Margaret Lothbury L41
          1689-94 Hampton Court Palace
                  East Wing V1
          1695 Morden College X2
         1696-1702 Royal Naval Hospital
                  Greenwich U3

     1671 Monument L22   1703

1661 NICHOLAS HAWKSMOOR   1736
            1695-c1705 King's Gallery and
            Orangery Kensington Palace I2

1664 SIR JOHN VANBRUGH   1726
    1668 THOMAS ARCHER   1743
       1682 JAMES GIBBS   1754
         1685 WILLIAM KENT   1748
           1694 LORD BURLINGTON 1753

| 1660 | | 1670 | 1680 | 1690 | 1700 | 1710 |

Eighteenth-century London

Three Georges of the Hanoverian dynasty occupied the throne of England from 1714 to 1811, giving their name to the 'Georgian' period and its architecture. The century was one of relative security and of economic and colonial expansion. The years between the Treaty of Utrecht in 1713 and the Battle of Waterloo in 1815 saw the emergence of England as a world trading power, with London its centre. With the new mercantile wealth, a new social order emerged. Country lords set up London houses, and artisans and shopkeepers proliferated to serve both the gentry and a growing middle class. In 1700 London's population was 670,500; by 1750 it had grown to only 676,750, but by 1801, the year of the first official census, it had increased dramatically to 900,000.

To celebrate the Tory Parliamentary victory over the Whigs in 1710, an Act of Parliament directed the building of 'fifty new churches in or near the Cities of London and Westminster or the suburbs thereof . . . churches of stone and other proper materials with Towers and Steeples to each of them'. Of the fifty only twelve were built (between 1712 and 1735), most of them by architects of the generation after Wren — Hawksmoor, Archer and Gibbs. The call for towers and steeples required them to continue Wren's attempts to reconcile the classical temple form with the Christian steeple.

The architecture of the first half of the century is distinguished by the flowering of Palladianism as the official taste of the ruling class, and by the continued shaping and extension of the city by speculators. The modern architectural profession has its roots in this century, when such gentleman-artist-architects as Lord Burlington and Sir William Chambers flourished. The architectural milieu centred round Lord Burlington and his associates, Colen Campbell (Burlington House K36 and Chiswick House T6) and William Kent (Horse Guards K50). Kent exemplified the universal designer – painter, architect, landscape gardener and furniture designer. Books published in the service of the new gentlemanly profession were to be the single most important agent in establishing the dictatorship of Palladian taste. In 1715 the first volume of Colen Campbell's *Vitruvius Britannicus* appeared, recording

Chiswick House T6

the best classical buildings erected in England, and in the same year Leoni made the first English translation of Palladio's *Quattro Libri*.

The force of Palladianism had waned by the middle of the century when, coinciding with England's increasing mercantile power, more exotic architectural influences developed. Architects like Chambers (the Pagoda, Kew T9), the Adam brothers (Syon House T10 and Osterley Park T11), and Horace Walpole and his Committee of Taste (Strawberry Hill V6) could digest oriental, classical and Gothic styles with equal facility. The beginnings of modern eclecticism — neo-Gothic, neo-classicism, and the Picturesque — were well established before the end of the century.

Following the great Building Act of 1774 the expansion of the city began in earnest in Bloomsbury (Bedford Square G12, 1775) and Marylebone (Manchester Square J15, 1776). Pattern books derived from *Vitruvius Britannicus* also appeared, giving instructions as to style, type and construction of buildings, and making the classical idiom accessible to the speculative builder, who might be a carpenter, actor, financier or lord. Besides the building on the Great Estates in central London, scattered developments also took place in what Sir John Summerson calls 'Greater Georgian London' — the villages of Hampstead, Highgate, Dulwich and Greenwich; along the roads from the centre to Islington, Highbury and Kennington; and in the parcels of land between the main radial roads: Somers Town, Camden Town and Canonbury. The ubiquitous Georgian terraced house, usually of four storeys including a basement, was arranged in streets, squares and crescents, and the grander terraces had an attic floor set back behind the parapet to accommodate extra servants. These narrow-fronted deep houses, unlike the houses built by master-craftsmen of the previous century, were early examples of industrial production, using standard sash windows, brick party walls, and iron railings. Beyond the composition of the street, architectural elaboration was restricted to the front door, the principal staircase, and the important rooms. In the following century John Nash used industrial methods and speculation to create picturesque urban scenery.

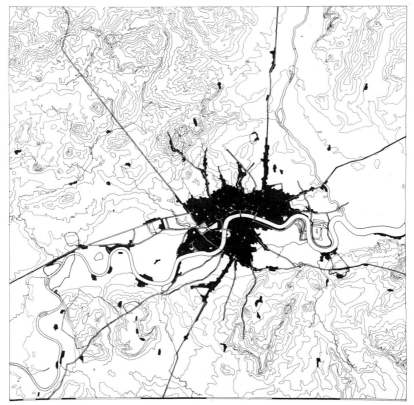

Eighteenth-century London

| WILLIAM III 1689-1702 | ANNE 1702-14 | GEORGE I 1714-27 | GEORGE II 1727-60 |

1700 population 674,500   17

1707 Union with Scotland

1713 Treaty of Utrecht

1716 THOMAS GRAY   1771

1727 THOMAS GAINSBOROUG

1728 JAMES COOK   1779

1736 JAMES WAT

1711 Church Building Act   1736 JOHN CON

1704 Queen Anne's Gate K31

1717 Cavendish Square J3

1720 Grosvenor Square J6   1739 Berkeley

1715-25 Colen Campbell *Vitruvius Britannicus*

1715 Leoni's translation of Palladio's *Quattro Libri*

1632 SIR CHRISTOPHER WREN —————— 1723   1726 Leoni's translation of *The Arc*

1675-1710 St Paul's Cathedral L27   1727 William Kent *Designs of Inigo*

1696-1702 Royal Naval Hospital Greenwich U3   1744 Va

1709-11 Marlborough House K33

1661 NICHOLAS HAWKSMOOR —————— 1736

1712-18 St Alfege Greenwich U5

1714-29 St George in the East V8

1714-30 St Anne Limehouse U9

1716-27 St Mary Woolnoth L51

1716-31 St George Bloomsbury G8

1735-45 West Tower

1664 SIR JOHN VANBRUGH —————— 1726

1717-20 Royal Arsenal Woolwich V10

1717-26 Vanbrugh Castle V11

1668 THOMAS ARCHER —————— 1743

1710-12 Roehampton House V2

1712-30 St Paul Deptford U6

1714-28 St John Smith Square K35

1682 JAMES GIBBS —————————

1714-17 St Mary-le-Strand K34

1721-6 St Martin-in-the-Fields K40

1730-59 St Bartholomew's

1685 WILLIAM KENT —————————— 1748

1733-6 Treasury Buildin

1744-5

1745

1694 LORD BURLINGTON —————————

1715-17 Burlington House with Colen Campbell K3

1722-30 College Westminster School K4

1725-9 Chiswick House T6

1697 HENRY FLITCROFT ——————

1731-3 St Giles in the Field

1700 GEORGE DANCE THE ELDER ——————

1736-40 St Leonard

1739-53 Mans

1741-4 St B

1717 HORACE WALPOLE ——————

174

1723 SIR WILLIAM CHAMBERS ——————

1728 ROBERT ADAM——————

1741 GEOR

1745

GEORGE III
1760-1820

population 676,750   1801 population 900,000

1763 Peace of Paris, Canada ceded to Britain

1776 Declaration of independence by USA

1757 THOMAS TELFORD   1834   1783 Peace treaty between USA and Britain

1788   1766 JOHN DALTON   1844   1789 French Revolution

1819   1775 JANE AUSTEN   1817

1778 SIR HUMPHREY DAVEY   1829

BLE   1837   1774 Great Building Act

1753 HUMPHREY REPTON   1818

1755 JOHN FLAXMAN   1826

1757 WILLIAM BLAKE   1827

1764 Hargreave's spinning jenny

1764 Watt's steam engine   1785 Crompton's power loom

re J8   1761 Portman Square J11

1775 Bedford Square G12

1776 Manchester Square J15

re of L B Alberti   1790-1812 Brunswick Square and
                           Mecklenburgh Square G14

igns of Inigo Jones and William Kent

1756 Ware *A Complete Body of Architecture*

1759 Sir William Chambers *Treatise on Civil Architecture*

1762 Stuart & Revett *Antiquities of Athens*

estminster Abbey K48

'54

al H12

keley Square J10

e Horse Guards K50

—1753

——————————————— 1769

——————————————— 1768

itch H14

use L55

Aldgate L57

———————————————— 1797

———————————————— 1796

0-8 Manresa House V7   1776-86 Somerset House K62

1761 Orangery & Pagoda, Kew T8 T9

———————————————— 1792

1761-8 Syon House T10   1793-8 Fitzroy Square G15

1763-7 Osterley Park T11

1764 Kenwood House R7

1768-74 The Adelphi with James & John K58

NCE THE YOUNGER ———————————————— 1825

1765-7 All Hallows London Wall L60

Y HOLLAND ———————————————— 1806

1754-8 Dover House K52   1777-8 Brooks's Club K63

752 JOHN NASH ———————————————— 1835

1753 SIR JOHN SOANE ———————————————— 1837

1778 WILLIAM WILKINS———————— 1839

1778 C R COCKERELL ———————— 1863

1781 SIR ROBERT SMIRKE——————— 1867

1794 HENRY INWOOD 1843

1795 SIR CHARLES BARRY 1868

Nineteenth-century London

The century which was to see London transformed from a typical European port and trade centre into the capital of a huge empire began with England at war with France. While the battle of Waterloo in 1815 brought an end to France's bid for European domination, the transformation of central London from a Georgian town into something grander had already started. In 1812 Regent Street was built with the encouragement of the Regent, but as a result of the initiative of the speculator-architect John Nash. His stuccoed streets and later terraces and villas brought a new, if theatrical, dignity to the city of uniform yellow-brick houses. The suburb of Regent's Park was finished in 1828 and opened to the public a decade later.

The 1820s and '30s in Europe saw the invention of new institutions of democracy, which required new building-types. London now acquired the British Museum G25, the Zoo F28, arcades, hospitals (St George's J28 and Charing Cross K87) and cemeteries. After these came the buildings for trade and transport: canals, the railway stations (Euston from 1836), markets, hotels, banks, offices, restaurants, and the hygienic parks. With the increased trade brought about by the Industrial revolution and the growth of the Empire, the population continued to grow. Many were housed in further speculative development of the Great Estates – Cubitt's Belgravia and extensions to Bloomsbury – or new ventures like the more open Ladbroke estate 17. Many more swelled the slums of the East End and notorious pockets of the West End. A series of cholera outbreaks in the 1840s and '50s showed that *laissez-faire* development would not provide adequate sanitation and in 1859 the Metropolitan Board of Works was established. Under its Chief Engineer, Joseph Bazalgette, a huge new system of sewers was built, with the main outfall at Becton, well to the east of the city. As a further precaution, the Victoria, Albert and Chelsea Embankments to the Thames were built to speed the river and rid it of putrid mud. In 1851, Prince Albert's Great Exhibition of Arts and Industry, housed in the Crystal Palace in Hyde Park,

St Mary, Wyndham Place F19

brought a flood of visitors to London, and promoted the West End as a centre of shopping and entertainment. The subsequent development of Kensington as a cultural showpiece and centre of imperial learning added impetus to the extension of London westward from Belgravia.

The Victorians attacked the slums in two ways. Philanthropist societies built model housing for artisans. The two chief societies were rivals: one had Henry Roberts as architect producing decent humane city-buildings like those at Streatham Street G33; the other, presided over by Baroness Burdett-Coutts, had H A Darbishire introducing models for the destruction of the city's coherence and its re-formation into freestanding 'blocks' – the precursors of today's tower blocks. The other attack was simply to remove slums by driving new roads through them, and the last quarter of the century saw the building of Shaftesbury Avenue, Charing Cross Road, and New Oxford Street in the West End; Queen Victoria Street (the continuation eastward of Bazalgette's Embankment) and King Street in the city; and the joining of Westminster with Hyde Park Corner by Victoria Street and later Grosvenor Gardens.

From the middle of the century, huge suburbs were built for the housing of artisans and clerks, who were enabled to commute to work in the city by an extensive but unplanned public transport system. New suburban railway lines were built, omnibuses ran on new highways and across and under the Thames by new bridges and tunnels. In 1863 the world's first underground railway opened: the Metropolitan Line from Paddington to Farringdon.

In 1870 the London School Board was set up to serve the new populations, and the type it established for the urban school is still recognizable. In 1889 the London County Council was established, taking over from the Metropolitan Board of Works, and was given increased powers to clear slums, and to provide rented working-class housing and parks. By the end of the century, London was physically much the city we inherit today. Its population had grown from under a million in 1800 to the 6.5 million of Greater London: the largest city ever known.

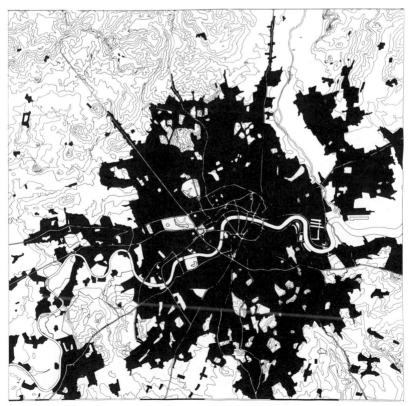

Nineteenth-century London

23

1790	**1800**	1810	1820	1830	1840

| GEORGE III | | | GEORGE IV | WILLIAM IV | VICTORIA |
| 1760-1820 | | | 1820-30 | 1830-7 | 1837-1901 |

1800 population 1,970,000

1775 J M W TURNER 1851   1815 Battle of Waterloo   18
1780 ELIZABETH FRY 1845   1819 JOHN RUSKIN 1900 1832 Reform Act
1781 GEORGE STEPHENSON   1848   1818 KARL MARX 1883   1832-3 Factory Acts
1801 SIR JOSEPH PAXTON   1865   1843 E
1806 I K BRUNEL   1859   1834 WILLIAM MORE
1809 CHARLES DARWIN   1882
1812 CHARLES DICKENS   1870
1813 DAVID LIVINGSTONE   1873

1752 JOHN NASH ——————————————————————1835
1812-28 Regent's Park F5   1836 A W Pugi
1816-18 Royal Opera Arcade K69   1840 Letar
1822-4 All Souls Langham Place F16   18
1827-32 Carlton House Terrace K77
1828- Waterloo Place K79
1831 Theatre Royal Hayma

1753 SIR JOHN SOANE ——————————————————————— 1837
1800-3 Pitshanger Place T12
1811-14 Dulwich Picture Gallery W3
1812-13 13, 14 Lincoln's Inn Fields K67
1814 Stables Royal Hospital N9
1816 Mausoleum G19
1823-5 St Peter Walworth P1
1825-8 St John Bethnal Green U18

1778 WILLIAM WILKINS ——————————————————————— 1839
1827-9 University College G30
1827-9 St George's Hospital J28
1832-8 National Gallery

1781 SIR ROBERT SMIRKE ——————————
1807-9 Royal Mint L67   1821-4 St Mary Wyndham Place F19
1823-47 British Museum G25

1788 THOMAS CUBITT ——————————
1820-60 Barnsbury C1, Bloomsbury G34 an

1795 SIR CHARLES BARRY ——————————
1826-8 Holy Trinity Cloudesley Sq
1829-32 Travellers' Club K82
1835-60 Houses of Pa
1837-41 Reform

1800 DECIMUS BURTON ——————————
1825-8 Screen & Arch Hyde Park C
1828-30 Athenaeum Club K80
1844-8

1811 SIR GEORGE GILBERT SCOTT ——————————

1814 WILLIAM BUTTERFIELD ——————————
1848

1824 GEORGE EDMUND STREET

1830 ALFRED WATERHOU

1831 R NORMAN SHAW

1831 PHILIP WEBB ——————————
18

1790	1800	1810	1820	1830	1840

EDWARD VII
1901-10

pulation 2,652,000   1900 population 6,501,000
               1869 Suez Canal opened
49 1853 1854 Cholera outbreaks   1880s London telephone system
   1851 Great Exhibition, Crystal Palace, Hyde Park   1888 London County Council established
ric Telegraph   1863 Metropolitan Underground Railway
   1896   1865 RUDYARD KIPLING   1936   1890 the motor car
50 SIR EBENEZER HOWARD   1928
          1857-66 Atlantic cable

ontrasts
y Edifice de Rome Moderne   1889 Camillo Sitte
oseph Gwilt An Encyclopedia of Architecture   City Planning According to Artistic Principles
48 Marx & Engels Communist Manifesto
          1856 Owen Jones Grammar of Ornament
K85

8
                    1867

855
lgravia J23 J25 J33
                1860
e G29

ment with A W Pugin (1812-52) K90
K91

J24 J27

House Kew Γ16
                                              1878
          1863-75 Albert Memorial J44
                1868-74 St Pancras Station G38
                1868-73 Government Offices Whitehall K105
                                                        1900
Saints Margaret Street K93 1870-77 St Augustine Queen's Gate N19
                                1881
          1860-1 St James the Less O4
                1868-78 St Mary Magdalene E3
                1874-82 Royal Courts of Justice K106
                                                        1905
                1873-81 Natural History Museum J48
                        1879 Prudential Insurance G39
                                1897-1906 University College Hospital G44
                                                                        1912
                1873-5 Royal Geographical Society J47
                1875 Hampstead Towers A1
                1875 Bedford Park with E W Godwin etc T18
                1876 Old Swan House N21
                        1879-86 Albert Hall Mansions J50
                                1886-90 New Scotland Yard K112
                                                                        1915
          1859 Red House X8
                1868-70 House I Palace Green I10
IR ASTON WEBB   1930
                        1899-1909 Victoria and Albert Museum J40
I C H TOWNSEND   1928
                        1896-1901 Horniman Museum X9
                        1897-9 Whitechapel Art Gallery L96
          1857 C F A VOYSEY   1941
                        1889-94 Studio houses Bedford Park T19 T20

Twentieth-century London

In the year 1900 London was firmly established as the capital of the world's largest empire. During the Edwardian era (1901–10) improvements to London befitting its imperial status were belatedly carried out – Kingsway K130, the Mall K17, Admiralty Arch K127 and a new front to Buckingham Palace K76 (completed, astonishingly, in three months). The architects of this confident decade were men like Aston Webb, Lutyens, Norman Shaw and Mewès and Davis. By then the English Arts and Crafts movement, originating in William Morris's reaction to the excesses of nineteenth-century industrialization, was widely admired abroad. Hermann Muthesius was commissioned by the *Deutsche Werkbund* to record English domestic architecture. His *Das Englische Haus* (The English House) was published in Germany in 1904. Without it, this significant indigenous English achievement, together with its life style, would have been mostly lost or undervalued. The Free Style of Shaw, Webb and C R Ashbee's domestic work had reached its prime by the end of the nineteenth century; in the early years of the twentieth century it was applied to public buildings – notably fire stations, colleges, hospitals and libraries.

London was also the world's largest city, with a population of 6.5 million, compared with 4 million in New York and 2.7 million in Paris. This massive population and the terrible slum conditions gave a fresh impetus to public housing schemes. The initiative for such work came from the philanthropic and public authority movements of the nineteenth century.

As a result of continued reformist and political pressure the London County Council was formed in 1889. The Housing for the Working Classes branch was established within the Architects Department of the LCC in 1893, following the Act of Parliament of the same name three years earlier.

At the turn of the century the LCC built the Boundary Estate H36 and the Millbank Estate to rehouse slum dwellers. They form the most conspicuous and celebrated evidence to support the claim that the LCC's output up to the First World War is one of the greatest achievements of the Arts and Crafts movement in English architecture. The socialist philosophy of William Morris and the architectural ideas of Lethaby and Philip Webb had finally been put into practice as urban design.

The suburb, that peculiarly Anglo-Saxon development for which the London prototype had been Norman Shaw's Bedford Park T18 of 1877, re-emerged. Ebenezer Howard's book *Tomorrow: A Peaceful Path to Real Reform*, published in 1898, pointed to the garden city as the prescription for the social and economic ills of city life. Raymond Unwin's Hampstead Garden Suburb R18 of 1906–9 was the closest Howard's prophecy came to being realized, and it has remained a model for similar developments to the present day. Unwin's own *Town Planning in Practice* of 1909 was also an important text. It was partly influenced by German developments, a point which underlines the widespread cultural interdependence and interest that existed between the two countries before the First World War.

By 1918, however, the British Empire was in decline, and architecture suffered along with everything else. Despite the continued high stature of architects like Lutyens, Townsend and Voysey, the ideals of the Arts and Crafts movement could not withstand the traumatic effects of the first mechanized war. Architectural initiative had passed to other European centres (notably Moscow, Paris and Berlin), but London, isolated during the war, was now suspicious of foreign influence.

During the 1920s and '30s building in London concentrated on continued suburban expansion. In these two decades England and Wales built 4 million houses, a third of the total national housing stock. Many of these 'homes for heroes', in the form of semi-detached single family dwellings, were made possible by major extensions to the London Underground ('Metroland'). The underground network in central London had been considered complete in 1914, but under the directorship of Frank Pick it was radically extended. Pick understood the value of the Underground in giving unity to a diverse and extended city. As Haussmann's boulevards were to Paris in the nineteenth century, so Pick's underground network was to London. The consistent quality of Charles Holden's many stations for this £40 million expansion and of Edward Johnston's typography for the Underground (commissioned by Pick in 1913 and designed by 1916) gave the network a unified image.

Modern architecture was gingerly introduced into the capital, principally as a middle-class experiment – *moderne* had to co-exist uneasily with neo-Georgian. From the end of the 1920s to the outbreak of the Second World War a number of distinguished emigré architects arrived in London – Gropius, Chermayeff, Breuer, Mendelsohn, Lubetkin and Moholy-Nagy among others. They brought with them an infectious enthusiasm for the 'new architecture'. Lubetkin and his firm Tecton were responsible for buildings at London Zoo F42, F45 and for the Highpoint flats R26, which were the best of their period. The Anglo-Saxon contribution from Connell Ward and Lucas, Emberton, Wells Coates, McGrath, Maxwell Fry and Owen Williams produced buildings of comparable quality but without the same intensity.

However the prolific output of the firm of Sir John Burnet, Tait and Lorne contributed an important middle-of-the-road modernity – seen in the mixture of frame construction with stripped classicism in Kodak House K133, and the influence of Dudok's brickwork in the Royal Masonic Hospital T24. At the same time the work of Giles Gilbert Scott offered another alternative path to modernity. The monumental brickwork of his Battersea Power Station N29, Guinness Brewery T27 and the elegant simplicity of Waterloo Bridge K154 are better appreciated today than they were by contemporary historians.

In 1940 the Blitz seriously damaged the City of London and virtually destroyed the Docks and the east End – curiously the West End of London remained relatively intact. The most conspicuous architectural casualties of the bombing were the City churches (twenty were destroyed), the halls of City livery companies (nineteen were badly damaged), and to the west Gray's Inn and the Temple. The evacuation of large sections of the population followed. In 1943 Abercrombie's plan was proposed for the reconstruction – regrettably its general intentions were neither valued nor implemented.

During the early 1950s the post-war reconstruction of London began, with the Festival of Britain buildings on the South Bank (1951) as its uneasy celebration (although the Festival Hall K157, the only remaining built evidence of the Festival, is still the best modern public building in London).

In domestic building the LCC were still taking the lead, devising housing programmes in the East End, South London and in Roehampton. However, the good intentions of the Welfare State, coupled with watered-down allegiances to Le Corbusier's principles and the democratic building style of Sweden, were not enough to produce good architecture. The lack of coherent architectural models, combined with mad planning policies, resulted in a further deterioration in the quality of building in London. At the same time began the continuing population decline as large numbers of people moved out to satellite New Towns like Harlow and Stevenage, established under the New Towns Act (1946). In the following decades the forms of speculative office and hotel developments have proved to be indistinguishable from the residential towers of the Welfare State. When viewed from Primrose Hill in the north or the plateau of Blackheath in the south, the skyline of London is now a depressing spectacle of stubby, evenly distributed towers. However, during the 1960s critical reaction to mixed development (towers and row houses) began to emerge in the form of 'low-rise high density' housing, supported by the research of Leslie Martin at Cambridge University, and produced most notably by the London Borough of Camden. The resulting solutions in the main are as alien to London as the tower blocks they wished to condemn. The current fashion for 'vernacular' forms or 'Noddyland', with some sentiment about building 'Merrie England' in the central urban areas and the vacated docklands, is also inauspicious.

The 1960s saw an orgy of motorway building, which came to a head with the

proposed motorway box (equivalent to the *Boulevard Périphérique* in Paris). For this, large and sound sections of St John's Wood and neighbouring areas were to be destroyed, but luckily vocal public opinion was beginning to act as censor to comprehensive redevelopment. Articulate local action groups prevented the construction of the motorway box and also saved the area of Covent Garden. In commercial building, the Smithsons' innovative Economist group (1965 K170), partly inspired by the organization of the Rockefeller Center in New York, was a welcome change from the general uncritical importation of the Lever House model (see for example Thorn House K161, New Zealand House K165 and Marathon House F49).

In the first edition of this book we noted that there had been little building in London in the 1970s and that the city was 'poised for fresh initiatives which should respect its architectural traditions'. These initiatives were taken in the huge area of Docklands, one of the few places where any significant public investment was made, and in the City, where towards the end of the 1980s a boom in office-building reached a climax. In neither case were traditions respected and very few new buildings of distinction were produced. There was very little public investment throughout the decade, with the exception of the construction of the M25, the orbital motorway which now nets London in a circle 50 kilometres (30 miles) across, providing new opportunities for development and speculation unhindered by the existing city. The failure to invest in London's public realm produced a squalor that compared very unfavourably with the continuing improvement of other European capitals. The private commercial market collapsed at the end of the 1980s, and the start of the 1990s saw very little public or private development being undertaken.

While in the 1970s architectural debate in Britain had been relatively pluralistic, the publication of HRH the Prince of Wales's *Vision of Britain* in 1990 helped polarize it between a synthetic architectural 'tradition', which was essentially reactionary, and modernism. This caricature has increased the opposition between the ingratiating 'neo-vernacular' style considered appropriate for most housing and some offices, and the mainly empty-headed modernism of the suburban 'business park'. Examples of both may now be seen all over London, although they may not be included here.

The City from Waterloo Bridge

Twentieth-century London

1890	**1900**	1910	1920	1930	1940

EDWARD VII	GEORGE V		GEORGE VI
1901-1910	1910-1936		1936-1952

1900 population 6,500,000　　　　　　　　　　　　　　　　　19

1914-18 First World War　　　　　　1939-45 Seco

1917 Russian Revolution　　　　1939 Evacuat

1904 Hermann Muthesius *Das Englische Haus*　　1940 The B

1831 R NORMAN SHAW ——— 1912　　　　　　　　　　I

1905-8 Piccadilly Hotel K123　　　1933 London Passenge

1849 SIR ASTON WEBB ———　　　　　　　1930　　　　1940 Siefri

1901-13 Queen Victoria Memorial K119 & Admiralty Arch K127

1912-13 Buckingham Palace front K76

1857 C F A VOYSEY ———　　　　　　　　　　　　　1941

1902 Voysey House T21

1857 SIR JOHN BURNET TAIT (SIR JOHN BURNET TAIT & LORNE)　　1938

1904-11 Edward VII Galleries G49　　1930-4 Royal Masonic Hosp

1911 Gallagher Building K133

1921 Adelaide House L107

1869 SIR EDWIN LUTYENS ———————————— 1944

1909-20 Central Square Hampstead Garden Suburb R21

1919-20 The Cenotaph K137

1924-7 Lutyens House H37

1924-39 Midland Bank Head Office L1

1928-30 Housing Page Street C

1935 Reuters and Pr

1875 CHARLES HOLDEN ———

1927-9 Broadway House K143

1930s Underground Stati

1932 Senate House G62

1878 ARTHUR DAVIES (MEWES & DAVIES) ———　　　　19

1906 Ritz Hotel K125　　　1928 Hasilwood House L110

1908-11 Royal Automobile Club K129

1922-31 National Westminster Bank L10

1880 SIR GILES GILBERT SCOTT ———

1929-55 Battersea Power Stati

1933-6 Guinness Brewe

1939-45 Water

1889 JOSEPH EMBERTON ———

1930 Olympia M4

1935 Simpsons Picc

1890 SIR OWEN WILLIAMS ———

1932 Daily Express Buildi

1934 Wembley Aren

1934-6 Peckham Hea

1895 WELLS COATES ———

1933 Isokon flats B27

1938 Flats 10 Pala

1895 LCC ARCHITECTS DEPARTMENT ———

1897 Boundary Street Estate

1899 E MAXWELL FRY ———

1935 Sun House A4

1936 Kensal House

1901 BERTHOLD LUBETKIN & TECTON ———

1933-8 Highpoint 1&2 F

1932-5 Gorilla House F

1938 Finsbury

1906 F R S YORKE (YORKE ROSENBERG MARDALL) ———

1908 SIR FREDERICK GIBBERD ———

1935 Pullman Court V

1914 SIR DENYS LASDUN ———

1926 JAMES STIRLING (STIRLI

1928 & 1925 ALISON & PET

1933 SIR RICHARD ROGE

1935 SIR NORMA

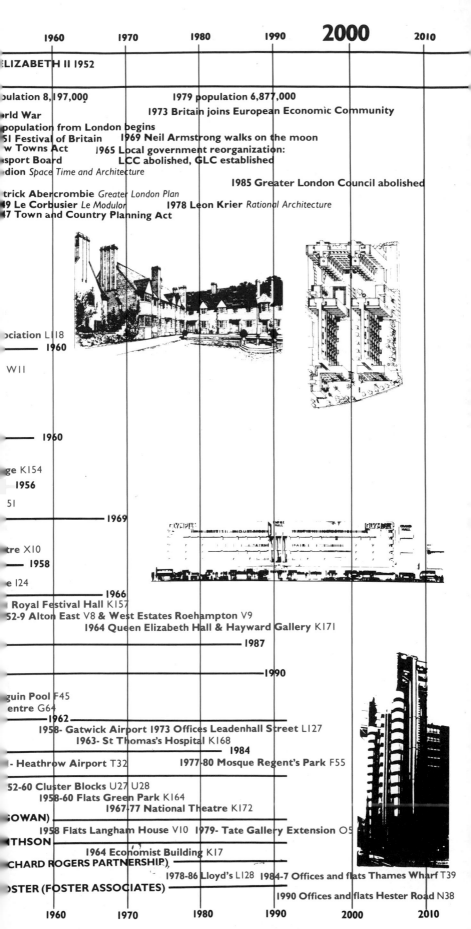

1960   **1970**   **1980**   **1990**   **2000**   **2010**

ELIZABETH II 1952

oulation 8,197,000   1979 population 6,877,000
orld War   1973 Britain joins European Economic Community
population from London begins
51 Festival of Britain   1969 Neil Armstrong walks on the moon
w Towns Act   1965 Local government reorganization:
sport Board   LCC abolished, GLC established
dion *Space Time and Architecture*
                          1985 Greater London Council abolished

trick Abercrombie *Greater London Plan*
49 Le Corbusier *Le Modulor*   1978 Leon Krier *Rational Architecture*
47 Town and Country Planning Act

ociation L118
———— 1960

WII

———— 1960

ge K154
   1956

51

———————— 1969

tre X10
   — 1958
e 124
   ———— 1966
Royal Festival Hall K157
52-9 Alton East V8 & West Estates Roehampton V9
     1964 Queen Elizabeth Hall & Hayward Gallery K171
                              ———— 1987

—————————————— 1990

guin Pool F45
entre G64
——— 1962
   1958- Gatwick Airport 1973 Offices Leadenhall Street L127
        1963- St Thomas's Hospital K168
                          ———— 1984
- Heathrow Airport T32   1977-80 Mosque Regent's Park F55

52-60 Cluster Blocks U27 U28
   1958-60 Flats Green Park K164
        1967-77 National Theatre K172
GOWAN)
   1958 Flats Langham House V10 1979- Tate Gallery Extension O5
THSON
      1964 Economist Building K17
CHARD ROGERS PARTNERSHIP)
        1978-86 Lloyd's L128 1984-7 Offices and flats Thames Wharf T39
OSTER (FOSTER ASSOCIATES)
                   1990 Offices and flats Hester Road N38

1960   **1970**   **1980**   **1990**   **2000**   **2010**

Childs'

continu

Trading Estate

a

b

Cricklewood Junc

Cricklewood

Carriage Shed

Depot

Sta

Sports Ground

Pav

Sports Ground

Pav

Athletic Ground

Pav

Posts

BS

BS

e

f

School

Hamstead Cemetery

Chap

Synagogue

Posts

Resr (covered)

Coll

West

Po

Brondesbury

i

j

West End Sidings

Station

Pavs

Hall

Sch

School

m

n

Sch

KILBURN GRANGE PARK

School

Hospl

Schs

Sta

Sch

School

contin

Wks

Chapl

Paddington Cemetery

Pavilion

Playing Fields

Netball Court

Kilburn

Section A: Cricklewood/West Hampstead/South Hampstead

The land slopes down from the favoured heights of Hampstead to the Roman line of Edgware Road. To the north of the railway lines (the North London Line and the main lines to the north from St Pancras and Marylebone) are the red-brick houses of West Hampstead; to the south are fancier red-brick flats, such as Greencroft Gardens.

To the west of Edgware Road (which becomes a High Street at Kilburn and Cricklewood) are the late Victorian and early Edwardian suburbs of Kilburn and Brondesbury. Between these and the Green Belt lies a ring of between-the-wars suburban semi-detached houses in which most Londoners now live, and in which most of the remainder would like to live. A sample is seen in the north-west, beyond Hendon Way, a quintessentially 1930s suburban motor road lined with flowering cherry trees.

West End Lane

Hampstead Towers 1875   A1h
6 Ellerdale Road NW3
R Norman Shaw
⊖ Hampstead

Hampstead Towers was built by Shaw for himself, and although he used the same Queen Anne style as in Old Swan House N21, the composition here is freer. The principal staircase divides the house into two halves with quite different floor heights, shown by two long oriel windows on the street frontage. One of these is in the same brickwork as the rest of the house, the other is stuccoed and contains

Studio house 1885   A2h
39 Frognal NW3
R Norman Shaw
⊖ Hampstead

The tile-hung exterior of this house, in the style of a Surrey Weald cottage, is appropriate to Kate Greenaway, the nineteenth-century children's book illustrator for whom it was built. The house faces north-east, but the studio within the attic has been rotated to face north.

Opposite is **University College School** (1907) by Arnold Mitchell, an impressive group of Edwardian baroque buildings.

more glass (reminiscent of Swan House). The remaining windows appear randomly placed, their position determined by the rooms inside. Hampstead Towers' pointed gables, tall chimneys, porthole windows and beautifully modulated brick-work are all characteristic of Shaw. Underneath the mezzanine studio where Shaw designed his subsequent buildings is the dining room which, with its low inglenook fireplace, is particularly fine. Unfortunately the house is difficult to visit as it is now an Italian convent, the Institute of St Marcellina.

Annesley Lodge 1896   A3g
Platts Lane NW3
C F A Voysey
⊖ Hampstead, West Hampstead

Voysey built this house for his father, and Pevsner calls it his best house in London. It is certainly a compendium of the elements of his style, with its long unbroken red-tiled roof, buttresses at the corners of the white pebble-dashed walls, and heart motifs on the front door. The plan is a response to its suburban corner site, the two wings enclosing the front garden, with the front door at their intersection. See also Voysey's Bedford Park houses T19, T20.

Sun House 1935   A4h
9 Frognal Way NW3
E Maxwell Fry
⊖ Hampstead

The first example of an expensive modern house in London – all earlier ones had been in the country. The site slopes up from the road, and the main rooms of the house are at the front, facing the view, and raised above the garage and retaining wall. The roof is 'accessible for the serving of tea'. The house is built of concrete, and the outside is smoothed and painted except for the steel balconies supported on slender columns. The railings were originally painted pale green, and the retaining wall grey. See also 66 Old Church Street N32.

Frognal Close NW3 1937   A5h
E L Freud
⊖ Hampstead

Approached from Frognal, this fine enclave of six brick houses in semi-detached blocks with front doors at each end suggests an enclosed courtyard, or M H Baillie Scott's close planning for Hampstead Garden Suburb R18. The raised brick band around the upper storey windows and the nautical handling of the front doors are the first clues to the period. The large windows set into dark brick walls are more like Mies van der Rohe's brick houses at Krefeld (1930) than the architecture of Hampstead Garden Suburb.

Hill House 1938   A6c
87 Redington Road NW3
Oliver Hill, garden by Christopher Tunnard
⊖ Hampstead

Hill, a stylistic chameleon (see his houses in Chelsea Square N31), here made Mies van der Rohe's brick style look as if it had originated in Hampstead instead of Krefeld. However, the soffits of the overhanging upper floor were originally painted an un-Germanic primrose yellow, and the window-frames were turquoise. The porches (originally for sleeping in the open air) have been filled in, reducing the dramatic effect of the curved roof-ends. Christopher Tunnard, who designed the garden, emigrated to the United States where he later wrote the celebrated *Man Made America*.

House 1938   A7h
66 Frognal NW3
Connell, Ward and Lucas
⊖ Hampstead

Le Corbusier's *Five Points of Architecture* are expressed in this house. The free ground floor plan, the long windows, the structure independent of the façade and the roof garden are all present to some extent as part of the necessary pedigree. From the outside it is convincing; however, the internal planning is merely sensible and bourgeois. It is touching to read the client's guarded justification of his completed house in the RIBA Journal of 1938: 'I can only regret that this building should offend the susceptibilities of some people and be beyond the comprehension of others'; and it is doubly regrettable that after such opposition Hampstead cannot claim a house of the calibre of Le Corbusier's Villa Stein in Paris! The windows on the street side were replaced in the 1970s, and the house is not now painted in its original colours.

House and swimming pool   A8c
1967
9 West Heath Road NW3
James Gowan
⊖ Hampstead

This strange and obsessive building was one of Gowan's first after the dissolution of his partnership with James Stirling. It uses piers of purple-grey brick rising through three storeys and separated by continuous strips of glazing, to define a series of spaces, each with a very specific function. The imagery would suit local authority housing rather than a residence for a successful furniture manufacturer. The circular swimming pool is housed in the glazed dome on the corner of the site.

Housing, Branch Hill   A9d
1970–7
Branch Hill NW3
London Borough of Camden Architects Department; Gordon Benson and Alan Forsyth
⊖ Hampstead

A steeply sloping garden, large and overgrown, in an affluent section of Hampstead was the improbable site for this local authority housing scheme of forty-two dwellings. The scheme adopts a well-tried section for building on slopes, deriving from traditional Mediterranean hill towns, and from Le Corbusier's *Roq et Rob* proposals (1948).

A miniature urban grid of alleys is established across and along the contours. The houses are arranged in pairs on either side of these pedestrian routes, the roof of the lower one becoming the garden terrace for the one above. The exteriors are a simple, almost utilitarian outcome of the logic of the plans – stained timber windows, with doors and balcony frames set in simple openings in the rendered walls. The virtuosity of the scheme is in its section and interiors, where specific planning contrasts with the neutral exterior in a way which reverses the traditional emphasis in housing design. The designers of Branch Hill are not alone in this, but their scheme is unusually easy to live in, and as such remains an outstanding achievement.

Section B: Hampstead/Hampstead Heath/Parliament Hill Fields/Belsize Park/Maitland Park/Gospel Oak/Chalk Farm/Dartmouth Park/South Hampstead

In the seventeenth century, Hampstead village, on the ridge of a steep hill overlooking London, was much favoured as a place of retreat from the city. At the beginning of the eighteenth century the villages of Hampstead and Kentish Town, the hamlets of the Vale of Health and North End, and the manors of Belsize and Chalk Farm were all surrounded by heathland and fields and were still quite separate from London. After the discovery of the Hampstead Wells the village rapidly became a fashionable eighteenth-century spa. Most of Hampstead's fine Georgian buildings have survived, owing both to a protective cordon of open land which hindered speculation, and to the steepness of Hampstead Hill, which prevented the incursions of trams and buses earlier this century.

By the early nineteenth century Hampstead was expanding beyond its village limits, and London was spreading northwards, beginning with the laying out of Regent's Park (see section F). With the development of the Eton College Estate in the 1830s, followed by the Belsize Estate in the 1840s, Hampstead's engulfment in the general expansion of London had begun, to be completed in the 1870s and '80s by the red-brick mansions of Fitzjohn's Avenue extending to Finchley Road, and to Belsize Park via Haverstock Hill.

Hampstead has attracted artists and writers as residents and still has great charm; its steep, labyrinthine alleys and well-preserved Georgian streets are best discovered on foot.

Inseparable from Hampstead are the heath and its hamlets, the Vale of Health and North End. In 1866 further building on the heath was restricted when 97 ha (240 acres) was bought by the government; Parliament Hill was added in 1890, Golders Hill Park in 1897, the Heath Extension north of Spaniards Road in 1905, and the Kenwood grounds in 1924, making a total of over 283 ha (700 acres).

Kentish Town was still a village on the road to Highgate as late as 1780, but by the beginning of the nineteenth century a series of brick terraces (notably Grove Terrace B15) was creeping along Highgate Road. In the second half of the nineteenth century Gospel Oak (the venue of traditional country fairs as late as the 1850s), Maitland Park and Dartmouth Park to the south of Highgate were developed. By the beginning of this century, the whole area of this section had been built up in a series of loosely connected estates, some of which fell victim in the 1950s and '60s to well-intentioned comprehensive redevelopment by local authorities. The most conspicuous and tragic example of this misplaced zeal is Gospel Oak B31.

Backs of houses, Church Row, Hampstead

Fenton House 1693   B1a
Hampstead Grove NW3
⊖Hampstead

The formal approach to Fenton House, one of the finest detached houses in Hampstead, is from the green triangle of Holly Bush Hill to the south. The wrought iron gates give a view of the southern front set deep in its site, but the entrance is from the side, in Hampstead Grove, where an opening in the high boundary wall reveals the house. It is square in plan with projecting wings, linked by a colonnade of later date; the eaves, cornice and hipped roof are found in several houses in Hampstead. The house is now owned by the National Trust and open to the public, and has musical and theatrical evenings.

Georgian Hampstead 1   B2a
18th Century
(west of Heath Street NW3)
⊖Hampstead

Apart from single buildings like Fenton House B1 and complete streets like Church Row B6, Hampstead to the west of **Heath Street** (note numbers 75–89 and 113–25) is a complex series of alleys and steps best appreciated on foot; the visitor will discover many small terraces and spaces not included in this guide.

Starting from Hampstead Underground station, north up Holly Bush Hill are **Volta House, Bolton House, Windmill Hill House** and **Enfield House**: an informal mid-eighteenth century terrace of nine bays. Set back from Holly Bush Hill behind long front gardens, they are a reminder that Hampstead was an eighteenth-century village. The front of the terrace is of brown brick, with red-brick dressings and straight door hoods on carved brackets.

Romney House

To the east is **Romney House** (1797), large and weatherboarded, and approached from the street through a walled courtyard. Built originally for the painter George Romney, it is one of London's earliest studio houses. The large north-facing windows at the back look over Heath Street.

Further to the north (past Fenton House) is **Old Grove House** in Hampstead Grove. The front of this complex early eighteenth-century house has an enlarged order of three bays, an attic floor of brown brick with red dressings, and a large doorway with a Tuscan pediment. In 1730 a wing of stables and cottages was added, surrounding a small yard.

Finally **The Mount** (c 1710) is a gentle ramp leading from Hampstead Square back to Heath Street, from which it is

Old Grove House

divided by railings and a strip of green. It contains **Cloth Hill**, an early eighteenth-century mansion with two projecting wings, and higher up and at right angles **Caroline House** and **Holly Cottage**, both two-bay mid-Georgian houses.

Georgian Hampstead 2 — B3e

18th century
(west of Holly Bush Hill NW3
and north of Church Row)
⊖ Hampstead

1–4 **Lower Terrace** (late eighteenth century), 1–6 **Mount Vernon** (early eighteenth century), **Holly Walk, Holly Place, Hollyberry Lane** (all mid-eighteenth century), **Benham's Place** (1813) and **Prospect Place** (1820), together form a dense and miniature composition of interconnected alleys and single-sided streets, the whole conveying the essence of eighteenth-century Hampstead. The painter John Constable lived at 2 Lower Terrace from 1835–8.

Benham's Place

Georgian Hampstead 3 — B4a

18th century
(east of Heath Street NW3)
⊖ Hampstead

An area which developed as a result of the discovery of the wells, and in the eighteenth century turned the village into a fashionable spa. Many of the place names (Well Road, Flask Walk, etc) derive from this time.

Flask Walk, a pedestrian street of eighteenth-century cottages, leads off Hampstead High Street to the south of the Underground station. At its end is the Flask Inn, the original meeting place of the Kit-Kat club (founded in 1705 by Whig politicians and writers), portraits of whose members are to be found in the National Portrait Gallery. Flask Walk continues into **Well Walk** (c1780) where, on the south side, is a fine terrace of eighteenth-century houses, with unusual protruding porches. Note also the Victorian fountain on the north side, commemorating the spring or wells. Also on the north side is **Burgh House** (1703), a large five-bay mansion approached from New End Square. Formerly the residence of the physician attached to the Hampstead Wells, the house is now open to the public.

Flask Walk

More Georgian houses are to be found in a group to the north, off East Heath Road, overlooking the heath. **Cannon Hall**, although much altered, is an early eighteenth-century house, with an impressive approach through a courtyard from Cannon Place. George du Maurier lived there. **Squires Mount**, a row of mid-eighteenth-century cottages forming a small court off East Heath Road, should also be noted. Also in East Heath Road is **Foley House** (1698), a fine house set back behind its walled entrance court,

Well Walk

Burgh House

Elm Row early 18th century   B5a
off Heath Street NW3
⊖Hampstead
A fine early eighteenth-century terrace, comparable to Church Row B6 in scale, although here the front gardens, enclosed with high walls, partly obscure the terrace from the street, and number 3 has an unfortunate roof extension. The windows of the houses are either straight-headed or segmentally arched. Elm Lodge (1700), on the corner, has a miniature Palladian entrance stair, and Vine House (1700–10) is an impressive five-bay, two-storey house, its doorway on carved brackets.

Church Row NW3 1720   B6e
⊖Hampstead
The best and most regular Georgian street in Hampstead, the houses on the south side all dating from about 1720. Of four storeys, they have low segmental brick arches to the windows, which seem to form a larger proportion of the façade than the brickwork. The north side of the street defines the southern boundary of Hampstead cemetery and is more irregular, both in form and period. The central reserve of the street is planted with a line of plane trees (unusual in London), and the terraces give a fine perspective view of the parish church of St John. In Hampstead's loose village structure Church Row's design is the closest thing to an urban set piece.

St John 1744–7   B7e
Church Row NW3
Sanderson(?) after Flitcroft's design(?)
⊖Hampstead
More remarkable for its position, closing the perspective of Church Row, than for its architecture (veiled by trees), the church is unexpectedly large with a tall east spire set behind battlements. The interior was much altered by S P Cockerell in 1872, the altar and reredos are by Sir T G Jackson, about 1878, and the ceiling was decorated in Renaissance style by Alfred Bell. Tall unfluted Ionic columns support arches which cut into the tunnel vault. The pulpit is original and particularly fine: an octagon on a square platform standing on four fluted Ionic columns. John Constable, George du Maurier and Norman Shaw are among those buried in the graveyard.

Admiral's House

B8a

mid-18th century
Admiral's Walk, west of Hampstead
Grove NW3
⊖ Hampstead

A conspicuously large, white stuccoed house with later additions. Its nautical associations are expressed by the galleries, railings, flagpole on the roof, and the large first-floor conservatory. The house was painted by Constable, and Sir George Gilbert Scott lived here for eight years. Grove Lodge, a cottage attached to the house and also painted white, further extends the composition, and was the home of John Galsworthy from 1918–33.

East Heath Lodge 1750

B9a

East Heath Road NW3
⊖ Hampstead

These two mid-eighteenth-century houses of plain brick have a surprisingly large common pediment facing south. Further to the west are Heath Lodge and Heath Side, two slightly larger cottages of symmetrical composition with bay windows. The latter is attributed to James Wyatt (1775).

Vale of Health NW3 1780

B10a

⊖ Hampstead

A village or hamlet within Hampstead Heath, the Vale of Health is more remarkable for its cohesion – a tight pattern of small streets and passageways – and the conspicuous absence of the twentieth century, than for any particular piece of architecture (although Vale Lodge, Manor Lodge and Woodbine Cottage are noteworthy). As a quiet backwater, it has attracted residents such as Leigh Hunt and D H Lawrence.

Keats Grove NW3 c1815

B11e

⊖ Hampstead, ≷ Hampstead Heath

Keats Grove is of a piece with Downshire Hill, although more loosely constructed and even more leafy. The houses, in mixed stucco and yellow brick and with very deep front gardens, give a good picture of the early nineteenth-century village suburb, designed for artists on aesthetic principles.

Keats House 1815–16　　B12e
Keats Grove NW3
⊖Hampstead, ⇄Hampstead Heath
It is unlikely that this two-storey stuccoed
house would have gained entry to this
guide without its literary associations: it
is not particularly distinguished, and was
rescued from destruction in the 1920s
only by courtesy of money from the USA.
When occupied by Keats and Fanny
Brawne it consisted of two semi-detached
houses, converted into one after Keats'
death. Decorated with period furniture
and wall-coverings, and open to the
public, Keats House gives a very good
idea of how such houses (many of which
still stand in London) were originally
equipped and used.

St Mary 1816　　B13e
Holly Walk NW3
⊖Hampstead
One of the first Roman Catholic churches
to be built in London after the
Reformation (and probably the smallest),
this beautiful and diminutive church is
recessed in the centre of a row of three-
storey cottages. The stuccoed front and
Tuscan doorway were added in 1830.
Note the statue of the Virgin Mary in a
niche above the door, and the segmental
pediment over the bell.

St John 1818　　B14e
Downshire Hill NW3
S P Cockerell(?)
⊖Hampstead, ⇄Hampstead Heath
This delightful cube-like chapel with
white stuccoed walls, portico and cupola,
and airy, light interior is one of London's
few remaining proprietary estate chapels.
Located at the acute corner of Downshire
Hill and Keats Grove, it is a reminder in
miniature of one of the twin churches of
the Piazza del Popolo in Rome.

Grove Terrace c1830　　B15d
off Highgate Road NW5
⇄Gospel Oak
An early but typical example of Georgian
ribbon development on the roads radiating out of London. Built originally in the
open countryside between the villages of
Kentish Town and Highgate, Grove
Terrace is well set back from Highgate
Road and has no overall formal
composition.

The Round House 1847   B16o
Chalk Farm Road NW1
Stephenson, Dockray and Normanville
⊖Chalk Farm
The Round House was originally an engine shed serving Euston Station. In the 1950s it was used as a warehouse for Gilbey's Gin, and in the 1960s it became a venue for London's first large hippy gatherings and concerts. It subsequently became a performance space. An ambitious plan to convert the building into a black arts centre was abandoned when the Greater London Council was abolished in 1985, and the building is now without a use.
The shed's robust engineering survives. Stalls for the engines are defined by a ring of cast-iron columns; these support both a gallery and the first level of the roof, which spans between them and the massive outer wall of stock brick.

St Stephen 1869–76   B17e
Rosslyn Hill NW3
Samuel Teulon
⊖Belsize Park
This almost derelict building is one of the most impressive nineteenth-century churches in London. The style is a mixture of thirteenth-century Gothic and Victorian invention, best shown by the massive tower with its capped roof, the ornamental brickwork of the interior, and the square-headed aisle windows. The materials are particularly uncompromising: various tones of Luton brick with granite dressings.
On the opposite side of Rosslyn Hill, in Lyndhurst Road, is another Victorian masterpiece, the **Congregational church** (1883–4) by Alfred Waterhouse. The plan is centralized and hexagonal, and the use of materials is unmistakably

Waterhouse – hard purple brick and terracotta. Happily, it is being renovated as a recital hall.

Belsize Park Gardens NW3   B18i
c1870–85
⊖Belsize Park
A long and majestically formal avenue of large Italianate semi-detached villas with informal tree planting. The white stuccoed façades of the closely packed villas have massive and almost identical first-floor bay windows, with small variations only in the detail, though many of the columns and their capitals have now been debased. The consistency of the white paintwork, often a surprise to the visitor, is due to the landlord's covenant, showing the continued influence of the Great Estates. As with many of London's grander houses most of the villas are now in multiple occupancy.

Mall Studios 1872 — B19k
Tasker Road NW3
Thomas Batterbury
⊖ Belsize Park

This row, apparently of seven cottages with a detached one at the end, is approached by a private pathway, or mall, behind the villas of Parkhill Road. It is a group of 'artisan' type studios, built originally to be leased to working artists. Inside, the double-height studios with galleries are unexpectedly impressive, as are their generous gardens. Much original detail remains – chimney pots bearing the monogram of the original owners on numbers 3 and 4, east-facing skylights, bull's-eye windows to the west – but the storage balconies in all except number 1 have been converted into an extra bedroom, and the models' changing rooms are now dining alcoves.

From the late 1920s to the beginning of the Second World War Mall Studios were a residence and meeting ground for artists of international repute. In 1927 Barbara Hepworth was a resident of number 7, to be joined by Ben Nicholson in 1931. In 1934 Herbert Read moved into number 3,

from where *Unit One* and *Circle* magazines were produced, edited by Leslie Martin, Nicholson and Gabo. Henry Moore (of 11a Parkhill Road), Moholy Nagy and Naum Gabo (of nearby Lawn Road Flats B27) and Piet Mondrian (whose time at 60 Parkhill Road is commemorated with a blue plaque) were among the frequent visitors to the Mall.

House 1878 — B20i
61 Fitzjohn's Avenue NW3
R Norman Shaw
⊖ Hampstead

A broad and generously composed red-brick house, entered from the side in Netherhall Gardens. With its two Dutch gables, high chimneys and projecting apsidal garden room, this house, together with Shaw's Three Gables at 6 Fitzjohn's Avenue (recently demolished), was the model for the red-brick expansion of Hampstead in the 1880s and 1890s.

Houses c1880 — B21m
1–9 and 43–73 Eton Avenue
NW3 (odd numbers only)
H B Measures
⊖ Swiss Cottage, Belsize Park

In contrast with the white stuccoed Italianate villas of Belsize Park Gardens B18, these red-brick buildings use Norman Shaw's Free Style with astonishing variety. They all have two bays to the street and cylindrical brick gate posts, but beyond this each house develops a different architectural arrangement within the genre – wilfully off-set entrances, conical corner windows, major and minor bay windows and side projections. In many of the façades it is possible to detect the features of the human face (the entrance bridge as tongue, the doorway as mouth, the chimney as nose and the oval windows either side as eyes), so that the street becomes a series of opulent Victorians looking out. The backs in contrast are quite ordinary. The magnificent studio at number 69, with leaded lights built into the side elevation, should also be noted. Built originally for single families, the houses are now converted into either flats or institutions. With their elaborate mass-produced ornamentation, they lend themselves as suitable models to those clamouring for greater variety and formal complexity in housing design. Note a further use of the type in Lyndhurst Gardens, NW3.

Wychcombe Studios c1880　　B22j
Englands Lane NW3
Sir Thomas D Becket, builder
⊖Belsize Park
Approached by a narrow, walled drive, this fine group of six studios forms an L-shaped court. They were built by Sir Thomas D Becket (see his terracotta monogram set in the front wall of each studio) on land leased from the Eton College Estate. The high Dutch gables are reminiscent of the contemporary Stratford Studios I 15 in west London.

Houses 1880s　　B23e
1–21 and 2–6 Hampstead Hill Gardens NW3
Batterbury and Huxley
⊖Hampstead
A very fine group of well crafted artistic houses, and in strong contrast to the earlier and soberer stuccoed Greek Revival terraces further down the street to the south (numbers 25–33).

All Hallows 1889　　B24g
chancel 1913
Shirlock Road NW3
James Brooks, chancel Sir Giles Gilbert Scott
⊖Belsize Park
'One of the noblest churches of its date in England' (Pevsner), All Hallows is, however, cramped on its site by later red-brick houses. It is a large shed without a spire and with aisles as high as its nave. The buttresses supporting the aisles give the west front a 'hunched' look.

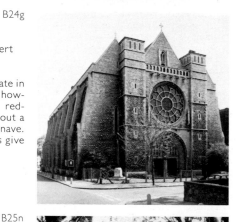

House 1890　　B25n
16 Chalcot Gardens NW3
C F A Voysey
⊖Belsize Park
An addition to the front of an existing house, built for the illustrator Arthur Rackham. The horizontal windows with leaded lights, the relieving brick arches and stone trim are typical of Voysey. The exaggeratedly steep pitched roof and brickwork are not, as the design had to blend in with the existing house. It is now covered with ivy and almost invisible.

Police Station 1896　　　　B261
Holmes Road NW5
R Norman Shaw
⊖Kentish Town

A simple three-storey yellow-brick building, with restrained baroque touches to
the stonework surrounding the two
arched entrances. The large archway leads
to the court behind (now disused), the
minor one being the principal street
entrance. Shaw was a major exponent of
the baroque revival (1890–1900s) and
showed more panache in his later works,
notably the Piccadilly Hotel K123.

Isokon Flats 1933　　　　B27f
Lawn Road NW3
Wells Coates
⊖Belsize Park

Set physically against the slope of Lawn
Road and ideologically against the neighbouring red-brick Edwardian villas, the
white stuccoed Isokon flats were prototype dwellings for the mobile intelligentsia of the 'new society'. The building
was planned as a 'collective', or long-stay
hotel for single professionals, with its own
bar and clubroom (designed by Marcel
Breuer but now altered). The social idea
derived from Le Corbusier's Pavillon
Suisse (1930) in Paris and Moisei
Ginzburg's Narkomfin apartments in
Moscow (1929). Despite such a pedigree
the building ironically conveys the feeling
of massive permanence and, notwithstanding its reputation in the history of
English modern architecture, is not a very
distinguished work. Its intention is best
expressed in the *existenz minimum*
planning.
The client, Jack Pritchard, was a pioneer of

English modernism who mass-produced
furniture, and the flats take their name
from his Bristol factory, in which the
furniture of Marcel Breuer was already in
production. This connection and the
contemporary furnishing of Lawn Road
are principally responsible for its
reputation.

Kent House 1936　　　　B28p
Ferdinand Street NW1
Connell, Ward and Lucas
⊖Chalk Farm

A major work, a rare and early example of
the new architecture applied to low
income housing. Despite the socialist
ideals of much early modern architecture
in Europe (notably Brinkman's Spangen
Housing, 1922, in Rotterdam, Moisei
Ginzburg's Narkomfin apartments, 1929,
in Moscow and Ernst May's Frankfurt
housing of the 1930s), pre-war modern
architecture in England was principally a
middle-class experiment. Kent House
consists of two identical buildings (except
for an extra storey to the street building),
representing a series rather than a static,
finite place. With their white stuccoed
walls, metal window frames and exaggerated cantilevered balconies, they come as
close as anything in London at the time to
the Heroic style.

Odeon Cinema 1937   B29m
Finchley Road NW3
Harry Weedon
⊖ Swiss Cottage

A grand streamlined *moderne* design, whose shape follows the street lines. The cinema's huge interior has, like most others outside the West End, been subdivided; its interior architecture is consequently destroyed, and its glamour lost.

Houses 1940   B30e
1–3 Willow Road NW3
Ernö Goldfinger
⊖ Hampstead

Built by Goldfinger for himself and others, this pleasant row of houses looks as if it might be one big villa. The projecting frames round the top-floor windows and the single frame uniting the windows of the first-floor living rooms both became worked-to-death clichés in other hands. Nevertheless, the houses have worn better than most English stucco-modern, perhaps because the imagery is as much Georgian as modern. They were built in spite of the opposition of the local authority, which was overridden by the LCC.

Gospel Oak Comprehensive   B31g
redevelopment 1954–80
Gospel Oak NW5
Metropolitan Borough of St Pancras, succeeded by London Borough of Camden Architects Department
⇌ Gospel Oak

This entry is included as representative of many well-intentioned architectural crimes committed on London since the war by the Welfare State. The area known as Gospel Oak, with Lismore Circus at the centre, was relatively intact until the early 1950s. It was made up principally of late nineteenth-century artisans' terraced housing, bounded by Mansfield Road to the north, Southampton Road to the west and Grafton Road to the east. Then for over twenty years the area was subject to the madness known as comprehensive redevelopment, believed in and subscribed to by almost everyone at the time. Gospel Oak can now be seen as a case study of almost every conceivable style of post-war housing: beginning with the mixed development of the Lamble Street tower and row houses of Powell and Moya

(1954); then the decks of the four-storey maisonettes and slabs of F Macmanus and Partners in the mid-1960s. The sad irony of Gospel Oak is that Lamble Street B38 completed in the late 1970s returns to the traditional pattern of the street and form of the London house – the very stuff that was condemned and swept away twenty years earlier.

Houses 1956   B32b
80–90 South Hill Park NW3
Howell and Amis
⊖Hampstead, ⇌Hampstead Heath

The terrace was designed by the architects for their own occupation when they were in the LCC Architects Department, working on the housing at Alton West V9. The houses have very narrow frontages of 3.6 m (12 ft) (one of Le Corbusier's *Modulor* dimensions) but they are deep. Their sections are designed ambitiously to exploit the site, which slopes down steeply to the ponds on the heath. Some houses have double-height living rooms with gallery bedrooms, giving them the sort of spatial intricacy which the architects would perhaps have liked to see at Alton West. The taller garden façades, now overgrown with creeper, are more satisfactory than those to the street because they are less utilitarian, but both are good examples of the short-lived English Brutalism.

House 1961   B33b
31 South Hill Park NW3
Michael Brawne
⊖Belsize Park, ⇌Hampstead Heath

A narrow-fronted terrace house, designed by the architect for himself. The steep slope of the site allowed an independent flat on the ground floor, while at the rear the first floor bridges an area to reach the garden, shared with the neighbouring house. The brick panels and timber screens on the exterior and the open ground-floor plan express the architect's preoccupation with Charles Eames, Japan and the Smithsons – formative influences on the English avant-garde in the late 1950s. The house to the south, while it shares many of the same concerns, is less memorable.

Centre Heights housing,   B34m
offices and shops 1961
Finchley Road NW3
Douglas Stephen and Panos Koulermos
⊖Swiss Cottage

During the speculative building boom of the early 1960s, when New York's Lever House was universally accepted as the model, this scheme offered a critical alternative. Le Corbusier and (less obviously) Terragni and the Italian Rationalists were the inspirations for the single, vertically layered form and its assertive precast concrete façade. The ground floor is devoted to shops, above which are five floors of offices and five floors of flats and maisonettes approached by galleries. It is unfortunate that the use of obscured glass in the galleries denies the magnificent view to the west. The building also has an ambiguous relationship with the street, its concrete mass and rhetorical stair tower making it more a freestanding object than part of a street façade.

Public library and   B35m
swimming pool 1964
Avenue Road NW3
Sir Bàsil Spence, Bonnington and Collins
⊖Swiss Cottage

These two buildings are all that was constructed of a much more extensive plan for the Borough of Hampstead's Civic Centre, stopped when London government was reorganized in 1964. The library and pool are in the practice's less flamboyant style, the exteriors consisting largely of precast concrete fins to protect the contents from the sun, which shines horizontally into the library and straight down on the pool. The interiors show some signs of 1960s largesse in well-finished and generous circulation areas; but they also show that it did not occur to the architects of the Welfare State, as it certainly had to the Victorians, that public buildings might be as good as private ones and perhaps even better.

Housing 1967–77   B36f
Fleet Road NW5
London Borough of Camden Architects Department; Neave Brown
⊖Belsize Park

Fleet Road is a definitive example of 'low-rise high density' design, which was fashionable in the 1960s as a reaction to mixed development (towers, slabs and terraces) and the excesses of high-rise living of the previous decade. In plan it is a series of alleys running parallel to Parkhill Road, supported by the beginnings of an upper-level walkway over Southampton Road (intended to connect with the main redevelopment of Gospel Oak to the east).

The scheme has an ingenious cross-section giving large balconies and communal gardens to all the residents. This exclusive semi-public realm results, however, in the visitor feeling intrusive, and the resident feeling invaded. The quality of the interiors is well above the usual in local authority housing (a unique aspect of the Camden School of design). The outside of Fleet Road is far less successful, looking like a large institutional building.

House 1968   B37b
78 South Hill Park NW3
Brian Housden
⊖Hampstead, ⇌Hampstead Heath

A strange and individual house on a sloping site overlooking the heath. Housden, building for himself and influenced by the Dutch architect van Eyck, made rooms defined by an exposed concrete frame, inset with panels of glass bricks and red-framed windows.

Lamble Street

Mansfield Road

Housing 1973–81   B38g
Mansfield Road NW3
London Borough of Camden Architects
Department; Alan Forsyth and Gordon
Benson
⊖ Belsize Park
This long street terrace appears to go
some way to repairing the damage in-
flicted on Mansfield Road by the part-
icularly unfortunate building by
F Macmanus and Partners to the east. The
first impression is of a 'normal' terrace of
houses, but the internal requirements of
the section do not allow this. The pavement is gathered into the building as an
access gallery at first floor, leaving a
curious no-man's-land between the building line and the street.
Note the nine terraced houses in *Lamble
Street* (1971), in Oak Village to the south of
Mansfield Road. Designed for Camden by
Gordon Benson and Alan Forsyth, they
have a characteristically complex internal
arrangement of half-levels and simple
abstract exteriors. They are united by a
continuous attic storey, like Winscombe
Street R29.

House 1975   B39e
49a Downshire Hill NW3
Michael Hopkins
⊖ Hampstead
The understatement of the architecture of
this house suggests that buildings do not
always need to carry the usual signs
(parapet, door, window and so on). Built
on a slope, the two-storey house is
entered via a metal bridge at first floor.
The street and garden elevations are
totally glazed, and the flanks are of stove
enamelled corrugated metal sheet.
Despite its conspicuous modernity this is
a nostalgic building, and is reminiscent
both of Charles Eames' house in Santa
Monica (1949) and of the English
nineteenth-century engineering tradition
of glass and iron. It has practical engineering virtues: low cost, speed of construction and flexibility, deriving from its
100 mm (4 in) square steel columns at
3.6 m (12 ft) centres and proprietary steel
beams. Whether it could be more than a

one-off in an urban context remains
doubtful. The house was built as both a
home and an office, and Hopkins was the
first of the exponents of 'high tech' to
realize a house from the techniques of
warehousing and offices.

Interaction 1975   B40 l
Dalby Street and Prince of
Wales Road NW5
Cedric Price
⊖ Chalk Farm
The first evidence of the 'indeterminate'
school of design, of which Cedric Price has
been the chief spokesman since his Fun
Palace project of 1961 (with Joan
Littlewood) and Potteries Thinkbelt of
1964. With the collaboration of the client,
Ed Berman, Interaction is an experiment
in spontaneous social events combined
with an improbable 'urban farm'. The
exposed steel trusses and random
windows and panels are intentionally
utilitarian and incomplete, conveying the
image of a building site.

House 1975–9   B41d
24a York Rise NW5
Jo van Heyningen and Birkin Haward
⊖ Tufnell Park

A tiny house originally built for the architects themselves, intelligently designed
on a tight site inside an envelope determined by the planning authority. The
living room, on the upper floor, is linked
to the ground-floor kitchen by a double-
height conservatory, underneath the
patent glazing of the roof at the street
end. In 1980 the house won an Eternit
International Architecture Award for a
single-family house.

Houses 1981   B42i
2c and d Belsize Park Gardens
NW3
Spence and Webster
⊖ Belsize Park

Two single-storey houses, one originally
for each of the architect-partners, are
joined round a courtyard, and shelter
behind the former garden walls of the
grand detached house to the north. They
are distant descendants of Mies van der
Rohe's court house studies of 1931–40,
but are built of very spindly steel and
aluminium sections, and lack the originals'
free plans.

TVam television studios 1981–3   B43p
Hawley Crescent NW1
Terry Farrell and Co.
⊖ Camden Town

The conversion of a large former garage
gave Farrell his first opportunity after the
dissolution of his partnership with Nicholas Grimshaw to develop his anti-
modern vocabulary of forms, both on the
exterior of the building, in the long
sinuous façade to Hawley Crescent, and in
the elaborately decorated interiors. The
problem with this vocabulary is that the
real materials of which it is constructed –

corrugated metal siding, painted rendering, glazed masonry blocks – carry their own lugubrious messages which often contradict the would-be playfulness of the forms. 'Depression Deco' always appeared tired, and the jokes, at best only one-liners, still fall flat. The giant eggcups used as finials on the elevation to the canal were briefly admired.

ZeNW3 1985   B44e
180 Hampstead High Street NW3
Rick Mather Architects
▽ Hampstead

That an improbable combination of 'nouvelle' Chinese cooking, purist architecture and aquatic sculpture could become a successful commercial recipe is a tribute to this restaurant designer, Rick Mather, and to his client, Laurence Leung. The transparent frontage reveals the cool white interior, animated by the playful cascading handrail, so reversing the normal London convention for eating and drinking in buried interiors. See also Now and Zen K161, the most recent and ambitious of the Mather-designed chain.

Houses 1986–9   B45d
Coutts Crescent, 23 St Alban's Road NW5
Chassay Wright Architects
▽ Kentish Town, Archway

Challenging a suburban street of Betjemanesque inter-war semis, this terrace of eleven large four-storey houses is arranged in a shallow crescent set back behind a walled yard for car-parking. The houses in the crescent are lavishly planned with south-facing terraces, while those at the ends are crowned with double-height 'studio' bedrooms. A wealth of traditional and fashionable influences have been absorbed and successfully synthesized, and the scheme is well detailed and well built.

The Blackburn House   B46e
1987–8
Rosslyn Mews NW3
Chassay Wright and the Wilson Partnership
▽ Hampstead

This long three-storey shoebox is tucked away behind Haverstock Hill and faces on to its own entrance court. The white-stuccoed wall provides a background for a series of metal protuberances; an 'anthropomorphic' drainpipe; a large canted oriel window; and so on. These give clues to the surreal world within, designed by Peter Wilson, incorporating a private art gallery, studios and residence for the owner. The house has been described as an 'ark' full of creatures at sea in the middle of London. The masonry wall facing on to the churchyard to the east is unexpectedly monumental.

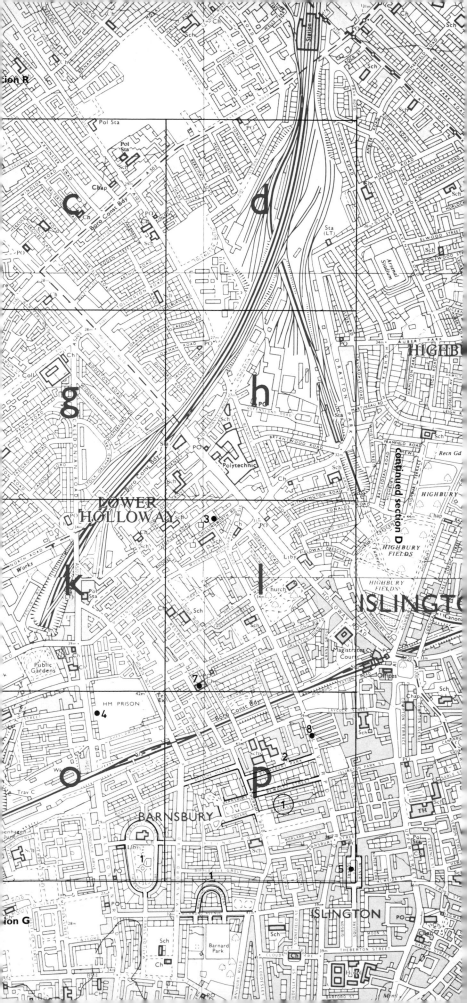

Section C: Camden Town (north)/Kentish Town/Tufnell Park/ Holloway/Barnsbury

Railways criss-cross this part of London: running north-south are the main lines from King's Cross (cut in 1851) and St Pancras (1868), while to the south runs the North London Line, mainly on viaducts. Before the railways there had been only villages and fields, although some of the village high streets had been lined with Georgian ribbon development: it is still possible to see these three- and four-storey houses behind the single-storey shopfronts of Camden and Kentish Town High Streets, in Holloway and Seven Sisters Roads, and in Caledonian Road (where some houses have remained unconverted).

The development of Barnsbury, to the west of fashionable Islington, was begun early in the nineteenth century and completed by 1835. Between the coming of the railways and the beginning of the First World War, the whole of the rest of the section was covered in houses. In 1845 began the building of large semi-detached houses around Camden Square in the south-west, and development then spread north and east along Camden Road, laid out in the 1820s. As a result, the prisons of Pentonville C4 and Holloway C6, and the Caledonian cattle market C6 (all of which had deliberately been placed outside the city), were enclosed by housing.

The eastern part of the section is the London Borough of Camden, and contains some of that authority's own recent housing designs (for example Maiden Lane C15 on abandoned railway land), and some of its more adventurous commissions (such as Colquhoun and Miller's infill at Caversham Road, Kentish Town C16).

Mountford Crescent

Thornhill Crescent

Richmond Avenue

Thornhill Square

Barnsbury N1 c1820   C1p
Thomas Cubitt
⊖Highbury and Islington
Lying between Liverpool Road and Caledonian Road, north of Richmond Avenue, Barnsbury was laid out by Thomas Cubitt before his more famous speculations in Bloomsbury and Belgravia, and is a rather loose composition of suburban open-cornered squares, crescents and streets either side of Thornhill Road.
Barnsbury Square (with the two partial crescents leading off its north-west and south-west corners), **Belitha Villas** and **Richmond Avenue** are the best parts. Although run down, Richmond Avenue has good terraces: sphinxes and miniature obelisks flank the entrances of numbers

46–72. In the north corner of Barnsbury Square is **Mountford Crescent** (c1830), an early pair of two-storey semi-detached villas, stuccoed, bow-fronted and set back from the street in their private garden. After 1830 the semi-detached villa became a popular model for developers, but here late nineteenth-century terraces have unfortunately destroyed the original image of villas standing in their own leafy gardens. To the west is **Thornhill Square** (c1850), the largest square in Islington, its elliptical composition completed by **Thornhill Crescent**. To the east note **Barnsbury Street** and **Bewdley Street**, where the condition of the houses varies from gentrification to seedy decay.

Barnsbury Park N1 1830s   C2p
⊖Highbury and Islington
Islington has many continuous late Georgian terraces, and was also the scene of experiments in various forms for housing. The south side of this street is an elegant two-storey terrace, with set-back entrances which give the effect of semi-detached villas.

St James 1837–8   C3l
Chillingworth Road N7
Inwood and Clifton
⊖Holloway Road
The eccentric south façade bears no relation to the main body of the church which is now exposed by demolition on both sides: the asymmetrical composition gives a central flat-pedimented portico with four Ionic demi-columns. The square tower on the left has a circular top decorated with grapes and ears of wheat. In the 1980s the building was converted into flats.

Pentonville Prison 1840–2   C4o
Caledonian Road N1
Major Jebb (first Surveyor General of Prisons)
⊖Caledonian Road
The prison's portico and massive, inclined wall dominate this section of the Caledonian Road. Behind, there are five brick wings radiating from a central control block. The plan is derived from Haviland's famous Eastern Penitentiary in Philadelphia (1829) and is the only surviving example of Bentham's Panopticon prison type in London.

Milner Square N1 1841–3   C5p
Roumieu and Gough
⊖ Angel, Highbury and Islington
With its continuous attic floor this is a
particularly European square, entered in
the middle of its ends like other small
squares in Islington. The houses are of
three bays separated by thinly proportioned pilasters, an arrangement which
gives the façades exaggerated height.

Caledonian Market Tower   C6j
1855
North Road and Market Road N7
J B Bunning
⊖ Caledonian Road
Only the gaunt white tower, the outer
railings and three (of the four) public
houses remain of this once famous market; it was designed by the City's architect to accommodate 34,900 sheep, 6,616
bullocks, 1,425 calves and 900 pigs on 6 ha
(15 acres) of granite paving. The tower
housed banks and a telegraph office at its
base. The public houses at the corners of
the enclosure are tall, robust and
Italianate.

At **Holloway Prison** (1849–51) on
Parkhurst Road, only a fragment of one of
the gatehouses remains of Bunning's City
of London Prison, demolished in the 1970s
complete with its central tower (a parody
on Warwick Castle). The reformist intentions of the stellar plan and its attendant
castellated architecture may now be
outdated, but at least the building looked
like a prison. The trouble with the new
Holloway is that it resembles a local
authority housing scheme with bars over
the windows. The demolition of Holloway
virtually completes the destruction of
works by this eminent architect: his
magnificent Coal Exchange was senselessly demolished in 1962 and the Caledonian market buildings were removed in
the 1960s.

St Clement 1863–5   C7 l
Davey Close, south of
Bride Street N7
Sir George Gilbert Scott
⊖ Highbury and Islington
'Far less conventional and well bred than
most of Scott's work' (Pevsner), this
church is now neglected, buried and
almost forgotten in a new housing estate.
The very tall, expressive, three-bay west
front is of stock brick with a bellcote
above, and the pitch to the nave is
exaggeratedly steep. The church has recently been converted into flats.

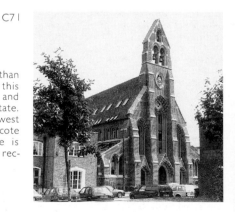

Samuel Lewis Buildings C8p
1910
Liverpool Road N1
⊖ Highbury and Islington

A small and late attempt by a charitable trust to bring high style to its housing: there are elaborate un-English mansarded gables, bay windows and sandstone trim. But the five blocks of flats are too close together for privacy – the spaces between them are mean.

Holloway Estate 1962–9 C9f
Parkhurst Road N7
McMorran and Whitby
⊖ Holloway Road

The 128 flats are contained in eight buildings (rather than blocks) of four storeys, forming three simple courtyards with open corners. Their neo-Georgian style (like the buildings in the Inns of Court), with arched public doorways in black brickwork (impervious to graffiti), simple openings and slate roofs, is a sane contribution to public housing. With McMorran's other London buildings – Lloyds, Pall Mall K160 and Wood Street police station L123 – they show that there is still mileage in the classical tradition.

Houses 1964–72 C10n
Murray Mews NW1
Team Four, Tom Kay and Richard Gibson
⊖ Camden Town

London mews were built from the seventeenth to the nineteenth century as stables for houses on the principal streets. As traffic and land values have increased, the relative calm and cheapness of mews properties has recommended them for residential use. Murray Mews is a good example of this transformation. However, the mews is not a street - it is narrower and lower, its ground floor is not defended by the typical 'area' and its back prospect is very limited indeed. It is interesting therefore to look at these houses, in the light of the 'low-rise high density housing' debate in the 1960s, and to see whether they suggest the development of a new type.

15, 17 and 19 Murray Mews

On the north side is a terrace of three houses, numbers 15, 17, and 19 (1964) designed by Team Four (Norman Foster, Wendy Foster, Richard Rogers, Su Rogers and Georgie Wolton) before the practice dissolved in 1967. The ground floor is protected from the mews by a solid red-brick wall, and a sloped patent glazed roof provides daylight to the principal living space behind. The houses follow the nineteenth-century studio tradition – a top-lit double-height space surrounded by secondary rooms. This is a very appropriate 'mews' type.

Number 22 was designed by Tom Kay (1972). The living accommodation is at first floor, surrounding an entrance court, and on the ground floor are a garage and small office, protecting the private domestic realm above. An ingenious section provides light to the deep plan and the principal rooms look to the rear.

22 Murray Mews

Almost merging with number 22, through the use of the same common stock brick, number 20 is a small house designed by Richard Gibson in 1965. The plan is a simple two-storey atrium, and the court is glazed at roof-level, supplementing the light to the rooms on either side. Despite their relatively complex interiors, all three houses present a neutral face to the mews.

House 1965 C11m
62 Camden Mews NW1
Edward Cullinan
⊖ Camden Town

For many architects London mews have offered the opportunity to realize personal ideas without the larger-scale responsibilities and restrictions of 'housing' schemes. In this case, the thesis was to prove a prototype for later work, notably Highgrove T34. Designed by the architect for himself, the plan is simple and hierarchic. The public rooms form a long gallery or *piano nobile* set over a plinth of bedrooms. The garden too is at first-floor level over the garage. The glazed timber screens and overhanging eaves have both elegance and directness. These planning and constructional concerns made the house a place of pilgrimage for students in the late 1960s. Number 66, designed by Peter Bell, is also of considerable architectural interest, and was occupied in 1985.

62 Camden Mews

66 Camden Mews

Studio apartments 1968–71 C12j
Cliff Road NW1
Georgie Wolton
⊖ Caledonian Road

Two of the first multi-storey groups of studios built in London since the Edwardian era. The building to the north is in the European tradition of six studios paired either side of a central staircase. The exterior is rendered and painted white, and the double-height studios are set back in section as they rise, facing north over the garden. Naum Gabo was a resident of this fine building, a type which is too rare in London.

Next door to the south a four-storey building provides generous single-storey studio apartments. A central core divides the floor plan in half; the studios face the street, and living accommodation looks out over the garden to the rear, with fine views of Highgate ridge in the distance. On top is a very beautiful roof garden with exotic vines and waving pampas grass. The elevation to Cliff Road is a painted concrete frame filled in with glass bricks; at one end are up-and-over industrial metal louvred doors (which when open turn the inside space into a balcony). Taken together this building and its neighbour are a valuable contribution to the lapsed London studio tradition.

Kentish Town Health Centre 1973
C13i

Bartholomew Road NW5
London Borough of Camden Architects
Department; Peter Watson
⊖ Kentish Town, Camden Town

More realistic than the social experiments of the Peckham Health Centre X10 and others of its kind in the 1930s, this building was a response to a new brief for local clinics, intended to relieve the burden of central hospitals and to foster a local sense of community. It provides for two group surgeries, a crèche, a teaching unit and other related health facilities, with a remarkable organizational clarity. The accommodation is planned around a central entrance and information bay. A pair of two-storey wings at right angles to each other form a diagonal and symmetrical entrance and a simple court for parking, prams and arrival.

The architecture is as rational as the organization: to the street, but separated from it by a vine-covered screen, there is a hard wall of white rendered panels, exposed concrete beams and industrial metal windows – a distant tribute by the designer to the architecture of Auguste Perret in particular and the 'Heroic' period of modern architecture in general. To the interior court there is a glazed entrance canopy. See also Finsbury Health Centre G64.

Flats 1975–80
C14e

14 Leighton Crescent NW5
Edward Cullinan Architects
⊖ Kentish Town

Built for the London Borough of Camden, this small block in the middle of the run-down crescent shows the architects grappling with the problem of designing housing without using the clichés of modern architecture. The windows (except for the attic strip under the overhanging roof) are treated as holes in the wall, and the wall is decorated with a trellis of balconies and rainwater pipes. While spare and assured in these hands, this format has quickly become debased in others'.

Maiden Lane Stage I 1976–81
C15n

Agar Grove, NW1
London Borough of Camden; Alan Forsyth and Gordon Benson

A large enclave of 225 dwellings on disused railway land behind Agar Grove, the Maiden Lane estate was designed by the same architects as Branch Hill A9 and adopts a similar site organization.

The scheme is divided in two by the extension of St Paul's Crescent, either side of which is a public network of footpaths and pedestrian decks. An outer 'wall' of three-storey terraces protects the housing in both parts from the railway to the south, and encloses small public piazzas and a continuous fabric of two-storey narrow-fronted terraces stepping gently to the west. However, while half of the dwellings look over open space to the west, the rest look out onto their backs.

Housing 1978 C16i
5 Caversham Road and
6–10 Gaisford Street NW5
London Borough of Camden;
Colquhoun and Miller
⊖ Kentish Town

Two small infill sites in a late nineteenth-century block, with large semi-detached villas on one side and terraced housing on the other, have resulted in two extremely successful and sane housing buildings. Refreshingly, they take their inspiration from the existing building types, completing the missing half of a semi-detached villa in Caversham Road and reinterpreting three houses as part of a terrace in Gaisford Street. In both sites, maisonettes are incorporated in the image of the large house or villa. Both buildings are beautifully detailed, the off-white rendering modulated by a series of grooves. Their

cool, abstract and modern appearance shows that the adoption of existing types does not inevitably result in pastiche.

House 1982 C17m
44 Rochester Place NW1
David Wild
⊖ Camden Town

An ambitious house which manages to combine public and private architecture. The two-storey portico and monumental corner column (carefully preserving an existing tree) establish a public scale to the street, while, set back within the portico, the glass brick panels, exposed concrete blockwork and glazed screens give the interior a domestic scale. It is a surprise, therefore, that this house was built by the architect for himself, as this usually results in a utilitarian appearance justified by the demands of economy. Number 42 was also designed by David Wild (1989), but built by a general contractor.

Sainsbury's supermarket C18m
1988–90
Camden Road NW1
Nicholas Grimshaw and Partners
⊖ Camden Town

The supermarket is part of the larger redevelopment of an irregular triangular site formerly occupied by a bakery. The shopping hall is a single bland volume without columns and with a curved ceiling which follows the line of the arched roof. The supports to the roof at either side are counterbalanced by the weight of the first floors, which contain rooms for staff. These floors are prevented from falling over by the cables which project from the face of the building. The façade to Camden Road fearlessly exhibits the consequences of the structural scheme to produce an uneasy mixture of industrial imagery and street architecture. The rest of the site is occupied by a service yard, a block of workshops to Kentish Town Road and, facing north-east across the Regent's Canal, a terrace of houses faced in what appear to be the re-cycled parts of aeroplanes.

Studios 1988–90   C19m
Cobham Mews, Agar Grove NW1
David Chipperfield Architects
⊖ Camden Town
Another contribution to the growing collection of small buildings of character in the environs of Camden Square, these three studios by a young architectural practice are arranged in parallel on a tight triangular site. The language and materials are cool and uncompromisingly modern: rendering, concrete beams, and massive steel window frames with inset panels of glazed blocks.

Section D: Stoke Newington/Highbury/Hackney/Canonbury/
De Beauvoir Town/Dalston

Two significant engineering works, nearly 2,000 years apart, divide this part of London into recognizable areas. Firstly, Ermine Street, the straight Roman road from Lincoln to the City of London, forms a north-south alignment along Stamford Hill (section U), Stoke Newington High Street, Stoke Newington Road and Kingsland Road. Secondly, at right angles to Ermine Street, the North London railway line (c1865) divides the section into its northern and southern parts. Ermine Street and the North London Line have no specific character, but they have proved significant and useful in defining districts.

To the east of Ermine Street and north of the North London Line is Hackney, and to the south-east is Dalston. To the east and west of Kingsland Road are Dalston and De Beauvoir Town – the south-west corner of the borough of Hackney (the majority of which lies in section U). The development of the De Beauvoir Estate in 1840 was the first large-scale building enterprise in Hackney. Here, unlike the other developments in Hackney, the Estate retained close control of the operation, giving it a conspicuous consistency (see De Beauvoir Square D8 and its surrounding streets). The urban villa – a semi-detached house in a variety of styles – was by the middle of the nineteenth century the typical form of development. The villa was more versatile than the terraced house, being suitable for both small and large sites. In the massive urbanization of the second half of the nineteenth century, Hackney's development was piecemeal, and its population rose from 120,000 to 370,000 between 1837 and 1901. Redevelopment after severe bombing in the Second World War has increased the fragmentary nature of the area.

The area to the west of Ermine Street and north of the railway line was essentially rural down to the middle of the nineteenth century. Stoke Newington was a medieval village with the parish church of Old St Mary D1 at its centre; its two reservoir ponds and Clissold Park still give the impression of a nineteenth-century suburb. Islington, to the south, was surrounded by the hamlets of Newington Green, Canonbury and Lower and Upper Holloway (see section C). From 1750 this rural picture changed dramatically with the building of the New Road: by 1805 there was a suburban nucleus south of St Paul's Road which was consolidated by the 1850s.

The district now known as Highbury had its origins in the eighteenth-century expansion of Islington along the main roads out of London. It has much late Victorian and early twentieth-century by-law housing (dwellings conforming to statutory light, ventilation and drainage), light industry, goods yards, the Arsenal football ground and, at its centre, Highbury Fields D6, forming a beautiful small park surrounded on two sides by fine eighteenth-century terraces.

In the sixteenth century wealthy Londoners built country houses in Canonbury, to the west of Islington, and the eighteenth century saw widespread development in the area, particularly the Canonbury House estates of the 1770s.

Highbury Fields

Old St Mary   D1c
from 14th century
St Mary 1858
Stoke Newington Church Street N16
Sir George Gilbert Scott
⊖ Manor House
Positioned either side of Stoke
Newington Church Street, the two
churches are an interesting pair: one the
church of a medieval village, the other
showing the aspirations of an emerging
London suburb. Old St Mary is picturesque; the nave is late medieval, the west
tower, south aisle and vestry were added
in 1560, Barry added the north aisle in
1824 and the timber spire is of 1829.
Scott's new church is run-of-the-mill
Gothic Revival; extensively damaged in
the war, it has since been repaired.

Canonbury House c1780   D2m
Canonbury Place N1
⊖ Highbury and Islington
The house is an elegant two-storey villa
built for the developer of the Canonbury
House Estate, which filled in the northern
triangle between Canonbury Road and
the earlier ribbon development of Upper
Street. The houses in **Canonbury Place**
are of the same date, and are interesting as
an early example of the use of stucco.

Highbury Terrace N5 1789   D3e
⊖ Highbury and Islington
A fine Georgian terrace with wide pavements faces the small park of Highbury
Fields. The first-floor windows are unusually slender (like Duncan Terrace in South
Islington H5), and accentuate its height.
The eighteenth-century terraces of
Highbury have an ethereal, lost quality,
embedded as they now are in dense
nineteenth-century artisan housing: they
recall the time when Highbury and much
of Islington was open country inhabited by
the wealthy few.

Canonbury Square N1 1800   D4m
Leroux (?)
⊖ Highbury and Islington
A completely preserved square of particularly beautiful proportions, distinguished by raised pavements on the south
side (reminiscent of Clifton in Bristol),
and a public garden at its centre. The
houses have tall first-floor windows with
arched brickwork. The square is now
divided and threatened by heavy traffic on
the Canonbury Road. George Orwell
lived at number 27b in 1945. To the east
note Canonbury House D2, Canonbury
Place, Alwyne Villas D7 and the fine
terraces in Compton Road and
Canonbury Grove.

Clissold House 1820–30   D5b
Clissold Park N16
J Woods
⊖ Manor House
This monumental portico of six Doric columns, superimposed on the three-storey stock brick villa overlooking Clissold Park, is a memory of Stoke Newington's more affluent and rural past.

Highbury Fields, Highbury   D6e
Park and **Highbury New**
Park N5
1830, 1850
⊖ Highbury and Islington
Highbury Fields is a pleasant surprise in dense semi-industrial surroundings: a small park with mature plane trees and broad gravel paths, it is nevertheless large enough to absorb normal community activities (a crèche, swimming pool, tennis, five-a-side football, and the occasional travelling circus or fair). The Fields developed with Highbury Park (c1830) and Highbury New Park (c1850). The large Victorian detached villas on its east side, in mixed Italo-Romanesque styles, are now in multiple occupancy, but speak of the district's more affluent past.

Canonbury 1835–45   D7m
Alwyne Villas, Alwyne Road,
Alwyne Place, Canonbury Park north
and south, New River Walk N1
⊖ Highbury and Islington
An early suburb, conveniently near the City, consisting mostly of semi-detached houses of two and three storeys in spare Italianate style, and with a loose and now leafy street pattern. To the south the pleasantly tamed New River forms a charming park. Canonbury Park is grander and more regular with good semi-detached houses.

De Beauvoir Square   D8o
N1 1838
Roumieu and Gough
⇌ Essex Road
This square, with its supportive pattern of streets, is Georgian in layout, but the architecture of its semi-detached villas is a curious Dutch/Jacobean mixture. The Tudor details of the oriel windows and mullions, the picturesque Dutch roof profile and the decorative stonework in no way anticipate Roumieu and Gough's strangely abstract and classical Milner Square C5, of only two years later.

Albion Square E8 1846–9   D9p
J C Loudon
⇌ Essex Road

Semi-detached villas, by the celebrated landscape designer Loudon, which according to Pevsner show 'the transition from late classical to the Italianate.' These simple brick boxes with mass-produced stuccoed embellishments were the prototype for the massive house-building boom in Hackney and the other outer boroughs in the second half of the nineteenth century. The urban villa – a grand house occupied by two or more families – lent itself to both small and large sites, and this versatility made it more appropriate than the terraced house for suburban development.

St Matthias 1851   D10g
Wordsworth Road,
off Matthias Road N16
W Butterfield
⇌ Dalston Junction

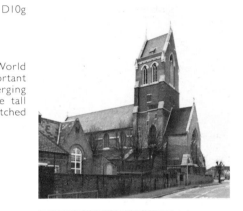

The church, damaged in the Second World War and since restored, is an important early example of Butterfield's emerging elemental Gothic style – note the tall gabled east tower and the steeply pitched gables over the aisles and nave.

Union Chapel 1888   D11m
Compton Terrace N1
Bonella and Paul
⊖ Highbury and Islington

The buildings in which Congregationalists first worshipped were as plain as the religion itself. This huge and wild Victorian Gothic chapel is therefore a surprise, especially as it erupts from the Georgian serenity of **Compton Terrace** (1806). The savage contrast is tempered by the narrow strip of park which separates both chapel and terrace from Upper Street.

Marquess Road Estate 1970   D12n
Essex Road and
St Paul's Road N1
Darbourne and Darke
⇌ Essex Road, ⊖ Highbury and Islington

The urban vernacular style of this estate goes back to Darbourne and Darke's entry 014 for the Lillington Gardens competition of 1961, and unfortunately has found widespread official approval as an antidote to the excesses of the tower block. Large sections of London, as at Marquess Road, are consequently being rendered inaccessible and incomprehensible by the construction of dense urban villages. The buildings are of brick with small window openings and slate roofs, but do not fall into the ordinary patterns of the city (street, house and so on). Instead they coagulate, giving the impression of an extremely large institutional building – the very form they were meant to avoid.

Section E: North Kensington/West Kilburn/Kensal Rise/Kilburn/Westbourne Grove/Maida Vale/St John's Wood (west)

The lines of transport connecting London to the west and north-west dominate this section. Edgware Road (the Roman Watling Street) runs straight north-west to St Albans and on to north Wales; now no longer a national route, it becomes tamed as a high street at Kilburn High Road, where the village of Kilburn used to be. To the south is the Paddington branch of the Grand Union Canal, constructed from 1795. Joined to the national canal network in 1805, it was extended eastwards via Regent's Park to the docks at Limehouse before being made obsolete by the railways. The original terminus of Brunel's Great Western Railway was built from 1832–8 at Paddington, then a village round its green, giving impetus to London's westward growth.

St John's Wood, to the east of Edgware Road, was developed as a suburb in the 1840s: at first villas stood alone in their own plots, later to form handsome streets like Hamilton Terrace E1. The suburb, fully developed by the 1850s, was never isolated: from the beginning it was served by buses to the West End and City, and in the 1870s the Metropolitan underground line was opened, further increasing its accessibility.

At the same time Little Venice, the first of the developments west of the Edgware Road, was growing around the junction of the canal with its branch to Paddington Basin. It was followed later in the nineteenth century by the huge areas of two-storey artisans' housing in West Kilburn, Kensal Rise (which had been an eighteenth-century spa) and Kilburn (see for example Queen's Park Estate E5).

In the 1960s Westway was built, the urban motorway following the line of the railway and connecting Euston Road (an eighteenth-century bypass) with the A40, the main road to Oxford. Raised on legs, its effect on the neighbourhood through and over which it passed was destructive, and its opening was marked by protests. Westway was probably largely responsible for the popular distrust of large-scale engineering schemes, which led to the abandonment of the proposed inner motorway 'box' – London's last big transport plan.

The villas of St John's Wood

Hamilton Terrace NW8

laid out 1830
St John's Wood NW8
↔ Maida Vale

A very long (1100 m/3600 ft), undulating, wide and tree-lined street, Hamilton Terrace developed from the south, first with terraces and later with detached villas, and shows that suburbs did not have to use picturesque forms or curved streets. None of the architecture is particularly good and the success of the whole relies entirely on the width of the street and the limited range of materials: stock brick and stucco. Number 58 (1934), by Francis Lorne of Burnet, Tait and Lorne, is the only 'modern' house in the street. Note the bow fronts of the houses in St John's Wood Road, terminating the south end, and the gentlemen's public lavatory at the junction of St John's Wood Road and Maida Vale, a Victorian public

convenience (now disappearing as a type) with polished brass handrails to the staircase, white and green glazed wall tiles and pavement lights.

Blomfield Road and
Maida Avenue W9 c1840

↔ Warwick Avenue

Blomfield Road and Maida Avenue, 'planned' streets on either side of the canal between Warwick Avenue and the Edgware Road, are unique examples (more Dutch than Venetian) of the canal's use as an extra ingredient in a London street. The buildings on either side vary from elegant nineteenth-century semi-detached stuccoed villas and terraced houses to Edwardian mansion flats. The secret of this special place lies in the mature trees forming a canopy to the canal, and the presence of boats and the bridge at either end of the wide space. To the south-west the canal continues and divides at the basin of Little Venice, where, with the visible proximity of both the Westway motorway and more recent building, the magic of Blomfield Road evaporates.

St Mary Magdalene 1868–78   E3o
Woodchester Square W2
George Edmund Street
Θ Royal Oak

One of the finest Gothic Revival churches in London, and a defiant landmark among the banal high-rise towers seen by the motorist from Westway. The exterior is banded with stone and dark brown brick and the tower and slender spire are positioned asymmetrically.

St Augustine, Kilburn   E4g
1870–80, tower 1897–8
Kilburn Park Road NW6
J L Pearson
Θ Kilburn Park

According to Pevsner, St Augustine's is one of the finest churches of its date in England. It is now surrounded by new housing and roads that have all but destroyed the coherence of the area, which the church used to dominate with its spire 77 m (254 ft) high. While the sources of its architecture (Early English and Albi Cathedral) are as scholarly as could be expected of a late Victorian building, the forms have an expressionistic baldness.

The interior is also very good: the nave is high, and the theme of brick and stone banding to the external walls recurs, with an astonishingly rich and decorative use of diagonally laid green and pink tiles below dado level. The columns on the north side are separated from the wall to form a screen, and there is a tall clerestory and vaulted ceiling. The crypt, by J N Comper, is notable for its elaborate timber screens, paintings and stained glass.

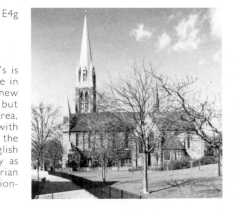

Queen's Park Estate NW6   E5a
1875–83
Austin, Roland Plumbe
⊖ Queen's Park

Built by the Artisans', Labourers' and General Development Company on land bought from All Souls College, Oxford, this 'improving' estate of 33 ha (76 acres) provided 2000 houses for 16,000 residents at a cost of £700,000. Although there was no public house and behaviour was firmly regulated, the estate was always successful, the early residents being 'of the regular employed class: railwaymen or police, artisans, small clerks ...' The houses have Gothic details, and there is a 1.6 ha (4 acre) park.

The Prince Albert c1880   E6 I
Formosa Street, Castellain Road
and Warrington Crescent W9
⊖ Warwick Avenue

Formosa Street is a remarkable shopping street, forming a grand but miniature urban block. Its east and west façades, stuccoed blank, have giant Corinthian pilasters; and on the south-west corner is the Prince Albert pub. The double-height ground-floor screen – a complex series of curves in bevelled, etched and inscribed glass set in a delicate timber frame – is especially fine and surprisingly intact. Inside, there are more screens dividing the large single space into four separate bars.

Housing, Alexandra Road   E7d
1969–79
Abbey Road, Boundary Road
and Loudoun Road NW8
London Borough of Camden Architects Department; Neave Brown
⊖ Swiss Cottage, ⇌ South Hampstead

Alexandra Road is probably the last (and the most ambitious) of the large comprehensive redevelopments of the inner city originating in the mid-1950s. The 6.6 ha (16 acre) site marks the northern boundary of St John's Wood, an area characterized by a loose pattern of nineteenth-century villas, and the development occupies an entire city block with a mainline railway cutting to the north. The planning brief required housing for 1660 people in 520 dwellings with garages, a training centre for mentally handicapped children, a community centre, a children's reception centre E9, a school and a local park of 1.6 ha (4 acres).

The site is conceived by the designer as a 'single gesture' and is organized linearly, like a giant centipede, in open rows of long terraces of varying height. The social buildings are grouped to form its 'head' at the eastern extremity, and its 'feet' are two pedestrian streets extending the length of the site, giving access to the dwellings on either side of the park. The principal terrace at Alexandra Road demonstrates the correct application of the stepped section: by forming an eight-storey wall to the railway cutting it develops a generous front of sun-filled terraces to the south. The interiors of the flats, like their antecedents at Winscombe Street R29 and Fleet Road B36, have a generosity of planning and quality in detail that are unrivalled in any post-war local authority housing.

Despite such accolades, we have reservations about the appropriateness of the architecture of the 'single gesture' to housing. At the scale of the individual dwelling it creates a fixed arrangement of rooms and their functions (and risks dictating a lifestyle); and on a larger scale it attempts to reduce hundreds of dwellings, with a complex social brief, to a single building.

Note also the two red-brick buildings by Tom Kay (1980) on Loudoun Road. The building to the south is another version of the stepped section and contains shops and housing; that to the north contains studio workshops.

Trellick Tower 1973   E8m
Golborne Road W10
Ernö Goldfinger
⊖Westbourne Park

When built, these were the tallest flats in England. Goldfinger was experimenting both with the 'deck' form, in which one access corridor serves three levels of maisonettes (like Le Corbusier's *Unité d'Habitation*, but with the corridor on the outside), and with his own language of the articulated concrete frame. The projection at the top of the separate lift and stair tower houses the gas-fired boiler, below which is a glazed meeting room for tenants. When journalists write of the horrors of tower block living, the inhabitants of this tower, mostly without children, write back saying how much they like it. If we must have towers (and this now seems doubtful), then this is one of the best.

ex **Children's Reception**   E9d
Centre 1976
Alexandra Road NW8
Evans and Shalev
⊖Swiss Cottage

Forming the 'head' to the 'centipede' of Alexandra Road E7, the children's reception centre provides short-stay accommodation for thirty-one children in care, aged five to eighteen, with sixteen residential staff. The architects (non-Camden Borough Council contributors to the Alexandra Road Estate) produced a compact organization to maintain a close relationship between staff and children. To this end, the section is all important, establishing a complex series of levels in which the small private rooms are related three-dimensionally through small communal areas to the main common space. The exterior is a neutral outcome, and is a good example of one of the principal concerns of modern architecture. This has shifted emphasis from the external appearance of buildings to the relatively exclusive internal domain: the form of the exterior is generated by the dynamic of the interior, rather than being designed separately and in its own right. Unfortunately the building was found to be unsuitable for its use and was closed in 1981.

Home for the Physically   E10d
Handicapped 1978
Boundary Road NW8
Evans and Shalev
⊖Swiss Cottage

Designed to provide a permanent home for thirty severely handicapped adults, aged from seventeen to fifty, the building has residential suites and staff flats arranged in section to form the community hall, and to provide a common roof terrace and a private outdoor space for each. The stepped terraces on Boundary Road face south, which is pleasant for the residents, but they destroy the continuity of the street and lend the building unnecessary significance.
Alexandra Road presents a microcosm of a much wider problem. The special architectural treatment of this home distinguishes it from the 'normal' terraces of the rest of the street. Such architectural segregation, though well-intentioned, reflects and exaggerates rigid social classifications: it is a pity that those unfortunate enough not to conform with a narrow definition of 'normality', including the physically handicapped, should not be allowed to live in more ordinary buildings.

Warehouses 1978–80   E11i
McKay Trading Estate,
Kensal Road W10
John Outram
⊖ Westbourne Park

The terrace of five porticoed warehouses, between Kensal Road and the Grand Union Canal, successfully challenges the contemporary tendency to give such buildings a bland, utilitarian appearance. The Kensal Road façade has monumental qualities: a massive brick central column supports the pediment, and the unsupported space either side is used for covered loading bays. The mixture of bands of blue, red and stock bricks gives the building an air of permanence by connecting it with the nineteenth-century warehouse tradition, while the steel portal frames and corrugated metal

roof structure represent contemporary technology.

Housing 1979–82   E12g
171–201 Lanark Road W9
Jeremy and Fenella Dixon
⊖ Maida Vale

A radical reproach to the urban model of the 1960s which it faces across Lanark Road, this row of what appears to be eight 'villas' actually contains flats. Their form paraphrases the nineteenth-century suburban housing types and street architecture with which Maida Vale was first developed. In the details there is a strong contrast between the 'traditional' forms of the front – deeply overhanging gables and arched windows with stucco surrounds – and the utility of the sides with their metal stairs and the backs, with their flush gables.

Shop 1985   E13p
Clifton Nurseries, Clifton Villas W9
Jeremy Dixon BDP
⊖ Warwick Avenue

Clifton Nurseries have several sites and have been imaginative patrons of small-scale architecture. This small shop, extended from an existing greenhouse, was elaborately wrought using materials which would wear well: the exposed structure is in oak and the whole is covered in a copper roof. The open framework which serves as entrance canopy is also by Dixon.

Saatchi Collection 1985   E14d
98A Boundary Road NW8
Max Gordon
⊖ Swiss Cottage

Although indebted to the art galleries of Manhattan's Soho (warehouse district) of the mid-1970s, this transformation of an industrial workshop behind a terrace of houses established itself as a bench-mark for the minimalist London art galley interior of the 1980s. The understatement of the entrance from Boundary Road enhances the drama and surprise of the very large dimensions of the gallery (100 m × 40 m/328 ft × 130 ft). The surprise has been further emphasized by the 1.2 m (4 ft) excavation of the principal sculpture gallery, which as you enter has the effect of making the works appear to be suspended in space. The dry lining of the galleries, set forward from the original and utilitarian structure, is the key to the minimalism of the interior. The portraits of Lucien Freud and the constructions of Richard Deacon are equally at home in this remarkably abstract universe.

continued

a

b

PRIMROSE

Reservoir
(covered)
Barrow
Hill

46

38

e

Sta
(LT)

PO

Synagogue

Hospl

35

St John's Wood

Convent

Hospl

10

f

38

Pol
Sta

36

60

Winfield
House

Tennis
Court

Ch

War
Meml

7

17

Larwood Cricket Ground

Ground
Car
Park

Pav

59

54

55

15

15

Lodge

Chap

i

Lisson
Green

27

Coll

j

Depot

Hospl

CITY OF WE
ST MARYLE

ROSSMORE ROAD

Ch

continued section E

58

Liby

33

Offices

57

Sch

m

Recn
Gd

Coll

Little
Venice

56

Hospl PO
Pol Sta

Lisson Grove

Sta
(LT)

n

Hospl

Ch

19

Paddington

Sta
(LT)

Goods Station

Sch

Bishop's Road
Bridge

Ingate Whar

Sta
PO

Paddington Basin

SOUTH WHARF ROAD

Synagogue

Hospl

Ch

PO

contin

Section F: St John's Wood (east)/Primrose Hill/Regent's Park/ Marylebone (north)/Camden Town (west)

The medieval village of St Mary-le-Bourne (the main street being part of the present Marylebone High Street, and Marylebone Lane a track meandering through open fields), the small settlement of Camden Town to the north, the mound of Primrose Hill set in open countryside and the Roman Watling Street (now Edgware Road) were the only developments here until the end of the seventeenth century. Between 1717 and 1817 two important enterprises transformed this rural picture, permanently connecting most of the area to central London.

In 1708 the Duke of Newcastle bought the Marylebone Estate; in 1717 he laid out Cavendish Square and the surrounding streets (see section J), which encouraged continuous residential building within its orderly grid of streets for the rest of the century. Portland Place F3 to the east, the grandest street in eighteenth-century London, dates from 1775, and Baker Street to the west was completed shortly before 1800. The northern boundary of the development was the New Road (now Marylebone Road, Euston Road and Pentonville Road), laid out in 1756 as an east-west bypass (London's first) of the West End. By the beginning of the nineteenth century Marylebone Road defined London's northern limits, as Oxford Street had done in the seventeenth century.

In 1812 the Prince Regent commissioned John Nash's plans for Regent's Park F5, to be carried out from 1817. An area of heathland in the eighteenth century, Regent's Park is now, thanks to Nash, London's largest and most impressive civic design: in contrast to most of London's civic spaces it is the result of a conscious plan rather than the fortuitous outcome of centuries of change. Included in Nash's plan for Regent's Park was Regent's Canal (see section E), which, apart from being an early example of industrial engineering, adds an unexpected touch of romance to the northern edge of the park. Much of the excavated material was intelligently added to the mound of Primrose Hill.

By 1830 Regent's Park was encouraging the growth (to the west) of St John's Wood, originally the Eyre Estate, which by 1855 was covered with white stuccoed detached villas, and (to the east) of Camden Town, completed by 1840. Here, as elsewhere, the railways had a significant effect: the London and Birmingham Railway, which originally terminated at Chalk Farm near the Round House B16, was ingeniously extended to Euston in 1836, cut in the seam between Camden Town and Albany Street, to the east of Regent's Park.

In a little under fifty years rough heathland had become an impressive new urban addition to the centre of London, its general form remaining unchanged up to the present. The area south of Marylebone Road has been rebuilt successfully many times, retaining the original layout of streets and squares and small households. But now this part of London is scarred by the housing redevelopments of the late 1950s and '60s – the worst being the monstrous Lisson Green Estate to the west of Regent's Park.

Sussex Place F14

Clarence Terrace F18

Chandos House 1769–71   F1p
Chandos Street W1
Robert Adam
⊖ Oxford Circus

At the same time as he was building the large Adelphi K58, Adam was developing a single plot: a serious, plain, four-bay stone-fronted house, its front decorated with a single band of carved waves. The stuccoed mews building decorated with sphinxes, in Duchess Street at the back, was built in the 1920s by Arthur Bolton. See also 20 Portman Square J14.

Houses 1770s   F2p
5–15, 18, 20–2 Mansfield Street W1
Robert Adam
⊖ Oxford Circus

Outside, only the fine and characteristic fan-topped doorways of these big, plain houses suggest their authorship, although the decorated ceilings of the first floors can be glimpsed from the pavement. The street is closed at the north end by a seven-bay composition of a pair of houses: symmetry is achieved by the left hand house having three bays, and the right four. Lutyens lived and worked at number 13.

Portland Place W1 1776–80   F3p
James Adam
⊖ Oxford Circus, Regent's Park

Started after the Adelphi K58, Portland Place is another of the Adams' speculative schemes: a single street, and very wide for its time (34 m/110 ft), designed as a whole from Foley House at the south end to the New Road (now Marylebone Road) at the north. The uniformity of the street has suffered from much rebuilding, which started with the enormous Langham Hotel (now used by the BBC) built on the site of Foley House in 1864. Twentieth-century building cut some of the delicate pediments in half, and bombing in the Second World War continued the destruction. The only fairly complete section is that between Weymouth Street and New Cavendish Street on the east side, although even here the attics are later additions. The brick house-fronts continue the stylistic innovations of the Adelphi: thin stucco pilasters with sunken panels decorated with honeysuckle support delicate flat pediments. By the 1780s fashion was beginning to turn against the Adams, but this particular decorative scheme continued in popular use for another twenty years. The street was incorporated by Nash in his grand route from Carlton House to Regent's Park, terminating Portland Place with the half-circus of Park Crescent F6.

St Mary 1788–91 F4m
Paddington Green W2
J Plaw
⊖Edgware Road

Now set forlornly between the ugly A40(M) motorway and the rebuilt north side of Paddington Green, St Mary's was restored to its eighteenth-century charm in the 1970s by Erith and Terry. In plan a Greek cross, the design is not of a particular school, although the extensive use inside of the segmental curve places it in the mainstream of the architecture of the end of the century. See also Quinlan Terry's Church Hall F56.

Regent's Park NW1 1812–28 F5
John Nash
⊖Regent's Park, Baker Street, Camden Town

John Nash's name is now automatically associated with his designs for Regent's Park, in its day one of Europe's most original architectural developments. The rough heathlands of Marylebone Park to the north of the New Road (Marylebone Road) were leased to the Duke of Portland for hunting up to the end of the eighteenth century. When the land reverted to the Crown in 1809, John Nash's plans for its transformation into a proper park were immediately accepted.

Nash's original intentions were far more extensive than the actual results. Park Crescent was planned as a giant circus (Europe's largest) to terminate Portland Place; the perimeter of the park was to be lined entirely by terraces; a second grand circus was projected on the site of the inner circle, with twenty-six villas scattered among the trees and two crescents at the north end; and the Prince Regent was to have a valhalla, churches and a pavilion. Seen as a whole the scheme was an early garden city of great originality, but a combination of factors, practical and aesthetic, constrained Nash's grand ideas. It was feared that too much building in the centre of the park would spoil the scenery – and in any case the speculative venture had run out of funds. The consequent reduction in building and modification of the grand circus to Park Crescent F6 proved to be successful revisions.

The Zoological Gardens F28 were laid out in 1827 by Decimus Burton and have been progressively enlarged ever since. The inner circle was leased to the Royal Botanic Society in 1839, and the open air theatre was built in 1932.

The people's park, like the museum, is an invention of the nineteenth century. In the seventeenth and eighteenth centuries parks had been the scene of pageants and hunts. Regent's Park, with its scholarly collections of exotic flora and fauna in the botanical and zoological gardens, provided a diverting educational spectacle for the Sunday promenade. At the same time, Nash's idea of the urban terraces looking out over an ideal landscape anticipated the garden city and suburb of the late nineteenth and early twentieth centuries.

Park Crescent   F6p
Regent's Park W1 1812
John Nash
⊖ Regent's Park, Great Portland Street
This crescent marks the formal entry to
Regent's Park. Intended as a circus, which
would have been the largest in Europe, it
has single-storey colonnades of paired
Ionic columns running the length of the
two wide quadrants, creating an almost
abstract architectural order. The
colonnades screen the individuality of the
houses' doors and areas, and the window
openings above are simple and unembell-
ished, unlike Nash's other terraces. All
other architectural features are merely a
background to the dominant idea of the
colonnade. As with many of the other

terraces in the park, the stuccoed front
has recently been repainted. Despite a
radical change of use to offices, and much
rebuilding behind the east façade, it keeps
alive the theatrical intentions of its
designer and is one of the finest architectural set-pieces in London.
In Park Square East, to the north, two
doors in the middle of the terrace once led
to the famous **Diorama**, designed by
Nash and the elder Pugin. Although neglected for many years, it has recently been
occupied by the Diorama Arts Centre.
Plans for its renovation, which would have
threatened the magnificent three-storey
octagonal atrium at its centre, have been
abandoned.

St John's Wood Chapel 1813   F7f
Park Road NW1
Thomas Hardwick
⊖ St John's Wood
The Ionic portico and turret of St John's
successfully close the view to the north up
Park Road. The churchyard is particularly
fine, although a recent two-storey brick
church hall to the east is unfortunate
(especially when compared with Terry's
hall F56 for St Mary, Paddington). Inside,
Tuscan columns support glazed galleries,
where Ionic columns in turn support the
slightly curved ceiling.

St Mary 1813   F8o
Marylebone Road NW1
Thomas Hardwick
⊖ Baker Street

In 1770, with the rapid expansion of the
parish, plans were proposed for rebuilding St Mary's, but only in 1813 was the new
building begun. The grand Corinthian six-
column portico looks up York Gate into
Regent's Park, thereby extending the
spirit of Nash's composition across the
New Road (now Marylebone Road). The
fine circular tower has a ring of freestanding columns, above which the dome is
supported by gilded caryatids. The choir
was remodelled by the Victorian 'rogue'
architect Thomas Harris in 1885; it gives
the east end an uncharacteristic 'high
church' and Byzantine effect.

Dorset Square NW1 c1815   F9n
⊖ Marylebone

Part of the northerly limits of the Portman
Estate, Dorset Square is a relatively intact
example of the late Georgian style. Rather
than being subordinate to the overall
composition of the façade the houses have
some individuality. On the east side they
have fine cast iron verandas: the growing
use of verandas in the early nineteenth
century was an early sign of the influence
of colonial life styles (particularly eastern)
on domestic architecture, which was to
flourish in the Regency period a decade
later (see houses in Park Lane J20).

Macclesfield Bridge c1815   · F10f
north gate to Regent's Park
from Prince Albert Road NW8
John Nash
⊖ St John's Wood

Marking the northern pedestrian
approach to Regent's Park across the
Grand Union Canal, this modest bridge
has symmetrically curved ends. The construction is a mixture of cast iron arches
and brick buttresses. The municipal railings, recently added, almost obliterate the
romantic view westwards to Burton's
Grove House F17, with barges in the
foreground.

The Holme 1818   F11k
Inner Circle, Regent's Park
NW1
Decimus Burton
⊖ Baker Street

Nash's original plan for Regent's Park had
included a large area to be given over to
villas; The Holme, St John's Lodge F12 and
Burton's Grove House F17 (now Nuffield
Lodge) are all that remain. The Holme is
Burton's first building, designed when he
was eighteen for his father, Nash's builder. Although the whole is less ambitious
than Grove House, the Corinthian portico on the entrance side is impressive.
Viewed from the north across the park, it
gives a good idea of the original appearance of the white classical villa standing in its own spacious grounds.

St John's Lodge F12g
Bedford College,
University of London 1818, 1847, 1890
Inner Circle, Regent's Park NW1
J Raffield, Sir Charles Barry, R Weir
Schultz
⊖ Baker Street

Only St John's Lodge, The Holme F11 and
Grove House F17 remain of the eight villas
built in Regent's Park. The original house
has been much altered – Barry added the
projecting wings and a second storey in
1847 – but it has a very fine entrance hall
leading to a beautifully enclosed garden.
Like The Holme, when viewed from its
garden St John's Lodge revives Nash's
vision of a very privileged suburb.

Cornwall Terrace 1821–3 F13k
Regent's Park NW1
John Nash with Decimus Burton
⊖ Baker Street

Cornwall Terrace is the most recently
restored (1980) of the terraces, and has
had its roof, parapets and chimneys put
back properly (unlike Park Crescent F6,
where the clean curve of the new roof
gives a curiously modern look). It is 171 m
(560 ft) long, and at the north end presents
an elegant bay window to the triangular
garden; it does not have a strip of garden
separating it from the Outer Circle, and
consequently seems more 'urban' than
the other terraces. The attribution to
Burton is strange: he was twenty-one and
working in the office of Nash, whose
builder was Decimus's father.

Sussex Place 1822 F14j
Outer Circle, Regent's Park
NW1
John Nash
⊖ Baker Street

It is no surprise that this terrace is
contemporary with Nash's Brighton
Pavilion (completed in 1823): with its
curved end wings, octagonal domes,
polygonal bay windows and Corinthian
central portico, Sussex Place (198 m/650 ft
in length) is the most eccentric terrace in
Regent's Park.

Hanover Terrace and F15j
Hanover Lodge 1822–3
Outer Circle, Regent's Park NW1
John Nash
⊖ Baker Street

This terrace, 140 m (460 ft) long, is of
simple composition: straight, with three
prettily decorated pediments, one at each
end and one in the middle, in a not very
refined Roman Doric. The only other
modelling is the ground-floor arcade,
rusticated with segmental arches.
Hanover Lodge, of the same date with
additions by Lutyens (1909), marks an
entrance to Regent's Park. An island lodge
with gates on either side, it is a delightfully simple stuccoed octagon with a
tall central chimney and steep pitched
roof. The open loggia on the park side has
been closed, and the building is now
overshadowed by Gibberd's Mosque F55
next door.

Hanover Lodge

All Souls 1822–4

F16p

Langham Pláce W1
John Nash
⊖ Oxford Circus

This is one of Nash's major works, partly because of the intrinsic originality of the design, but principally because it manages to give Regent Street a satisfactory conclusion on a difficult site. Nash used the quadrant to change direction from Lower Regent Street to Regent Street; here he also enlisted the circle as a device to change direction between Upper Regent Street and the existing line of Portland Place. The church's circular portico acts as a pivot, and its rectangular nave is rotated on the north-east axis and thus concealed from the principal views. The conical spire surrounded by a Corinthian peristyle, a diminutive version of the portico below, caused a storm of controversy at the time, prompting the famous cartoon of Nash sitting on his spire. As Summerson has observed, 'It is nevertheless a curiously ambiguous design . . . both modern French and old English'. With the building of Broadcasting House F41 in 1931 the church was overwhelmed and much of its town planning importance lost. Inside, the flat coffered ceiling is reminiscent of Wren; it is carried on Corinthian columns, the galleries on chamfered piers. The new glass doors and screen to the entrance are unfortunate. Note the bust of John Nash by the entrance, looking south down Regent Street.

Nuffield Lodge

F17f

ex Grove House 1822–4
Prince Albert Road NW1
Decimus Burton
⊖ St John's Wood

The purest of the surviving villas in Regent's Park, Grove House is also one of the few remaining examples of the Edwardian 'artist's house'. Burton's designs for the original owner, G B Greenough, were modified in 1877, and as a result have lost their former strict neo-Palladianism.

Grove House was designed to meet the requirements of a cultivated and liberal-minded bachelor, who enjoyed mapping out obscure areas of the globe as much as he enjoyed his weekly soirées at home, which had the atmosphere of a small London club. The ground floor was dedicated to entertainment, scholarly pursuits and the exhibition of Greenough's extensive collection of fossils and minerals. The billiard room, drawing room, library, museum and mineral room were arranged *en suite* around the beautiful circular hall, all the rooms having carefully composed views of the garden. In the basement the same area was allocated to service rooms, and the first floor had a minimum number of bedrooms.

The four elevations are all different – the most imposing was the south front to the garden, a portico of four Ionic double columns. After Greenough's death the house was extended (1877) by Burton's cousin Henry Marley Burton. The bachelor's villa was transformed into a family house by the addition of windows and bedrooms, and it was bought by the Nuffield Foundation in 1953: See also the Studio F36.

Clarence Terrace 1823

F18k

Outer Circle, Regent's Park
NW1
Decimus Burton
⊖ Baker Street

Burton's invention of three-bay attached screens either side of the central pavilion is the special interest here. They have an arched base, paired columns and a flat entablature, and behind each is a single bow-fronted house. The device anticipates Burton's Ionic screen J24 for Hyde Park Corner two years later. Clarence Terrace has recently been insensitively rebuilt; its new back can be seen from Park Road.

St Mary 1823   F19n
Wyndham Place W1
Sir Robert Smirke
⊖ Baker Street
The semicircular portico of Ionic columns and the slim round stone tower and cupola of St Mary's have a well-planned, monumental relationship to Bryanston Square J18 to the south. The main body of the church to the north is square and built of stock brick, with two-tier windows, and forms part of the adjoining pattern of streets. The interior, with its gallery and the Doric columns supporting the gently curved coffered ceiling, is further evidence of Smirke's successful use of the Greek Revival style.

Smirke's glorious portico now sits on a paved forecourt. Part of this recent and modest urban improvement is **Tarrant Place** (1989–90) to the west by Quinlan Terry. These eleven houses arranged around a granite cobbled courtyard are a reinterpretation of the traditional mews.

Ulster Terrace and   F20l
Ulster Place 1824–5
Outer Circle and Marylebone Road
NW1
John Nash
⊖ Regent's Park
Ulster Place is a very plain stuccoed terrace, fortunately set back from the torrential traffic of Marylebone Road. Ulster Terrace faces Regent's Park, and is a more ambitious design, though the engaged Ionic columns to the ground floor are distinctly un-grand. The bay windows providing emphasis at the ends are unique in the Nash terraces.

Ulster Terrace

York Terrace, F21k
Upper Harley Street and
York Gate 1824–6
Regent's Park NW1
John Nash
⊖ Regent's Park

This long composition (430 m/1410 ft) is arranged axially round the York Gate entrance to Regent's Park F5, but is not seen to advantage from the park because one looks south into the sun. The two terraces have giant Ionic features in the centres and at the ends, between which runs a Greek Doric colonnade on the ground floor. Between the eastern range and Upper Harley Street is a fine pair of Doric semi-detached houses. York Gate was designed to frame Hardwick's earlier St Mary, Marylebone F8 and successfully does so, but the vista is now spoilt by the anachronistic street furniture required to direct traffic into the park: this short street could well be pedestrianized. Between York Terrace and Marylebone Road are the delightful two-storey stuccoed mews houses built for the servants; these are all that remain of Nash's small domestic buildings.

York Gate

York Terrace

Holy Trinity 1824–8 F22l
Marylebone Road NW1
Sir John Soane
⊖ Great Portland Street

Of Soane's three churches built at the same time, Holy Trinity is the least interesting, and much less idiosyncratic than St Peter Walworth P1. The shallow Ionic porch here projects, rather than being recessed into the plane of the front, and the tower is less geometrically pure: only the finials to the columns of the first stage show the strangeness characteristic of Soane. The interior has been converted to offices for the use of the Society for the Promotion of Christian Knowledge. See also St John, Bethnal Green U18.

Chester Terrace 1825 F23h
Regent's Park NW1
John Nash
⊖ Regent's Park

The longest unbroken façade in the park (287 m/940 ft), Chester Terrace has a complex alternating system of bays (ABCBABCBA), marked periodically by giant Corinthian columns. At either end are projecting wings, connected to the main façade by theatrically thin triumphal arches. It is sobering to reflect that immediately after the Second World War the Regent's Park terraces were so run down that the Crown Commissioners seriously considered demolishing them.

St Katharine's Hospital   F24h
1826
Outer Circle, Regent's Park
NW1
Ambrose Poynter
⊖ Camden Town

This early example of the Gothic Revival brings further variety to the buildings surrounding Regent's Park. Despite a medieval air the plan is Palladian, with a large central chapel and curved 'collegiate' wings connecting to the domestic quarters. The Royal College of St Katharine was moved to Regent's Park when its original site, next to the Tower of London, was excavated to make way for St Katharine's Dock.

Cumberland Terrace 1826–7   F25h
Regent's Park NW1
John Nash, James Thomson
⊖ Regent's Park

The grandest of Regent's Park's eleven terraces, Cumberland Terrace is 244 m (800 ft) long and embodies the idea of a palace confronting a 'natural landscape' within the city. The centre block has a giant order of ten Corinthian columns capped with a pediment of exuberant sculptures; on each side of these are symmetrical - terraces, terminated by pavilions and detached triumphal Ionic arches. It is the most daring, theatrical and successful terrace in the park.

Gloucester Gate and   F26d
Gloucester Lodge
Regent's Park NW1
John Nash
⊖ Camden Town

The two-storey Lodge is asymmetrically composed: to the right of the central portico of attached Ionic columns is a pavilion of three bays; to the left is a more substantial building which turns the corner into Parkway, and from which the Lodge is entered. Gloucester Gate is the most northerly of Nash's terraces, secluded behind a well-planted garden. The familiar stuccoed façade is modulated by Ionic pilasters, with attached columns to the three projecting bays.

Kent Terrace 1827   F27j
Park Road NW1
John Nash
⊖ Baker Street

The only terrace to face outwards from the park, and one of the last to be built. Its long (112 m/368 ft) and stuccoed façade is usually described as plain and dull, but it would be no bad thing if London had more buildings of this quality and from this period – when, perhaps for the last time, middle-class taste was good and homogeneous.

The Zoo (Royal Zoological Society Gardens)
F28c
started 1827
Regent's Park NW1
laid out by Decimus Burton
⊖ Camden Town

The Zoo is the British Museum of live animals and, like that institution, an invention of the early nineteenth century. The private Zoological Society employed Burton to lay out the gardens, and his building work survives only in the restored stock brick Buffalo and Giraffe Houses on the terraces overlooking the Regent's Canal. The layout is a 'campus': the buildings are loosely arranged, with patches of grass and trees in between.

There is no structure of blocks like those of a city, but the buildings are too close together for it to be a park. The Society has patronized many distinguished architects, including Belcher and Joass (the fake mountains of the Mappin Terraces with the Aquarium underneath); Sir John Burnet (Camel House); Sir Hugh Casson and Partners (the Elephant House in ribbed concrete); Tecton and Lubetkin (Penguin Pool F45 and Gorilla House F42); and Price, Snowdon and Newby (Aviary F51). Most recent are the Lion Terraces where the dozing cats can be seen at close quarters through glass, and where the unusually dense landscaping makes up for undistinguished architecture.

Park Village East and West 1829
F29d
Albany Street NW1
John Nash, J Pennethorne
⊖ Camden Town

Nash established a model for the suburban Victorian villa in these two park villages, once separated by a branch of the Regent's Canal (now filled in). With their various styles, these villas were Nash's final contribution to Regent's Park. Park Village East is linear, bounded by the street and the canal; Park Village West is picturesquely arranged along a winding 'country' road. The interiors have been altered, but it is the romantic, classical, Tudor and Italianate mixture of the exteriors that is important – cream stucco, projecting eaves, and black lattice pergolas. Such stylistic variety was much imitated by Victorian suburban builders.

Christic Church 1838,   F30h
altered 1868
Albany Street NW1
Sir J Pennethorne, alterations by
W Butterfield
⊖ Great Portland Street
Successfully marking the bend in Albany
Street, Christ Church is decidedly understated, despite its classical pretensions.
There is no portico, the entrance being
marked by two giant pilasters, above
which rises a simple thin tower and spire.
On the west side are two tall secondary
doors, and the north and south façades
have high arched windows. The marble
floor is by Butterfield, and the glass of one
of the south windows is by Rossetti.

Circular Factory c1860   F31d
Oval Road NW1
⊖ Camden Town
Once a famous piano factory (Camden
Town specialized in pianos and still does),
this magnificent five-storey cylindrical
building is a fine example of the Victorian
functional tradition.

Primrose Hill Studios 1882   F32c
Fitzroy Road NW1
Alfred Healey
⊖ Chalk Farm
A colony of twelve studios occupying the
back gardens of Fitzroy Road: by the 1880s
the tradition of artists' studios appro-
priating either the mews or the ends of
gardens was well established in London.
Here, they vary in size and complexity:
those on the south side of the 9 × 19 m
(30 ft × 64 ft) court are exclusively top-lit
studios with minimal living accommodation; on the north side and at the ends are
more ambitious 'studio houses' with their
own gardens.
The combination of the two-storey
cottage style – simple red-brick gables and
slate roofs – and the quiet of the surrounding back gardens created the de-
sired illusion of being in the country.
The painters J Waterhouse, R Talbot

Kelly, Arthur Rackham, Lord Methuen
and the conductor Sir Henry Wood are
some of the former residents.

Marylebone Station 1898–9   F33n
Melcombe Street NW1
Colonel R W Edis
⊖ Marylebone
Outside the City of London, Marylebone
Station is the latest and smallest Victorian
terminal. The glass and iron *porte cochère*
spanning Melcombe Street and connecting the station to the former Great
Central Hotel opposite is memorable, as is
the discretion with which the building fits
into the eighteenth-century street pattern of Marylebone.

Arlington House F34d
ex Rowton House 1905
Arlington Road NW1
H B Measures
⊖Camden Town

Under the philanthropic patronage of
Lord Rowton, Arlington House still provides accommodation for 1000 men in
single rooms, with sixty-six resident staff.
Although the original Rowton House at
Mount Pleasant has been converted to an
ordinary hotel, other working men's
hostels still exist at Vauxhall and Whitechapel. The elaborate red-brick detailing
to the street façade and the marvellously
decorated front door are rare examples of
the Free Style applied to a public building.
This massive building serves as a reminder
that nineteenth-century philanthropy is
still alive: the building dominates
Arlington Road as strongly as its residents
influence the subculture of Camden
Town. See also Measures' villas B21 in
Eton Avenue.

House and studio 1907 F35e
40 Grove End Road NW8
Sir Lawrence Alma Tadema
⊖St John's Wood

Alma Tadema built himself this remarkable house and studio. Although much
altered externally, the silver-domed
studio and atrium (with fountain) remain
intact, as do many of the Graeco-Egyptian
external embellishments. The building is
an eminent addition to the late Victorian
tradition of artists' studios and houses in
St John's Wood.

Studio Nuffield Lodge F36f
ex Grove House 1908–10
Prince Albert Road NW1
Sidney Tatchel
⊖St John's Wood

Sigismund Goetze, the painter and penultimate private owner of Decimus
Burton's fine Grove House F17, converted
the stables into a studio for himself.
Despite the restrictions imposed by the
curved wall, the studio house has two
highly distinctive and original exteriors.
From Prince Albert Road it is immediately apparent, with tall arched windows and
a large pyramidal lantern rooflight (below
which is an oval lay light).
From the garden side, the house is
picturesque and more of a cottage. The
doors and windows, conceived on a
domestic scale, are placed at random in its
slowly curving stuccoed wall. This is
extended, by an attached trabeated
screen of Tuscan columns, to the semicircular freestanding greenhouse which
forms the back wall.

Royal Academy of Music F37k
1910–11
Marylebone Road NW1
Sir Ernest George
⊖ Regent's Park

A composition of three pavilions in red brick with stone quoins, George's late work might pass as that of Lutyens, who, although younger, had already invented his 'Wrenaissance' style. However, the heavy central pediment and sculpture obviously derive from the nineteenth century or from Michelangelo.

Flats 1910–70 F38f, b
Prince Albert Road NW8
⊖ St John's Wood

With the common ingredients of a south front and a magnificent view across Regent's Park, it is interesting to see how these large apartment buildings either value this relationship or offer alternatives to Nash's original vision.

First, from the east, is **Northgate** (1910), a large Edwardian mansion building occupying a whole block. It is self-centred with no obvious acknowledgement of the park apart from decorative balconies, although its gabled and turreted profile is very impressive from the park. At its east end **104–14 Northgate** (1936), by Mitchell and Bridgwater, is an elegant and

104–14 Northgate

restrained modern red-brick building with a central curved bay window addressing the park. The building has seven floors making the same height as the five floors of its neighbour. **Oslo Court** (1938) by Robert Atkinson follows, bounded on either side by Culworth Street and Charlbert Street. This is the first of the 'democratic' versions: within the site depth the building is stepped in plan, to give every apartment a balcony with sun and a view.

Next is **Viceroy Court** (1937) by Marshall and Tweedy: the curved corners and large balconies give this fine building a genuinely European feeling – it could be in Vienna or Berlin.

Two more recent apartment buildings follow: **Imperial Court**, 55–6 Prince Albert Road (1965) and **2 Avenue Road** (c1970). With their exaggerated balconies both conspicuously celebrate the value of sun and the view; resembling the holiday architecture of the Costa del Sol, they are a retreat from the spirit of the pre-war buildings.

Stockleigh Hall (1937) by Robert Atkinson is the most interesting group of all, arranged around a deep four-storey entrance courtyard framing a collective view to the park. This building and Viceroy Court are very important ad-

Viceroy Court

ditions to Regent's Park, showing that the forms of modern architecture are sometimes capable of consolidating rather than destroying the city.

The sequence is concluded by **King's Court** and **Prince Albert Court**, the most recent additions: these utilitarian and architecturally indifferent buildings are exclusively concerned with financial profit, like countless other post-war speculations.

Council House

Library

Westminster Council House
F39n

Marylebone Town Hall
1914–21 and
Public Library 1939
Marylebone Road NW1
Sir Edwin Cooper
⊖ Baker Street

Two buildings in the classical tradition occupy a block to the north of Georgian Marylebone. Together they demonstrate how public buildings should be arranged on an important street, and how much mileage there was (and still is) in the classical tradition. The twenty-five year interval between the two buildings shows a good Edwardian architect working in good Portland stone, and stripping down his classical repertoire from the elaborate Wren tower of the earlier building to the smoothness and near-modernity of the later. The two buildings are a reproach to the thin modernity and unfortunate composition of Marathon House F49 opposite.

Rudolph Steiner House
F40j

1926–37
Park Road NW1
Montague Wheeler
⊖ Baker Street

The only example of expressionism in London, and a fairly tame one. Steiner's dislike of the right-angle shows only in a few curved eyebrows over the irregularly placed windows of the flat ashlar façade.

Broadcasting House 1931
F41p

Portland Place W1
Val Myers and Watson-Hart
⊖ Oxford Circus

The monolithic Portland stone façades, the Georgian proportions of the window openings and the sculptures of Eric Gill represent a compromise between deference to the architecture of Nash's Regent Street, and a building style appropriate to the heroic days of national broadcasting. Broadcasting House successfully overcomes an extremely complicated site, and its massive, prow-like, rounded shape gives the building a semi-marine quality. The spirit of the new medium was better expressed inside – Wells Coates, Chermayeff, McGrath and others contributed interiors which have unfortunately been removed by the BBC. The rigorous requirements for soundproofing, isolation, artificial lighting and air-conditioning of the studios produced further technical innovations in this building, which was to become a potent symbol of national unity in the 1930s and '40s.

Gorilla House 1932

F42c

London Zoo, Prince Albert
Road NW1
Lubetkin and Tecton
⊖ Camden Town

Lubetkin's first English building was for apes, not people. In 1932 Tecton was commissioned by Sir Julian Huxley, Director of the Royal Zoological Society, to design a new Gorilla House to accommodate two Congolese gorillas. It was the first of a series of zoo buildings by Tecton: in the face of widespread human opposition to, and scepticism of, modern architecture, it was the animals of London and Whipsnade Zoos that benefited. The brief for the cylindrical Gorilla House, situated between the Outer Circle and the canal, called for the strictest climatic control. After intensive quasi-scientific research – Tecton's typical method – the cylinder was divided into two halves, the ends of one sealed with an open mesh of caged steel, and those of the other with solid white concrete walls. Within the cylinder was a semi-circular shield which could be rotated to protect the animals from the English winter. The prospect of ape and human viewing each other through Lubetkin's cylinder is not without humour. See also the Penguin Pool F45.

Royal Institute of
British Architects 1932–4

F43p

66 Portland Place W1
Grey Wornum
⊖ Regent's Park

The winner of a competition, Wornum's design is everything an institute should be: it is clearly not a house, and the large plain features of the Portland stone front establish its importance. Models for buildings of this kind were then scarce (it would have been very strange to have found an example of continental modern among the competition entries). Wornum used those available from Sweden – in particular Asplund's Stockholm Public Library, 1920–8 – especially in the eclectic, complex and elaborately detailed section and interiors, which incorporate many decorative works of craftsmanship. The building combines the functions of learned institute (library, lecture halls and committee rooms) with those of a club for members. If impressive size and generosity of circulation are a measure of learning, then RIBA members are very

knowledgeable, but they are less well served as members of a club (here a subsidiary function), with accommodation which cannot match other London clubs for style. On the ground floor, open to the public, is a good architectural bookshop and a notice board with information about lectures, trips and events.

Houses c1933　　　　　　　F44b
1, 3, 4, 6, 8, 10 Wells Rise NW8
Francis Lorne and Tait
⊖St John's Wood
These stuccoed terrace houses are a
fragment of a 1930s bourgeois street,
stepping down the hill to Regent's Park.
The combination of vertical and horizontal elements (the double-height
windows to the staircases contrasting
with the entrance canopies) is reminiscent
of the Dutch De Stijl movement in
general, and J J P Oud's terraces at the
Weissenhof Siedlung at Stuttgart (1927) in
particular.

Penguin Pool 1934–5　　　　　F45g
London Zoo,
Prince Albert Road NW1
Lubetkin and Tecton
⊖Camden Town
The Penguin Pool, on the park side of the
Zoo, manages to combine the principles of
modern architecture, the results of
behaviourist research, structural virtuos-
ity and humour. It was the result of
Lubetkin's collaborations with Ove Arup,
the Danish consultant engineer, and Felix
Samuely, employed by the general contractor J L Kier, and recently arrived from
Berlin. The exuberance of the pool's
narrow spiral ramps, oval plan and rendered screen walls was inspired partly by
Cubism and partly by Lubetkin's Beaux
Arts training. The architects' behaviourist
research shows in the design of the long
curved ramps, which encourage the penguins to promenade or form patient
queues, displaying their comic resem-
blance to English City gents. The floor
surfaces vary from slate to rubber to
concrete, and are designed to agitate the
penguins' feet, thereby (it is hoped)
helping to relieve boredom.
Built of unsupported reinforced concrete,

the ramps (14 m/46 ft long, 1.2 m/4 ft wide
and tapering from 150 mm/6 in to
75 mm/3 in in section) were technical
innovations. See also the Gorilla House
F42.
The pool has recently been renovated and
restored successfully by Avanti architects.
This transformation is due principally to
the initiative and generosity of Peter
Palumbo.

Dorset House 1935　　　　　F46o
Gloucester Place and
Marylebone Road NW1
T P Bennett with Joseph Emberton
⊖Baker Street
Dorset House conveys an optimistic 1930s
image of modern urban life. Above a two-
storey plinth of shops and entrances, the
plan of nine storeys of flats is formed by a
series of interconnected Ts. Emberton's
involvement is immediately noticeable in
the elevations – curved corner balconies,
green-painted metal balustrades, and
mannered structural details. **Berkeley
Court,** another block of mansion flats
next door across Glentworth Street, is of
a similar scale with a continuous privet
hedge and a roof garden; and across
Marylebone Road, **Bickenhall Mansions**
(1896) by W H Scrymgeour uses the Free
Style of Norman Shaw, with many bay
windows and gables all in red brick and
terracotta.

The White House 1936 F47 l
Albany Street NW1
R Atkinson
⊖ Great Portland Street

The White House was built as a number of small service flats, supported by recreational facilities, shopping and restaurants, and displays this period's preoccupation with constructing a 'city within a city' (see also Dolphin Square O12). The star-shaped nine-storey plan occupies a whole city block and has two main effects: first, following functionalist principles, the increased area of the façades provides optimum light and ventilation, avoiding the need for light wells; second, it breaks away from the usual continuous street façade, thus isolating itself from the traditional city. The façades of the White House (unlike those of many of its contemporaries) are not white stuccoed but beautifully made of cream faience tiles with no sign of deterioration.

The corner windows, projecting eaves and elegantly detailed handrails further contribute to the building's suave and urbane appearance.

Gilbey's Offices and F48d
Warehouses 1937
Oval Road and Jamestown Road NW1
Serge Chermayeff
⊖ Camden Town

Apart from a slightly curved plan and a north elevation which has an unexpectedly impressive relationship with the Regent's Canal, this large corner building is generally nondescript. Built of white stucco on a reinforced concrete frame, it incorporates technical innovations by Felix Samuely, the consulting engineer; the foundations, for instance, were floated on 100 mm (4 in) of cork insulation to protect Gilbey's wine stocks from the vibrations of trains in the nearby cutting. The entire building was also air-conditioned to combat the noise and dirt from the railway. The training of engineers of the period was less specialized than it is today, allowing them to be

scientific consultants, and more than just calculators. Samuely was particularly concerned with acoustics, services and insulation.

Marathon House F49n
ex Castrol House 1960
174 Marylebone Road NW1
Gollins, Melvin, Ward and Partners
⊖ Baker Street

By the mid-1950s the planning laws in London permitted buildings above the previous height restriction of 30 m (100 ft); the fifteen storeys of Castrol House took early advantage of this new legislation. Bearing superficial resemblances to New York's Lever House (1952), it was one of London's first towers on a podium – a solution with many subsequent imitators. Despite our strong criticisms of the form, the curtain wall of Castrol House is elegantly reductive, and at the time it was impressive that this industrial refinement should come from an English architectural firm.

Royal College of Physicians   F50 I
1960–4
Outer Circle and St Andrew's Place,
Regent's Park NW I
Sir Denys Lasdun and Partners
⊖ Regent's Park

The oppositions of street versus park,
brick versus mosaic, transience versus
permanence, day-to-day versus
ceremonial and wall versus pavilion are
some of the concerns of this ambitious
building. The ceremonial functions of
entrance hall, library, dining room and
conference room are seen as permanent in
their relationship to the park: they form a
pavilion on *piloti* covered in white mosaic.
The day-to-day administrative offices have
a transient, terraced form on Albany
Street – a wall of dark brickwork. The
half-submerged lecture theatre, ceremonial but in dark brickwork, is
inconsistent with the scenario.

Aviary 1963   F51c
London Zoo,
Prince Albert Road NW I
Lord Snowdon, Cedric Price, Frank
Newby
⊖ Camden Town

A wide range of Indian and African birds
are housed in this large, netted, irregular
enclosure. Despite the aviary's experimental 'tensegrity' structure (in the
Buckminster Fuller tradition), the tight-
angled corners have always seemed
hostile to flight; the birds themselves are
rendered rather pathetic, like leaves
blowing in the wind.

Flats, Albert Court 1963–6   F52c
23 Prince Albert Road NW I
Property and Development Ltd,
Martin Richmond and Malcolm Higgs
⊖ Chalk Farm

One of the better apartment blocks built
recently on the valuable land round
Regent's Park. It is curious that the
building should take its inspiration from
the red engineering bricks and tiles, the
industrial windows and balustrades of
Stirling and Gowan's engineering laboratories at Leicester (on which Higgs
worked as an assistant) rather than from
Nash's white stuccoed terraces down the
road. Although the building has a recognizable back and front, the principal
entrance is from the back and has the
diminished status of a service entrance.
The entrance hall is similarly understated, having the same dimensions as the lobbies
on the intermediate floors.

Flats 1964   F53d
37 Gloucester Avenue NW I
James Stirling
⊖ Camden Town

Four identically planned floors of flats,
built for the London Borough of Camden,
are raised on columns above a car park.
Only the hard red brick, symmetrical
planning, and characteristic entrance
ramp suggest that this modest infill,
designed to be repeated on either side, is
the work of one of England's internation-
ally renowned architects. The living
rooms face the garden behind, and their
windows are larger than those to the
street.

Flats 1970   F54j
125 Park Road NW1
Farrell and Grimshaw
⊖St John's Wood, Baker Street
The significance of this slim tower (containing thirty-six one- and two-bedroom flats and four one-bedroom penthouses) lies in the simple idea of building around a single central core, with one internal escape stair ventilated by a shaft. The beneficial results are firstly, that the entire periphery is given to habitable rooms (as opposed to corridors and staircases) and secondly, that the flat plans acquire real flexibility. In appearance the tower is a period piece. The façade banded with corrugated metal and the indifferently inclined patent glazed penthouse roof are in the 'high tech' fashion of the mid-1960s, and with the passage of time the paucity of these architectural ideas is exposed: metal sidings are characteristic of the factory and not of housing.

Mosque 1978   F55j
Park Road and Hanover Gate
NW1
Sir Frederick Gibberd and Partners
⊖Baker Street
The winner of an open competition, Gibberd's scheme was conventionally 'Arabized' between the competition and final designs, and as built has a cardboard thinness and lack of architectural inventiveness in the detail. It will not be remembered in histories, but its minaret and gilded dome make a curious addition to the skyline of Regent's Park, and complement Nash's more sober fantasies.

St Mary's Church Hall 1981   F56m
Paddington Green W2
Quinlan Terry
⊖Warwick Avenue, Edgware Road
Seen by the motorist from Westway, Quinlan Terry's modest church hall appears to be a remnant of an eighteenth-century village. On closer examination the hall is brand new, the bricks seconds, the window sills reconstructed stone, the rainwater pipes plastic and the niches at either end *trompe l'oeil*. It is pivoted around the centre of the semicircular west portico of Plaw's parish church of St Mary F4, renovated by Erith and Terry in 1973.
The classical work of Terry currently induces a mixed reaction, sometimes verging on hysteria, from purists and diehard modernists. However, the legitimacy of designing in a non-'modern' idiom no longer seems worth arguing. The building is eminently sane and practical, and if plastic is all you can afford for the drainpipes and guttering, it does not discredit the entire proposition – history is full of such expediency.

Housing Marylebone 1984   F57n
Ashmill Street NWI
Jeremy and Fenella Dixon
⊖ Edgware Road

This terrace of fourteen tiny two-storey houses set over seven basement flats is built on a very narrow strip of land. The white stuccoed base sliced by a series of tall staircase windows lends considerable character and a larger scale to the whole. The project is for the same client as the villas at Lanark Road E12. In the absence of a local authority housing programme, these dwellings are sold at the bottom end of the market to people on the local authority waiting list.

Offices 1985   F58n
Broadley Street NW8
Michael Hopkins and Partners
⊖ Edgware Road, Marylebone

These offices were built to house Michael Hopkins' practice which had outgrown its previous accommodation – the architect's Studio House B39 of 1975. The office building follows the same matter-of-fact ethos as the house: low cost, speed of construction and flexibility, but with the added ingredient of a generous double-height volume. Here Hopkins develops further the 'Patera' building system, in which an identical composite metal panel is used for both walls and roof.

Mound Stand,   F59i
Lord's Cricket Ground 1985–7
St John's Wood Road NW8
Michael Hopkins and Partners, consulting engineers Ove Arup and Partners
⊖ St John's Wood

Until this new stand was built, there were few distinguished buildings for sport in London. The lower part of the new work is a remodelling of an earlier open terrace whose arcade in stock brick was extended in a curve to the east. Above this, a new white-painted steel structure supports private boxes and a second cantilevered terrace protected by a white fabric roof suspended from masts.

Ionic, Veneto and Gothic Villas   F60f
1988–91
Outer Circle, Regent's Park NW1
Quinlan Terry
⊖ Baker Street

As they were built for the Crown Estate Commissioners, it is not surprising that the style of these villas should reflect the preferences of our future monarch. They neither detract from nor significantly enhance the Outer Circle. They do however raise questions of authenticity. When seen next to Gibberd's Mosque F55 they become part of a cloying and complacent world of make-believe.

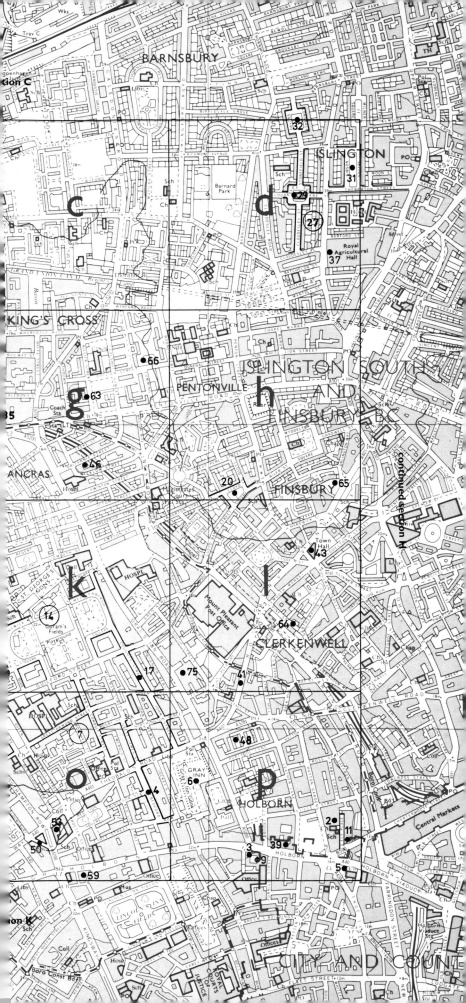

Section G: Camden Town (south)/Somers Town/King's Cross/ Islington (south-west)/Finsbury/Clerkenwell/Bloomsbury/Holborn

New Road, now Marylebone Road, Euston Road and Pentonville Road, was started in 1756 to connect Bayswater Road with the City while bypassing the West End. It divides this section in half: to the south (north of the line of the Roman road, Holborn) lies the eighteenth-century development of Bloomsbury. To the north are the railway termini and Victorian Somers and Camden Towns. This neat scheme is upset only by Islington and Barnsbury, which grew north from the City from the seventeenth century onwards.

The earliest remaining building (although much restored) is the Norman church of Old St Pancras G1, which still stands in open ground. Ely Place marks the site of the Bishop of Ely's house, whose chapel was St Etheldreda G2. Nothing remains of the original fourteenth-century foundation of Gray's Inn, the most northerly of the three Inns of Court which lay to the west of the City, beyond its boundaries.

The first urban developments north of Holborn were Bloomsbury Square (1660) and Red Lion Square (1684), both now much changed. Over the next forty years, the land to the north was built over, giving us the fine houses of Queen Square, Great Ormond Street and Great James Street G7. In 1742 the Foundling Hospital was built in fields north of Great Ormond Street, and its demolition in this century has left one of the area's largest open spaces: Coram Fields, Brunswick Square and Mecklenburgh Square G14. Bedford Square G12 to the east was begun in 1775, and remains a magnificent, unscathed example of Georgian planning. The development of Bloomsbury continued over the next fifty years, and was completed by Cubitt. London's first evidence of the Industrial Revolution was the Regent's Canal (1814–20), running at first from Limehouse to Paddington, where it connected to the Grand Union and hence to the national canal network.

In the years of peace after the Napoleonic Wars, the British Museum was founded, to be followed, two years later, in 1827, by the foundation of University College with its new building south of the New Road. Between them, these two institutions transformed the domestic character of Bloomsbury over the next 150 years. At about the same time the development of Barnsbury was beginning, with Cloudesley Square G27 (1825) followed by Lonsdale Square G32 (1845). In thirty years three major railway termini were built to the north of the New Road: Euston G67 in 1836, King's Cross G35 in 1851 and St Pancras G38 in 1868.

A pall of soot and smoke hung over the early Victorian workers' dwellings of Somers Town and Camden Town, and was dispelled only by the electrification of the railways in the 1960s. The slums of Somers Town became the object of late nineteenth- and early twentieth-century experiments in housing reform.

The twentieth century has not much altered the physical pattern of this part of the city. The biggest single change has been the conversion of Bloomsbury from private residences to the campus of the University of London, the most striking evidence of which is Holden's Senate House G62 (1932). In the 1930s the socialist Borough of Finsbury, with some of London's poorest and unhealthiest citizens, commissioned from Tecton architecture for a new and more enlightened age: a Health Centre G64 and housing at Collier Street G66.

Camden Town, traditional stopping place for waves of settlers, is now being gentrified; Somers Town is being improved as a large council estate, and the Greater London Council is intent on widening Marylebone Road into something resembling Paris's Boulevard Périphérique; on the north side, to the west of St Pancras Station, the new British Library G73 is nearly complete. A plan by Foster Associates was prepared in 1987 for the development of the vast vacated railway lands to the north of St Pancras and King's Cross Stations. A new district is proposed which may include a new terminus for the Channel Tunnel.

Old St Pancras Church GIb
11th century
Pancras Road NWI
restored 1848 by Roumieu and Gough
⊖ King's Cross
The chief interest of Old St Pancras is that
it is the sole remainder of medieval St
Pancras: thirteenth-century fragments
can be seen in the Norman doorways
(north and south) and a lancet window in
the chancel. The churchyard (now a park)
contains interesting period monuments,
the most remarkable of which is the Soane
Mausoleum GI9.

St Etheldreda c1300 G2p
restored 1874
Ely Place ECI
⊖ Chancery Lane
St Etheldreda is almost all interior apart
from its façade and east window set back
behind the building line of Ely Place. Built
as the private chapel of the town house of
the Bishops of Ely, it is a single volume of
great beauty, dimly lit through the fine
stained glass of the east and west
windows. The entrance bay from the
south is separated by a simple timber
screen, and the plain undercroft has
nineteenth-century columns. See also Ely
Place GI1.

Houses 1586, G3p
restored 1866, 1937
Staple Inn, Holborn ECI
⊖ Chancery Lane
This small group is London's only remaining domestic architecture of the sixteenth
century, showing typical half-timbering,
strip windows, gables and overhangs.
They are now almost completely rebuilt,
and face a street which is much too wide
for them.

Bedford Row WCI G4o
laid out 1680
Nicholas Barbon
⊖ Chancery Lane
Although many of the houses in this sober
street, 23 m (75 ft) wide and 198 m (650 ft)
long, were rebuilt after the Second World
War, its form survives. Much of the west
side is original, in brown brick with red
trim to the flat-headed windows. Note
the paired front doors and fine detailing of
numbers 12 and 13.

St Andrew Holborn 1684–90   G5p
Holborn Viaduct EC4
Sir Christopher Wren
⊖Farringdon
This church was sumptuously rebuilt after
being bombed in the Second World War.
The Corinthian architecture starts above
the dado of woodwork, which includes
the galleries, and the east end is dominated by the huge double-decker Venetian window. Used on Sundays for Coptic
services, during the week St Andrew's is a
regular City church.

Gray's Inn late 17th century   G6p
Holborn and
Gray's Inn Road WC1
⊖Chancery Lane
The Society of Gray's Inn came into
existence on this site in the fourteenth
century. A curiously public private place,
the most northerly of London's Inns of
Court is also the easiest to see as a whole
(from Theobald's Road across Gray's Inn
Fields).
With Staple Inn, Lincoln's Inn, the Law
Courts and the Temple, Gray's Inn forms
an almost continuous band of lawyers'
colleges separating the City of Westminster from the City of London. The
buildings here are more formally compre-
hensible than those of the Temple K4, but
also suffered severe damage in the Second
World War.

The raw new brickwork and absence of
trees give **Gray's Inn Square** (first built
1678–88) a rather blank quality. Originally
a cross range (demolished in 1685) divided
the square into two courts; on the south
side are the hall and chapel. The main
approach is from the Gatehouse in
Holborn via **South Square** (built 1685),
where number 1 is mid-eighteenth-
century, and all the other houses, destroyed in the war, have been rebuilt to
the original plans. Number 10 is by
Raymond Erith.
In the south-west corner of Gray's Inn
Square a passageway leads to **Field
Court**, which lacks architectural
coherence (number 2 dates from 1780 and
its neighbour from 1936) but is open to
the spacious gardens of Gray's Inn Fields,
approached through an extremely elegant
iron gate (1723).

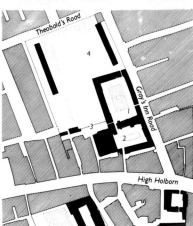

1 Gray's Inn Square   3 Field Court
2 South Square   4 Gray's Inn Gardens

Holborn early 18th century   G7o
area bounded by
Guilford Street, Southampton Row,
Gray's Inn Road and Theobald's Road
WC1
⊖Russell Square, Chancery Lane
This area formed the eastern edge of the
eighteenth-century expansion north of
Gray's Inn. At the centre is **Great James
Street** (1720–30), the best-preserved,
longest and most uniform early
eighteenth-century street in London. The
houses are built of red brick with segmental arches to the windows, and most
have complete bracketed door hoods. To
the east is **John Street** (1760) which is
also well preserved, with its mews intact.

Great James Street

The street is very wide and leads into Doughty Street G17 of the following century. To the west of Great James Street the streets retain their original pattern but are less well preserved. **Lamb's Conduit Street** has the fine early nineteenth-century Lamb public house, opposite which **Great Ormond Street** leads into **Queen Square**. The Italian hospital (founded in 1884, rebuilt in 1900) and the church of St George the Martyr (1723, transformed inside in 1867) are noteworthy.

John Street

St George 1716–31
Bloomsbury Way WC1
Nicholas Hawksmoor
⊖Holborn

G8n

The two equal cross-axes common to all Hawksmoor's churches were here used to reconcile the restrictions of a deep, narrow site with the direction of liturgical east. The altar was originally on the short axis (in the semicircular niche on the right of the entrance through the portico), as were entrances through the tower. In 1781 the altar was moved to the northern recess and the northern gallery was removed; but the characteristic flat-ceilinged central space nevertheless maintains the coherence of the interior. The arrangement and nature of the exterior elements are unique: none of Hawksmoor's other churches uses the grand Corinthian portico (for which see St Martin-in-the-Fields K40 and St George, Hanover Square J5, both built at the same time). The tower, which comes down to the ground, is square, not rectangular, and is crowned with a paraphrase of the Mausoleum of Halicarnassus and a statue of George I. The sooty-black north façade to Little Russell Street is a wonderfully Roman two-storey arcade over the massive keystones of the crypt windows. An obscure side passage leads back past the tower to Bloomsbury Way.

Inner Court, Staple Inn 1734   G9p
Holborn EC1
⊖Chancery Lane
Approached through an arched opening in the best surviving timber façade in London G3, Inner Court has been extensively renovated over the years. The only buildings to survive the Second World War were the east side (1729–34), with rubbed brick detailing, and the Hall (1581) with its fine hammerbeam roof. The others were indifferently rebuilt by Maufe (1954–5). Through a small arched opening in the south side is the garden court, and beyond a short cut to Chancery Lane. See also the Temple K5.

Colville Place 1766   G10m
off Charlotte Street W1
⊖Goodge Street
A rare survival: a small Georgian alley of houses, some with shop fronts, partly and badly rebuilt after damage in the Second World War.

Ely Place 1773   G11p
Holborn EC1
Charles Cole and John Gorham
⊖Chancery Lane
Built on the site of the Bishop of Ely's town house, Ely Place is an almost intact eighteenth-century close of great charm and tranquillity. It retains its delightful miniature lodge, centrally positioned, with working wrought iron gates to either side. The houses on the east side are very regular with clipped bay trees marking each front door; on the west side Ely Court leads to Hatton Garden, which is also gated. In this passageway is Ye Olde Mitre pub, dating from 1546. See also St Etheldreda G2.

Bedford Square WC1 c1775   G12n
Thomas Leverton(?)
⊖Tottenham Court Road
A completely preserved square (162 m × 117 m/530 ft × 385 ft), the next to be developed on the Bedford Estate after Bloomsbury Square of a century earlier. The square is made up of plain four-storey houses in brick, with ornaments in Coade stone. Although the yellow stock brick looks handsome when cleaned, recent research suggests that the houses may

originally have been painted black with the tuck-pointing outlined in white. The centre houses on each side are stuccoed, with pediments supported on pilasters, and the end houses on the south side are capped with balustrades. The result is that, in spite of the repetitive front doors, the square can be seen as four palace fronts facing each other. Number 1, at the south-east corner, is in a different style, and was built by Leverton for himself. It has a charming entrance hall and stair.

When the square was built, the streets approaching it were gated, for the exclusive use of residents. Coaches and services were accommodated in the now-demolished mews behind. Owners and tenants of the houses still have keys to the oval garden, which is filled with mature London plane trees – a place of rural magic in one of the densest districts of London, and a vestige of the power of private landlords.

The houses are now used as offices and publishing houses, and numbers 34–6 are occupied by the Architectural Association and its School, where there are frequent exhibitions open to the public. Visit the bar and first-floor front rooms for a good view over the square from a high-ceilinged and elegantly ornamented Georgian living room.

Alfred Place WC1 1790   G13n
George Dance the Younger
⊖ Goodge Street
The buildings of Dance's street schemes have mostly been destroyed and none remain here. His plans, however, are relatively indestructible – here a broad street with a shallow crescent at each end. See also The Crescent L59, Seven Dials K25, Finsbury Square H18.

Mecklenburgh Square and   G14k
Brunswick Square WC1
1790–1812
S P Cockerell, Joseph Kay
⊖ Russell Square
The squares, a speculative development by the Governors of the Foundling Hospital on fields either side of the hospital, were planned and supervised by Cockerell. The east side of Mecklenburgh Square by Kay, Cockerell's pupil, is the most complete composition: it follows the example of Adam's Fitzroy Square G15, but in brick and stucco, and with fine Greek detailing. With **Coram's Fields**, the two squares form the largest open space in central London outside the parks (larger than Lincoln's Inn Fields or Russell Square G16), but the present division into three prevents this being appreciated.

On the south side of Coram's Fields are the entrance gates and loggias of the **Foundling Hospital** (1742–52), which once stood in the Fields but was demolished in 1928. The hospital was one of several established around London in the first half of the eighteenth century and, like the others, stood in its own grounds in the fields outside the City.

Mecklenburgh Square

Coram's Fields

Corner Pavilion

Fitzroy Square

Fitzroy Square W1   G15m
1793–8, 1827–35
Robert Adam
⊖ Warren Street

While planned as an entity, Fitzroy Square was not built all at once. The east side (1793–8) was built in Portland stone by the Adam brothers as a unified *palazzo* of individual houses, the centre pavilion having attached unfluted columns. The south side was built in 1794, with a central tripartite window. The north and west sides were built in 1827–35 and have stuccoed fronts. While the use of stone in residential building was typical of Bath and Bristol in the eighteenth century it was unusual in London.

More recently, zealous planners have excluded cars from the square, and it now seems strangely empty. Termed an 'environmental area', it has been given miserable street furniture: benches, street lamps, and the inevitable bollards to keep out the traffic. Many blue plaques record earlier illustrious and artistic residents: Maddox Brown, William de Morgan, Roger Fry of the Omega Workshops, Virginia Woolf and George Bernard Shaw.

Russell Square WC1   G16n
laid out 1800
James Burton, Humphrey Repton
⊖ Russell Square

Few of the houses which enclosed London's largest square – 210 m × 205 m (690 ft × 673 ft) – remain, and those on the south-east and north-west corners are not in their original state. Terracotta ornaments were added as part of the Bedford Estate's attempts to make Georgian Bloomsbury more acceptable to Victorian taste, which found it gloomy, with the windowpanes too small. Gross hotels now line the eastern side, and face the unfinished wing of Holden's Senate House G62 on the west. To the north, Lasdun's Institute of Education G73 presents its end to the square. The gardens are open to the public, but their early 1960s design is not as successful as a pastiche of Repton's style might have been.

Doughty Street WC1   G17k
early 19th century
⊖ Chancery Lane

Doughty Street consists of continuous late Georgian terraces. A few houses have been cleaned, but it is a pity that 'planning' has not prevented some of the brickwork from being painted. Charles Dickens lived at number 48, which is now a small museum.

Tavistock Square WC1   G18j
1806–26
Thomas Cubitt
⊖ Euston

Only Cubitt's west side survives in this 165 m × 110 m (540 ft × 360 ft) Bloomsbury square, and his terrace shows the drift towards more individual houses which emerged in the nineteenth-century recipe for the architecture of squares; the numerous pilasters and features both at the ends and in the middle fragment the composition more than uniting it. The other sides of the square were rebuilt in the twentieth century, and the only building of significance is the BMA headquarters G54 on the west side.

Soane Mausoleum 1816   G19b
Old St Pancras Churchyard,
Pancras Road NW1
Sir John Soane
⊖ King's Cross

Although modest in scale, Sir John Soane's tomb for his wife, his son and himself is typically complex. A shallow domed canopy with four pierced pediments surrounded by low stone railings barely contains the cube-shaped monument. The decoration is minimal, and where it occurs (on the capitals and the knobs to the railings) there is no obvious historical reference.

The level of the churchyard is raised above Pancras Road, and in winter, when the trees are bare, the profile of St Pancras Station G38 and the large form of Cecil Rhodes House opposite are revealed, creating a touchingly incongruous combination, typical of London.

Lloyd Square WC1 1819 · G20h
⊖ King's Cross

The square was laid out as part of the development of the Lloyd Baker Estate, with houses less stylish than their pedimented neighbours in Lloyd Baker Street. Note Cumberland Gardens off the north-west corner of the square: a single-sided paved alley (unusual in London) whose houses look across the back gardens of the block.

To the north-east is **Myddleton Square** (1827), a well-preserved, large and regular square, with St Mark's Church by W Chadwell Mylne standing in public gardens at the centre. Off the north-west corner of Myddleton Square is **Claremont Square** which has a reservoir in the middle.

St Pancras 1819–22 G21j
Euston Road and
Upper Woburn Place NW1
H W and W Inwood
⊖ Euston

The earliest and probably the finest Greek Revival church in London, St Pancras was built as part of the southern expansion of the borough, superseding the parish church G1 on Pancras Road to the north. Following the model of Gibbs' St Martin-in-the-Fields K40, the octagonal bell tower (based on the Tower of the Winds in Athens) stands above the giant six-column Ionic portico. Two lower additions to the east, duplications of the portico of the caryatids of the Erechtheum, confirm the pagan inspiration.

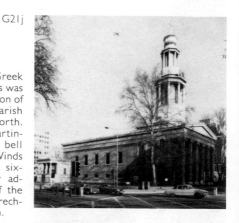

Montague Street and G22n
Bedford Place WC1 c1820
James Burton, builder
⊖ Russell Square, Holborn

The houses of the two Georgian streets leading into Russell Square from the south are plain and well proportioned, with rusticated stuccoed ground floors. Bedford Place is perfectly preserved; Montague Street lost its south-west corner with the building of the British Museum, but has intricate cast iron balconies on the south-east corner.

Woburn Walk and G23j
Duke's Road WC1
early 1820s
Thomas Cubitt
⊖ Euston

Cubitt was responsible for the development of the Bedford Estate north and east from Russell Square. His work is distinguishable from the earlier Georgian of the area by its extended use of stucco, and the articulation of the elevations of his squares (for example Gordon Square G34 and Tavistock Square G18). Here, however, he was working to the tiny scale of a short pedestrian street, one of the few designed as a whole in London. He used a restrained Greek style, the dryness of which was revealed by restoration in the 1960s.

Woburn Walk

All Saints, Camden Town G24a

1822–4
Camden Street NW1
W and H W Inwood
⊖ Camden Town

A disappointment for those who have seen the Inwoods' masterpiece, St Pancras G21, All Saints is now a Greek Orthodox church serving Camden Town's Greek Cypriot settlers. Its interior, while still retaining its original gallery, has been fitted with a screen bearing icons and separating the sanctuary and the nave (the iconostasis). The yellow stone exterior and semicircular portico are unaltered.

British Museum 1823–47 G25n

Great Russell Street WC1
Sir Robert Smirke and others
⊖ Tottenham Court Road

The nation, to which several connoisseurs had left their collections of art and antiquities in the late eighteenth and early nineteenth centuries, and to which George IV had sold the Royal Library, found in Smirke a neo-classical architect whose style matched the new programme of a public museum.

At the time the site was occupied by Montague House, which had served as a disorganized museum since the mid-eighteenth century. Smirke planned a quadrangle extending north from the house, and this plan was carried out in stages. The east side was built first to house George IV's library, and this is the most handsome original room in the building, 90 m (295 ft) long. It is spanned with iron beams clad in concrete, an early use of the material. The west and north wings off the quadrangle, for antiquities, were built between 1831 and 1838, and later filled with a remarkable collection of architectural trophies from Rome, Greece and Asia Minor. (The splendid west wing was redecorated to Smirke's original colour scheme when the Egyptian collection it housed was rearranged in 1980.) It was only in 1842 that Montague House was demolished and the magnificent Ionic colonnade and portico of the façade begun. Smirke probably knew of Schinkel's Ionic colonnade on the front of the Berlin Altesmuseum, built twenty years previously, and both buildings probably derive from Durand's academic project for a museum of 1808. Smirke's quadrangle was filled by his brother, Sidney, who designed the great circular domed Reading Room, finished in 1857. The museum expanded north during the nineteenth century until, with the building of the Edward VII Galleries G49 in Montague Place in 1914, it occupied a complete block of 4.6 ha (11.3 acres). The new restaurant and gallery for temporary exhibitions, west of the main entrance and opened in 1979, are by Colin St John Wilson.

It has always been a worry that Smirke's great façade cannot be seen from the distance it deserves, and there have been schemes by Nash, and most recently by Sir Leslie Martin, to clear the area in front of its shops, dwellings and publishing houses as far south as Hawksmoor's St George G8. These plans have always faltered, and now that a site on the Euston Road has been found for a new British Library, they will probably not be revived in this century. Meanwhile, the façade is floodlit, and the orange sodium lamps render the daytime's chaste Ionic authentically Asiatic and pagan.

St Mary 1824–7   G26e
Eversholt Street NW1
H W and W Inwood
⊖ Euston

The symmetrical west front has a centre tower of London stock brick, and the thin cast iron columns in the interior support vaults. When compared with the stronger Greek Revival style of St Pancras G21 and All Saints, Camden Town G24, the undeveloped scraped Gothic of this church illustrates the Inwoods' versatility in response to the various desires of their patrons.

Cloudesley Square,   G27d
Cloudesley Street and
Stonefield Street N1 1825
⊖ Angel

A set-piece development immediately west of Liverpool Road. The square is entered in the middle of its sides, on the seventeenth-century model, and is exceptional for its wedged corners on the west side and Barry's Holy Trinity G29 in the centre.

To the south of Cloudesley Square are Batchelor Street, Cloudesley Road, Barnsbury Street, Cloudesley Place and Bewdley Street, a good pattern of minor streets, relatively untouched except by the local council's recent environmental area strategies, which have rendered them inaccessible to outside traffic. The condition of the houses varies from 'gentrification' to seedy decay. The north end of Cloudesley Road, with its wide pavements, is particularly fine.

Cloudesley Square

Woburn Square

Torrington Square

Woburn Square WC1 1825   G28j
⊖ Russell Square

This poor relic south of Gordon Square (only the modest terraces on the north-east and south-west sides are original) is included only to catalogue the squares of Bloomsbury. The University of London is the destroyer (now threatening to demolish the remaining houses as well), and Lasdun's School of Oriental and African Studies G72 to the south is merely an 'object in space', rather than one of the 'space-defining' elements which originally constituted Bloomsbury.

To the west is the contemporary **Torrington Square**, now a square only in name, with the remains of an original terrace on the north-east corner. The square was to have been included in Holden's grandiose plan for the University, which included the Senate House G62, but instead it now entertains the ugly brick backs of Birkbeck College and the Students' Union.

Holy Trinity 1826–8 G29d
Cloudesley Square N1
Sir Charles Barry
⊖Angel

Set in the middle of the square like a miniature King's College Chapel, Holy Trinity is the third of Barry's Islington churches. The flimsiness of these churches from the beginning of the Gothic Revival shows the difficulties that classical architects experienced in dealing with Gothic forms. It was not until Barry's collaboration with Pugin on the Houses of Parliament K90 that neo-Gothic became more accurate and scholarly.

University College London G30i
1827–9
Gower Street WC1
William Wilkins, J Gandy-Deering
⊖Euston Square

University College, the founding institution of the present University of London, was established in the early 1820s. Its private sponsors, modelling its constitution and curriculum on current German education practice, were concerned to extend the range of subjects taught at universities; to free university education from the influence of the Church of England; and to extend its franchise to Jews, Roman Catholics and, later, women.

It is appropriate therefore that Wilkins won the competition for the design of the new college's buildings: his radical neoclassical style matched the institution's aims and newness. Here, however, unlike his earlier Downing College, Cambridge (1807), but like his later National Gallery K88, he was unable to rise to the occasion; his lofty portico, centrepiece of the design, has always been criticized for having its columns too close together. The interior spaces behind it are also disappointing; the dome seems cramped and the cloisters (largely rebuilt after destruction in the Second World War) are nondescript.

The north and south sides of the quadrangle were built between 1869 and 1881 by Hayter Lewis. The frontage of early twentieth-century buildings to Gower Street remained unfinished until 1987, when the ends of the two wings were completed in an appropriately elegant classical style, and the two brick lodges were rebuilt, by the Casson Conder Partnership. The opportunity of finally ridding the handsome quadrangle of academics' cars was not taken.

Gibson Square and G31d
Theberton Street N1
1830–40
⊖Angel

To the east of Cloudesley Square, Theberton Street leads into Gibson Square, the corner houses of which have giant pilasters.

In the middle of the square is Raymond Erith and Quinlan Terry's **Victoria Line ventilation shaft** (1970), derived appropriately from the Temple of the Four Winds. The building is in brick and stone, its roof netted for ventilation.

Gibson Square

Lonsdale Square N1 1838–45   G32d
R C Carpenter
✚Highbury and Islington
Carpenter departed from Georgian tradition by giving the houses in the square Tudor styling: the façades have recesses for the entrances, there are gables on the face, and the windows are square or horizontal with stucco surrounds and Tudor 'eyebrows'. He later became a successful if cramped church architect.

Model Dwellings for   G33n
Families 1849
Streatham Street WC1
Henry Roberts
✚Tottenham Court Road
The Society for Improving the Condition of the Laboring Classes was one of several set up in the 1840s as a result of progressive agitation, including that of Roberts. Some of the Society's earlier model dwellings were built as two-storey cottages, but this was their first experiment on a dense urban site. The courtyard is lined with open galleries giving access to the flats, which have a living room, kitchen and scullery, and mostly two bedrooms. Construction is fireproof: brick load-bearing walls and arched hollow-brick floors. The galleries are supported by brick piers which span two floors, more in the tradition of the Georgian engineer than the Victorian speculative builder. The top floor is a later addition. It is interesting to speculate on

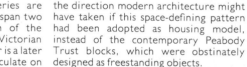

the direction modern architecture might have taken if this space-defining pattern had been adopted as housing model, instead of the contemporary Peabody Trust blocks, which were obstinately designed as freestanding objects.

Gordon Square WC1 1850   G34j
Thomas Cubitt
✚Euston
The last of the Bloomsbury squares to be completed, Gordon Square shows Cubitt drifting into Victorian fashion; the east side, especially the five-storey section to the south, is more like the contemporary Italianate houses of Kensington. The Tudor-style building on the west side, Dr Williams' Library, was built by Professor Donaldson in 1848 as a hall of residence for the new University College. The rendering of the terrace north of the library is unpainted; this is unusual. See also University Church of Christ the King G36.

King's Cross Station 1851–2   G35g
Euston Road NW1
Lewis and Joseph Cubitt
✚King's Cross
King's Cross was the terminus of the Great Northern Railway, opened in 1850 to accommodate the massive tourist influx to the Great Exhibition. It is a bold engineering building, memorable for its façade (best seen from the other side of Euston Road) and the vaulted Arrival and Departure Halls. The no-nonsense builder's approach to King's Cross (compared with the romantic Gilbert Scott façade of St Pancras G38 next door) has been severely undermined by the recent insensitive additions to the forecourt, and

earlier additions to the west approach. The principal features of the façade are the great arched roofs of the Halls, each spanning 26 m (71 ft), and separated by the

central clock tower 37 m (120 ft) high. The original cast iron brackets supporting the arches are still there, but the timber roof construction has been replaced by steel.

University Church of Christ the King 1853 G36j
Gordon Square WC1
Raphael Brandon
⊖ Goodge Street

Originally built for the Catholic Apostolic Church, a sect which broke away from the Catholic Church after the announcement of Papal infallibility in 1870, this huge Victorian Gothic church is strangely empty of the accumulated bits and pieces which would normally by now have softened its harshness. The unbuilt steeple was to have been 90 m (295 ft) high, and would have topped Holden's Senate House G62.

Agricultural Hall 1861–2 G37d
Islington High Street and
Liverpool Road N1
F Peck; engineered by Heaviside
⊖ Angel

The huge 117 m × 66 m (384 ft × 217 ft) hall, with its central clear span of 46 m (150 ft) in iron, lies back from Islington High Street, from which it is reached via a giant entrance arch with angle towers. The roof profile can best be seen from Liverpool Road to the west. The building is disused, and its redevelopment is being discussed.

St Pancras Station 1866–8 G38f
hotel and offices 1868–76
Euston Road NW1
Hotel, Sir George Gilbert Scott; train shed, W H Barlow and R M Ordish
⊖ King's Cross

This station, originally the terminus of the Midland Railway, and one of the three to the north of Euston Road, was built during the 1860s boom in railway and terminus construction. Broad Street, Cannon Street, Charing Cross and Victoria were also constructed in this decade, but St Pancras is architecturally the most important. Scott, at the peak of his career and public esteem, was designing the Foreign Office K105 at the same time, and his Albert Memorial J44 was under construction. Here he could exhibit his masterly synthesis of Gothic motifs, both in the craggy, wilfully picturesque composition (best seen from Pentonville Road), and in the details which partial cleaning has revealed.

The complex multi-level planning and circulation is startlingly assured. The materials he chose – bright red bricks from Nottingham, red and grey granite and beige stone – demonstrate the Victorians' passion for colourful buildings which would be visible through the smoky atmosphere of the nineteenth-century city, and which would resist the attack of pollution.

The inclusion of that quintessential Victorian building type, the hotel, in the station's accommodation was part of the

boom in London hotel building of the 1860s and '70s, to serve an increasingly mobile, international and imperial society. Its fine interiors, at present used for offices, cannot be visited.

The uninterrupted shed, 210 m (689 ft) long and 75 m (245 ft) wide, was extremely ambitious, being for many years the widest span in the world. Its ingenuity lies in concealing the ties necessary to hold the vault together under the platforms.

The straightforward juxtaposition of shed and high-art building worried the Victorians, and can now be seen, as Donald J Olsen suggests, as a direct indication of the schizophrenia of a period obsessed both with the past and its styles (architecture), and with the glamour of technology (engineering).

The building of Euston, St Pancras and King's Cross stations drastically affected

the area to their north: for a century it consisted of grimy, soot-infested workers' housing, until the railways started to use electric and diesel trains in the 1950s.

Behind the station in Camley Road are the **St Pancras gasholders**, started in 1824 by the Imperial Gas, Light and Coke Company, and the largest gasworks in London until 1869. They have been repainted in their original colours and are still working.

Prudential Assurance G39p
1879, 1899–1906
Alfred and Paul Waterhouse
Holborn EC1
⊖Chancery Lane

In a city made principally of stock brick, Portland stone and stucco, Waterhouse's vibrant, blazing-red terracotta Gothic palace for Prudential Assurance is a remarkable and rather forbidding exception. Its size is a consequence of the wealth and self-importance gained by insurance in the nineteenth century. The redness may be Waterhouse's whim, but it is more probably the result of Victorian architects' desire for materials which would resist London's polluted atmosphere and could be seen through it. The 1879 scheme at the corner of Brooke Street (rebuilt in 1932) was extended in 1899–1906 to encompass the whole block. The principal Holborn façade is symmetrical, with prefabricated terracotta units, three-storey ranges of of lancet windows, a roof profile of gables and spires, and a big central tower crowned by a pyramidal roof. Waterhouse's son Paul finished the building after his father's death in 1905.

Clinic c1885   G40m
35 Langham Street W1
⊖ Oxford Circus
The Victorian concern for materials which
would not be destroyed by London's
polluted air here reaches its absurd and
extreme conclusion – the façade is entirely of shiny white glazed brick and
looks as if it will last another century.

Rosebery Square 1889–92   G41l
Rosebery Avenue EC1
⊖ Chancery Lane
Rosebery Avenue was one of the last
Victorian 'Improvements', cut through
slums north of Clerkenwell Road. Rosebery Square is a pathetic widening of the
rows of dreadful walk-up dwellings with
which the avenue is lined.

Mary Ward Settlement   G42j
1895–8
Tavistock Place WC1
Smith and Brewer
⊖ Russell Square
This is a major work and one of the best

examples of the Free Style applied to a
public building in the 1890s. Although
owing something to Charles Rennie
Mackintosh (though it predates his
Glasgow School of Art by three years),
C H Townsend and Norman Shaw, the

language of this building is handled with great sophistication and originality.

The overall composition of the street façade is symmetrical, with local asymmetries to the entrance (reminiscent of Townsend): the tripartite window arrangement is typically Norman Shaw; the stepping windows for the staircases at either end are not. Wedged into the surface of the building is the side door, with projecting canopy and stepped stonework, all very good indeed.

Finsbury Town Hall 1895–9   G43 1
Rosebery Avenue EC1
G Evans Vaughan
⊖ Chancery Lane

The turn of the century was a period of architectural experiment, and the revived Tudor style used here associates itself ultimately with the glory of Elizabethan England. The Borough of Finsbury lost its identity when London's local government was reorganized in 1965, and its exuberant and wilfully asymmetrical town hall no longer serves the symbolic function it had when built.

University College   G44i
Hospital 1897–1906
Gower Street NW1
Alfred Waterhouse
⊖ Euston Square, Warren Street

Set in Georgian Bloomsbury and opposite the Greek Revival of Wilkins' University College, Waterhouse's eccentric turrets and spires in red terracotta are a lesson to the 'in keeping with' lobby, which of recent years has justified much timid and mediocre building. As with all his London buildings, the sheer virtuosity of the forms and the precision of buildings are overwhelming. The X-plan of seven storeys connects the four corners of the square site diagonally. It was an exemplary hospital model in its day, but the triangular spaces left over between the building and the street are problematic.

Russell Hotel 1898   G45n
Russell Square WC1
C Fitzroy Doll
⊖ Russell Square

The construction of this hotel (a characteristically Victorian building type), was the first large incursion into Georgian Bloomsbury. Twice as high as its then domestic neighbours, it is in the uncertain late Victorian style – a confused mixture of eclectic motifs in beige faience, from which Shaw was able to show a way out in his cooler Piccadilly Hotel K123 of only seven years later. See also Russell Square G16.

Derby Lodge G46g
late 19th century
Britannia Street WC1
⊖ King's Cross
A recently renovated six-storey tenement building with fine iron arches to the staircase landings.

Fire Station 1901–2 G47j
Euston Road NW1
LCC Architects Department; W E Riley
⊖ Euston
The English 'Arts and Crafts' Free Style originated in the second half of the nineteenth century in the domestic work of Philip Webb and R Norman Shaw, among others. It was later applied to public buildings: the LCC Architects Department was an influential early advocate of the movement, and this building is one of the best examples. As Gavin Stamp writes, 'The style came to be regarded as essentially utilitarian and informal, suitable for a fire station but not for a bank, excellent for flats but not for a town mansion.' The Eversholt Street elevation should be noted for its complex handling of windows, relieving arches, gables and projections, all in very good red brickwork and Portland stone – a remarkable composition.

Bourne Estate 1901–7 G48p
Clerkenwell Road EC1
LCC Architects Department, Owen Fleming
⊖ Chancery Lane
This is the only pre-war LCC estate that approaches Boundary H36 and Millbank in size. 3900 people are housed behind the extensive façade to the Clerkenwell Road; from the road the arched openings reveal perspectives through a series of courtyards. The five-storey tenement blocks are laid out north-south and although the flats have gallery access their living rooms receive maximum sunlight. But compared with the Boundary and Millbank Estates it feels overcrowded, and marks a retreat from the previous Free Style ideals of the young LCC architects. The buildings are also more in the Edwardian grand manner than in the tradition of Shaw or Webb.

Edward VII Galleries G49n
British Museum 1904–11
Montague Place WC1
Sir John Burnet
⊖ Tottenham Court Road

The galleries were built to extend the museum and, continuing the replacement of Bloomsbury's Georgian houses with large institutions, completed the block on which it stands. The composition of the façade, with its flat higher ends framing the Ionic screen, owes as much to Schinkel's Berlin Altesmuseum as to Smirke's south front of this museum G25, but it has a specifically Edwardian Beaux Arts flavour: there are straightforward commercial windows between the engaged columns. The interiors are competent, and it is planned to restore their original colours and splendour. The lions terminating the balustrade and flanking the entrance are particularly fine. See also Kodak House K133.

Sicilian Avenue 1905 G50o
between Bloomsbury Way and
Southampton Row WC1
W S Worthy
⊖ Holborn

A corner is sliced through with an 8 m (27 ft) wide pedestrian street separated from the main roads by spindly Ionic screens. The five storeys of offices (originally flats) above the shops are clad in a mixture of bright red brick and white terracotta, newly cleaned. The Italian restaurant provides that rare thing in London, a nice place to sit outside – a fragment of Italy, but with a view of the plane trees of Bloomsbury Square. Sicilian Avenue demonstrates that the means of making a civilized public place removed from traffic can be quite modest, making the 'decks' of the South Bank K171 seem unnecessary.

Working Men's College 1905 G51a

Crowndale Road NW1
W H Caroë
⊖ Mornington Crescent
One of a series of such colleges for the
further education of adults, set up under
Fabian socialist and self-help auspices. This
one sports the full Edwardian apparatus
for public buildings, and could be a town
hall or library.

Department of Health and G52i
Social Security ex London,

Edinburgh and Glasgow Assurance 1907
Euston Road and Melton Street NW1
E Beresford Pite
⊖ Euston
Pite started his career as assistant to John
Belcher, who combined a commitment to
the Arts and Crafts movement with his
own fine baroque style, and Pite's early
work followed that of his master. This
strange concoction of archaic and classical
Greek motifs departs wildly from the
earlier baroque. The remarkable tiled
entrance hall is in a strange style of its
own.

Central School of Arts and G53o
Crafts 1907–9

Southampton Row WC1
LCC Architects Department;
W E Riley with A Halcrow Verstage
⊖ Holborn
Although normally attributed to Lethaby
(who as Principal of the Central School
was influential on the design and consultant for the specification), this is another
example of the formal variety of buildings
produced by the LCC under the direction
and supervision of W E Riley. The massive
stone façade has segmental arches in
shallow relief and, almost as an afterthought, a curious domed entry system on
the corner. Lethaby's preoccupation with
symbolism emerges in some of the decorative details.

British Medical Association G54j

ex Theosophical Society
Headquarters 1911–13, 1922–9
Tavistock Square and Burton Street
WC1
Sir Edwin Lutyens, completed by
C Wontner Smith
⊖ Euston, Russell Square
The Burton Street façade is all that
Lutyens built for the Theosophical Society
(of which his wife was a founder member)
before construction was interrupted by
the First World War. Mostly in brick with
stone dressings, it is truly monumental.
The large and simple window openings are
formed in what appears to be a *piano nobile*
four storeys high, below which is a plinth
of open arches. After the war the building
was taken over by the BMA, and the
equally grand brick façade to Tavistock
Square was added by Wontner Smith.

Burton Street façade

Heal's 1916   G55m
196 Tottenham Court Road
W1
Smith and Brewer
⊖ Goodge Street

The firm founded by Ambrose Heal has a distinguished history of promoting the functional qualities of vernacular furniture – the large-scale craft workshops of Heal's kept the Arts and Crafts Movement alive and were a rebuke to the cheap revivals in the other furniture stores on Tottenham Court Road. As Le Corbusier observed in *Towards a New Architecture*, 'The existing plan of the dwelling ... is conceived as a furniture store. This scheme of things, favourable enough to the trade of Tottenham Court Road, is of ill omen for Society'.

The façade to Heal's aptly expressed the sober, functional and craft-based preoccupations of its owner. The stone casings to the steel frame running the full height of the store are divided by decorative blue spandrels depicting the tools of the trade; note also the ingenious curved display window on the ground floor and the elegantly crafted internal staircase. The building has since been extended and with each extension some of the quality of the original has been lost.

Friends' House 1925–7   G56j
Euston Square NW1
H Lidbetter
⊖ Euston

The range of buildings on the south side of Euston Square, from Gordon Street to Woburn Place including Friends' House, shows how the neo-Georgian style – red brick with stone dressings for important features – could successfully be used for most urban building types: a bank, Post Office, Trading Standards Office and a religious centre. Friends' House provides a meeting place and offices for Quakers. The main rooms are in the middle, with rings of offices round light wells on either side.

School of Hygiene and   G57n
Tropical Medicine
University of London 1926–8
Gower Street and Keppel Street WC1
Morely Horder and Vernon Rees
⊖ Goodge Street

With its 'stripped classical' Portland stone façade, this building works well as an example of neutral town planning. In one direction it maintains the continuity of Gower Street; in the other direction, with Keppel Street as its central axis, it anticipates the Beaux Arts composition of Holden's massive Senate House G62. The gold insects and other fauna decorating the balconies are an interesting detail.

Levita House, Chamberlain House and Walker House

G58f

1928
Chalton Street, Phoenix Road and
Ossulton Street NW1
G Topham Forrest
⊖ Euston

A palatial set-piece of local authority housing, combining formal street façades, arched entrances to internal courts and diminutive avenues of trees.

Although badly in need of repair, the scheme might not seem out of place in a benevolent Marxist mid-European state.

Offices

G59o

ex W S Crawford Limited 1930
233 High Holborn WC1
Frederick Etchells and Welch
⊖ Holborn

It is appropriate that Crawford's, one of London's most progressive advertising agencies in the 1920s, should have commissioned one of the earliest examples of the 'new architecture' for their offices. The building handles the corner site traditionally and its use of materials is both urbane and sensuous. Unlike the more abstract rendered contemporaries, the building has a polished black marble ground floor or plinth, above which are alternating bands of white stucco and continuous windows. The windows are subdivided by structural mullions with chromium steel cover-strips (see Mies van der Rohe's Barcelona pavilion of 1929). As a result of its external detail, the building has weathered extremely well.

This was unfortunately Etchells' only

building of consequence in London. His reputation as a pioneer of modernism is attributable more to his translation into English of Le Corbusier's *Vers une Architecture* and his association with Vorticism.

American Express Garage

G60j

ex Daimler Car Hire Garage
1931
Herbrand Street WC1
Wallis Gilbert and Partners
⊖ Russell Square

In this quiet back street there rises unexpectedly a baroque 1930s façade. Car ramps are contained in cylindrical forms, complete with striped rendering and horizontal metal windows: a palace for the motorcar, when compared with today's more utilitarian equivalent.

Wellcome Building 1931

G61i

Euston Road NW1
Septimus Warwick
⊖ Euston Square, Euston

A well-mannered, late example of classicism, used appropriately for an institution. Originally of four storeys, the building has been spoilt by the later addition of two attics. The Wellcome Foundation is an offshoot of the drug company, and the building houses a small museum. See also Warwick's Brixton Town Hall W9.

Senate House University of   G62n
London, started 1932
Malet Street and Montague Place WC I
Charles Holden
✪ Tottenham Court Road

Soon after Holden's London Transport building K143 was finished, he was employed by the University to make a plan for its new administrative centre in Bloomsbury. In line with Store Street Holden proposed, as a landmark for London, a tower from which a high spine block would have extended north as far as Torrington Place. At right angles to this block, lower wings would have run to the streets bounding the site to the east and west. In the event, work was interrupted by the Second World War, and neither the northern extension of the scheme nor Holden's design for a ceremonial hall on the west side of Russell Square was built.

Stuart Mills House c1937   G63g
Killick Street N1
Joseph Emberton
✪ King's Cross

This six-storey slab building – with access galleries at every floor and an asymmetrically positioned lift shaft – is a reminder that even the 'heroes' of the 1930s were capable of indifferent designs when called upon to produce low-cost housing. The building is distantly influenced by Brinkmann, van der Vlugt and W. van Tijen's Bergpolder apartments in Rotterdam (1933).

The elaborately modelled tower houses many different functions, and its structure allows for changing the internal arrangement; even the steel-beamed floors were designed to be moved up and down. The style is Holden's late stripped-classical, here so stripped that the only horizontal mouldings remaining are those of the parapets and balustrade-cappings. Holden was particularly concerned to control the weathering of Portland stone, and although the buildings have been cleaned several times since their completion, his skill in anticipating the inevitable effects of pollution and weather is clearly visible. The ceremonial interiors are splendid, using travertine for floors and wall panelling, and have excellent examples of light-fittings (for which Holden had gained practice from his Underground stations R23, T25).

Finsbury Health Centre   G64 I

1938
Pine Street EC1
Lubetkin and Tecton
⊖ Angel

With the approach of the Second World War this building was to be Tecton's last in the optimistic spirit of the 'new architecture' of the 1930s. The health centre, partly indebted to the Peckham experiment X10, was a pioneering idea of the time. This project, for a slum clearance area of Finsbury, was the first to coincide with Tecton's declared socialist ideals. Its symmetrical two-storey H-plan, withdrawn from the existing street pattern, is reminiscent of the public buildings Le Corbusier projected for the continuous parklands of the *Ville Radieuse*. When the centre was built it stood as a shining white rebuke to the decayed area of Finsbury, but it is important for a less obvious reason. Its symmetrical plan and the baroque exuberance of its entrance

sequence reaffirm the autonomy of architecture: they are not dictated by the programme (that is, form does not follow function) but show instead the inevitable presence of 'historical' or Beaux Arts planning techniques in pioneer works.

Research Building   G65h

ex Metropolitan Water Board
1938
Rosebery Avenue EC1
Sir Howard Robertson
⊖ Angel

A grandiose curved arrangement on a prominent site, but a disappointment from the only architect since Durand to attempt a book describing the art of 'composition'. He later designed the South Bank's Shell Centre.

Priory Green Estate 1938–52   G66g

Collier Street N1
Tecton: Skinner, Bailey and Lubetkin
⊖ King's Cross

Although planned and started before the Second World War, the Priory Green Estate was postponed and subsequently revised. The 269 flats occupy 3.5 ha (8.7 acres) and unlike the later Hallfield Estate 126 follow the alignment of the original street pattern. They form two eight-storey set-back formations, with four identical four-storey blocks adjacent.

Note also **Bevin Court**, in Holford Place south of Pentonville Road, built by Tecton in 1953. Named after Ernest Bevin, this seven-storey block of flats is triangular in plan. The façades have alternating panels of brick and pre-cast concrete.

Euston Station and offices   G67i

1960–80
Euston Road NW1
British Rail Architects Department and
R Seifert and Partners
⊖Euston

Philip Hardwick's great Euston Arch (1836–40) was senselessly demolished by British Rail in 1961, together with the other front buildings. The reason given was that it would get in the way of the station 'improvements', notably the extra platform lengths which were required. However, following the demolition of the arch the track lengths were not increased, leaving the site untouched.

The new station hall (1965) by British Rail and Seifert's offices (1979–80) are a particularly glib and depressing replacement. Unlike Hardwick's arch they fail to convey any sense of arrival or departure.

London Telecom Tower   G68m

1963–6
Howland Street W1
Architects Section of the Ministry of
Works
⊖Warren Street

This structure is one of a series dotted across the country, linking the large cities in the UK by microwave transmission of telephone and other messages. When completed, it was widely admired as an example of pure, 'innocent' engineering; why this was, given its poorly proportioned and clumsily detailed curtain wall, is not now clear. At 174 m (580 ft) high, it was the tallest building in London until the National Westminster Tower L129 was finished in 1981. The observation gallery was a good place from which to appreciate London's loose structure (compared with Paris or New York), but has been closed since a bomb explosion.

Brunswick Centre 1965–73   G69k

Brunswick Square and
Guilford Street WC1
Patrick Hodgkinson (design),
Bickerdyke Allen (construction)
⊖Russell Square

Like much recent British housing, the Brunswick Centre is a heroic failure. It is a sad conclusion to Hodgkinson's long, complex and spirited inquiry (starting in the early 1960s under Sir Leslie Martin in Cambridge) into high density, low-rise alternatives to the universal prescription of high-rise towers for the inner city areas. Despite frequent changes of client and Hodgkinson's resignation before the building was finished, it is still just possible to detect some of the early passion for an 'ideal' city block. The two parallel blocks follow the existing street pattern, facing each other across a raised internal plaza. The extruded nature of the stepped section, with its monumental back-of-stadium effect on the surrounding streets, and the emptiness of the central plaza are some of the Centre's problems. The Brunswick Centre and Alexandra Road E7 are probably the last of London's concrete dinosaurs.

Housing and **showrooms**   G70m
1966–71
Clipstone Street W1
Frederick Macmanus and Partners,
designed by Michael Gold
⊖ Great Portland Street
Housing for 800 people, in a six-storey
ring with basement car parking below,
stands apart from a two-storey triangular
block of showrooms. The housing is a
fortuitous illustration of Sir Leslie
Martin's theories of the usefulness of
building along the edges of sites to
produce high densities, here about 720
people to the hectare. The buildings are
reticently styled: the painted concrete
frame shows on the outside, but on the
inside the well-planted courtyard has
continuous projecting balconies.

College of Engineering and   G71m
Science Polytechnic of
Central London 1970
Clipstone Street W1
Lyons Israel and Ellis
⊖ Great Portland Street
This building shows a mixture of in-
fluences. The towers housing offices and
laboratories are separated from smaller
attendant towers housing services (stairs,
ducts, lifts and so on), recalling the
'served' and 'servant' spaces of Louis
Kahn. The patent glazing, cantilevered
lecture theatres and external gantries and
boiler flues pay homage to the celebrated
Leicester University engineering laboratories (1964) designed by Stirling and
Gowan (one-time assistants in the firm of
Lyons Israel and Ellis). While the industrial and constructivist imagery may
be appropriate to an engineering faculty
and a red-brick university campus, the
same forms are incongruous in the streets
and squares of eighteenth-century
London. However, the entrance hall with
flying galleries is quite spectacular.

School of Oriental and   G72n
African Studies University of
London 1973
Woburn Square WC1
Sir Denys Lasdun and Partners
⊖ Russell Square
The school comprises teaching rooms
arranged round a double-height rooflit
library. Built in concrete and clad in white
precast concrete panels which seem to
have been designed for a Mediterranean
climate, the building disregards the pattern of streets and squares that character-
izes what remains of Georgian Bloomsbury. It suggests only a future pattern of
isolated and unrelated objects – a still life.

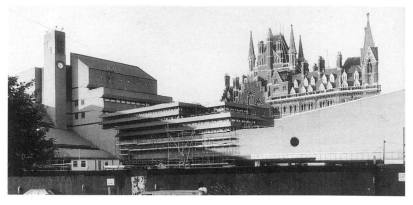

British Library 1974–   G73f
Euston Road NW1
Colin St John Wilson and Partners with
Property Services Agency
⊖ King's Cross
The British Library will not be established
in its new premises on Euston Road until
1993. Meanwhile it has drawn attention to
itself as the building with the highest
recorded state investment (£445 million),
the building that has induced premature
criticism from the Prince of Wales, and the
building that has inspired heroic perseverance from its architect for over three
decades.

Institute of Education   G74j
University of London 1975–9
Bedford Way WC1
Sir Denys Lasdun and Partners
⊖ Euston Square, Russell Square

Contemporary with Lasdun's National
Theatre K172, the Institute provides
offices, classrooms and lecture rooms.
One side of Bedford Way, to which it
presents a suave continuous curtain wall
236 m (770 ft) long, is punctuated by
aggressive triangular features in concrete.
The detailing at ground level is not so
satisfactory. The side away from the street
is planned to grow by receiving a series of
stepped wings. One has been built,
extending towards Lasdun's School of
Oriental and African Studies G72.

ITN offices 1987–90   G75l
200 Gray's Inn Road WC1
Foster Associates
⊖ Farringdon

Now mainly occupied by Independent
Television News, these offices were
originally a speculation. The office accommodation is arranged round a full-height
and roof-lit atrium. To the street, the
office floors present their sheer skin: an
energy-efficient 'neutralizing wall' of two
planes of widely separated glass. Below
this at pavement level the entrance is
recessed behind painted concrete
columns.

Imagination offices and   G76n
gallery 1990
Alfred Place, Store Street WC1
Ron Herron and Associates
⊖ Goodge Street
The provocative roofscape of fabric domes seen from Bedford Square is the only external expression of one of London's most celebrated recent works. An inauspicious light well has been trans- formed into an atrium of extraordinary qualities. The combination of heavy masonry walls, light steel and inventively designed bridges spanning the brilliant white interior, topped by the tented roof structure, produces a breathtaking spatial effect of remarkable luminosity. When there are public exhibitions it is possible to appreciate this central space from the rooftop gallery.

Offices 1991   G77i
388 Euston Road NW1
Sheppard Robson Architects
⊖ Warren Street, Great Portland Street
Just as the retention of 'historic' façades has become a familiar compromise for many London developments, so the oppo- site tendency of providing new façades to existing buildings might be seen as less conservative and more didactic (see also Orion House K161). Here we have one of the more successful attempts, which goes some way to moderating the miseries of this section of Euston Road. The building is also dramatic when floodlit.

Section H: Finsbury/Shoreditch/Spitalfields/Islington

The historic boroughs of Shoreditch and Finsbury to the north and the hamlet of Spitalfields to the east were among the first outer districts of London to merge with the medieval City. It is ironic that the most historic areas of London should, as a result of continuous development, be the most confusing and architecturally disappointing, and nowhere is this more evident than in the areas adjacent to the City.

Shoreditch today has no architectural links with its medieval and Elizabethan past, its earliest buildings dating from the late seventeenth century. Hoxton Square, where no original houses now remain, was laid out shortly after 1683 in an attempt to emulate developments to the west, and acquired for the district a reputation for genteel living. Many almshouses were built in the eighteenth century, but only the Geffrye Museum (Ironmonger's Almshouses) H7 survives, built in 1715 on Kingsland Road, the borough's boundary with the country. In the nineteenth century the population of Shoreditch rose abruptly, indicating a rise in trade and a corresponding decline in gentility. The area is still characterized by warehouses, offices and workshops, and retains the timber and furniture trades which started in the nineteenth century. Badly bombed in the Second World War, Shoreditch has been reconstructed in a piecemeal fashion.

Spitalfields was a silk-weaving area, settled by French Huguenots exiled largely as a result of the revocation of the Edict of Nantes (1685), and was one of the nine hamlets in the parish of Stepney. Some silk weavers' houses – identifiable by large windows to the upper storey to light the looms – survive near Bethnal Green Museum. By the late eighteenth century it had developed, like Shoreditch, into a desirable residential area. Evidence of this more salubrious past remains in the few early eighteenth-century houses in Spital Square, Folgate Street, Elder Street, Fournier Street H9 and Wilkes Street H8 immediately north and east of Spitalfields Market. By the nineteenth century, however, Spitalfields had followed the East End's general pattern of industrialization. In the 1980s, many of London's railway stations and markets were redeveloped. Broad Street Station was demolished for part of the new Broadgate H43 and Liverpool Street Station H33 was surrounded by new offices in an extension of the same scheme. The market at Spitalfields closed and has since been the object of proposals and counter-proposals for its comprehensive redevelopment.

Sixteenth-century Finsbury, next to the City but outside its jurisdiction, was (like Southwark, section L) popular for theatres – Sadler's Music House started in 1685. In the early seventeenth century it attracted religious and nonconformist groups. However, nothing remains today of this romantic past, with the exception of the Charterhouse, Finsbury's only surviving medieval monument. The urban development of Clerkenwell and Finsbury was encouraged by reconstruction after the Great Fire of 1666: Charterhouse Square H4 dates from about 1700, and Finsbury Square H18 was laid out by the younger Dance in 1777 in an attempt to emulate the development of the great estates to the west. Unfortunately no houses remained after the Blitz. Finsbury Circus, laid out to the south in 1815, retains only the plan of the younger Dance's original proposal: its mediocre twentieth-century transformation is now complete with the exception of Lutyens House H37. Standing on the fringes of London, the traditional site for hospitals, Finsbury acquired two in the same year, 1751: St Luke's and the Lying-In Hospital.

Islington to the north, meanwhile, had remained a village, but by the beginning of the nineteenth century it too was becoming absorbed in London's growth. Expansion to the north and west was accelerated by two important engineering works, the New Road (1770) and the Regent's Canal (1814–20). Both were concerned with the practical matter of bypassing the congested centre of London, to facilitate the passage of goods from the expanding West End to the City and finally to the Docks. At the same time they bridged the historic divide between the cities of London and Westminster (see section K).

St Bartholomew the Great HIm
1123
West Smithfield EC1
restored by Sir Aston Webb 1880–1900
⊖Farringdon

In 1123 the Augustinian Priory and Hospital of St Bartholomew the Great were founded. The present church is the remains of the Priory, whose precinct lay to the south. The nave has been demolished, leaving a T-shaped arrangement, and the apsidal east end was completely rebuilt in the late nineteenth century. Nevertheless, St Bartholomew's is London's only surviving monastic church from the twelfth century, and its only example of large-scale Norman work – for the small scale see the Chapel of St John in the Tower of London L3. The half-timbered gatehouse (rebuilt) in Little Britain marks

the position of the original entrance to the nave.

St John 1721, crypt 1140 and H2i
1180, gate 1504
St John's Square EC1
⊖Farringdon

Only the crypt remains of the twelfth-century priory church of the order of St John of Jerusalem, its rib vaulting showing that the church had the circular nave then customary. The massive vaulted gate from St John's Lane (restored by John Oldred Scott in 1903) suggests the size of the original priory which, although it was damaged during the Peasants' Revolt in 1381, survived until the dissolution of the monasteries during the reign of Henry VIII. The present church is eighteenth-century, unexceptional and understated, and stands behind a fine red-brick wall with rubbed brick detail. In the wall is a memorial gateway to the Doewra family

leading to a small garden. Prior Doewra rebuilt the priory in 1504.

Houses mid-17th century H3m
41–2 Cloth Fair EC1
⊖Barbican

The timber houses destroyed by the Great Fire were replaced in brick. These houses escaped the Fire, and their timber construction gives an idea of what early seventeenth-century London was like. On a corner site, adjacent to the typically narrow alleys of Cloth Court and Rising Sun Court, they have four two-storey timber bay windows capped by pediments. Numbers 39–45 Cloth Fair are owned by the Landmark Trust.

Houses c1700 H4m
4–5 Charterhouse Square EC1
⊖Barbican

Standing in one of London's few remaining gated squares, these houses are more severe than their contemporaries at Queen Anne's Gate K31, and 1 and 2 Laurence Pountney Hill L48. The doorcases are later.

Colebrook Row

Charlton Place

Colebrook Row and   H5e
Duncan Terrace N1
c1710 and 1786
✚ Angel

The pride of eighteenth-century residential Islington, these two long terraces faced each other originally across the New River: a garden now follows the course of the culverted river. Duncan Terrace, on the west side, is a sequence of impressive façades, regular but for the interruption of the massive church of St John the Evangelist (1843) which Pugin described as 'the most original combination of modern deformity that has been erected for some

Christ Church 1714–29   H6p
Commercial Street E1
Nicholas Hawksmoor
✚ Aldgate East

The church was savagely altered in 1850 by Ewan Christian (better known as architect of the National Portrait Gallery K116), who removed the galleries, blocked in the windows at the corners of the central space, and lowered the main windows. After years of neglect, it is at present being restored to its pre-1850 condition, using the original building documents where possible. The restoration will reveal the most complex and sumptuous of Hawksmoor's interiors. The central space with its flat ceiling is lit by a clerestory, and flanked by aisles. These are roofed with elliptical barrel-vaults carried on a raised Composite order (see also Wren's St James, Piccadilly K21). This order is used for the screens across the east and west ends. The Venetian window at the east end may

time past'. The raised pavements accommodating the slope either side of **Charlton Place** are particularly good. Charlton Place itself is a little street of Georgian cottages made special by the shallow curve on the south side, its uncertain stepped cornice line following the slope of the street towards the New River.

To the east of Colebrooke Row are Cruden Street, Chantry Street, Queen's Head Street and St Peter's Street, a triangular area of small-scale streets best appreciated as part of an extended Islington walk.

show the growing influence of the Palladians, or it may be a rhyme with the arched pediment of the entrance portico, repeated in the wide main stage of the tower.

Geffrye Museum   H7h
ex Ironmongers' Almshouses 1715
Kingsland Road E9
✚ Old Street

A two-storey group of fourteen almshouses forms three sides of a generous courtyard; in the centre is a chapel, approached by a formal avenue of lime trees (planted in 1719) from the gated entrance with fine lampholders on Kingsland Road. A statue of Sir Robert Geffrye, the benefactor, stands benignly in a recess above the entrance. In 1910–14 W E Riley of the LCC converted the almshouses into a museum: by removing the first floors, stairs and much of the party walls he produced a long sequence of small galleries.

Houses 1721　　　　　　　H8p
Wilkes Street E1
⊖Shoreditch
In this street are good and atypical examples of Stepney's surviving eighteenth-century housing stock. Number 1 has tall windows in the roof to illuminate work at the loom; number 2 has a generous frontage, although the house inside is cramped and only one room deep; and the wooden doorcase to number 11 is one of the few surviving examples in London.

Fournier Street 1722–8　　　H9p
Spitalfields E1
⊖Aldgate East
Running alongside Christ Church H6, this is the least damaged of the many surviving early eighteenth-century streets in the district. The four-bay rectory on the south side is by Hawksmoor.

House c1725　　　　　　　H10k
16 Charles Square N1
⊖Old Street
The only original house in the square, number 16 was refurbished in 1980: it has five bays, a good doorcase, and rather unfortunate painted keystones to the windows.

St Luke 1727–33　　　　　　H11j
Old Street EC1
Nicholas Hawksmoor and John James
⊖Old Street
The ruined St Luke and the demolished St John, Horsleydown, formed a pair of late Commissioners' churches. The bizarre fluted obelisk steeple is attributed to Hawksmoor who had a reputation for strange tower-terminals; in 1730 he had proposed a similar but unfluted design for St Giles-in-the-Fields K45. James was architect of St George, Hanover Square J5.

St Bartholomew's Hospital   H12m
1730–59, 1834
West Smithfield EC1
James Gibbs, Philip Hardwick
⊖ Barbican, St Paul's

With its long history of adaptation and its formal entrance sequence, St Bartholomew's resembles other English institutions, particularly the Inns of Court and the colleges of Oxford and Cambridge. The first buildings dated from 1123, but the earliest surviving are the fifteenth-century tower and vestry of the hospital church, St Bartholomew-the-Less. The octagonal body of the church was added in 1823 by Philip Hardwick, to plans by George Dance the Younger. It now forms the north-east side of the hospital's first courtyard, entered through the boundary wall to West Smithfield. Over the entrance is the magnificent but eccentrically tall gatehouse, entirely rebuilt by Hardwick in 1834. A Venetian gateway leads from here to the principal courtyard.

The Gibbs court was originally four detached stone buildings, spare and Palladian in detail, with a fountain and large plane trees at the centre. In summer the trees form a canopy, and the combination of water and shade encourages patients and visitors to use the space as a grand salon. The statues and urns which once stood on the parapets and the big arches connecting the open corners have unfortunately disappeared. In 1934–5 Lancaster, Lucas and Lodge replaced the south side with the George V building, a dull and uninspired copy of the original. The three surviving Gibbs buildings (recased by Hardwick in 1856) were London's earliest large-scale examples of the use of Bath stone.

The most interesting interiors are the main staircase and the great hall, both good secular examples of English baroque.

Honourable Artillery   H13j
Company
1735, 1828, 1857
City Road and Bunhill Row EC1
Jennings (?)
⊖ Moorgate

The HQ building (1735) is a large five-bay house of London stock brick, with a parapet decorated with cannonballs instead of the customary urns. Originally it was freestanding, and faced artillery grounds to the south (now a cricket field). In 1828 a wing was added to the house, and in 1857 the barrack buildings on City Road were built, in an appropriate castellated fortress style.

To the west, on Bunhill Row, is 21–9 Artillery Row, a four-storey early nineteenth-century terrace, and a further extension of the Artillery Company. The original house is now almost totally concealed, and the best view of it is from Finsbury Street across the playing fields to the south.

St Leonard 1736–40   H14l
Shoreditch High Street E1
George Dance the Elder
⊖ Liverpool Street, Old Street

Since at least the twelfth century a church has existed at the junction of the two main Roman roads north out of the City, now Kingsland Road and Old Street. The present St Leonard's, while as grand as one of Hawksmoor's, is not a Commissioners' church but was built to replace the one which collapsed in 1713. The outside is notable for its multi-staged and obelisk-finished steeple nearly 60 m (200 ft) tall and its fine Tuscan portico, both in Portland stone and arranged like Gibbs' St Martin-in-the-Fields K40. The interior is very plain and emptier than it should be: the galleries, which were supported by the Tuscan arcade between nave and aisles, have been removed. It is St

Leonard's 'Bells of Shoreditch' that are mentioned in the nursery rhyme *Oranges and Lemons*.

Whitbread's Brewery H15n
from 1749
Chiswell Street EC1
⊖Moorgate

This famous English brewery straddles
Chiswell Street. The eighteenth-century
buildings, on the south side, form an
internal courtyard which has recently
been restored by Wolf Olins, Roderick
Gradidge and Julian Harrop. To the north
of the archway is the original house, a fine
early eighteenth-century building in the
carved . brick 'artisan' style with a
canopied door and arched window above.
Of the early brewing buildings only the
Porter Tun Room of 1774 survives, 49 m
(160 ft) square, and with a magnificent
timber truss roof. The south yard has a
ramped and colonnaded entrance (previously an exit for barrels) and has also been
very well restored.

St Mary 1751–4 H16a
Upper Street N1
Launcelot Dowbiggin
⊖Angel

Set back behind a line of plane trees, St
Mary's is a curious architectural hotch-
potch. The rather fine steeple is all that
remains of the original church: the under-
scaled porch was added in 1903; and the
remainder, including the nave, was destroyed in the Second World War and
replaced by a stripped classical design.

Wesley's Chapel 1777 and H17k
House 1770
47 City Road EC2
⊖Old Street

The architecture of Methodism? No: the
chapel is a straightforward late Georgian
design for a public building, in brick,
altered in the 1890s when the present
porch was added. John Wesley, the
founder of Methodism, lived in the house
(now a museum) and is buried in the
churchyard.

Finsbury Square EC2 H18o
laid out 1777
George Dance the Younger
⊖Moorgate

As with his other schemes, all the original
houses of Dance's only large square have
been destroyed. Even the central space
has been humiliated by an ugly underground car park. See also Alfred Place G13
and America Square L59.

Clerkenwell Conference H19m
Centre
ex Middlesex Sessions House 1779–82
Clerkenwell Green EC1
Thomas Rogers
⊖Farringdon
An early example of a court house, carried
out in a very late Palladian style, com-
manding what remains of Clerkenwell's
village green.

Cross Street N1 c1780 H20a
⊖Angel
Sloping gently from Upper Street, the
pavement and carriageway at the east end
of Cross Street are separated in a manner
more characteristic of Bristol and Bath
than of London. The dilapidated houses on
the south side are mostly late eighteenth-
century, and the doorways of numbers 33
and 35 are imitations of the Adams'
Adelphi K58, as Sir John Summerson has
observed.

St Botolph 1788–9 H21m
Aldersgate Street EC1
Nathaniel Wright
⊖Barbican
A stuccoed and very rural-feeling parish
church with a pleasant interior containing
the original woodwork to gallery and
organ.

St James 1788–92 H22i
Clerkenwell Close,
Clerkenwell Green EC1
James Carr
⊖Farringdon
A typical London church in the tradition
of Wren, Hawksmoor and Gibbs, St James
stands on prominent ground at the north
end of Clerkenwell Close. Its square stone
tower, fine obelisk-like spire and entrance
gate close the view from the Green down
Clerkenwell Close. The stock brick
exterior to the remainder is consistent
but unexceptional. The interior has a
curved west end and a gallery with two
fine staircases, approached unexpectedly
from rooms either side of the tower.

Warehouses ex East India   H23o
Company 1798–1820
New Street, off Bishopsgate E C2
W Jupp, Henry Holland
⊖Liverpool Street
Only the façade of these grand warehouses remains after their internal rebuilding as offices. They have lost the
workmanlike character which remains
in the earlier Bengal Warehouses (1764)
on the south side of the street.

Almeida Theatre   H24a
ex Literary Institute 1837
Almeida Street N1
Roumieu and Gough
⇌Essex Road
Not much to look at now, this is a good
example of a secular public building of the
period in the inevitable Greek Revival
style with which both learning and religion were associated. After an undistinguished history it has been restored for
use as a small theatre.

Warehouse 1858   H25m
12 Little Britain EC1
T Young and Son
⊖St Paul's
Little Britain is at present threatened by
the westward extension of the dual
carriageway, London Wall. Most of the
commercial buildings have less charm
than number 12, with its arcades on
freestanding columns and Florentine
cornice.

Model Dwellings 1860–2   H26h
Columbia Road E2
H A Darbishire
⊖Shoreditch, Old Street
Baroness Burdett-Coutts was one of the
aristocratic agitators behind the Metropolitan Association for Improving the
Dwellings of the Industrial Classes, set up
in 1852 as a rival to the Society for
Improving the Condition of the Laboring
Classes, which had started building in
1845 and was responsible for the
Streatham Street flats G33 using Henry
Roberts as architect. The Baroness's
favourite architect was Darbishire, who
was later to provide the dreadful model
for the freestanding 'Peabody' blocks of
flats in Greenman Street H29. However,
these flats, a continuous four- and five-
storey block with open staircases and
access from short galleries, are along a
street, and originally formed part of an
ambitious plan which included

Darbishire's famous Columbia Market,
since demolished. Again with Darbishire,
the Baroness built houses for her staff at
Holly Village, Highgate R11 – the smarter
end of London.

Holborn Viaduct EC1   H27m
1863–9
William Heywood, engineer
⊖Farringdon, St Paul's

The Victorians' concern with making London's traffic circulation efficient concentrated on improving the connection between the Cities of London and Westminster. The main route – Fleet Street and the Strand – had become hopelessly congested, and two bypass schemes were instituted: to the south, the Embankment K103, to the north the improvement of the line of the old Roman road between Marble Arch and the Post Office, north of St Paul's. Holborn Viaduct and the cutting

of New Oxford Street were important links in the latter. The viaduct spans the valley of the Fleet river which runs, culverted, under Farringdon Street.

It is notable for its integration of engineering and architecture (see also Waterloo Bridge K154), evident in the decorative use of the cast iron beams which comprise the main span, and in the tastefully Italianate 'houses' at its abutments (only those on the south remain), which actually contain the staircases connecting Farringdon Street and High Holborn. Fine art is represented in the improving statues on the parapets.

Shops and **houses** 1863   H28o
91–101 Worship Street EC2
Philip Webb
⊖Old Street

Work by the architect who designed the Red House X8 for William Morris is unexpected in commercial Shoreditch, and Webb's short terrace actually resembles the high street of a quiet country town. The buttressed façade divides the terrace into six bays, and the ground floor shops have a continuous shallow pitched roof, behind which the remaining floors are set back. There are two arched windows to the first floor, the second floor has three extremely small square apertures, and the roof has high dormers. At one end of the terrace is a drinking fountain.

Housing for Peabody Trust   H29a
1865
Greenman Street N1
H A Darbishire
⇌Essex Road

The Peabody Trust built large numbers of 'improving' sanitary housing schemes to many designs, and it is surprising how many survive. This is one of the nastiest: four five-storey blocks (called 'Block A', 'Block B' etc) face each other round a tarmac square. The scant Italianate styling does nothing to lessen the prison-like effect of the deeply recessed windows. Contrast with the nearby refurbished Theberton Street G31.

Charterhouse Street façade

Grand Avenue, Smithfield Market

Smithfield Market 1866   H30m
Farringdon Street,
Charterhouse Street and Smithfield
Street EC1
Sir Horace Jones
⊖ Barbican

Smithfield is London's principal meat market, located on the site of a horse and cattle market dating back to 1200. Unlike Covent Garden (London's main fruit, flower and vegetable market, now moved ignominiously to the 'industrial zone' of Nine Elms) and Billingsgate fish market (now on the Isle of Dogs), Smithfield is active as a traditional city market, complete with arcaded avenues of raw meat. The market buildings are impressively straightforward and typically mid-Victorian in scale; the four massive trading halls are organized around Grand Avenue, East Poultry Avenue and West Poultry Avenue, all lit from above by linear glazed lanterns.

The exterior, of red brick with stone dressings, has domed corner turrets. The new market hall (1962–3) by T P Bennett has lost the arcaded quality of the original, despite its massive central dome.

Peabody Trust Dwellings   H31j
1870
Chequer Street, Dufferin Street,
Whitecross Street and
Roscoe Street EC1
⊖ Old Street

'Tough' and 'grim' are the adjectives generally applied to this six-storey tenement building – a standard philanthropic housing recipe. Although the buildings provide little in the way of light and air, they nevertheless form identifiable streets with proper addresses. The recent swing of the philanthropic housing pendulum means that the resident suffers from a surfeit of light and air at the expense of isolation from the city.

Liverpool Street Station EC2   H32o
1874–5, extended 1891–4
Hotel 1884, altered 1901
E Wilson, extension by W N Asbee;
hotel originally Charles Barry,
but altered by R Edis
⊖ Liverpool Street

One of the last major stations to be built in London (only Marylebone was to follow), Liverpool Street consolidated the pattern of rail termini which persists today. It served as the metropolitan terminus for what was to become the Great Eastern Railway, and more locally for trains which put the north-eastern suburbs – Enfield, Stamford Hill, Tottenham and Edmonton – within easy commuting distance of the City.

The buildings are not particularly fine – the Gothic is more restrained than that of St Pancras. In the 1980s, as a result of the massive Broadgate Develpment H43, the station was partly rebuilt and significantly

renovated. Like other redevelopments of the capital's railway stations – see Charing Cross K102, Cannon Street L78 – the original building has been diminished in character.

Bishopsgate Institute 1894   H33p
Bishopsgate EC2
C H Townsend
☉Liverpool Street

The beige faïence façade is a mixture of
Victorian and proto-art nouveau motifs.
The composition is symmetrical: a large
round arch for the entrance is recessed
between narrow towers. The art nouveau
decoration of this conventional scheme is
rare in London: there are flat trees on the
towers, and under the steep roof between
the towers is a fine panel of lettering. See
also Townsend's Whitechapel Art Gallery
L96 and Horniman Museum X9.

City University College   H34i
Building 1896
ex Northampton Institute
St John Street, Spencer Street and
Northampton Square EC1
Edward Mountford
☉Angel

This massive and ambitious building by
one of the principal architects of the
Edwardian baroque revival (see also
Mountford's Old Bailey L97 and Battersea
Town Hall) responds successfully to a
demanding site – the acute corner of
Spencer and St John Streets to the north of
Northampton Square. The resolution of
this corner is a *tour de force* – turret,
cupola and walls interlock with the big
curved gable of the hall behind. The front
to St John Street is asymmetrical and very
grand; the central entrance tower (reminiscent more of Townsend than of the
baroque) is topped with massive brick and
stone striped drums surmounted by a
shallow dome. Unlike more recent City
University buildings to the east, the
Institute has a direct formal relationship
with Northampton Square.

Boundary Street Estate   H35l
1897–1900
Arnold Circus E2
LCC Architects Department;
Owen Fleming
☉Shoreditch

The first and probably the best of many
large housing estates designed by the
LCC at the turn of the century is also the
least well known. The scheme, which
replaced the infamous 'Jago' slum immediately east of Shoreditch Parish
Church, is a series of streets radiating
from Arnold Circus. The buildings are
five-storey tenements and their architecture reflects the designers' taste for
the work of Street, Shaw and Philip
Webb: high gables, good quality brickwork and, around Arnold Circus, bands of
yellow brick to give the façades greater
elaboration. 5524 people were rehoused
at a density of 200 people per acre, with all
the support facilities of shops, surgery,
school and so on. This estate, despite its
conspicuous neglect, is a very fine
example of urban design. It supports the
claim that the output of the early LCC is
to be counted among the highest achievements of the Arts and Crafts movement in
English architecture.

Britannic House H36o

ex Lutyens House 1924–7, 1987–9
Moorgate and Finsbury Circus EC2
Sir Edwin Lutyens
Peter Inskip and Peter Jenkins Architects
⊖ Moorgate

Only the oval plan remains of George Dance the Younger's and William Montague's Finsbury Circus (1815), once part of an ambitious extension to the City including Finsbury Square H18 to the north. On the north-west side is Britannic House, Lutyens' first large London building. The classical repertoire is stretched to seven storeys, to form a magnificent curved frontage to the circus. Two rus-ticated storeys rise through a further two, to conclude in a three-storey Corinthian screen of attached columns – a pity he did not do the whole circus.

The recent renovation introduces an impressively large-scale semicircular atrium to increase the penetration of natural light to an otherwise deep and dark office. This intervention is a good example of the contemporary approach, based on discontinuity and surprise, to the appropriation of dormant space in City office buildings. The circular void brings to mind, albeit in modern dress, Vignola's rotunda at the Palazzo Farnese at Caprarola, one of the inspirations for the original building.

Stone House 1927 H37o

136 Bishopsgate EC2
Richardson and Gill
⊖ Liverpool Street

A large, handsome corner building: the ornate curved metalwork above the double-storey plinth refers to art nouveau, while the generous curved corner with large and simple openings anticipates later commercial street architecture.

Spa Green Estate 1950   H38e
Rosebery Avenue and
St John Street EC1
Lubetkin and Tecton
⊖ Angel

Three slabs run north-south; two straight
ones of eight storeys with, between them,
a sinuous one of four storeys. In this
housing for Finsbury Borough Council,
Lubetkin and Tecton were unable to
adopt Le Corbusier's ruthless social
programme – the self-contained housing
unit – and, in spite of their politics, their
housing done after 1945 shows no clear
idea of what a partly reconstructed city
should be like. The obsessive pattern-
making of the façades is as arbitrary as the
arrangement of the blocks – both are
examples of the practice's decline from
the clarity of Highpoint 1 R26 into busy
formalism.

Barbican Estate 1959–79   H39n
bounded by London Wall,
Beech Street and Moorgate EC2 and
Aldersgate Street EC1
Chamberlin Powell and Bon
⊖ Barbican, St Paul's, Moorgate

That the area of the City most devastated
by the Second World War should be
developed into a new quarter of 24 ha (60
acres) comprising 2113 flats for 6500
people is indicative of the good intentions
of post-war socialism. That the forms for
this memorial should be 125 m (412 ft)
high towers loosely mixed with slab
buildings (the tallest residential buildings
in Europe when planned and the only high
density housing models available in the
late 1950s) is the predictable and depressing outcome. Whatever the merits of the
restored St Giles church with its new
churchyard, the excavated Roman wall
and the initiatives of the new Arts and
Conference centre (completed in 1981),
they do not ameliorate the emptiness of
the Barbican and its meaningless severance
from the rest of the City.

London Wall 1963–91   H40n
between St Martin-le-Grand
and Moorgate EC2
City of London Planning Department;
various architects
⊖ Moorgate, Liverpool Street

London Wall was part of a huge redevelopment area in the City, much of which
had been bombed in the Second World
War. To the north is the residential part,
the Barbican H39, but the southern portion, called in planners' jargon the 'Barbican Commercial fringe', was originally
devoted to six office buildings, arranged
on either side of a road. This dual carriageway is part of a proposed bypass to the
City from Holborn and Kingsway – the
northern counterpart of the widened
Lower Thames to the south.
With hindsight, it is possible to regard
London Wall either as a plausible idea let
down in its realization by poor architecture, or as a proposal so bizarre and
problematical as to be incapable of success. The plan was for six office buildings
of similar format, 18 m × 43 m × 66 m
(58 ft × 142 ft × 220 ft), placed on two-
storey podia in a staggered arrangement,
not at right angles to the road but parallel
to Moorgate to the east. The roofs of the

podia, when connected with bridges
across roads, were supposed to provide a
new traffic-free ground level. It was intended that this format should be extended
to most new buildings in the City and
some, such as the Commercial Union
building L124, still bear the scars of the
scheme, now mostly abandoned.
The difficulties were first, that the English
climate made life on the podia unpleasant
for a large part of the year; second, that
only architects with the skill of Mies van

der Rohe have been able to relate a building to its podium successfully; third, that a main entrance to a building was impossible to design (witness the Museum of London's H41 unsatisfactory arrangements); fourth, that the street was destroyed, even for the motorist; and fifth, that there never was the slightest chance that a substantial portion of the City could have been rebuilt in this way. Barbican and London Wall remain islands approached by inadequate flights of stairs.

Only twenty-five years after the completion of London Wall, and in the wave of speculation which overtook London in the late 1980s, some of the office buildings have now been rebuilt, drastically altering what now appears to be the modest scale of the original scheme. The huge Lee House, by Terry Farrell and Co., contributes a muddled form and bridges the road, destroying the original pattern and offering nothing in return but sheer bulk.

Museum of London 1975   H41n
London Wall EC2
Powell and Moya
⊖ Barbican, St Paul's
The Museum of London is sited inaccessibly in the middle of a traffic intersection and is approached at an upper level by bridges. Its banal and utilitarian architecture represents an opportunity sadly lost. Don't be put off. The museum contains an extraordinary fund of material on London's history and social life from prehistoric times to the present, though this material deserves better housing. See also London Wall H41.

Offices and flats 1976–9   H42m
24 Britton Street EC1
YRM Partnership with
Fitzroy Robinson and Partners
⊖ Farringdon
On a steeply sloping backlands site next to a small churchyard, the three-storey office building sits on a two-storey podium, the roof of which forms a courtyard at the level of Britton Street. The frame of the building is covered with well-made aluminium panels. The six-storey block of flats and shops facing the street was built behind the reconstructed façade of a former gin distillery, designed by E W Mountford about 1900.

Broadgate,   H43o
Finsbury Pavement
Finsbury Pavement EC2: 1984–6, Arup Associates
Broadgate stage 1: 1984–88 between Sun Street, Finsbury Avenue, South Place/Eldon Street and west of Liverpool Street Station, Arup Associates
Broadgate stage 2: 1988–91 between Bishopsgate and Appold Street, Skidmore Owings and Merrill
⊖ Liverpool Street
Two contiguous and ambitious schemes on the northern edge of the City and extending its commercial value, by two of the few London developers who patronize good architecture: Greycoat and Rosehaugh Stanhope.
For the Finsbury Pavement buildings and the first stage of Broadgate, Arup Associates ignored the models of the city as a machine and instead revived the urban forms last used in the 1950s. 150,000 square metres (1,615,000 square feet) of office buildings of modest height are effortlessly connected with the existing city. They are informally arranged to compose two new linked squares, one empty, the other filled with an elaborate

Broadgate stage 2

terraced circular feature containing shops and with a skating rink at its centre. These outdoor spaces are finished with fine materials previously only seen in Europe and north America (compare for example the Barbican H39 and London Wall H40). The offices are entered through semi-public atriums whose glazed roofs are the pretext for virtuoso displays of engineering. The outsides of the buildings became

Broadgate stage I

progressively more mannered through the various phases: the earlier façades of Finsbury Pavement are in metal with refined sunbreakers, while those of Arup's Broadgate attempt a more decorative treatment with implausible 'curtains' of fretted granite.

To the north and east of Liverpool Street Station the second stage of Broadgate, by SOM, while following the same urban model introduces a new and overbearing scale, particularly in the very long fourteen-storey block to Bishopsgate whose vacuous architecture does little to disguise its bulk.

House 1987   H44m
44 Britton Street EC1
CZWG Architects (Campbell,
Zogolovitch, Wilkinson and Gough)
⊖ Farringdon
This is an improbable part of London for a highly individual house, planned on four floors with a studio in its pitched roof. The yashmak of diagonal screens, the lintels of concrete logs, and the grading of the exterior brickwork from dark to light are just some of the building's conspicuous elevational devices.

Offices 1987–90   H45n
1 Moor Lane, Chiswell Street EC1
Denys Lasdun, Peter Softley and
Associates
⊖ Moorgate

An impressive but enigmatic speculative
office building in a style completely unprecedented and unexpected in Lasdun and
Softley's work. The building is one of a
contemporary series developed along
Chiswell Street and fully occupies the
block on which it stands. It is clad entirely
in two layers of glass, the outer one green
and frameless with patch fixings, the inner
one framed and visible only at night. The
lower parts of the exterior are sheer, but
the glass on the upper storeys is thrown
into a wildly picturesque and faceted
silhouette with corner towers, the whole
suggesting the forms of defence. It is
surmounted by an enormous pitched roof.
The only tokens of the style of Lasdun's
earlier work are to be found in the two,
round brick-clad columns which mark the
entrances at the corners.

contin

Brunel E

North Kensington

a

b

Notting Hill

7

23

e

f

Ladbroke Square
Gardens

Avondale
Park

8

29

5

Offices

ROMAN ROAD

i

j

20

1

HOLLAND PARK
Holland
House

Cricket
Field

14

13

9

m

n

3

Olympia

conti

continued section T

Section I: Notting Hill/Ladbroke Grove/Bayswater/Holland Park/Kensington/Kensington Gardens

The first developments here were royal and aristocratic: Henry VIII enclosed Hyde Park, including what is now Kensington Gardens, for hunting grounds; in 1600 Holland House I 1 was started, as a country manor and estate (now Holland Park); and Kensington Palace I 2 was enlarged for William and Mary in the 1690s.

The westward development of the area was a nineteenth-century enterprise, and illustrates the changes in housing layouts in the period. In the 1820s Orme Square, north of Kensington Palace, was laid out as a simple and traditional rectangle open to the south. But the most important contribution to Victorian ideas of town-planning was the Ladbroke Estate I 7 started in 1840: in contrast to contemporary Pimlico, houses were laid out on sloping ground in a loose and picturesque way, using Italianate styling. Both the pattern and the style became very influential.

In the 1840s and '50s Bayswater was laid out north of Hyde Park. The model was Georgian, based on squares, but the houses were huge, Italianate and very un-Georgian – all are now hotels or subdivided into flats. At the same time, Kensington Palace Gardens was developed, with opulent and very large detached houses and lavish planting of trees. These private mansions (now occupied mainly by embassies and consulates) are perhaps London's nearest equivalent to Beverly Hills.

To the west, the streets north of Holland Park were laid out and lined with sumptuous Italianate terraces, still with their own mews, and later in the century the streets on either side of Addison Road became the site of more adventurous experiments (for example houses by Norman Shaw I 13 and Halsey Ricardo I 20).

In 1863, London's first underground railway was opened, from Bishop's Bridge Road near Paddington to Farringdon. Its successor, the Circle Line, runs partially in an open cutting along the western edge of the section.

The museums were established in the 1850s (see section J), and South Kensington's long streets of Italianate houses (Queen's Gate and Queen's Gate Terrace, for example) followed in the 1860s and '70s. The stuccoed homogeneity of these large houses (subdivided soon after they were built and probably always too big for their intended occupants) was broken only by the later red brick of Norman Shaw (see I 12).

By the end of the nineteenth century Kensington High Street was a fashionable shopping street and a rival to the West End. Its commercial heyday was in the 1920s and '30s, and it has good examples of department stores of the period, from the modernistic Barkers I 19 to the art deco Derry and Toms I 22.

Gateways to back gardens, Ladbroke Estate

Holland House 1606–7 11j
Holland Park W14

⊖High Street Kensington

The ruins of Holland House are the only remaining example in central London of an E-plan Jacobean manor. The front court was south-facing and graced with a loggia, and the house is set in its own large and pretty grounds – the first park west of Kensington Gardens. The west wing has been rebuilt as a youth hostel. For a complete Jacobean house see Charlton House U1.

Kensington Palace

Orangery

Kensington Palace W8 12k
1661–1702
Sir Christopher Wren,
Nicholas Hawksmoor, William Kent,
Thomas Ripley(?)

⊖High Street Kensington

In 1689 the bronchitic William III withdrew from Whitehall Palace to the purer air of Kensington. There he bought Nottingham House (built for the Earl of Nottingham in 1661) as his permanent residence. The King did not, however, bestow any royal magnificence on Kensington, unlike Hampton Court. Pevsner observes, 'never did any powerful monarch of the age ... build a less ostentatious palace ... If on the other hand the social and political implications of the building are considered, this sensible, domestic, one is tempted to say democratic, structure assumes a new meaning, even if not a higher architectural value.'

Kensington Palace is the result of a series of pragmatic additions, begun with William III and continued by George I, producing a disjointed overall composition grouped around three courtyards. Wren's south and east façades have some monumental ambition, but the remainder, built entirely of brick with rubbed brick detailing, resembles almshouses more than a royal palace. The interiors by Wren (c1690) and William Kent (1723–7) are correspondingly simple.

The grandest addition is the King's Gallery (1695–6). With the **Orangery** (1704–5), this is attributed by Downes to Hawksmoor. The fine brick exterior and austere white interiors of the Orangery link the design with those at Easton Neston, Northamptonshire, and Blenheim, Oxfordshire.

Edwardes Square W8 13n
1811–20

⊖High Street Kensington

A modest late Georgian square, Edwardes Square derives its name from William Edwardes, the second Lord Kensington, who leased land from the Holland House Estate. It has the quality of a large back garden formed by the back walls of Earls Terrace to the north, a medley of nondescript buildings to the south, and two consistent terraces to the east and west. The Tuscan garden house or Temple is particularly delightful.

Houses 1823–4   14h
3–5 Porchester Terrace W2
J C Loudon
⊖ Queensway, Lancaster Gate

This apparently detached villa (designed
by Loudon, the famous landscape architect) is an example of the well-established
English tradition of domestic architectural illusion. With the symmetry of the
central domed conservatory, side verandas and dummy windows masking the
party walls, Loudon ingeniously concealed
the pair of semi-detached houses within
(one of which he lived in). During repairs
in 1972 later Victorian additions to the
sides of the house were removed, revealing the clarity of the original design.

Norland Square 1837–46   15i
also Royal Crescent,
St James's Gardens, Addison Avenue
and Queensdale Road W11
Robert Cantwell
⊖ Holland Park

Royal Crescent's regular four-storey stuccoed façade with cylindrical turrets,
Norland Square's shallow bow fronts, St
James's Gardens' stone-faced connected
pavilions, and Addison Avenue's generous
dimensions and plane trees are all conveniently connected by Queensdale Road and
Princedale Road. This remarkable combination of urban types – crescent, gardens, avenue and square – could be a
useful model for the reconstruction of
London after the comprehensive disasters
of the 1960s.

Royal Crescent

Kensington Palace Gardens   16g
W8 1843
laid out by Sir James Pennethorne
⊖ High Street Kensington

Private roads with lodge gates at either
end were common in the eighteenth and
nineteenth centuries; this street of opulent villas in spacious gardens is a rare
survival. It was laid out on the site of the
kitchen gardens of Kensington Palace 12,
and between 1844 and 1870 the following
architects contributed: entrance lodges
and numbers 18–19, Wyatt and Brandon;
number 8a, Owen Jones; number 15,
Knowles; numbers 12 and 18, Banks and
Barry; number 12a, Decimus Burton,
Sidney Smirke and James Murray; number
13, C F Richardson. At the south end of

Kensington Palace Gardens

the road is **Palace Green**, where in 1868
Philip Webb built number 1 110 for the
Earl of Carlisle. Number 2 is the neo-

Georgian house Thackeray designed for
himself (1861).

Ladbroke Estate   17e
started c1850
bounded by Kensington Park Road,
Clarendon Road, Cornwall Crescent
and Holland Park Avenue W11
Thomas Allom
⊖ Notting Hill Gate, Holland Park,
Ladbroke Grove

The Italianate houses of the Ladbroke
Estate are large, but lack architectural
distinction. However, the Estate was one
of the most important contributions to
early Victorian suburban planning. Since
(like the later Bedford Park T18) it was
such an influential and much-copied
model, its virtues are easy to overlook. Its
early success was due both to its site – on a
healthy breezy hill as opposed to the

29½ Lansdowne Crescent

contemporary development on Belgravia's drained swamp – and to its informal, fairly low density layout. The north-south axis of the Estate is **Ladbroke Grove**, a wide street which rises over the hill and passes beside the very large **Ladbroke Square** on the site of Ladbroke's racecourse, the Hippodrome. The Ladbroke coat of arms can still be seen on the iron gates leading into the square from **Kensington Park Gardens**. Individual houses on the south side are large and stuccoed.

To the north of the square are **Lansdowne Crescent, Elgin Crescent** and **Clarendon Road**. The houses range from semi-detached villas to groups of four, and follow the curves of the crescents to make very pleasant streets. The remarkable communal gardens contained by the houses are one of the most congenial arrangements in London: in a sense the traditional London square has been inverted, as access to the gardens (exclusive to the residents) is through each dwelling's private back garden.

Lansdowne House c1860   18e
Lansdowne Road W11
H Flockhart
⊖Holland Park
A multi-storey group of studios, rare in London, but more familiar in Paris and Brussels. The tall composition of stock brick, with stone detailing, turreted corners, north-facing studio windows and the seventh floor set back to form a pediment, is an unexpected urban addition to the leafy Arcadia of Lansdowne Road. Charles Ricketts, Charles Shannon and Glyn Philpot were among artist-residents here.

Leighton House 1865–79   19n
12 Holland Park Road W14
George Aitchison
⊖High Street Kensington
Leighton House was the home and studio of Lord Leighton (1830–96), one of the most successful and fashionable painters of his generation. The classical exterior was very unusual for the time (Webb's Gothic studio for Val Prinsep was next door) and was like an Italianate villa, reflecting the style of Leighton's own paintings. The richly coloured interiors – red walls and black woodwork – imitated a Venetian *palazzo*. In 1877 Aitchison added the Arab Hall, based on the hall of the twelfth-century Moslem Palace of La Zisa at Palermo, to display Leighton's collection of Saracenic tiles. William de Morgan designed new tilework, Boehm carved the capitals, and the mosaic frieze is by Walter Crane. The house established Aitchison as a master of decoration. Note also the window with a sliding, mirrored shutter, positioned above a fireplace (the flue ingeniously concealed by an S-bend) and looking out to the garden on the ground floor. The back door for the models, the generous promenades for the clients and the luxurious studios are a reminder of the successful artist's social position in the mid-Victorian era.

Kensington Park Gardens

29½ Lansdowne Crescent, by Jeremy Lever (1973), ingeniously fills a left-over wedge with a 3 m (10 ft) frontage to the street in an existing crescent. Its stuccoed front, bay window and simple openings unite it with its neighbours without recourse to period pastiche.

The Arab Hall: section

House 1868–70   110k
1 Palace Green,
Kensington Palace Gardens W8
Philip Webb
⊖ High Street Kensington

Built for the Hon. George Howard (later ninth Earl of Carlisle), this is Webb's most important town house. The original design was turned down by the Commissioners (headed by the architect James Pennethorne) because of the absence of stone as a relief to the brick façade, and Webb finally conceded some stonework in the elevation. The tall red-brick building has an exceptionally deep plan and an asymmetrical front with a pointed pediment to the porch, a three-storey bay window to the right and open battlements above. In the side elevation is a tall arched niche with a staircase leading to the garden; either side of the niche are modulated chimney breasts. The combination of tall Queen Anne style windows and pointed arches considerably pre-dates Norman Shaw's use of them, but it has been said that Webb subscribed more to the rational principles of Pugin than to the artistic and empirical methods of Shaw. Gavin Stamp observes that 'many of Webb's buildings have a certain awkwardness which was proof of his Gothic revival and puritanical conscience'.

St Mary Abbots 1869–72   111k
Kensington High Street and
Kensington Church Street W8
Sir George Gilbert Scott
⊖ High Street Kensington

In this church Scott was designing in Gothic while his classicist Foreign Office K105 was being built. It is a dull design in Early English style, with a very tall spire 85 m (278 ft) high.

House 1875   112p
196 Queen's Gate SW7
R Norman Shaw
⊖ High Street Kensington

A characteristically asymmetrical composition of superimposed Dutch pilasters, early Renaissance decoration and Shaw's by then typical window motif. The result is a complex arrangement of projecting balconies and local symmetries, built in red brick with terracotta decorative panels. With 180 Queen's Gate (demolished in the early 1960s) this house set the style – known as Pont Street Dutch – for speculative developments in Kensington up to the end of the century.

Studio house 1875–6   113n
8 Melbury Road W14
R Norman Shaw
⊖High Street Kensington
Built for the painter Marcus Stone, this is the Queen Anne style at its most fluent and memorable – contemporary with Shaw's own house at 6 Ellerdale Road A1 and the Swan House N21. The composition of the ground floor is asymmetrical, with narrow vertical windows, above which three symmetrical oriel windows are cut through the cornice. At the same time, across the road at **number 31**, Shaw designed another studio house for the painter Luke Fildes. It is less notable and has been considerably altered.

Tower House 1876–81   114n
29 Melbury Road W14
William Burges
⊖High Street Kensington
Built by Burges (a convinced Gothicist) for himself, the Tower House contrasts with the new Queen Anne style of its contemporary neighbours (numbers 8 and 31) by R Norman Shaw. The exterior, of massive and picturesque brickwork, with the corner dominated by a circular staircase tower topped by a conical roof, shows all Burges's preoccupations with medieval castles and the theoretical work of Viollet le Duc. But the magic of the house is in the interiors, as described by Gavin Stamp: 'All the rooms tell a story. The dining room was meant to convey an idea of Chaucer's House of Fame; the library, with its birds painted by H. Stacy Marks, has an elaborate castellated stone chimneypiece illustrating the dispersal of the parts of speech ... A staircase window

illustrates the storming of the castle of love. Burges finished his own bedroom so that he could imagine himself – when in an opiate haze – at the bottom of the sea.'

Stratford Studios c1880   115o
off Stratford Road W8
⊖High Street Kensington
A gated, miniature close of ten high, Dutch-gabled studios: a reminder of the area's artistic tradition, given impetus by the Great Exhibition of 1851. The buildings have now been gentrified and converted into family houses, although their original use is unmistakable.

Studios 1882   116j
77–9 Bedford Gardens W8
R Stark Wilkinson
⊖Notting Hill Gate
In the 'suburban' context of the early nineteenth-century villas and cottages of Bedford Gardens, this five-storey group of eleven artists' studios is exceptional for its 'urban' scale: as the foundation stone records, the building is 39 m (128 ft) deep (north-south) and 11 m (34 ft) wide. The working studios are approached by a public central staircase around a generous well, daylit by a large glass lantern above. The street façade is formed by north-facing studio windows, set back in section between robust red-brick piers.

House 1887–9 117p
170 Queen's Gate SW7
R Norman Shaw
⊖South Kensington
The elongated windows to either side of
the central bay are the only clues to the
authorship of this large and restrained
classical house: 170 Queen's Gate is the
bridge between the free composition
characteristic of Shaw's earlier designs
and the baroque revival of his later works.

Linley Sambourne House 118n
late 19th century
18 Stafford Terrace W8
⊖High Street Kensington
The house of illustrator Linley Sambourne
(1844–1910), with interiors preserved
much as he left them. They give a rare
opportunity to see how the interior of an
otherwise characteristic Kensington
house was furnished by an 'artistic'
owner.
The house was bought by the GLC in
1980, and is now managed by the Victorian
Society and open to the public.

Barkers Department Store 119k
1904–38
Kensington High Street W8
Bernard George 1937–8
⊖High Street Kensington
George's façade and remodelling of
Barkers store (previously designed by
John Barker, 1904, and Sir Reginald
Blomfield, 1912–13) completed its long
building history. Barkers and Derry and
Toms 122 next door gave London a
fragmentary art deco commercial
frontage, a reminder that England during
this period was less innovative than at the
turn of the century and was reverting to
her previous role as a sympathetic re-
ceiver of European ideas – in this case the
jazz modern of Paris in the later 1920s.

Debenham House 1905–7 120i
8 Addison Road W14
Halsey Ricardo
⊖High Street Kensington
This masterpiece of coloured ceramic
architecture was originally designed for
Sir Ernest Debenham, whose department
store in Wigmore Street was faced in
white tiles. The exterior of the house is
remarkable in that all the surfaces are in
Burmantofts Staffordshire bricks and
Doulton's tiles – even the capitals, cornices and medallions are moulded and
glazed. The white tiles delineate the two-
storey superimposed arcade, attic and
chimneys; the panels of blue and green
glazed bricks echo the colours of the sky
and the trees in the garden, giving the
house an ethereal, transparent quality.
Ricardo was a member of the Art
Workers' Guild, and many of the interior
furnishings were executed by his friends –
the peacock blue tiles by William de
Morgan's firm, plaster ceilings by Gimson,

timber staircase by William Aumonier
and lead rainwater heads by the
Birmingham Guild. The house is now
occupied by the Richmond Fellowship,
and has been used as an 'exotic' set for
numerous feature films.

Whiteleys Department Store 1908–12, 1989
121c

Queensway W2
Belcher and Joass, Building Design Partnership

⊖ Queensway, Bayswater

The old conflict between the shopkeeper's desire for large areas of glass and the architect's wish to produce large buildings with strong bases was partly resolved at Whiteleys by the use of metal (rather than stone) facings to the intermediate floors. Daniel Burnham's contemporary contribution to Selfridges J60 is more vigorous and single-minded by comparison. Had Hitler's invasion of England succeeded, Whiteleys might have achieved a kind of celebrity, for it is said that the Führer was particularly fond of it and wished to make it his HQ. Despite closure in 1981, the store has been recently and ambitiously renovated, transforming the staid Edwardian interior into a north American shopping mall 'experience', complete with ramped auto drop-off at the rear.

Department Store
122o

ex Derry and Toms 1933
Marks and Spencer and British Home Stores, Kensington High Street W8
Bernard George

⊖ High Street Kensington

A large dull rectangle by the designer of the much more exuberant Barkers 119 to the east, the store was famous for its roof garden. This has recently been restored, but it is now part of the night club which occupies the top floor and so is not open to the public. A lift car and its doors from the store are now in the Museum of London as an example of the splendid *moderne* internal fittings.

Flats c1933
123e

65 Ladbroke Grove W11
E Maxwell Fry

⊖ Ladbroke Grove

The five-storey façade, comprising access galleries and an asymmetrically positioned lift and stair shaft, is now mostly hidden by dense and mature trees. The combination of materials – yellow stock brick, steel tube and mesh balustrading, and blue-tiled dados – is very well handled. The ramped approach to the semi-basement for cars, a motorized 'area' in very tight dimensions, is also ingeniously planned. The flats follow the same programme as Lawn Road B27 but with more architectural ability: the well-serviced anonymity of Le Corbusier's *machine à habiter*. See also Kensal House T30.

Flats 1938
124p

10 Palace Gate W8
Wells Coates

⊖ Gloucester Road

These flats, together with those at Lawn Road B27, are Coates' most important extant London works. He used an ambitiously complex section on a difficult narrow site. Three floors of service rooms, bedrooms and access galleries are set against two floors of living rooms. Coates handles the exterior with more style than his contemporaries, using direct quotations from Le Corbusier's Pavillon Suisse in Paris. The small facing panels of reconstituted stone were used as permanent shuttering to the reinforced concrete frame.

House 1938

32 Newton Road W2
Sir Denys Lasdun
⊖ Bayswater
Set among mid-Victorian semis, Lasdun's
incredibly early work on his own account
(he was twenty-four) is more influenced
by Le Corbusier than by the work of his
first employer, Wells Coates. However,
its interior does not have the dynamic
spatial complexity of its apparent model,
the Maison Cook in Paris.

Hallfield Housing Estate

1951–9
Bishop's Bridge Road W2
Tecton: Drake and Lasdun
⊖ Westbourne Park, Queensway
One of the early large and comprehensive
post-war redevelopments which should
have been an early warning to the well-
intentioned bureaucratic appetite for
such excesses. Although bearing superficial resemblances to Highpoint 2 R26,
and carrying watered-down quotations
from Le Corbusier's *Ville Radieuse*, the
fifteen large slabs and attendant social
buildings are a permanent scar on a fine
nineteenth-century district of London.
They show the last use of Tecton and
Lasdun's elevational composition – at last
it was seen to be merely arbitrary pattern-
making as a device to relieve the mass of
the buildings. The Hallfield primary
school (1951–4) with a ramped entrance

from Inverness Terrace is also by Lasdun.
The two-storey building is linear and
curved in plan, with vertical *brises soleil* to
protect its south-facing classrooms.

Maisonettes 1964

13–16 Craven Hill Gardens W2
Douglas Stephen and Partners,
Associate Architect Kenneth Frampton
⊖ Queensway
The transition of the Stephen practice
from cragginess to a smoother manner
was marked by the Kensington housing
1 28, and this much larger block. The
arrangement is derived from the LCC's
'scissors' section, in which the dwellings
cross over and under central access
corridors in half-level jumps. This allows
all the living rooms of the forty-eight
dwellings to face the street, and all the
bedrooms, each with a balcony, to face the
garden at the back. The corridors are
reached via a stair and lift at the north end
of the block, but the disadvantage of this
format is that the entrance lobby is only as
large as the landings above. The façades
are sober and smart, even if their subdivision suggests a hostel or an office building,
and the concrete, originally exposed, has
now been painted.
Across the road note the dummy façade of
20 Leinster Gardens, concealing the gap in
the terrace caused by the Circle Line
Underground.

Flats, The Mount 1965   128j
Bedford Gardens and
Campden Hill Road W8
Douglas Stephen and Partners
⊖ Notting Hill Gate

These four-storey flats are one of the first
in a line of eclectic reworkings of European modernism (especially the work of
Giuseppe Terragni and the Italian Rationalists) from the office of Douglas
Stephen. After the Second World War
such work had been beyond the pale,
stigmatized by Fascism. The flats represent an early reaction to the whimsy and
provincialism of the Festival of Britain era.

Peter Eaton Bookshop 1973   129i
80 Holland Park Avenue W11
Rick Mather
⊖ Holland Park

A deep single-storey building on the site
of a front garden is the basis of this
beautiful antiquarian bookshop, the first
bespoke modern one in London. The
section of the shop is developed skilfully:
excavation has produced seven levels,
with the bookcases forming walls and
balustrades. The 'purist' language of white
plaster, chromium handrails and plate
glass acts as a foil to the leather-bound and
gilded spines of the books. The glazed
shop front extends 1 m (3 ft) into the
pavement of Holland Park Avenue.

Phillips West 2 1976   130c
10 Salem Road W2
Campbell, Zogolovitch, Wilkinson and
Gough
⊖ Queensway, Bayswater

A conversion of a two-storey warehouse
into a flamboyantly styled art nouveau
building of mixed uses. The combination
of pink painted brickwork, grey window
frames and sensuously curved dark blue
metalwork to the balconies and principal
entrances was a sign of the emergence in
the mid-1970s of architectural dandyism.
The auction rooms are on the ground
floor behind a series of bay windows, with
offices on the first floor. Seven duplex
apartments form a remarkable enclosed
court on the second floor, reached by a lift
with a pantiled 'hat'. The court is surrounded by an arcade, also with a pantiled
roof, and at the centre is a miniature
tropical jungle.

Kensington Place restaurant   131g
1987
205 Kensington Church St W8
Tess and Julyan Wickham
⊖ Notting Hill Gate

A splendid single space lit by 'industrial'
windows the length of the façade to the
street and entered through a superbly
minimalist revolving door. Inside, the most
elaborate feature is the ceiling, which is
nearly outclassed by the colourful mural
occupying the whole of the north wall. A
rare conjunction of good architecture and
good food.

Section J: Marylebone (south)/Paddington/Mayfair/Knightsbridge/Belgravia/Imperial College/Hyde Park/Green Park

At the beginning of the seventeenth century the West End of London was open countryside, with two small rivers (the Westbourne and Tyburn), two Roman roads (now Edgware Road and Oxford Street), the medieval villages of Paddington and St Mary-le-Bourne, various manors standing in their own estates, and the royal hunting ground of Hyde Park.

The rivers now run in underground culverts and are no longer visible. The Westbourne (later dammed to form the Serpentine in Hyde Park) was bridged at Knight's Bridge, on the approaches to St James's Palace. The Tyburn Brook, to the east, gave its name to Tyburn Hill (now Marble Arch), in the north-east corner of Hyde Park, which until the end of the eighteenth century was London's place of public execution.

By the mid-seventeenth century the City of Westminster was contained to the north by Lincoln's Inn and to the south and east by the Thames and its marshy ground. Although the initiative of the King was significant in expansion to the west, most of the building was the result of the aristocracy's development of the Great Estates. Green Park J1 and St James's Park K9 were first enclosed by Henry VIII as hunting grounds for St James's Palace, and by the mid-eighteenth century they had become fashionable places for promenades and building: the large and noble houses along the north and east edges date from this time, notably Spencer House K51 and Buckingham House K76.

Hyde Park J2 was abbey land until it too was enclosed by Henry VIII as a deer park. In the eighteenth century its overall area was reduced by the formation of Kensington Gardens (see section I), and in 1730 the Serpentine was created. Rotten Row, the other large-scale device from this period, derives its name from *Route du Roi*, the king's route from St James's Palace to Kensington Palace.

Mayfair's early eighteenth-century development was given impetus by Lord Burlington, who built up the streets behind his house on Piccadilly. The square with its supporting network of streets was the format for development: Hanover Square, Grosvenor Square J6 and Berkeley Square J8. In 1720 New Bond Street was started as an extension of Old Bond Street.

Running like a fault line through Mayfair is the course of the Tyburn Brook (now South Molton Street and Avery Row). The marshy ground on its banks was never developed by the Great Estates, and thus was available for less salubrious building and for service trades to the estates. By the middle of the eighteenth century the urbanization of Mayfair was complete.

In 1708 the Duke of Newcastle bought the Marylebone Estate to the north of Oxford Street (then Tyburn Road, the processional route to the place of public execution). In 1717, in relatively open countryside, he laid out Cavendish Square J3 and the surrounding streets. His daughter Lady Margaret Cavendish married the second Duke of Portland, and the estate remained in the hands of the Portlands until 1879, when it passed to Lord Howard de Walden, to whose family it still belongs.

There is evidence of seventeenth- and eighteenth-century building to the north and south of Hyde Park, but it was not until the nineteenth century that the areas known as Belgravia to the south and Tyburnia to the north were developed, as a further stage in the western extension of London under the agency of the Great Estates. The builder Thomas Cubitt was to Belgravia what his contemporary Nash was to Regent's Park. In 1810 Belgravia – then the Grosvenor Estate – was mostly open fields. With its free composition of large-scale stuccoed crescents (Wilton J26), squares (Belgrave J23) and avenues (Eaton Square J25), Belgravia was completed by 1825, and remains one of London's most architecturally impressive districts (see also section N).

Until 1820 Paddington was still a village. In 1825 part of the Bishop of London's estate, the triangular area described by Praed Street to the north, Edgware Road to the east, and Bayswater Road to the south (later known as Tyburnia), was developed to the plans of S P Cockerell, surveyor to the

Bishop. Although much rebuilt since 1945, Tyburnia, with Bloomsbury and Belgravia, is one of London's finest early nineteenth-century planned districts, combining English squares and crescents with monumental European avenues (see Sussex Gardens and Westbourne Terrace J30).

By the mid-nineteenth century the Industrial Revolution – particularly the advent of the railways – had caused the further expansion of London. Paddington Station J39, the terminus of the Great Western Railway, was begun in 1850, and the rapid growth of Paddington and the areas to the west (see section I) in the 1840s and '50s can be directly attributed to the railway. A population of 6,500 in 1831 had by 1881 increased to 100,000.

Following the Great Exhibition of 1851, plans were drawn up for the area now known as the Imperial College campus, south of Hyde Park. This agglomeration of cultural and educational institutions is compressed into the area from the Albert Memorial J44 in the north to the Victoria and Albert Museum J40 in the south, and from Exhibition Road in the east to Queen's Gate in the west. The museum and technical institution were inventions of the nineteenth century, and this dense area represents the Victorian passion for cataloguing and analysing the world.

The Royal Mews

Green Park SW1   J1
16th century
⊖ Green Park
With St James's Park K9, Green Park was part of Henry VIII's hunting grounds. It was never subsequently developed and remains a large patch of grass with many plane trees, some of them arranged in an avenue from the Queen Victoria Memorial in front of Buckingham Palace to a pair of fine eighteenth-century gates onto Piccadilly. The two sides of the park provide 'good addresses', commercial on the north and residential on the east (see Spencer House K51 and Lasdun's flats K164).

Hyde Park W2, SW1, SW7   J2
16th century onwards
⊖ Hyde Park Corner, Marble Arch, Knightsbridge and Lancaster Gate
Originally another of Henry VIII's hunting grounds, enclosed by him and stocked with deer, Hyde Park with Kensington Gardens is London's largest park, about 250 ha (600 acres) in area. It has been open to the public since the mid-seventeenth century, but 'improvements' were not carried out until 1730, when the Serpentine was formed by damming the Westbourne River. Throughout the eighteenth century the park remained the 'natural' western edge of London, which began properly at Hyde Park Corner. Only in the early nineteenth century, after the building of Belgravia and Pimlico, did development spread beyond it to Kensington, Bayswater and Notting Hill. The park became ringed with the five- and six-storey terraces which, until the hotel and barrack-building boom of the 1950s and '60s, successfully maintained the fiction of 'the country in the town', for their roofs were lower than mature plane trees. The wonderful distant view of the Houses of Parliament from Rennie's elegant masonry bridge (1826) across the Serpentine was tragically destroyed by the erection of government offices in Petty France (designed by Sir Basil Spence) in the 1970s. To the north of the bridge is the Magazine, a little stock brick pavilion with a Doric colonnade, remodelled by the young Decimus Burton in 1825. He also designed (at the age of twenty-one) Grosvenor Gate, Stanhope

Gate and Cumberland Lodge, and culminated his work with the grand entrance to the park, the Screen J24 and Arch J27, at Hyde Park Corner.

The park was the site of Paxton's Crystal Palace for the 1851 Great Exhibition, which stood south of the Serpentine opposite Kensington Road. Its royal sponsor is commemorated in the Albert Memorial J44 in Kensington Gardens on the other side of the Ring. Hyde Park has had a richer social history than the other London parks, and has seen the passing of many fashions. In the early nineteenth century it was a favoured place for rioting, but its activities now are generally more sedate: oratory at Speakers' Corner in the north-east near Marble Arch, horse-riding along the sanded Rotten Row and American baseball.

Cavendish Square W1 1717   J3d
John Prince
⊖ Oxford Circus
The first square to be built on the Marylebone Estate north of Oxford Street, Cavendish Square established both the pattern of surrounding streets and monuments and a planned relationship with Hanover Square, the other side of Oxford Street. Apart from two magnificent stone-faced houses of about 1770 in the middle of the north side, the square has little architecture of interest. The unexceptional John Lewis department store (1939) on the south side is by Slater, Moberly and Uren. Most of the trees in the middle of the square were uprooted in the 1960s to make way for an underground car park.
In nearby Vere Street is the charming

St Peter

church of **St Peter** (1721–4) by James Gibbs. Built as a chapel for Cavendish Square, it sits confidently on its island site. The small double-cupola tower is well proportioned with the simple rectangle of the body of the church, built in the brick tradition started by Wren. The plan, with a broad nave, is also indebted to Wren. Sir John Summerson has observed, however, that its interior – the curved ceiling, giant columns, and decorative plasterwork – look forward to Gibbs' more important work at St Martin-in-the-Fields K40.

Curzon Street WI c1720   J4h
☉Hyde Park Corner, Green Park
Enough Georgian terraced houses remain here – numbers 21–3, 28–30, 47 and 48 – to recall Curzon Street's elegant eighteenth-century origins. Number 30 (1771–2) was designed by Robert Adam, and has a magnificent first floor and entrance hall. The most distinguished building is **Crewe House** (c1730) further to the east: built by Edward Shepherd, it is a rare example of the large detached mansion set back from the street behind a generous garden. Its white stuccoed classical façade, with seven bays and a central pediment, was added in 1813; when floodlit at night it is unexpected and surreal. Opposite is the **Curzon Cinema** (1963) by Sir John Burnet, Tait and Partners. For those who remember the restrained and stylish Dutch modern façade and mysterious dark blue velvet interior (with double seats) of the original cinema (1933), the new one by the same architects is unfortunate.

Shepherd Market

In 1735 Shepherd laid out **Shepherd Market** just to the south, a development of small shops to serve the grand residences of Piccadilly which retains its eighteenth-century scale.

St George, Hanover Square WI   J5d
1721–4
John James
☉Oxford Circus
At St George's, a Commissioners' church, James first introduced the portico to the west front of a London church. It was soon to be followed by St George, Bloomsbury G8 and St Martin K40, but only here does the portico span the level pavement. James's solution to the difficult problem of adding a tower to a Roman temple is not as stylish as Gibbs'. The side elevation to Maddox Street, while sooty, is more robust than those of James's later churches, which by comparison seem thin and poverty-stricken. The interior arrangement loosely follows Wren's St James, Piccadilly K21, but was restored by

Sir Arthur Blomfield in 1894. See also St Luke, Old Street H11.

Grosvenor Estate WI 1720–5   J6g
Grosvenor Square, Upper Brook Street, Brook Street, Upper Grosvenor Street, Grosvenor Street, North Audley Street, South Audley Street, Carlos Place, Carlos Street and Duke Street
☉Marble Arch
At the beginning of the eighteenth century the Grosvenor Estate was agricultural land bounded by Oxford Street, Park Lane and, to the east, the Tyburn Brook. Grosvenor Square, laid out in 1720, followed the initiative of Hanover Square and was twice its size. The streets listed above were part of this ambitious development and all date from about 1725. With Brook Street and Carlos Place making connections to Hanover Square and Berkeley Square respectively, the principal urban network of Mayfair was established. These houses are original, although many have been refaced:

Grosvenor Square

Upper Brook Street, numbers 35–6; Brook Street, numbers 25 (residence of Handel), 41, 43, 66–76 (residence of Colen Campbell, editor of *Vitruvius Britannicus* and architect of the original south side of Grosvenor Square), and 86; Upper Grosvenor Street, number 48; Grosvenor Street, numbers 16 and 34; North Audley Street, numbers 11 and 12, refaced about 1820, but with one of the finest Georgian interiors in London.

33 Upper Brook Street, Sir Robert Taylor's first London town house (c1765 – the second was Ely House K60), is a grand affair in brick, occupying two standard house frontages. The placing of the front door in the middle of the three bays is unusual. The ground-floor arches are particularly elaborate: instead of Palladian rustication, Taylor used a complicated layering of recessed arches, the main ones supported on Tuscan columns. The whole façade appears to be twice as big as its earlier neighbours to the east.

Grosvenor Chapel 1739   J7h
South Audley Street W1
Benjamin Timbrell
⊖ Marble Arch

Built to serve the newly developed Grosvenor Square to the north, this little chapel, set in its small park, is the work of builders and craftsmen rather than architects. Seen down Aldford Street from Park Lane, it appears transported from New England. The Ionic screen in the otherwise original interior is by Sir Ninian Comper. Behind the chapel are St George's Gardens J57.

Berkeley Square W1   J8h
started 1739
⊖ Green Park

Berkeley Square was never conceived as an architectural entity: the east side (known as Berkeley Row) was built first and the west side followed in 1745. Today the houses on the west side and the magnificent plane trees, over 200 years old, are the square's main points of interest. Of the houses, number 44 J10 by William Kent is the *pièce de résistance*. Numbers 45 and 46 are original, dating from 1744, and have especially good rusticated stonework and wrought iron railings. Number 47 is a good example of imitation Italian Renaissance (1891); numbers 49–51 have particularly fine lampholders; and number 52 has two bays to Charles Street and a pedimented Ionic doorway to the square.

Chesterfield Street W1   J9h
c1740
⊖ Green Park

Remarkable for its complete and regular Georgian terraces (though number 10 is slightly later and has different details), Chesterfield Street terminates in **Charles Street**, also remarkably intact and richly decorated, and of the same period.

44 Berkeley Square W1   J10h
1744–5
William Kent
⊖ Green Park
Built for Lord Burlington's cousin, Lady Isabella Finch, this has been called the finest terrace house in London. The exterior is modest, the only clues to the palatial arrangements inside being the pediments to the first-floor windows and a large rusticated surround to the front door. The principal staircase and drawing room are the grandest and most technically ingenious of any eighteenth-century private house in London. See also Berkeley Square J8.

Portman Square W1   J11c
laid out 1761
⊖ Marble Arch
A regular square 170 m × 143 m (560 ft × 470 ft) in which no ordinary houses remain. On the north side, numbers 20 and 21 are two grand Adam houses J14. The huge and unremarkable Portman Hotel on the west side recently extinguished the other remaining eighteenth-century houses.

Stratford Place c1770   J12d
off Oxford Street W1
⊖ Bond Street
An almost complete eighteenth-century close, offering a welcome relief from the bustle of Oxford Street. The north end is concluded by **Derby House** (1773), a stone-faced classical mansion by R Edwin in the style of Adam: the view of its dignified Ionic pilasters and central pediment is a reminder that Oxford Street was once a relatively calm spot on the northern edge of London.

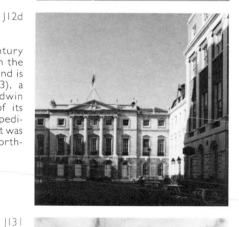

Apsley House (Wellington   J13l
Museum) 1771–8, 1828–9
Hyde Park Corner SW1
Robert Adam, Benjamin and Philip Wyatt
⊖ Hyde Park Corner
By the end of the 1820s, Apsley House (postal address Number 1, London) formed part of an extraordinary group of neo-classical monuments on the edge of Hyde Park: St George's Hospital J28 (1827–8), the Screen J24 (1825) and the Arch J27 (1825). Built by Adam for Baron Apsley, it was originally a much smaller brick building; in 1828 Benjamin and Philip Wyatt transformed and enlarged it for the Duke of Wellington, facing it in stone, and adding the Corinthian portico and the west side extension. Much of Adam remains in the interior, however, notably the semicircular staircase, the drawing room with its eastern apse and the portico room. The Wyatts' principal contribution to the interior is the Waterloo Gallery, which houses many

trophies from a grateful nation – the most impressive is Canova's 3.4 m (11 ft) statue of Napoleon as a near-naked hero holding out a golden victory emblem. Apsley House is now marooned in the midst of the Hyde Park Corner traffic intersection, and the former neo-classical ensemble has been all but destroyed. In the 1960s the adjoining buildings on the east side were demolished for road widening, and the exposed flank was refaced with a copy of the Wyatts' west extension. The house is now open to the public as the Wellington Museum.

Houses 1775–7   J14c
20 and 21 Portman Square W1
Home House, number 20, Robert Adam; number 21, James Adam
⊖ Marble Arch

Home House (now housing the Courtauld Institute) and Chandos House F1 are the only remaining great houses in London designed by Robert Adam. Here he was able to develop both the planning of a continuous sequence of rooms, differentiated by function, shape and style, and his delicate, flat, linear decoration which he started at Syon. Summerson proposes that the Music Room represents the summit of this development. Number 21, its entrance in Gloucester Place, accommodates the RIBA's magnificent Drawings Collection (containing among others most of Burlington's Palladio collection), and the Heinz Gallery, scene of continuous exhibitions of architectural drawings. The first-floor rooms, while not as suave as those of number 20, are well worth visiting. The top floors of both houses are later additions.

Manchester Square W1   J15c
laid out 1776
⊖ Marble Arch

The form of this square, with three streets entering at the mid-points of the sides (rather than at the corners, as at the contemporary Bedford Square G12), is a throwback to the seventeenth-century forms (For example St James's Square K18). The south and east sides are complete, with grand houses but no attempt at composition. The square was developed by the Duke of Manchester, who built himself a commanding free-standing house on the north side. In 1882 the house was altered to its present form by Sir Richard Wallace, whose collection of paintings, objects and armour it now contains.

Great Cumberland Place W1   J16c
1789
⊖ Marble Arch

A circus was originally planned in the middle of Great Cumberland Place, but while the crescent on the east side was built in 1789, the opposite side followed the straight line of the road. As part of the planned composition of the Portman Estate the road was extended northwards (1810–15), creating the oblong Bryanston Square J18 and terminating at Smirke's St Mary's in Wyndham Place F19. The lamp-holders and railings are among the best in London.

Gloucester Place W1 and NW1   J17c
late 18th and early 19th
centuries
⊖ Baker Street

It was this sort of street, 1.4 km (1 mile) long, that confirmed the Victorians in their belief that Georgian architecture was rigid and boring. This street of grand houses escaped their recipe for improvement (the insertion of red brick), which can be seen in Harley and Wimpole Streets. It remains remarkably intact, with the only interruption at Marylebone Road.

Bryanston Square and   J18b
Montagu Square W1 1811
Joseph Parkinson, Albert Richardson
⊖ Baker Street, Marble Arch

Bryanston Square, the westerly extension of the Portman Estate, forms part of an axial composition from the older Great Cumberland Place in the south to Smirke's fine church in Wyndham Place F19 to the north. Parkinson's original houses remain on the east side and at all four corners. The square was designed as two grand palaces with stuccoed end pavilions and giant Ionic columns confronting each other, but this image has been impaired by Albert Richardson's replacement of the houses in the centre section of the west side with a particularly bleak affair, consisting of a neo-Georgian façade to a large apartment building. To the east is Montagu Square, a companion to Bryanston Square, with shallow bay windows to the houses.

Bryanston Square

Stirling Street and   J19n
Trevor Square 1818
Montpelier Square and
Montpelier Place 1837 SW7
⊖ Knightsbridge

A small collection of Regency houses, which look more appropriate to the seaside than to their site between busy Brompton Road and Knightsbridge.

Trevor Square

Houses 1820s   J20g
91–9 Park Lane W1
⊖ Marble Arch

The only complete collection of individually designed and built terrace houses remaining on Park Lane, these have the Regency bow windows and fine cast iron verandas which used to be characteristic of the street.

Dudley House 1824-7   J21g
100 Park Lane W1
William Atkinson
⊖ Marble Arch
Park Lane was originally lined with aristocrats' detached houses built along the edge of the Grosvenor Estate. Dudley House, small but pretentious with an Ionic colonnade and first-floor glazed iron loggia, is the only one left.

St Mark 1824-8   J22c
North Audley Street W1
J P Gandy-Deering
⊖ Marble Arch
The very fine tall Greek portico, with two Ionic columns, a straight entablature without pediment and an elegant octagonal lantern behind, is best appreciated from Green Street opposite. The interior was 'Normanized' by Sir Arthur Blomfield in 1878 and is of no special interest. The whole church is in need of repair.

Belgrave Square SW1 1825   J23o
Thomas Cubitt
⊖ Hyde Park Corner
The diagonal approaches, marked by four corner mansions, are Belgrave Square's distinguishing feature. It is also large, nearly 4 ha (10 acres), and grand – its name synonymous with the high society of the area as a whole. All the terraces are of four storeys with the attic set back behind the cornice, but Cubitt, in collaboration with the architect George Basevi, was deter-

mined to break the uniformity of the Georgian square. The entrances are individual, and the elevations employ various different motifs. The houses in the corners are by various architects: the north-west by Sir Robert Smirke (1830), the south-west by H E Kendall (1826), the south-east by Philip Hardwick (1842) and the north-east by George Basevi (c1840).

Screen 1825 — J24k
Hyde Park Corner SW1
Decimus Burton
⊖ Hyde Park Corner

Hyde Park Corner was always regarded as the important entrance to London from the west, and a number of schemes for improving it were proposed during the eighteenth century. We are lucky in that the present arrangement is the consequence of the building boom in the years following the battle of Waterloo: nowhere else in London is there a group of buildings of such high quality of this period. It is, however, characteristically English that this important place should be called merely a 'Corner' – perhaps it was this name which allowed the traffic engineers of the 1950s to rape it so shamelessly. The Screen and Arch J27 are the culmination of Burton's work in Hyde Park, for before them he had designed many of the lodges. The combination of delicacy and correctness in the Ionic Screen is perhaps a happy consequence of Burton's youth – he was twenty-five when designing them. The busy Greek sculpture on the attic above the central arch is by John Henning Junior, who with his father carried out the magnificent frieze on Burton's Athenaeum K80.

Eaton Square SW1 1826–53 — J25p
Thomas Cubitt
⊖ Victoria, Sloane Square

One of the grandest architectural set pieces in London (originally the formal beginning of the route from St James's Palace to Hampton Court), Eaton Square is more of a triumphal way than a typical square. King's Road forms its central axis from Hobart Place in the east to Sloane Square in the west, and parallel streets on either side (like a European boulevard) serve the generously composed and varied terraces (see also Tyburnia J30). The north side was developed by Thomas Cubitt, the south side by Seth Smith (1825–30).

At the north-east corner of the square is Henry Hakewill's church of **St Peter** (1824–7), a standard Greek Revival work with a giant portico of six Ionic columns. Fire gutted the building in the 1980s, thereby removing Sir Arthur Blomfield's unfortunate Norman interior of 1872.

St Peter

Wilton Crescent SW1 1827 — J26o
Seth Smith
⊖ Hyde Park Corner

Approached via Hyde Park and Wilton Place to the north, Wilton Crescent is a typical nineteenth-century device to give the visitor a grand introduction to the Estate. However, where Nash's Park Crescent F6 has a vista onto Regent's Park, here the south side is blocked by buildings, which confuse the entrance to Belgrave Square. The north side was refaced with stone by Balfour and Turner in the early twentieth century. The stuccoed fronts and giant pilasters of the south side are typical of Belgravia.

Constitution Arch 1827–8   J27l
Hyde Park Corner SW1
Decimus Burton
⊖ Hyde Park Corner

The Arch was built as a northern gate to the grounds of Buckingham Palace, and originally stood opposite and to the south of Burton's Screen J24, where its solidity and Corinthian order complemented the delicacy and openness of the Ionic Screen. In this position, it formed an orthogonal composition with the other buildings of the 1820s (St George's Hospital J28 and the portico of Apsley House J13) which, before Belgravia was built, marked the entrance to London from the west. The Arch was moved to its present position at the head of Constitution Hill in 1883. The Quadriga – the magnificent imperial bronze chariot carrying Victory – replaced the original statue of the Duke of Wellington in 1912. Since the reconstruction of Hyde Park Corner as one of the biggest and busiest traffic roundabouts in Europe in the late 1950s the setting of the Arch has been less than satisfactory.

St George's Hospital 1827–9   J28k
Hyde Park Corner SW1
William Wilkins
⊖ Hyde Park Corner

While the London hospital is largely an eighteenth-century building type, several were built or rebuilt in the years of peace following Waterloo. St George's was founded in 1719 and Wilkins' building replaces that of 1732–4. The Greek stuccoed façade to Hyde Park Corner has a central porch of square columns, with two side wings curiously divided into two bays by a central pilaster. The top floor is a later addition. There are some good Grecian interiors. The hospital was enlarged in the mid-nineteenth century, but closed in 1980. It has been redeveloped as a hotel, and Wilkins' façades restored.

Marble Arch 1828   J29c
Oxford Street and Park Lane W1
John Nash
⊖ Marble Arch

Marble Arch was designed to stand in front of (its material in contrast to) the Bath stone façade of Nash's Buckingham Palace, but was moved to its present site when the Palace was extended after Nash's death. It is based on the three-arched Roman model and like this was intended to have more sculptured decoration than it now sports. A statue of Victory was to be placed on top, but this was replaced by one of George IV, which eventually found its place in Trafalgar Square. While it suits the delicacy of the design, marble is not a good material to use outdoors in London as it is vulnerable to frost and sulphuric acid. The lack of polish, and its miserable setting in the middle of a poorly designed traffic roundabout, make it look a little wan.

Tyburnia 1828–35   J30b
Connaught Square, Connaught Street, Kendal Street, Hyde Park Square, Sussex Gardens, Westbourne Terrace, Sussex Square, Hyde Park Street, W2
S P Cockerell and George Gutch
⊖ Paddington, Edgware Road

The special interest of the district, best appreciated as a whole, lies in the combination of the established eighteenth-century patterns of domestic streets and squares (stuccoed after Nash) and the larger-scale European-style avenues such as Sussex Gardens and Westbourne Terrace (tree-lined, with service streets on either side, separated by strips of green). In the eighteenth century squares were never seen as through-routes, and were often gated and exclusive to their residents.

Pantechnicon 1830   J31o
Motcomb Street SW1
Seth Smith
⊖ Knightsbridge

An extraordinarily large Doric façade to a warehouse, until recently Sotheby's Belgravia auction rooms.

ex **Pimlico Literary Institute** 1830   J32p
22 Ebury Street SW1
J P Gandy-Deering
⊖ Victoria

The Institute, now converted into flats, uses a Greek Doric propylaeum format, set in a stuccoed street frontage. The towers at the sides rise higher than the portico – not a satisfactory arrangement – but make a tastefully modelled secular public building, as good as any of Nash's similar, contemporary works.

Chester Square SW1 1835   J33p
Thomas Cubitt
⊖Victoria
Although Chester Square, very long and thin, is divided by the traffic of Eccleston Street, it is the most intimate of Belgravia's squares, with differing details in the frontages.

Lowndes Square SW1   J34o
laid out in 1836
⊖Knightsbridge
The few houses on the east and south sides (by Lewis Cubitt, 1841) are all that remain of the original. In 1931 Messrs Joseph completely redeveloped the west side of the square with large red-brick blocks of flats. Despite their inconsistencies with the earlier houses – double-storey rust-ication and greater overall height, for example – these stripped classical build-ings are impressive.

St Paul 1840–3   J35k
Wilton Place SW1
Thomas Cundy III
⊖Hyde Park Corner
One of the dignified churches of the Grosvenor Estate. The castellated west tower is open at the ground floor, forming a grand porch. Inside, the three galleries are supported by fine cast iron columns, and the construction of the timber roof is exposed.

Church of the Immaculate   J36h
Conception 1844–9
Farm Street W1
J J Scoles, High Altar by
Augustus Welby Pugin
⊖Bond Street, Green Park
A remarkably beautiful and unexpectedly large Gothic interior is to be discovered behind the Immaculate Conception's un-exceptional street façade. The nave and aisles are of eight bays, with red granite columns and tall clerestory windows; the east window and the porch and rose windows at the west are supposedly inspired by Carlisle Cathedral. The ceil-ing, white with a spare red geometric pattern, is quite ethereal. The church has two later outer aisles: to the right by Henry Chilton (1878) and to the left by W H Romaine Walker (1898–1903). The buttressing to the nave subdivides both into independent polygonal chapels. There is a secondary entrance from the

north (from St George's Gardens J57) ingeniously positioned between the chan-cel and the chapel – a short cut for those who know.

Houses 1845   J37g
1–2, 26–32, 64–9 South
Audley Street W1
⊖ Hyde Park Corner
The street's architecture is a mixture of
calm Georgian remains (see numbers 71
and 72) and the wilder Victorian in-
sertions listed above. The ensemble is
characteristic of Mayfair, and is held
together by the right-angled street grid of
the Grosvenor Estate, laid out in the
eighteenth century.

1–2 South Audley Street

All Saints 1846–9   J38n
Ennismore Gardens SW7
L Vulliamy; front by C H Townsend 1892
⊖ Knightsbridge, South Kensington
A rare, early example in England of a copy
of a primitive Christian basilica (they were
more common in Germany), All Saints is
decorated in Arts and Crafts sgraffito by
Heywood Sumner, and has surprisingly
secular stained glass. It has recently been
bought by the Russian Orthodox Church.

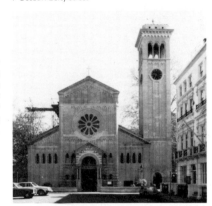

Paddington Station 1850–4   J39a
Eastbourne Terrace and
Praed Street W2
Isambard Kingdom Brunel,
Matthew Digby Wyatt, Owen Jones
⊖ Paddington
The hotel marking the south front to
Paddington Station is an earlier and
separate building by Philip Hardwick, and
established the railways' tradition of
putting hotel fronts to the large engineering sheds behind (see St Pancras G38,
Charing Cross K102 and so on). The
station is the work of Brunel, the engineer
of the Great Western Railway; Wyatt and
Jones added the architectural decorations.
It had three parallel sheds (the fourth was
added in this century), with roofs of
wrought iron and glass and columns of cast
iron. Originally the inner platforms were
reached by retractable drawbridges, as
there was no concourse at the south end,
and the station master's lookout was
behind a second-floor oriel window on
platform 1. The station has a northern
approach from Bishop's Bridge Road – a
miniature elevated road for taxis, and a
bridge for pedestrians. Externally the east
side of the station is very impressive, like a
long, curved whale's back, the front or
head visible from London Street to the
south. To the east, in London Street, are
P G Culverhouse's **Great Western
Railway Offices** (1933), a delightful and
rare example of a *moderne* office building.

Great Western Railway Offices

Victoria and Albert Museum

J40m

ex South Kensington Museum
1856–1909
Cromwell Road SW7
Captain Francis Fowke, Godfrey Sykes and others, main quadrangle 1856–84; Sir Aston Webb, Cromwell Road entrance range 1899–1909
⊖South Kensington

The Victoria and Albert Museum was promoted by Prince Albert to improve the technical and art education of designers and manufacturers, at a time when Britain was beginning to lose her industrial supremacy to other European countries. The extensive collections of ceramics, furniture, tapestries and other *objets d'art* from around the world were assembled by the museum's energetic first director, Sir Henry Cole. Cole profoundly distrusted architects, preferring to commission engineers and decorative artists for the buildings: it is this combination that gives the first galleries for South Kensington Museum their distinctive style.

Until Webb's Cromwell Road façade was built (1899–1909) the museum presented an extremely utilitarian appearance to the public. Known disparagingly as the 'Brompton Boilers' because of their cast iron structures and corrugated iron facings, the buildings were dismantled and moved to form the Bethnal Green Museum U21 in 1867.

The earliest surviving gallery is the Sheepshanks (1857–8) by Fowke. North of this are the Vernon and Turner Galleries (1858–9), east of these are North and South Courts (1861–2), and to the south is the great East Court (1868–73) by Lieutenant-Colonel Scott. All the courts were 'engineered' utilitarian iron structures, decorated later by artists including Moody and Leighton. Even the main quadrangle, the principal architectural space, was built in stages as part of the museum's slow growth. It is a good example of the South Kensington style of terracotta, red brick and mosaic. First was the West Side (1862–3), then the North (1864–6) with an arcaded loggia designed by Sykes, mosaic lunettes by Townroe, terracotta detail by Gamble and the great bronze doors designed by Sykes and modelled by Gamble and Townroe. The

South Side remained open until 1879 when it was filled by the Art Library range. The East Side was formed by the 'backs' of the Sheepshanks and Vernon and Turner Galleries until 1901, when Aston Webb faced them by reproducing the west side.

There are some very remarkable interiors on the north side of the main quadrangle. The New Refreshment Room (1866) and the Grill Room (1865–73) are both splendid examples of the use of glazed ceramic tiles. The Green Dining Room (1866–9), designed by William Morris's firm (his first major secular commission), was unnecessarily redecorated in 1978. The stained glass window is by Edward Burne-Jones.

In 1891 Aston Webb won the competition to complete the principal Cromwell Road façade. The design is exceptional for its pomp and mixture of historical motifs, and the interiors of the entrance hall are very tall and impressive in their oversized way. As the capital of the British Empire, London was thought to require such grand civic gestures.

The Cromwell Road elevation was cleaned in 1991, revealing Aston Webb's original façade; and a pair of handsome new steel gates (designed by the Royal College of Art project office, 1980) has been introduced to the Exhibition Road elevation, thereby clearly announcing the secondary entrance to the museum.

Grosvenor Crescent SW1

J41k

1860
Seth Smith, Thomas Cubitt
⊖Hyde Park Corner

Beginning with the fine Greek Revival façades of Wilkins' St George's Hospital J28 on Hyde Park Corner, Grosvenor Crescent is the diagonal approach to Belgrave Square from the north-east. The north side, by Seth Smith, is a fine continuously curving elevation. Cubitt's south side, consisting of individual houses, is more fragmentary.

Grosvenor Hotel

Victoria Station

Victoria Station 1862   J42p
partially rebuilt 1898–1908
Victoria Street SW1
J Fowler

Grosvenor Hotel 1860
Buckingham Palace Road SW1
J T Knowles
⊖ Victoria

Victoria Station was run originally by two railway companies, which had no connection until 1923. To the east are two fine vaulted iron and glass structures, built by J Fowler for the London, Chatham and Dover Railway Station (now platforms 1–8). To the west is the London, Brighton and South Coast Railway station (platforms 9–17), which was entirely rebuilt in 1898–1908. The railway line was built on the course of the Grosvenor Canal, which allowed access to the Thames; the Southern Railway Companies were thus enabled to build the first railway crossing of the Thames in central London. Romantic associations with journeys on the

Flèche d'Or to distant European capitals have unfortunately now been subsumed by the present-day squalor caused by the station's over-use in the service of Gatwick Airport.

The Grosvenor Hotel, although not the first station hotel in London, was one of the first examples of the 'Second Empire' style. The large-scale design, an elaborately decorated large rectangle of brick and stone, expresses the confidence of the railway age. On the first and top storeys, between the arched windows, are medallions with portraits of Queen Victoria, Prince Albert and Lord Palmerston, among others. At either end of the curved and dormered roof are four French pavilions. The Grosvenor Hotel proved to be an influential building (see the Langham Hotel, Portland Place, by Giles and Murray) and as Summerson writes, 'is one of the representative monuments of Victorian London'.

Henry Cole Building   J43m
ex Huxley Building 1863–73
Exhibition Road SW7
Lieutenant-General Scott
⊖ South Kensington

The Henry Cole Building was first occupied by the School of Naval Architects, then the Science School, followed by the Imperial College of Science, and at the time of writing is being renovated internally as a further extension to the Victoria and Albert Museum. The building is truly monumental: seven central bays are flanked by pedimented corner pavilions and topped by a continuous loggia. To the left an arched gateway leads through to the (original) Royal College of Art, its name and the Imperial College of Science's inscribed in the stonework above. The exterior is extensively decorated with terracotta panels ornamented in Minton majolica.

Albert Memorial 1863–75   J44i
Kensington Gardens,
Kensington Gore SW7
Sir George Gilbert Scott
⊖ Knightsbridge

That the Prince Consort should be commemorated by a monumental interpretation of a medieval shrine, normally associated with the relics of saints, is typical of High Victorian idealism. Scott's idea was 'to erect a kind of ciborium . . . on the principle of the ancient shrines', encrusted with precious metals and enamel.

The 53 m (175 ft) high memorial has a Gothic spire decorated with angels, and a 4.2 m (14 ft) high seated bronze statue of Prince Albert forming the apex to a remarkable pyramid of sculpted figures representing the ideals, aspirations and achievements of the Victorian age. In the four projecting corners groups of marble figures symbolize the Imperial colonies and the four corners of the globe: Asia (by J H Foley), Europe (Patrick MacDowell), America (John Bell) and Africa (William Theed). Below, figures at the corners represent Agriculture (W Calder Marshall), Manufacture (Henry Weekes), Commerce (Thomas Thornycroft) and Engineering (John Lawlor). Between them is a continuous frieze of painters, poets, composers, architects and sculptors. The poets, musicians and painters are by H H Armstead, the rest by J B Philip. All this stands on a massive granite plinth of twenty-four steps.

The memorial has provoked hostility and affection, but has finally gained acceptance as a relic of the age it so accurately portrays. So many artists and craftsmen were involved that it is as much a memorial to the Arts and Crafts movement as it is to Albert. It is best seen either at close quarters, or from the east (the site of the original Crystal Palace) framed by the majestic avenue of London plane trees.

Royal Albert Hall 1867–71   J45m
Kensington Gore SW7
Captain Francis Fowke, carried out by
Major-General H Y D Scott
⊖ Knightsbridge, High Street
Kensington

The vast elliptical Albert Hall holds 8000
within its 225 m (735 ft) circumference.
Together with Norman Shaw's Albert
Hall Mansions J50, Sir George Gilbert
Scott's Albert Memorial J44, and in spite
of the recent Royal College of Art (1962),
whose chief virtue is to expose the
beautiful end wall of the Royal College of
Organists, the Albert Hall forms one of
the best Victorian set-piece designs in
London. The central axis runs from the
front steps of the Natural History
Museum J48 on Cromwell Road through
Queen's Tower to the Imperial College
campus. The simple domed brick cylinder
and terracotta decoration has been attributed to the influence of the architect
Gottfried Semper, a political refugee
befriended by Prince Albert. The frieze,
running the full circumference and depicting *The Triumph of Arts and Letters*, is a
particularly fine work by Armitage,
Pickersgill, Marks and Poynter. The interior of the Hall has three tiers of boxes,
including the balcony and the gallery
above. The dome is of glass and iron.

Grosvenor Gardens SW1   J46p
1870
Thomas Cundy III
⊖ Victoria

Grosvenor Gardens and Grosvenor Place
were laid out as a north-western extension of Victoria Street to Hyde Park
Corner. The Grosvenor Estate seems to
have started its experiments with French
styles at about this time (and continues to
do so – see Grosvenor Square J6). For
Grosvenor Gardens it introduced not
only the clothing of a French apartment
building, but also the *maison meublée* of
about 200 rooms to be let off in various
numbers to form apartments. There was a
restaurant on the ground floor to serve
both residents and public. The social
experiment has long been discontinued,
and the building is now used as offices.

Royal Geographical Society　　J47i
ex Lowther Lodge 1873–5
Kensington Gore and
Exhibition Road SW7
R Norman Shaw
⊖Knightsbridge, High Street
Kensington

With its skilfully asymmetrical elevations and masterful brickwork, Lowther Lodge is a *tour de force* of the Queen Anne style. When the house was built (for William Lowther MP) Kensington was almost fully developed, although the adjacent sites were still empty. Unlike Shaw's other (more urban) London houses, this seems to be a country mansion encroached on by the town. The Hyde Park front is set back behind an entrance court with the stable wing to the east. The façade of fine brickwork has no stone dressings, and the pediments, gables, pilasters, massive chimneys and exaggerated cornices are made from 50 mm (2 in) cut brickwork. The external details are reminiscent more of Shaw's partner Nesfield's Lodge at Kew T17 than of his own contemporary work in Queen's Gate 112 and Melbury Road 113.

Following Lowther's death in 1912, the house was bought by the Royal Geographical Society. In 1928–30 an inoffensive lecture hall was added by Kennedy and Nightingale on the site of the stables at the corner of Kensington Gore and Exhibition Road. The statues of Shackleton and Livingstone, also on the corner facing Exhibition Road and Kensington Gore, are by C Sargeant Jagger (1932).

Natural History Museum　　J48m
1873–81
Cromwell Road SW7
Alfred Waterhouse
⊖South Kensington

The first public building in London by this eminent Victorian architect, the Natural History Museum dominates the Cromwell Road, and its terracotta slabs in the Romanesque style were new to the city's streets. When compared with neighbouring buildings (notably Aston Webb's loosely composed front to the Victoria and Albert Museum J40) the Natural History Museum has a breathtaking tough consistency. It has beautiful and varied zoological decoration along its 206 m (675 ft) frontage. Inside the huge entrance hall, the monumental staircase, steel and glass roof and large exhibition halls are particularly impressive. The Department of the Environment's recent extension at the south-east corner is deplorable, as is their projected programme of expansion.

It is unfortunate that the museum has adopted the current clichés of contemporary museum display in many of its principal exhibition halls. The visitor is distracted from the exhibits by an over-diagrammatic and populist presentation.

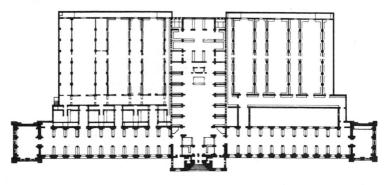

0　　20　　　　　　　　　　　　　　　　　　　　　200m

Royal College of Organists   J49m
1875
Kensington Gore SW7
H H Cole
⊖ South Kensington

A strangely eclectic four-storey, three-bay building, whose effect derives more from its decoration in cream, maroon and pale blue sgraffito by F W Moody than from its form. The College's decorative frieze of musicians curiously contains no organ. H H Cole was a soldier in the Royal Engineers, like so many of the designers of the buildings erected round the Albert Hall.

Albert Hall Mansions   J50i
1879–86
Kensington Gore SW7
R Norman Shaw
⊖ High Street Kensington,
Knightsbridge

In their sheer mass and scale these buildings are reminiscent of a fragment of a European city: their swirling shapes contain the Albert Hall J45 and offer a grand façade to Kensington Gardens. Shaw had studied the French apartment type before taking this new departure, which influenced flat development in Kensington up to 1910. The double-storey plinth (supporting the main storeys with twice repeated double arches) and the tall Dutch gables above show Shaw's inventive use of the Queen Anne style.

House 1879   J51o
4 Cadogan Square SW1
George Edmund Street
⊖ Knightsbridge

Grandly occupying a corner, Street's house makes few concessions to the prevailing 'Pont Street Dutch' – only the use of red brick and perhaps the restrained window arrangements. His Gothic is given full rein in the magnificently asymmetrical porch to the front door. See also Norman Shaw's houses, numbers 60a, 62, 68 and 72 N24 and J J Stevenson's numbers 63–73 N23.

The London Oratory   J52n
1880–93
Brompton Road SW3
Herbert Gribble; house by J J Scoles
⊖ South Kensington

The Oratory was the first large new Roman Catholic church to be built in London after the Reformation. Its building was the culmination of the influence of the Oxford Movement which set up branches of St Philip Neri's Oratorians at Birmingham and London in 1845, when John Henry Newman and Frederick Faber became Catholics. Rather as Islam is associated today with a particular style, so Gribble's huge church, chosen in competition by Alfred Waterhouse, is studiedly Roman, using a domed nave (each dome with a central rooflight) to which vaulted side chapels are attached. The vaults and domes are in concrete (see also Westminster Cathedral K118). The Roman atmosphere is enhanced by the skilful recycling of genuine Italian ornaments and statues, but the seven-branched candlesticks are by Burges. The painting of Saints Thomas More and John Fisher in St Wilfred's Chapel is by Rex Whistler.

Mount Street W1 c1885　　　　J53g
Sir Ernest George
⊖ Bond Street, Hyde Park Corner
The most complete and lavishly decorated
red terracotta tiled street in London,
largely by Sir Ernest George, though
numbers 125–9 by W H Powell (1889) and
J T Smith's numbers 118–21 (1886) are the
most astonishingly ornate examples. The
Connaught Hotel (one of the best in
London) is by Isaacs and Florence (1901).
From Carlos Place the street is more
regular; numbers 87–102, three-storeyed
and gabled, are by A T Bolton (1893). On
the south side of Mount Street are the two
gated entrances to St George's Gardens
J57.

Imperial Institute Tower　　　J54m
1887–93
Imperial Institute Road SW7
Thomas Edward Collcutt
⊖ South Kensington
The tallest marker on the (invisible) axis
extending south from the Albert Hall to
the Natural History Museum, this 85 m
(280 ft) tower (now surrounded by the
1960s redevelopment of Imperial College)
is all that remains of the building erected
after the 1886 Colonial Exhibition.
Collcutt's striped style is more restrained
here than in his contemporary Palace
Theatre K115.

Ukrainian Catholic Cathedral　　J55d
of the Holy Family in Exile
ex King's Weigh House Chapel 1889–91
Duke Street W1
Alfred Waterhouse
⊖ Bond Street
Waterhouse's style and materials are
unmistakable — a curious mixture of
Gothic and Romanesque in brick and buff
terracotta tiles. The Duke Street façade is
asymmetrical, with a tall tower on the
south-west corner. Inside, the principal
space is oval, with an impressive gallery
carried on iron piers encased in
terracotta.

Albert Court c1890　　　　J56m
Prince Consort Road SW7
⊖ South Kensington
With Norman Shaw's Albert Hall Mansions J50, Albert Court follows the line of
the Albert Hall, establishing around it a
ring of civic space (which unfortunately is
not continued by the Royal College of Art
to the west). The large, brick, seven-
storey apartment building is exceptional
for its entrance corridor
(90 m × 7 m/296 ft × 23 ft) connecting it
with the steps from Prince Consort Road
to the Albert Hall: this impressive internal street is furnished with large fireplaces, post-boxes, grandfather clocks and
minstrel galleries, and is lit by internal
light wells. The façade to Prince Consort
Road is remarkable for its corner turrets
and three-storey tiered loggias of attached columns.

St George's Gardens c1890   J57h
entrances on South Audley
Street, Mount Street and
South Street W1
ϴHyde Park Corner

A beautiful meticulously maintained
irregularly shaped secret garden, walled
in by the backs of mansion flats and by
Grosvenor Chapel J7 and Liddon House to
the west. For those who know, it is a
tranquil place to sit in the middle of
Mayfair; all the benches face south, and
the enormous 200-year-old plane trees
give it a leafy ceiling in summer. The
bronze fountain is by Sir Ernest George
(1892).

Houses 1891–2   J58n
14–16 Hans Road SW3
C F A Voysey
House 1894
12 Hans Road SW3
Arthur Mackmurdo
ϴKnightsbridge

These houses by Voysey are among his
earliest works in London, contemporary
with his Studio House, Bedford Park T19.
They distinguish themselves from the
verticality of their Dutch surroundings by
the emphatic horizontals of their grouped
windows and their squat, smooth
porches. Mackmurdo's house is less radical: it displays a mixture of Queen Anne
style motifs, with others, like the oriel
windows, derived from Norman Shaw.

Harrods Department Store   J59n
1901–5
Brompton Road SW3
Stevens and Munt
ϴKnightsbridge

Although they are architecturally and
technically less adventurous than their
continental equivalents of the same
period – Samaritaine in Paris and Messel's
Wertheim store in Berlin – the London
department stores are impressive for
their sheer size and Edwardian splendour.
From its modest beginnings in 1849 as a
small grocer's shop, Harrods expanded
vigorously to become the largest store in
Europe. It now occupies a whole city block
of 1.8 ha (4.5 acres), with over 5.5 ha (13.5
acres) of sales space on its five floors, the
214 departments and staff of 4000 seeming
to justify the store's motto, *omnia, omni-
bus, ubique* (everything for everyone,
everywhere). With its eight public entrances, sixty-six window displays and
complex internal organization of lifts and
escalators, it seems like a miniature city
within the city.

Inside, the Food Halls are a *tour de force*:
the mosaic friezes and tilework (designed
by W J Neatby) combine magnificently
with the sensuous display of food. Recalling Harrods' original trade, they are an
oblique memorial to the energies of
Henry and Charles Harrod. The
gentlemen's hairdressers in the basement
and the ladies' lavatories on the first floor
are unexpectedly fine art deco designs.
The exterior is made with red terracotta
tiles of small-scale decorative relief (also
by Neatby), and is impressive when
adorned with its festive lighting at Christ-
mas, like a giant Pandora's box.

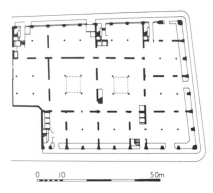

0   10   50m

Plan of the first stage

Selfridges Department Store
J60c

1907–28
Oxford Street W1
R F Atkinson with Daniel Burnham; supervised by Sir John Burnet
⊖ Marble Arch

The design and building of Selfridges, London's grandest shop façade, has a complex history. Although R F Atkinson is credited with the design, there are significant contributions by Daniel Burnham of Chicago (with Francis Swales), the internal steel frame is attributed to Albert Miller, and the first stages of construction (the east section) were supervised by Sir John Burnet. The massive and richly decorated Ionic columns of the façade are set forward from the three intermediate floors, which are concealed by metal panels. The store follows the nineteenth-century tendency for a single building to occupy a whole city block, and this extraordinary temple of the retail business was promoted with Edwardian zeal by Mr Gordon Selfridge. As commercial street architecture it has a generosity of scale which is still unmatched.

Royal School of Mines
J61m

1909–13
Prince Consort Road S W7
Sir Aston Webb
⊖ South Kensington

The last of Webb's three buildings in Kensington – the earlier ones are the Victoria and Albert Museum J40 and Imperial College – carried out in hard white stone during the Edwardian classical revival suggests that he was losing his touch. The monumental central semicircular niche with sculptures is impressive but cramped.

Science Museum 1913
J62m

Exhibition Road S W7
Office of Works; Sir Richard Allison
⊖ South Kensington

Allison used the department store as the model for the inside of his building, and the Edwardian office building (those in Kingsway K130 for example) for the outside. The combination works well, and the generous circulation spaces using well finished, practical materials easily accommodate the flocks of mainly young visitors. The rooflit central well is good for the display of large engines, and the open galleries at the sides used also to be naturally lit. Fashion now requires that exhibits are best looked at under artificial light, if not in near-darkness.

Grosvenor House Hotel J63g

1926–8
Park Lane W1
Wimperis, Simpson and Guthrie;
consultant Sir Edwin Lutyens
⊖ Marble Arch

Built on the site of Lord Grosvenor's early nineteenth-century mansion, Grosvenor House Hotel was one of the first in a series of grand hotels on Hyde Park. Although it avoids the conspicuous mass of the high-rise towers and slabs of its successors (the Hilton J74, Royal Lancaster and so on) the building is deceptively large. The 478 bedrooms and 160 apartments are contained in four closely packed blocks angled obliquely (east/west) to Park Lane.

Lutyens, who was responsible only for the elevations, marked the end of these blocks with square roof pavilions, and these four belvederes are very impressive when seen across Hyde Park, riding above the trees like a fragment of a much larger order. The massive and abstract base to Grosvenor House, the disappearing pilasters, and the quadrant screen of giant Corinthian columns to the first-floor terrace, are further contributions by Lutyens to this fine urbane building. R D Russell's interiors (1955–61) with their generous foyers have since, predictably, been replaced by ubiquitous international chic.

Tudor House 1929–31 J64h

6–10 Mount Row W1
Frederick Etchells
⊖ Green Park, Bond Street

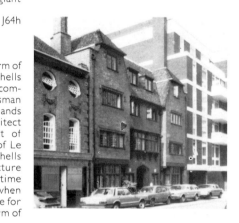

This curious group of offices in the form of an Elizabethan house confirms the Etchells enigma and also John Betjeman's comment, 'at heart Etchells was a craftsman who enjoyed making things with his hands ... he was an artist first and an architect *faute de mieux*'. As the architect of Crawfords G59 and the translator of Le Corbusier's *Vers une Architecture* Etchells also confirmed that modern architecture was for most English architects at the time a style like any other, to be used when appropriate. The rear court is notable for the decorative plasterwork in the form of trees.

Dorchester Hotel 1930 J65g

Park Lane W1
W Curtis Green
⊖ Green Park

In its time the hotel was thought very modern. Owen Williams designed the structure, but resigned from the job when there were objections to his plans for covering the frame. London lost a potentially modernist hotel on the park, but it is still the best building on Park Lane. It fills the block to the pavement line, and the convexity to the south is just enough to mark the entrance. The exterior, faced in faience, is well-mannered and decorated in the *moderne* style.

C&A Department Store J66c
ex British Industries House
and Hereford House 1931–3
200 Oxford Street W1
Messrs Joseph; elevations by Sir Edwin
Lutyens
⊖ Oxford Circus
Lutyens was one of the last great architects in England to do 'styling': here he
designed the exterior proportions and
decoration of a very large part of a block.
Viewing the successful if bland results,
both here and at the Grosvenor House
Hotel J63, one must regret that the
practice has gone out of fashion.

Aldford House 1932 J67g
Park Lane W1
Val Myers and Watson Hart; Sir Edwin
Lutyens consultant for elevations
⊖ Hyde Park Corner, Marble Arch
Lutyens and Val Myers were the principal
contributors to the appearance of Park
Lane in the 1920s and '30s. The superimposition of a scraped classical façade on a
utilitarian plan was not unusual at the
time, and it was also quite usual for the
designer of the façade to be a celebrated
architect while the internal organization
of the building was delegated to those less
well known (see Lutyens' façades to C&A
J66 and Grosvenor House Hotel J63, and
Myers' 80 Park Lane and Fountain House).
The façade has broad bands of stone and
red brick, capped at either end by
pavilions with stone pediments on a scale
appropriate to Park Lane.

Mount Royal Hotel 1932–3 J68c
Oxford Street and
Bryanston Street W1
Sir John Burnet, Tait and Partners;
designed by Francis Lorne
⊖ Marble Arch
The hotel is an excellent example of how
Beaux Arts planning round light wells,
smart streamlined Dutch styling, and the
influence of Mendelsohn enable a very
large building occupying a whole block to
be assimilated into the structure of the
city and the surrounding buildings.
From Oxford Street one sees only shops,
as the hotel entrance is at the back in
Bryanston Street.

Flats c1935 J69m
59–63 Princes Gate SW7
Adie, Button and Partners
⊖ South Kensington
A rare example of the language and
tradition of London's nineteenth-century
white stuccoed terraces applied to an
early twentieth-century apartment building. The building is set back from the
pavement by a traditional area, and the
top two of its nine floors are further set
back to form an attic. The façade is
rendered to acknowledge the rustication
of the neighbours' ground and first floors
(the striped banding aligns with the
transoms of the metal window frames);
and, appropriately, the basement car park
is entered from the mews. On the other
hand, the waffle slabs and cantilevered
balconies and corners are contemporary
aspects of this fine building.

Time & Life Building 1952   J70h
New Bond Street and
Bruton Street W1
M Rosenauer
⊖ Bond Street, Green Park

The London Time & Life Building, unlike its stridently commercial New York counterpart, is well-mannered and unexceptional: a Portland stone façade sitting on a marble plinth. Many contemporary artists and designers contributed to its interiors, coordinated by Sir Hugh Casson and Sir Misha Black: the frieze panels are by Henry Moore, sculpture by Geoffrey Clarke, furniture by R D Russell, rooms by L Manasseh and a cafeteria by Casson and Neville Conder. The building combines with the Westbury Hotel opposite (in the same style) and is like a fragment of a mid-European socialist city.

United States Embassy   J71g
1956–9
Grosvenor Square W1
Eero Saarinen and Associates, with Yorke Rosenberg and Mardall
⊖ Bond Street

Although by the firm which had designed the clean-cut certainties of General Motors' Detroit headquarters ten years earlier, the Embassy is muddled and unsatisfactory. The building is shorter than the sides of the square it attempts to command, and the left-over spaces at the corners are only now being filled by plane trees. The exterior combines fussy, demonstratively non-structural Portland stone facings, supported on the ground-floor structure of diagonal beams, with flimsy 'gilded' aluminium trim. Its appearance suggests a large department store rather than the pomp and circumstance appropriate to an Embassy.

Halls of residence   J72m
Imperial College 1960–3
Princes Gardens SW7
Sir Richard Sheppard, Robson and Partners
⊖ South Kensington

These two residential buildings are all that was built of an ambitious scheme for the whole of Princes Gardens. The grandiose arrangement of the one on the south side of the Gardens, with its third-floor 'deck', is completely characteristic of the period. The northerly one, however, has a scale more like the remaining houses in the square. The style is an accomplished late English 'Brutalism', satisfactory for the outside of each building, but very overbearing inside.

Royal College of Art   J73m
1962–73
Kensington Gore SW7
H T Cadbury-Brown, Sir Hugh Casson
⊖ South Kensington

One of several educational institutions established in Kensington after the Great Exhibition of 1851 under the patronage of Prince Albert, the College was intended to supply British industry with trained designers, and soon outgrew its original accommodation next to the Victoria and Albert Museum. The various functions of the new building – workshops, hall and library – are arranged in three linked buildings round a courtyard. Seen from the park, the massing was intended to complement Norman Shaw's huge Albert Hall Mansions J50 on the eastern side of the Albert Hall J45; seen from Kensington Gardens the seven-storey workshop block successfully does so. Close to, however, the detailing combines fussiness and crudity: the first in the glazing of the tall block, the second in the squat Gulbenkian Hall which faces the Albert Hall. Since its completion, the ground floor has been converted into a cool exhibition space, called the 'Henry Moore Gallery'. Some departments had never been housed in the main building, and in the late 1980s the conversion of three of the large houses in Queen's Gate and a new building in Jay Mews finally provided space for these. The architects for these works were Colquhoun and Miller.

London Hilton 1963   J74l
Park Lane W1
Lewis Solomon Kaye
⊖ Hyde Park Corner
An early arrival of Manhattanism. The chief attraction of the view from the rooftop restaurant and bar, one of the earliest in London (by Casson, Conder and Partners), is that this particularly inept building is for once absent from the skyline (as Victor Hugo remarked of the Eiffel Tower).

Playboy Club 1963–5   J75l
45 Park Lane W1
Cotton Ballard and Blow, with Walter Gropius, Benjamin Thompson and Llewelyn Davies and Weeks
⊖ Hyde Park Corner
Gropius always advocated teamwork, but it is ironic that the founder of the Bauhaus should find himself collaborating with the least distinguished speculator architects of the decade (see what they did to Notting Hill) and with the planners of Milton Keynes to produce premises for the Bunny Club. The banality of the eight-storey precast concrete façade – the rounded end to Stanhope Gate being its only distinction – was a great disappointment to those weaned on the belief, further subverted by his Pan Am building in New York, that Gropius was one of the masters of modern architecture.

Household Cavalry   J76j
Barracks
1967–9
South Carriage Drive, Hyde Park SW1
Sir Basil Spence and Partners
⊖ Knightsbridge
These barracks replaced the outworn but unobtrusive four-storey red-brick Victorian buildings previously on the site. It is not clear why living accommodation for soldiers should have been allowed to spoil 400 years of Crown and public investment in Hyde Park: until the late 1950s, it was still possible to stand in the middle of the park and, not seeing any buildings, to pretend one had left the town. First the Hilton Hotel, and then the Barracks' tower destroyed this illusion. (Sir Basil's later government office building at Petty France, Westminster, seriously interfered with the wonderful long view of the Palace of Westminster from the Park's Serpentine bridge.) The loose arrangement· of red-brick buildings, strung out from the foot of the Tower along Knightsbridge, contributes nothing to the street or the park.

Danish Embassy 1977   J77o
55 Sloane Street SW1
Arne Jacobsen, Dissing and Weitling
⊖ Knightsbridge

A strange work by Denmark's best-known
international architect and the only
example of his work in London. Jacobsen's
style was distinguished by an extreme
delicacy and refinement of the parts, and
the several parts of this building are
treated as individual exercises in product
design. To Sloane Street are presented
four floors of offices behind ochre-
coloured aluminium panels, above which,
set back, are a further two floors of offices
and flats clad in a flush dark brown curtain
wall. The building is inoffensive but has
little to do either with London or with its
immediate context, and Jacobsen's better
work is to be found in St Catherine's
College, Oxford.

Esprit 1978   J78o
6 Sloane Street SW1
Foster Associates
⊖ Knightsbridge

Fosters were originally employed to produce a new image for the fashion shop
Joseph, but in a game of fashionable musical chairs, Joseph have moved to number
20 Sloane Street, where a spectacular stair
designed by Eva Jiricna occupies most of
the volume of the shop. The subsequent
proprietors of number 6 have retained the
white-painted shell containing all the
paraphernalia of modern retailing: the
'kit-of-parts' – bolted frames and clip-on
lighting – but which for the first time
included some of the furniture of the
Heroic period of modern architecture.
The exterior openings were filled with
large undecorated sheets of glass: there
are no cupboarded window displays.

Kenzo 1990   J79d
28 Brook Street W1
David Chipperfield Architects
⊖ Bond Street

The depth and the original two floors of
the shop are exploited with a subtle play
of volumes, small changes of floor level
and both natural and artificial lighting.
The whole is finished in Chipperfield's
restrained but luxurious modernist pal-
ette of materials: fine cream plaster walls,
Portland stone flooring and pine fittings.
The architecture provides an appropriate
setting for the lavish sobriety of the
merchandise.
To the east of Kenzo, the smaller shop at
number 26, **Equipment**, was also designed by Chipperfield. It was opened in
1991.

Section K: Westminster/St James's/Soho/St Giles/Strand/ Covent Garden/Lincoln's Inn/Temple/Lambeth/South Bank

The line of the Roman road from London to the west, now Oxford Street, forms the upper boundary of this area, but there is little evidence that the Romans occupied the flat marshy area which was to become the administrative hub of the British Empire, and which, as Westminster, is now the royal, religious, legislative and administrative centre of the United Kingdom. The first Abbey was one of many founded outside the City and owned the land up to the City boundary. It was probably established in the tenth century, but acquired importance only when it was rebuilt in 1065 by Edward the Confessor. Edward's successor William Rufus confirmed the royal presence by building Westminster Hall K5 nearby in 1097–9. The twin poles of the Cities of London and Westminster have existed side by side for 900 years, and for 800 years the slow growth of links between them shaped the development of London. First the Temple K4 was built alongside the Thames in the twelfth century, followed in the thirteenth by a hospital near Charing Cross. In 1245 Henry III began the Gothic rebuilding of the Abbey K2, a work continued through the following 300 years, finishing with the Chapel of Henry VII K8 in 1512.

The present large-scale planning of Westminster is the result of Henry VIII's ambitious activities. He enclosed St James's Park, Green Park and Hyde Park as a chain of royal hunting grounds; he dissolved the monasteries and confiscated their land, making the Abbey's strip north of the Thames ripe for development; he established the Palace of Westminster as England's administrative centre, and started work on St James's Palace K10. Under the Tudor dynasty and with the beginnings of imperial exploration, England prospered, and London began to expand. By 1600 there were houses as far north as St Giles, and in the century up to 1605 the population quadrupled to 225,000.

At the beginning of the seventeenth century, the Renaissance struck London in the person of Inigo Jones, whose white buildings (the Banqueting House K12, Queen's Chapel K13 and St Paul, Covent Garden K15) must have made the Tudor brick muddle look provincial and old-fashioned. London's growth was now the result of two methods of development: aristocrats speculated with land from their own estates (as at Covent Garden), while builders bought land and built speculative houses (as at Lincoln's Inn).

Westminster survived the Great Fire of 1666 undamaged, and the century also saw the consolidation of the pattern of streets and squares south of Oxford Street. The grid-iron pattern of St James's was laid out in the 1660s, and with the completion of Wren's St James, Piccadilly K21, north of St James's Square K18 in 1684 it was fully established as a district. Soho followed in the 1680s and '90s, growing round Golden Square K20 and Soho Square K24, which now give little sense of their originally spacious style.

North of the aristocrats' mansions of Piccadilly, speculative development continued to the end of the century, with the laying-out of Berkeley Square J8, Albemarle Street, and Sir Thomas Bond's Bond Street.

A century after Jones's assault on Tudor muddle, Lord Burlington, from his headquarters in Piccadilly, launched his attack on the seventeenth century's debasement of Jones's correctness. In 1715–17 he had Burlington House K36 remodelled and to the north he laid out streets where his protégés could build. Houses were now built south of Westminster Abbey around Smith Square K38 and Archer's St John K35; many remain, their dolls' plainness a contrast to the pomp with which Mayfair was being developed.

At the same time a wave of churches, all of architectural significance, was built to serve these new districts: St George, Hanover Square J5, introduced the pavement portico to Mayfair; Gibbs' St Mary-le-Strand brought Rome to the royal route from Westminster to St Paul's, and St Martin-in-the-Fields K40 solved the Anglican problem of combining temple and steeple. Whitehall's government offices were now rebuilt to suit their functions (the

Admiralty in 1722–6, for instance, and Kent's Horse Guards K50). Westminster Bridge joined Westminster to Lambeth and the south in 1749. Whitehall nearly lost its administrative supremacy when Somerset House K62 was built between the Strand and the river (to house a large number of government departments); the Adams' contemporary Adelphi K58, also on the river, formed a private speculative counterpart.

The introduction of Greek taste to London can be dated exactly to James Stuart's exquisite house at 15 St James's Square K56, but Greek and second-generation Palladian architecture (exemplified by Sir Robert Taylor's houses J6, K60, and his magnificently dour Stone Buildings K61 at Lincoln's Inn) were able to co-exist.

The building activities of the Prince Regent, Nash's patron, mark the years of peace after the Battle of Waterloo (1815), providing in Regent Street the first north-south axis to connect London's three main east-west routes (Oxford Street, Piccadilly and the Strand). Nash rebuilt Buckingham Palace K76, planned Trafalgar Square K70 and, with Repton, restyled St James's Park. Just before his death he built Carlton House Terrace K77 as the magnificent southern end to his north-south route.

The 1820s and '30s saw the peak of the classical taste, coinciding with invention of new building types, from barracks to gentlemen's clubs. In the Travellers' Club K82, Barry introduced his Italianate, which provided one of the routine styles for the rest of the century. In 1834 the Old Palace of Westminster burnt down and the Gothic Revival was launched with Barry and Pugin's competion-winning design (K90) for its replacement.

The reforming conscience of the Victorians showed itself in concern for hygiene; sewers were built to prevent cholera, slums were cleared by building roads through them, and the displaced poor were rehoused by charitable trusts in more or less horrible blocks of flats. Shaftesbury Avenue K107, Charing Cross Road K113, New Oxford Street and Victoria Street K95 were all cut through and redeveloped, giving the West End its present pattern. Victorian efficiency and engineering zeal is exemplified in the Embankment K103 (designed to bypass the congested Strand), then the single most ambitious engineering work ever undertaken in the capital. It combined a wide road, a finely detailed retaining wall, a large sewer, and a tunnel for the underground railway. By the beginning of the twentieth century the last of the metropolitan improvements was finished, as Kingsway and Aldwych K130 provided sites for commercial palaces and a subway for trams.

The royal route was upgraded by the construction of Admiralty Arch K127 and the Queen Victoria Memorial K119 and Buckingham Palace was given a new front in time for George V's coronation in 1911; at least part of the capital now had architecture appropriate to the centre of a huge and prosperous empire. Westminster escaped devastation in the Second World War, and plans were made (notably by Forshaw and Abercrombie in their *County of London Plan*, 1943) for grand post-war rebuilding: but in the exhaustion that followed nothing came of them.

Lambeth and the South Bank
Lambeth Palace K3 stood alone on the South Bank until houses and factories were built in the mid-eighteenth century. In 1769 the works for Coade stone (to provide the architectural ornaments for Bloomsbury) were set up on the future site of County Hall, and St Thomas's Hospital K168 was established in the 1860s. In 1951 the land at the southern end of Waterloo Bridge, where the river bends sharply, was used for the attempt at national cheering-up, the Festival of Britain. The Royal Festival Hall K157, the most distinguished of the Festival buildings, was the only permanent one and it is still one of the few good modern buildings in London. The cultural ghetto established next door with the building of the Hayward Gallery and Queen Elizabeth Hall K171 and the National Theatre K172 is unsatisfactory, although it may in future offer relief from the relentless walls of offices being considered at the time of writing for the entire river front from Vauxhall Bridge to Tower Bridge.

Temple Church K1d

c1160–85, c1220–40,
19th and 20th century
Inner Temple EC4
Sir Robert Smirke 1825, E Blore 1841–3,
Walter H Godfrey 1948–58
⊖Temple

A Norman and Gothic church, extensively renovated in the nineteenth century. The tradition of the circular nave derives from the church of the Holy Sepulchre, Jerusalem, and two other examples survive in English parish churches: Holy Sepulchre, Cambridge, and Holy Sepulchre, Northampton. The building as a whole is one of the earliest in London to be built according to strict Gothic principles – the triforium with its small marble columns is worth noting, as are the piers surrounding the circular nave, 18 m (59 ft) in diameter. The nave and porch date from about 1160. Below the chancel is the Undercroft (c1170) and to the south the underground Chapel of St Anne (thirteenth century). The present chancel (1220–40) was an enlargement of the original and, with very fine marble piers and capitals and high lancet windows, is one of the best thirteenth-century examples in England.

The church was restored by Smirke in the nineteenth century and was further renovated following extensive damage in the Second World War.

Westminster Abbey K2n

from 1245
Parliament Square SW1
⊖Westminster

The Abbey and Westminster Hall K6 across the road were to become the nucleus of the City of Westminster, 3 km (2 miles) upstream from the site of the (Roman) City of London. While Roman remains have been found at Westminster the first building of which evidence exists is the abbey built by Edward the Confessor (1042–66) on the site of an earlier one. A Norman church was built between 1110 and 1150, but this was demolished under Henry III's huge building programme, and a new church started in 1245. It is this church with its later nave which we see today. The chancel, transepts and crossing, and the first five bays of the nave were built between 1245 and 1260. The polygonal apse with its radiating chapels originally forming a *chevet* (the first of its kind in Britain), its tall (31 m/103 ft high) section (the highest of all England's Gothic churches) and its lavish decorations are all of French derivation and reflect Henry III's interest in the French Court. The architect, Henry of Reynes, may have been French.

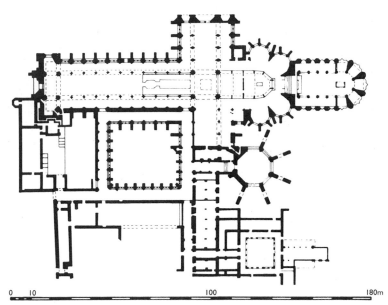

For a hundred years the abbey church had a Gothic east end and a Norman nave, and it was only in 1375 that the Norman work was demolished. The master mason for the new nave was Henry Yevele, who instead of building in the current Decorated style, modestly built in keeping with the earlier work. The nave was completed in the 1390s, when the west window, much altered since, was done in Perpendicular style. The last significant additions to the Abbey were the Chapel of Henry VII K8 and Hawksmoor's west towers K48.

The Abbey's continued existence is the result of its role as the religious centre for coronations, royal weddings and burials; for a time it acted as Treasury, and Parliament sat in the Chapter House. Its appearance has changed drastically. When completed, the interior was painted white, the carved decoration picked out in bright colours and gilded, the windows filled with stained glass; there was a delicate screen across the chancel, quite unlike the present massive one which supports the organ, and the place was as yet empty of 700 years' accumulation of monuments, about which critics including Pugin and William Morris were to complain.

The Abbey was built of soft Reigate stone, and the exterior has been refaced several times – cleaning and patching is going on at the time of writing.

Wren was Surveyor for a time; he made designs for completing the crossing, but it was his pupil Hawksmoor who completed the exterior with his west towers started in 1735.

Lambeth Palace 1297, 1495, 1660, 1829   K3o
Lambeth Palace Road SE1
⊖ Vauxhall

The fine medieval, Tudor and Jacobean buildings of Lambeth Palace have been the official residence of the Archbishop of Canterbury for seven centuries. Before the building of the Albert Embankment, with its bridges and traffic roundabouts, the Palace was approached from the river (boats were moored on the site of the pier now used by the river police); it must then have seemed considerably more impressive than it does today.

Immediately to the north of the tower of St Mary K96 is the red-brick gatehouse, known as Morton's Tower, built by Archbishop Morton in about 1495. On either side of the gateway are five-storey brick wings; inside, on the south side of the cloisters, is the Hall, rebuilt by Archbishop Juxon in about 1660–3, and the Palace's finest building. The magnificent hammerbeam roof was restored after damage in the Second World War. The Chapel, which probably dates from about

1230, was also gutted in the war.

The neo-Jacobean extensions to the north and east of the Hall, incorporating the cloisters and partly medieval guard-room, are by E Blore (1829–33); they give the Palace an unfortunate lugubrious quality. The extensive Archbishop's Park, to the east, is now open to the public.

Temple Church

Master's House

The Temple c1350 and c1500 onwards

K4d

Fleet Street and Victoria Embankment
⊖ Temple

With its many gated and controlled entrances, the Temple is an exclusive English institution dating back to the fourteenth century, when it was leased to students of law by the Order of St John. At the Dissolution the Temple reverted to the Crown, and Templar lands on the west side of the Fleet became the site of Henry VIII's Bridewell Palace. In 1608 the Temple was leased by James I to the Benches of the Inner and Middle Temple. Its position, midway between the merchants' City of London and the royal City of Westminster, is no coincidence.

There is now no visible distinction between the Middle Temple (to the west) and the Inner Temple (to the east), and the buildings are linked by a labyrinth of passageways and courts almost as complex as the legal system they encompass. There was much destruction in the Second World War, and many buildings have been either renovated or replaced. A leisurely walk is the best way to appreciate the area.

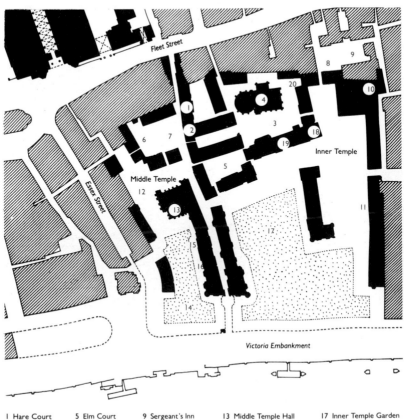

1 Hare Court	5 Elm Court	9 Sergeant's Inn	13 Middle Temple Hall	17 Inner Temple Garden
2 Pump Court	6 Essex Court	10 Niblett Hall	14 Middle Temple Garden	18 Inner Temple Library
3 Church Court	7 Brick Court	11 King's Bench Walk	15 Middle Temple Treasury	19 Inner Temple Hall
4 Temple Church	8 Mitre Court	12 Fountain Court	16 Middle Temple Library	20 Master's House

Plan of Inner and Middle Temple

Westminster Hall 1394–1402   K5n
St Margaret Street,
Parliament Square SW1
Henry Yevele, mason; Hugh Herland,
carpenter
⊖Westminster
The Hall replaced that built in 1097 by
William Rufus, while the Tower was being
finished at the other end of London; only
some eleventh- and twelfth-century masonry survives of the original. Richard II's
rebuilding involved the construction of a
spectacular hammerbeam roof with
massive timbers: restored after fires and
bombings, it survives as London's earliest
example of this kind of roof. All the
openings in the extremely thick walls
have been altered from the original. See
also Eltham Palace X1 and Guildhall L7.

Old Hall

Gatehouse

Lincoln's Inn WC2 c1400   K6d
⊖Chancery Lane
Lincoln's Inn, between Street's Law
Courts K106 and Lincoln's Inn Fields, is
one of London's three districts now
devoted to the law (the others are the
Temple K5 and Gray's Inn G6). The
original nucleus of the district was a
Dominican friary (1221–76), later the Earl
of Lincoln's house, which in the fourteenth century became a hostel for
lawyers. The lawyers' offices are now in a
number of buildings of all ages, loosely
arranged around four connected spaces,
forming a delightfully picturesque ensemble like the colleges of Oxford or
Cambridge.
The **Gatehouse** (1518) has massive doors
in a central, four-centred arch. Much of
the red brickwork patterned with blue
diapers is original, as are the doors, but
the windows were inserted in the seventeenth century. It leads to the east
court and **Old Buildings** beyond, a
collection of picturesque and turreted
brick houses of the early sixteenth and

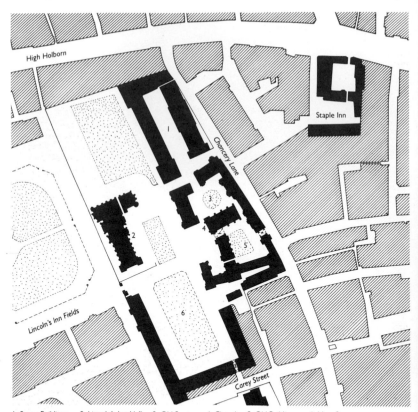

I Stone Buildings   2 Lincoln's Inn Hall   3 Old Square   4 Chapel   5 Old Buildings   6 New Square

seventeenth centuries. The north side of the courtyard is formed by the stone **Chapel** (1619–23), from the curious period in English architecture when late Perpendicular Gothic coexisted with continental classical imports (usually Tuscan, as here, until Inigo Jones showed how to do the other orders). Note the unusual vaulted ground floor.

St Margaret, Westminster   K7n
founded 1120–40, rebuilt 1480–1523
Parliament Square SW1
⊖Westminster
The 'parish church' of the House of Commons since the seventeenth century, St Margaret's is dwarfed by neighbouring Westminster Hall and Westminster Abbey. The church is a strange mixture of late Perpendicular Gothic and eighteenth-century Gothick. The nave and aisles, although restored in the eighteenth and nineteenth centuries, are original. In 1735–7 John James rebuilt the tower in the Gothick style of William Kent, and in 1758 Kenton Couse added an apse, which was altered by S P Cockerell in 1799–82. The degree to which this small church has been renovated and extended over the years (the interior was restored by Giles Gilbert Scott in 1877, for instance) and the lavish inventory of its fittings befit its national status and promi-

The **Old Hall** (1492), bay-windowed and buttressed, was the living room of the original residential community of lawyers. Its interior furnishings are of the seventeenth century. The thirteenth-century arch between the Hall and the Chapel is re-set from the original hall. See also New Square and Taylor's extraordinary Stone Buildings K61.

nent site in Parliament Square. Samuel Pepys, John Milton and William Shakespeare are among those who have been married here.

Henry VII's Chapel K8n
Westminster Abbey 1503–12
Parliament Square
Robert Vertue(?)
⊖ Westminster

While Bramante was designing the first centralized Renaissance plan for St Peter's in Rome, England's last Tudor kings, Henry VII and Henry VIII, built King's College Chapel, Cambridge, the Chapel of St George at Windsor, and this, London's finest complete late Perpendicular chapel. Widely spaced piers support the extraordinary fan-vaulted, cusped and pierced vault and define the nave, returning at the east end to make an apse in the shape of half a hexagon. Very large windows span between them so that the interior is like a brightly lit cage, combining practical and elegant engineering with a taste for intense, busy decoration. Most of the original extensive statuary has survived, although it has lost its bright colour.

On the outside the buttresses supporting

the vault are exposed, but are pierced and carved to reduce their structural effect. The outer piers, carrying the load from the buttresses, are folded, panelled and crowned with playful turrets which originally carried gilded weathervanes.

St James's Park SW1 K9
from 16th century
⊖ Charing Cross, Westminster,
St James's Park

Like so many of central London's parks, St James's was originally Crown land, enclosed by Henry VIII as hunting grounds for St James's Palace. It was remodelled in French style under Charles II, with a straight, tree-lined canal and the first setting-out of the Mall, and opened to the public. The park's present picturesque arrangement dates from Nash's work of 1828; he converted the canal into an irregular lake which, like that of Regent's Park, is now a sanctuary for resident and visiting wildfowl.

St James's Palace 1530s K10i
Cleveland Row, Marlborough
Gate SW1
⊖ Green Park

The Palace is another of Henry VII's building projects – he emerges as the monarch who shaped more than any other the future pattern of central London, even more than Nash's patron, George IV. The original Palace had four courts, and while fire and rebuilding have now reduced these to two, the outdoor Tudor work is all visible from the street, most notably the toy-like gateway to Cleveland Row. The state rooms, which face south and can be seen over the wall to the Mall, were rebuilt in 1703, possibly by Wren.

Gough Square and K11d
alleys Hind Court,
Bolt Court and St Dunstan's Court
17th century
off Fleet Street EC4
⊖ Blackfriars

A remarkable network of pedestrian alleys winding between modest three- and four-storey buildings; the most notable is the seventeenth-century house in which Dr Johnson lived from 1748–59.

Dr Johnson's house

Banqueting House 1619　　　　K12j
Whitehall SW1
Inigo Jones
⊖ Westminster

Jones's first work, the Queen's House U2 at Greenwich, stood alone. Three years later the Banqueting House started James I's ambitious plan for the rebuilding of Whitehall. When first built, it stood among a medieval and Elizabethan jumble of small-scale buildings: its startling newness in this setting is unimaginable today, when the surrounding buildings are faced in the same fine Portland stone. Jones is credited with having introduced the material to London and first used it here, perhaps in imitation of the white stone with which Palladio's urban palaces were covered. The building is a box with two levels: the lower a crypt for the King's less formal parties, the upper a sumptuous room for masques and banquets. This is one of London's great seventeenth-century rooms; a double cube 17 m × 34 m × 17 m (55 ft × 110 ft × 55 ft) with a flat ceiling. The room's only features are the gallery, the fine Ionic porch to the entrance and the decoration of two orders – Ionic below, Corinthian above, as on the outside. The panelled ceiling was painted by Rubens in 1634–6 and, like the decoration in Palladio's buildings, appears today to have a robust gaiety which the architecture denies.

The exterior owes much to Vicenza, but perhaps in Jones's hand English versions of Palladio were becoming more correct than those of the master, although its crispness is due in part to Sir John Soane's refacing of 1829.

Queen's Chapel 1623–7　　　　K13i
Marlborough Road SW1
Inigo Jones
⊖ Green Park, St James's Park

The chapel was built for James I's wife Queen Anne, and belongs to St James's Palace – Marlborough Road was cut through to the Mall in the early nineteenth century. With the Queen's House U2 at Greenwich, and the Banqueting House K12, it is part of Jones's successful campaign to drag English architecture into the (Italian) sixteenth century, and a marvellously pure work. The interior is a double cube volume, the coffered ceiling a segmental tunnel vault, and the whole is lit from a full width Venetian window (the first in England) at the east end. The exterior has the same primitive quality as St Paul, Covent Garden K15, the front having a simple

pediment over stucco walls reinforced with Portland stone quoins.

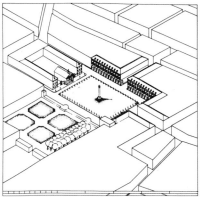

Covent Garden Piazza WC2   K14c
1631
Inigo Jones
⊖ Covent Garden

Covent Garden is one of London's more romantic districts, associated with the opera, Pygmalion, and (until 1974) London's principal fruit and vegetable market. Architecturally it is significant because the piazza was London's first real square, built under the patronage of one of the great estates which reshaped London in the following 250 years.

The land was formerly a convent garden, belonging to the Abbey of St Peter. After Henry VIII's confiscation of all land belonging to the monasteries in 1552, Covent Garden was given to the first Earl of Bedford. The idea of a residential square is attributed to the fourth Earl, who in 1631 commissioned Inigo Jones to produce plans for the square. Bedford apparently knew the Place Royale in Paris (the present Place des Vosges) built by Henri IV twenty years earlier. However, Inigo

Jones's proposal was classical, unlike the Place Royale, and its origins were Italian (as the name 'Piazza' suggests). The square of individual houses behind the continuous classical façade was very successful, and inhabited by the highest society in London. The façades are like the walls of a big public room, governed by the large temple of St Paul K15. In 1671 the Earl obtained the right to hold a daily vegetable market, and by the end of the century the square was no longer a respectable residential area. The arcades, however, remained so popular that the word piazza came to be associated with them rather than with the square itself.

The central market building K81 (1831) has been lovingly restored, but its demolition and the restoration of the Piazza, which has kept its original proportions through several rebuildings, might have been better. The 'post-modern' garden centre in the north-east corner is by Terry Farrell (1982).

St Paul, Covent Garden   K15g
1631–8
Covent Garden Piazza WC2
Inigo Jones
⊖ Covent Garden

The monumental portico to this Etruscan temple, with projecting timber beams forming the pediment and eaves, constitutes the headpiece – a shelter and meeting place – to Jones's original Covent Garden Piazza K14. It is not the main door to the Church of St Paul: this is through Inigo Place off Bedford Street to the west. Whether Jones intended this deceit (following Scamozzi's idealized illustrations of urban Etruscan temples), or whether, as contemporary evidence suggests, the church was planned originally with the altar at the west end and was revised following ecclesiastical objections, is not clear. In any event Jones's famous saying, 'You shall have the handsomest barn in England', is vindicated by this revision and by the building's further modifications over the years.

In 1795 a fire gutted the interior, and in his restoration Thomas Hardwick omitted to replace the side galleries and on the exterior substituted stone for the original brick facing. It was later re-restored in brick by Henry Clutton.

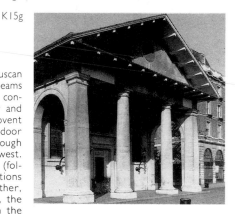

Lindsey House 1640   K16c
59–60 Lincoln's Inn Fields
WC2
Inigo Jones(?)
⊖Holborn

This is the earliest town house in London to use a giant order on a rusticated base, and is the only remaining example of the type developed in Lincoln's Inn Fields in the early 1600s. This type was to be used for at least two centuries (see also Bedford Square G12), and was repeated in stone a century later at numbers 57–8, but in Palladian taste.

The building is of brick, which was originally exposed but later stuccoed. It is in the style of Jones, but the authorship is disputed.

Following the initiative of Covent Garden Piazza K14, Lincoln's Inn Fields were London's first garden square, laid out by William Newton in 1640. By 1658 there were houses established on three sides; the fourth side (east) had already been appropriated by Lincoln's Inn. The central garden is now a public place with tennis courts and a tea pavilion.

The Mall SW1 1660 and 1906   K17i
Le Nôtre(?) and Aston Webb
⊖Charing Cross

Surprisingly, the processional route from Trafalgar Square to Buckingham Palace is less than a hundred years old, and its history is a typical example of English empiricism. The early democratic traditions of land ownership and the power of the great London estates impeded the development of royal triumphal routes, but by the end of the nineteenth century their absence was becoming a national embarrassment to the world's largest capital. The original alignment of the Mall was part of Charles II's plan for St James's Park and its avenues, laid out in 1660 and attributed to Louis XIV's great landscape gardener, Le Nôtre. Nash's Carlton House Terrace K77 was the only building with a planned, formal façade to the park; the remaining buildings along the north edge (Marlborough House, Schomberg House, St James's Palace and Lancaster House) all have an informal, low-key

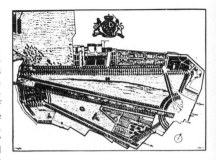

relationship to it. Until 1900 a narrow and unimportant street called Spring Gardens separated St James's Park from Trafalgar Square. It was here that Aston Webb's magnificent Admiralty Arch K127 brilliantly reconciled the shift of axis from the Mall to the Strand. With his less than magnificent façade to Buckingham Palace K76 and Rond Point K119 to the west, the capital's principal processional route was established with minimum disruption.

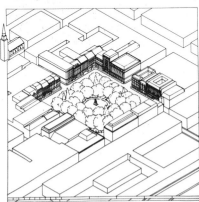

St James's Square SW1   K18e
started 1665
⊖Piccadilly Circus

London's most regular seventeenth-century square which, unlike those of eighteenth-century Bloomsbury, is actually square, with the connecting streets approaching the centre of each side (except the south). The north-south axis is on the line of Wren's St James's, Piccadilly K21, and the east-west axis was later

extended by Nash to his Theatre Royal, Haymarket K85. The streets and squares of this period were designed as settings for fashionable perambulation; here, the views from the square are stopped by either monuments or churches, while services are provided by a labyrinth of mews and alleys at the back. Unlike its contemporaries (Soho Square K24 and Red Lion Square) St James's Square has remained very fashionable.

Leicester Square WC2   K19f
1670
⊖ Leicester Square

One of London's earliest squares, laid out by the Earl of Leicester on ground known as Leicester Fields to the south of Leicester House. The square now represents the heart of London's West End, and its buildings, which have been renewed continuously, are mediocre; the Odeon (1937), with a *moderne* black tower and lettering, is the most memorable.

Golden Square W1 1673   K20e
⊖ Piccadilly Circus

Golden Square was not completely built up until the early eighteenth century. Except for numbers 11 and 21, which are original, the buildings are mostly of this century and undistinguished. The 'Cotswold' walls to its raised and redesigned garden (1952) are particularly feeble. At the centre is a diminutive statue of George II in Roman costume by Nost, erected in 1753.

St James, Piccadilly 1676–84   K21e
Piccadilly and Jermyn Street SW1
Sir Christopher Wren
⊖ Piccadilly Circus

Designed to hold 2000 people, St James is one of Wren's best known and most influential works. It was built in connection with Lord St Albans' contemporary scheme for the development of the St James's area, and the tower and general siting of the church were intended to 'stop the view' from St James's Square, when seen in perspective along Duke of York Street.

The rows of five two-tiered windows on the north and south elevations express the longitudinal plan. Although this was a practical arrangement for the Anglican church, it indicated Wren's retreat from his earlier, and more idealistic, centralized plans. Largely as a result of its economy, it was taken up by Gibbs (see St Martin-in-the-Fields K40), and through his influence was copied in many British colonies (Harrison's Christ Church, Boston, USA, of 1723, and Richard Munday's Trinity Church, Newport, USA, of 1725–6 for example). The brick exterior is restrained, with its simple stone detailing and square tower added by Wren's office in 1700; a new spire was completed in 1968 by Sir Albert Richardson. The church was badly damaged in the war and restored in 1947–54.

One rezes that St. James's Piccadilly is the only "City Church" by Wren outside of the tiny "City of London"? See St Clement Danes, K-22, p 208.

Christ Church [The Old North Church – of Paul Revere's "Midnight Ride to Lexington and Concord] in Boston's North End was designed by Boston draftsman William Price. Cornerstone laid April 1723. opened 29 Dec 1723. [Peter Harrison was the architect of King's Chapel in Boston, 1749–1754.]

St Clement Danes 1680　　　K22d
Strand WC2

Sir Christopher Wren, tower by Gibbs
1719–20

⊖ Temple

Wren's church recased some of the masonry of its predecessor, but it illustrates a
stage in his development of the section of
the two-storey church, which culminated
in the definitive St James, Piccadilly K21.
In this development the columns supporting the vault and side galleries were
progressively raised on plinths above the
fixed pews of the nave. Unique among his
churches, the aisles of St Clement's return
at the east end in semicircles. The upper
stages of the tower were added by Gibbs,
in a style owing more to the Italian
baroque (which he used in his earlier St
Mary-le-Strand K34 further west along
the Strand) than to his predecessor Wren
or to his contemporaries, the Palladians.

The church was bombed in the Second
World War, and was rebuilt as a memorial
to the Royal Air Force.

Houses 1680–1766　　　K23j
10, 11 and 12 Downing Street
SW1

⊖ Westminster

That the official residences of the Prime
Minister and the Chancellor of the
Exchequer should be unremarkable
houses in a nondescript cul-de-sac could
be regarded as a fine example of English
understatement. That the Georgian
London house can perform such a function
and acquire symbolic importance carries a
still-unlearned lesson for today's architects. The houses, all interconnecting,
have been continually altered over three
centuries: William Kent and Soane were
among those who refitted rooms. Kenton
Couse refaced them in 1766, and Raymond
Erith repaired the outsides in 1962–4.

Soho Square and　　　K24b
Greek Street W1
laid out 1681

⊖ Tottenham Court Road

Soho's two squares (the other is Golden
Square K20) were started at about the
same time, and both have now been
almost completely transformed. Soho
Square always seems gloomy. There are
two churches – St Patrick K117 and the
French Protestant church on the north
side – and few early houses. Some regret
the changes of scale since the square's
setting-out, and some admire its present
interesting diversity, as the Victorians
who contributed most to the change
would have done. The statue under the
plane trees in the centre is of Charles II by
Cibber. It was originally flanked by per-
sonifications of English rivers, which were
transferred in the 1870s to Norman
Shaw's Grims Dyke Q3.
Number 1 Greek Street (the House of St
Barnabas for destitute women) turns the
corner into Soho Square. Built in 1746 it is
the most distinguished building in the
street and has very fine interiors. The

exterior is restrained, with large, simple
window openings. Two obelisks stand
either side of the doorway, added by
Richard Beckford MP after he bought the
house in 1754; by the mid-eighteenth
century stone consoled doorcases and
obelisks had become fashionable for grand
houses. Numbers 50 (1736) and 48
(1741–2) are also noteworthy.

Seven Dials WC2 K25b
laid out 1690
Thomas Neale
⊖ Leicester Square

A few houses survive of this early and, for London, rare example of French street planning. The layout consists of a rectangle bordered by Shelton Street, Neal Street and Tower Street, and the later Shaftesbury Avenue, crossed at right angles by Mercer Street and Shorts Gardens and on the diagonal by Earlham Street and Monmouth Street. In the 1980s the crossing was consolidated by undistinguished rebuilding on the corners on the west side and substantial work on the many late seventeenth and early eighteenth-century houses of the 'Comyn Ching triangle' K175. Finally, a replica by Whitfield Partners of the column which

originally stood at its centre was erected, complete with new sundials.

New Square c1690 K26d
Lincoln's Inn WC2
Henry Serle
⊖ Chancery Lane

This remarkably well preserved early 'square' (actually a north-facing U-shape) was built between Carey Street, to which it is connected by an arched passage, and Lincoln's Inn. It has always been occupied by lawyers, originally as flats, now as offices, their names painted on boards at the foot of the staircase. The ensemble represents an important stage in the development of the London square. There is no private open space (gardens, back yards or mews) and on the west the houses back directly on to the pavement of Serle Street. This arrangement is characteristic of the colleges of Oxford and Cambridge (perhaps one of the origins of the London

square) and it suits the present semi-collegiate habits of the legal profession.

Schomberg House c1698 K27i
Pall Mall SW1
⊖ Charing Cross

Built for the German Duke of Schomberg, this is a rare surviving example of a house of the period which is not in the routine terrace format. Schomberg House is built of the customary brown brick with red trim, but has tall windows of Dutch proportions (abandoned by the eighteenth century, but revived by the Shavians), and decoration derived from contemporary French sources. The central porch with caryatids is later.

St Anne, Soho K28b
Late 17th century, tower 1801–3, 1991
Wardour Street W1
S P Cockerell; the Westwood Practice
⊖ Leicester Square

The outer walls and tower are all that survived the Second World War. The nave, which remained a car park for over forty years, has now been replaced by two wings of residential building. The yellow-brick tower of the church has at its apex an eccentrically bulbous form from which bulge four clock faces. The garden, raised above street level on the west side, is an unexpectedly tranquil place.

Savile Row W1 K29e
laid out early 18th century
⊖Piccadilly Circus

Laid out soon after Burlington House K36 was built, the streets north of the house were inhabited by many of Burlington's circle. William Kent lived in Savile Row, of which numbers 3–17 are the only originals to survive. The street is now known as the centre of London's bespoke tailoring trade, whose activities can be viewed from the pavements – the tailors work near the basement windows lit from the 'areas' typical of Georgian London. See also Old Burlington Street K43.

Greycoat School 1701 K30m
Greycoat Place SW1
⊖Victoria, St James's Park

Another example of early philanthropy (see also the near contemporary Blewcoat School K32 in Caxton Street). Following extensive damage in the war, the charming centre section, with its lantern and wings, was rebuilt in twentieth-century Queen Anne style. The miniature buildings are a reminder of the scale of early eighteenth-century London. Note the two wooden statues of charity children.

Queen Anne's Gate and K31n
Old Queen Street SW1
started 1704
⊖St James's Park

The best and most complete street of regular houses of its date in London. In 1704 Queen Square was developed in an L-shape, entered from Broadway and with a gate into St James's Park. Although the widths of the houses vary, they are all regular in design and built in brown brick with stone bands marking the division of the storeys. The decoration is pre-pattern book, as can be seen from the intricate carved rustic foliage surrounding the doorways, and the pendants, arches and frieze (see numbers 17, 19, 23 and 25 and opposite numbers 26, 28 and 30). In the south-east corner of the square stands a statue of Queen Anne, to the east of which the character of the street changes, becoming more uniform (owing to the emergence of pattern books). On the south side numbers 5–13 (1773–5) have doorways marked by Doric pilasters carrying pediments with open architraves. On the north side numbers 14–24, of the same date, have magnificent bow windows facing the park. Also of the same date is 34 Old Queen Street, the narrow eastward continuation of Queen Anne's Gate. 9–11 Old Queen Street are earlier and more modestly detailed.

Blewcoat School 1709 K32m
23 Caxton Street SW1
⊖St James's Park

A marooned relic, this tiny elegant brick schoolhouse was built as a charitable act by a brewer. It is one of the earliest examples of this building type extant in London. Now, stranded among new offices, it is a reminder of the minuscule scale of the early eighteenth-century city. The school is owned by the National Trust.

Marlborough House K33i
1709–11, 1861–3
Pall Mall SW1
Sir Christopher Wren,
Sir James Pennethorne
⊖ Green Park

In gratitude for his victories against the Dutch and the French, Queen Anne commissioned Vanbrugh and Hawksmoor to build the first Duke of Marlborough a monumental palace at Blenheim, and Wren to build his London residence on the Mall. Wren's Marlborough House has been much altered: in the nineteenth century the original house, with thirteen bays to the south front, was extended by two extra floors and further stables and outbuildings to the east. To the north of the main entrance court is a fine red-brick screen of arched recesses and pediments. In 1861–3 the north side of the original house was almost totally concealed by a range of rooms with a deep porch, added by Pennethorne for the Prince of Wales. The interiors were mostly altered in the nineteenth century, but the salon, the almost cube-shaped principal room, still has wall paintings of the Battle of Blenheim by Laguerre. Pennethorne added the balcony to this room, where formerly there had been a screen of columns.

St Mary-le-Strand 1714–17 K34c
Strand and Aldwych WC2
James Gibbs
⊖ Temple

Though twenty years his junior, Gibbs was Hawksmoor's working contemporary, and from 1713–15 acted as his fellow surveyor to the Commissioners' fifty new churches. His architectural training had been in Rome, unlike Hawksmoor's, and the body of this delicate little church is clearly derived from Mannerist models – the porch from Cortona's Santa Maria della Pace. The tower, not part of the original design, owes more to Wren. Gibbs quickly changed his style after this early effort and produced Palladian designs more likely to appeal to the Whigs in power. The original setting, cramped between houses, was destroyed in the Edwardian 'Improvements' to Kingsway and Aldwych, and the church is now a large traffic island (GLC road engineers please note). See also St Martin-in-the-Fields K40.

St John 1714–28   K35n
Smith Square SW1
Thomas Archer
⊖Westminster

Built at the same time as the square which
it still dominates, the church marks an
extreme of baroque London: its design
owes as much to Rome as to Wren.
Externally, the plan appears to be a Greek
cross, but the north and south 'transepts',
marked by wild fractured pediments, are
porticoes to the entrances. The interior is
rectangular, the east and west ends having
huge Venetian windows. Burned in 1758
and bombed in 1941, the church has been
rebuilt as a concert hall. The four towers
– drums with circular entablatures over the
corner columns, topped by pineapples –
have been much criticized; we like them.

See also St Paul, Deptford U6.

Burlington House   K36e
refaced and remodelled
1715–17;
extended and remodelled in 19th century
Piccadilly W1
Colen Campbell and others
⊖Piccadilly Circus

Richard Boyle, third Earl of Burlington
(1694–1753), first visited Italy at the age of
twenty, and on his return immediately
employed Colen Campbell to remodel the
façade of the family house in Piccadilly.
Gibbs, who had been working on curved
colonnades (demolished in 1728) connecting the house to the street, was sacked.
Campbell became the first member of
Burlington's circle of artists; William
Kent, at first as painter, and the sculptor
Rysbrack were to follow. In 1715
Campbell had begun to publish *Vitruvius
Britannicus*, his illustrated descriptions of
British 'regular buildings' – those showing
the direct influence of Antiquity, Inigo
Jones, or Palladio. Leoni's English trans-
lation of Palladio's *Quattro Libri* was
published in the same year. The remodelling of the first Earl's seventeenth-century
house was therefore the beginning of
Burlington's successful campaign to shift
English architecture from the pragmatic
baroque of the Wren school towards a
more correct Italian (ancient Roman and
sixteenth-century Vicentine) – a style
judged appropriate to George I's new
Hanoverian dynasty. Campbell's two-
storey façade was based on Palladio's
Palazzo Porto-Colleoni in Vicenza, but
with details from Jones. It was in Portland
stone, of seven bays with a rusticated
ground floor, an Ionic order above, and

Venetian windows in the projecting wings
at either end.

The radical, cool elegance of the original
design can now be appreciated only in
drawings of the period, for at the beginning of the nineteenth century a series of
remodellings was started, and in 1867 the
building became the Royal Academy's
headquarters. The interior was then
remodelled by Robert Smirke, who also
added the present storey with its statues
of artists. The arched building fronting
Piccadilly was added in 1873 by Banks and
Barry. The most recent addition, the new
Sackler Galleries by Foster Associates, of
1991, provides three top-lit vaulted
rooms at roof level. They are reached by a
new glass lift and stair set in what had
become a light well. The result is a masterly synthesis of space and fine modern
detailing, which is effortlessly juxtaposed
against the classical masonry.

Arcade 1716–17   K37i
Stable Yard, St James's
Palace SW1
Nicholas Hawksmoor
⊖Green Park

One of Hawksmoor's few surviving
secular buildings, this little arcade in stock
brick, with a stone trim and turrets at the
corners, was ruined in 1980 by the
Department of the Environment's crude
restoration. The inside was gutted, and
the exterior pointing in modern mortar
clumsily smudged.

Smith Square,
Lord North Street and
Cowley Street SW1 c1720

K38n

⊖Westminster

Dominated by Archer's magnificent church K35, Smith Square takes its name from Sir James Smith, who developed the square and streets around. The south and east sides were damaged in the Second World War and unfortunately redeveloped as twelve-storey offices, which have destroyed the relationship between the church and the square. With the exception of numbers 1 and 2, rebuilt after the war, the north side is original, as are the ironwork and lampholders. Numbers 6–9 are almost identical with each other and date from 1726, and 36 is by Lutyens in his neo-Georgian style. On the north-west corner of the square is a neo-Georgian house (1930) by Oliver Hill.

Lord North Street and Cowley Street are

almost complete early Georgian streets, like rows of dolls' houses in brown brick with red-brick dressings to windows and arches.

Houses c1720

K39d

14–15 Tooks Court,
off Cursitor Street EC4

⊖Chancery Lane

Two unexpectedly grand small houses, both of three storeys and three bays with segmental window heads of rubbed brick. The grand elements are the three-storey Ionic pilasters *in antis*, marking the party walls, and the ornate rubbed and carved brick cornice to number 15 (known as Dickens' House), which also retains its original mansard roof.

St Martin-in-the-Fields

K40f

1721–6

Trafalgar Square WC2
James Gibbs

⊖Charing Cross

Gibbs' synthesis of influences from Rome, Wren and Palladio here produced a type which has had widespread and continuing influence in the English-speaking world. The interior scheme was derived from Wren, but improved on its models – the giant order is raised on pedestals and the galleries firmly relegated. The exquisite plasterwork of the ceiling is by the Italian craftsmen Artari and Bagutti. Outside, Gibbs provided the definitive model for the relationships between the tower and the steeple and the portico. In his introduction to the exterior of the round-headed window edged with dies (to be known as 'Gibbs surrounds') and of the coupled columns at the corners, he considerably extended the architectural repertoire for the sides and backs of churches. Because of its position, St Martin's is one of the few London churches that still gives the Italian feeling of being *used*: the steps are good for resting on and the portico provides shelter from the rain.

James Gibbs (1682-1754) - a Scot, born in Aberdeen, a Roman Catholic, and a Tory. St Martin-in-the-Fields is his masterpiece - it was widely copied in the American colonies because his Book of Architecture (1728).

College, Westminster   K41n
School 1722–30
Little Dean's Yard SW1
Lord Burlington
⊖Westminster

Gutted in the Second World War and much altered – the ground-floor arcade has been glazed in and the first-floor windows, originally blank, have been opened up – Burlington's only surviving early work in London nevertheless shows his fastidious interpretation of his models: Palladio, via Scamozzi and Inigo Jones. The flat, fifteen-bay stone façade is proportioned 4:1, but the rainwater pipes make this difficult to read.

House 1726–8   K42e
4 St James's Square SW1
Edward Shepherd
⊖Piccadilly Circus

The five-bay elevation to the square is strangely horizontal, a consequence of the deep band of brickwork above the first-floor windows. The delicate balance of vertical and horizontal which was later to mark Georgian compositions is here absent.

Old Burlington Street W1   K43e
started c1730
⊖Piccadilly Circus

Almost completely rebuilt, and now a pleasant mixture of styles and uses, the architectural interest of the area north of Burlington House is now one of association rather than of buildings. Burlington laid out the streets up to Clifford Street, and many of the artists he worked with or patronized (Colen Campbell and William Kent for example) took or built houses in them. Numbers 30 and 31 are original, with a fine lampholder and ironwork to the doorway of number 31, but the stucco surrounds to the windows look heavy and Victorian. See also Savile Row K29.

Pickering Place 1731   K44i
off St James's Street SW1
⊖Green Park

A surprising tiny enclave of houses arranged round a paved court, reached down a timber-lined passage from St James's Street: it would be less surprising in a cathedral town than in the centre of London.

St Giles-in-the-Fields K45b
1731–3
St Giles High Street WC2
Henry Flitcroft
⊖Tottenham Court Road

The church is a standard eighteenth-century galleried box for preaching and being preached at. Its interior arrangement follows the model of Wren's St James, Piccadilly K21, and its vault that of Gibbs' St Martin-in-the-Fields K40. Flitcroft was a clerk in the Office of Works which Wren had left in 1719, and Gibbs' designs had been published in 1728.

The original wooden model stands in a niche in the vestibule under the tower, and Flitcroft's name is carved above the west door under the pediment. The arch outside the west door was built in 1800, incorporating a sooty wood-carving of the Resurrection of the Dead (1687).

Treasury Building 1733–6, K46j
1824–7, 1844
Whitehall SW1
William Kent; Sir John Soane,
Sir Charles Barry
⊖Westminster

The symmetrical flanking wings and pavilions of Kent's original design unfortunately were never built, but the central building has great Palladian elegance. The façade is curiously mannered and vertical, with overall stone rustication and a diminutive portico of four Ionic columns on the second floor. Inside there are three rooms of note on the first floor, two facing north and the third to the west. Their design – unusually for Kent – is very simple: restrained plaster panelling to the ceilings, and simple coves and marble fireplaces. The building overlooks Horse Guards Parade and can also be reached from Treasury Green via Treasury Passage.

In 1824–7 Soane built a new Board of Trade and Privy Council facing Whitehall. The building proved too small, and was dismantled in 1844, to be replaced by Sir Charles Barry's new Treasury, incorpor

ating Soane's columns and frieze. Fortunately the interior still has Soane's remarkable entrance halls from Downing Street and Whitehall. The modest relief of Barry's façade is typically early Victorian, showing the insecurity of Victorian neoclassicism in the face of neo-Gothic's growing popularity. It has far less authority than Soane's designs for the same building two decades earlier.

Houses 1734 K47e
9, 10 and 11 St James's
Square SW1
Henry Flitcroft
⊖Green Park

Flitcroft was one of Lord Burlington's circle, so it was appropriate that he should use Palladian for these large houses, whose spare refined façades make the earlier number 4 K42 look clumsy by comparison.

West Towers   K48n
Westminster Abbey 1735·45
The Sanctuary SW1
Nicholas Hawksmoor
⊖Westminster
Hawksmoor's last public work before he died in 1745 is one of the two examples of his Gothick style in London – the other is his tower for St Michael, Cornhill. The flatness of the corner buttresses, their interruption by broad string-courses, and the oval arch over the clock betray the towers' eighteenth-century, rather than medieval, origins. See also Westminster Abbey K3.

Houses 1736 and 1740–55   K49e
16 and 22 Arlington Street
SW1
James Gibbs and William Kent
⊖Green Park
Number 16 has a plain brick elevation to Green Park. It is now part of the Overseas Club, entered from Park Place, but the main entrance used to be through the big arch at the end of Arlington Street. Number 22, Wimbourne House, has been partly obscured by a new seven-storey office building, and Kent's interiors are inaccessible. Its interest lies in the unusual plan: it has two large rooms of similar size with bay windows facing the park; and, on the entrance side, a vaulted passage along the north side of the filled-in court connects the front door to the street.

The Horse Guards 1745–55   K50j
Whitehall SW1
William Kent, John Vardy
⊖Charing Cross, Westminster
Built by John Vardy after Kent's death in 1748, this building demonstrates the dryness of English Palladianism when not in Burlington's hands. Its picturesque composition is built up from arched openings housing either Venetian or pedimented windows, both set in rust-icated masonry without columns. The façade to the Parade, through the arch from Whitehall, with the backs of Downing Street to the south and the Admiralty to the north, now forms an impressive background for pageantry like Trooping the Colour. It is scandalous that this fine open space is cluttered during the week with the cars of privileged government officials. On the Whitehall side, the Horse Guard is changed twice a day.

Spencer House 1752–4   K51i
27 St James's Place SW1
John Vardy; altered by Sir Robert Taylor
1772 and Henry Holland c1785
⊖ Green Park

This fine double-fronted mansion for the
Earl of Spencer is strictly Palladian; the
entrance faces the confines of St James's
Place, and a rhetorical façade gives onto
the open spaces of Green Park. Of the two
façades the elevation to the park is more
memorable and public, having a rusticated
ground floor, and an upper floor of seven
bays separated by engaged Tuscan
columns, with a five-bay pediment. The
entrance hall, with rounded corners and
plaster ceiling, and the staircase, with Ionic
pilasters and a tunnel vault, are especially
fine. The latter was an alteration by Sir
Robert Taylor in about 1772, and Henry
Holland remodelled the rooms to the
west of the entrance in 1785. In 1991 a
restoration of the whole house was completed. This included the decoration and
furnishing of nine of the state rooms and
these can be visited.

Dover House 1754–8, 1787   K52j
Whitehall SW1
James Paine, Henry Holland
⊖ Charing Cross

The original house was built as a private
residence by James Paine, one of the most
prolific Palladian architects. When the
Duke of York bought the house in 1787 he
appointed Henry Holland to add new
façades, with the result that the courtyard
was filled in, and of the original only the
inner block now remains. With this
transformation of the façade Holland gave
Whitehall its finest architecture (excepting Inigo Jones' Banqueting House K12),
modest in scale and very un-English. The
Greek Ionic portico flanked by attached
columns and the rusticated wall strongly
resemble the French *hôtel particulier* of
the early eighteenth century. The domed
entrance hall (abstract and unorna-
mented, like the early work of Ledoux) is
formed by a circle of Tuscan columns in
pink marble, behind which rises a staircase with an intermediate landing. The
central dome is glazed, creating the
illusion that the vestibule is an exterior
space, and illuminating the brilliant white
marble floor, patterned with radiating
black insets.

House 1756–60   K53n
6–7 Old Palace Yard SW1
John Vardy
⊖ Westminster
Portland stone, Palladian, and now
stranded out of context.

Admiralty Screen

Admiralty House

Admiralty Screen 1759–61 K54j
Whitehall SW1
Robert Adam
⊖Charing Cross
In 1758, after returning from Rome and a visit to Diocletian's Palace at Spalato, Adam set up in private practice, and his first work at the age of thirty-one was a public one. The screen hides the court-yard of Ripley's feeble Admiralty from Whitehall. The seriousness of its correct Roman Doric order anticipates none of

Adam's departure from Palladianism to-wards a new delicacy, which is so evident in the screens at Osterley T11 and Syon T10. Decoration is restricted to the seahorses on top of the piers flanking the central arch, and to the sculptured pedi-ments of the astylar end-pavilions. To the south of the Admiralty is S P Cockerell's **Admiralty House** (1786–8), which has good but inaccessible interiors and pre-sents only its side to Whitehall.

Shop ex Fribourg and Treyer K55f
c1760–70
34 Haymarket SW1
⊖Piccadilly Circus
A very fine and rare example of a mid-eighteenth-century shop front, now marooned in an increasingly seedy West End. The house dates from about 1760 and the shop front and its elegant internal screen were added later (about 1770). Fribourg and Treyer, the tobacconists who originally occupied the shop, have recently moved.

Lichfield House 1764–6 K56e
15 St James's Square SW1
James 'Athenian' Stuart, interiors Samuel Wyatt, 1791–4
⊖Piccadilly Circus
James Stuart visited Greece with Revett in 1751–3, surveyed the ancient monuments, and in 1762 began publishing the results as *The Antiquities of Athens*. Built shortly afterwards, this suave stone façade capped with a single pediment uses Greek motifs. The capitals of the Ionic giant order are exact copies of those of the Erechtheum.

Boodles Club 1765   K57e
28 St James's Street W1
J Crunden
⊖ Green Park

The London club is an eighteenth-century invention, with its origins in the coffee houses and inns of the previous century. Boodles – named after the original proprietor – is one of the best and earliest examples of the type. Designed in the style of Robert Adam, it is the only building in London attributed to Crunden. The fine yellow-brick façade to St James's Street, with a central arched Venetian window and flanking porches, represents the main 'upper room' of the club. The interior, partly remodelled by Papworth, is also good. The modern buildings for *The Economist* next door K170 draw Boodles into their composition of small towers on a raised podium, and the new, faceted bay window is built on to the club's newly exposed wall as a gesture of continuity.

Original engraving

The Adelphi 1768–74   K58g
Adelphi Terrace; John Adam, Adam and Robert Streets WC2
James, John and Robert Adam
⊖ Charing Cross

Only a few fragments remain of one of eighteenth-century London's most ambitious and important urban designs, but these are of such high quality that its history is given here. In 1768, the Adams, concerned that their work, with the exception of the early Screen K54, had been either outside London or domestic and private, became developers. They leased land between the Strand and the north bank of the Thames, where they built a quay and four storeys of set-back vaults for warehousing. On the platform created by the roofs of the vaults (nowadays it would be called a 'deck'), they raised four streets, two parallel to the river and two at right angles. Set back from the edge of the platform, a terrace of eleven four-storey brick houses faced the river, its ends closed by the projection of the terraces in Robert and Adam Streets. The centres and ends of the terraces projected slightly, and were decorated in the new style with flat bands of stucco, both horizontal and vertical, and pilasters with sunken panels of very pretty honeysuckle strands. These can be seen in 1–3 Robert Street, all that remains of the composition to the Thames. Even better is 7 Adam Street where, because the dark brick has not been cleaned, the light stucco carries the architecture's prettiness and also the Adams' strange, sometimes chill, archaeological neo-classicism. Further fragments of the scheme remain on either side of this last house and at 4–6 John Street, next to the Royal Society of Arts building. This has a stone façade (a serious Ionic order and pediment) and some good original interiors, particularly the library.

The Adelphi was disliked by the contemporary architectural establishment, headed by Sir William Chambers, but liked by the artistic (for example Garrick, who in 1772 moved in). The houses did not sell and the Adams were saved from bankruptcy only by disposing of them by lottery. Chambers went on in the same decade to design Somerset House K62, using the Adelphi's format, and the Adams to speculate again at Portland Place F3. In 1872 many of the houses were stuccoed, and in 1936 the central block was demolished for the present offices. An LCC blue plaque on 9 Robert Street records that 'Robert Adam, Thomas Hood, John Galsworthy, Sir James Barrie and other eminent writers and artists lived here'. The street names, given by the brothers themselves, record their achievement. 'Adelphi' is the Greek for 'brothers'.

The Albany 1770–4, 1803–4   K59e
Piccadilly and
Burlington Gardens W1
Sir William Chambers, Henry Holland
⊖ Piccadilly Circus

Built for Lord Melbourne and originally known as Melbourne House, the Albany has two approaches, one from Piccadilly and the other from Burlington Gardens, and is the product of two architects of the golden age of late English Palladianism. Seen from Piccadilly through a formal gateway, the house is set behind a fore-court, on either side of which is a two-storey nine-bay building. The principal façade is of seven bays with a projecting three-bay pediment. The general arrange-ment of the house is like a Parisian *hôtel particulier*, or miniature palace in the town, but here the square openings in a brick façade are relatively restrained.

The Albany's most original feature is at the back where, instead of the garden of the Parisian *hôtel*, there is an elongated court giving access to a series of apart-ments. In 1803 Henry Holland converted the house into apartments and built two parallel rows of chambers leading to a gated entrance off Burlington Gardens. The apartments are approached by a

covered way down the middle of the court, branching off to a series of en-trances and terminating in the back of the original house, where common dining facilities were available for residents. The buildings are stuccoed, with segmentally arched windows, and the elevation to Burlington Gardens is of one-storey lodges either side of the fine entrance gate, also by Holland. One of the lodges is still a florist's for the residents; the other formerly a cigar shop, is now a gallery.

House 1772   K60e
37 Dover Street W1
Sir Robert Taylor
⊖ Green Park

Set between two lower stuccoed houses, the tall house built by the Bishop of Ely for himself looks as authentically Vicentine as a work from a second-generation Pal-ladian architect should. The very high first floor alters the expected balance of solid and void in the façade, emphasizing the flatness against which the precise archi-tectural features are placed. The central medallion between the first and second floors bears the Bishop's coat of arms. The interiors are much altered.

Stone Buildings 1774–80   K61d
Chancery Lane and
Lincoln's Inn WC2
Sir Robert Taylor, Philip Hardwick
(additions in 1842)
⊖ Chancery Lane

One of the best examples of Palladianism in a public building in London, built entirely of Portland stone, with a two-storey rusticated base, above which are two plain storeys topped by a cornice and open balustrade. The west front to Lincoln's Inn Gardens is impressively restrained, and the ends are articulated by projecting pedimented pavilions with giant Corinthian columns. The internal court (91 m × 18 m/300 ft × 60 ft) has two entrances from Chancery Lane: a gate, and a concealed pedestrian passage in the north-east corner. The centre of the east side is stone-faced, while the ranges either side are of brick, giving the court a lopsided emphasis. The offices' moated entrances, complete with cast iron lamp-holders, are particularly fine.

Somerset House 1776–86, K62g
1830–5, 1856
Strand, Lancaster Place and
Victoria Embankment WC2
Sir William Chambers, Sir Robert
Smirke, Sir James Pennethorne
⊖Temple

Somerset House – purpose-built offices for several government departments – offered the challenge to Sir William Chambers of designing the greatest English public building since the Royal Naval Hospital U3. Several factors increased this challenge: firstly, the need to demolish the Protector Somerset's house (1547–72) with its fine chapel (1630–5) by Inigo Jones and the magnificent riverside gallery by John Webb; secondly, the recent success of Robert Adam's Adelphi K58 upstream (Chambers was openly Adam's rival); and finally Chambers' lack of experience in the grand tradition of monumental design. His work prior to Somerset House had been concerned with smaller-scale domestic architecture for the nobility.

The Strand block and the central court were begun in 1776 and completed in 1780 and 1786 respectively. The Strand façade occupies only a third of the total site width and seems like a gatehouse to the large interior court behind. The triple-arched gateway to the court is particularly fine, and reminiscent of Le Vau's entry to the Louvre. Apart from its sheer size, 106 m × 95 m (350 ft × 310 ft), with equal emphasis on three sides and central Corinthian pavilions, the court is more like a grand square for domestic residence than a *cour d'honneur* for principal administrative offices. By London standards the river front is extremely long (244 m/800 ft), including Smirke's extension to the east for King's College and the western extension by Pennethorne. Like the Adams' Adelphi it has the repetitive imagery of a grand and dignified housing scheme. The building stood originally on large arches rising out of the river, between which Chambers positioned water gates, thereby linking the separate pavilions in the façade. When the Victoria Embankment K103 was built the building's main relationship to the river was lost.

Most of the sculpture in Somerset House was drawn by Cipriani and carved by Carlini, Wilton and Bacon, friends of Chambers. Inside there are a number of excellent rooms, whose ceilings and fireplaces (inspired by Louis XV ornamentalism) are among the finest of Chambers' decorations. While highly cultivated in parts, as a whole Somerset House is not entirely successful. English architects generally have built much more assertively when abroad (as in Lutyens' work in New Delhi and Stirling's in Germany).

In 1990 London University's Courtauld Institute moved to Somerset House. The Courtauld Gallery is open to the public and contains fine Impressionist paintings housed in the refurbished suite of rooms above the wing facing the Strand. The most splendid of these, the 'Great Room' with its huge lantern, was first used to display paintings by the Royal Academy in 1780. Although the room's architecture was carefully restored, its effect was then destroyed by the tatty new screens installed to display the present collection.

Brooks's Club 1777–8   K63e
St James's Street SW1
Henry Holland
⊖ Green Park

Holland's work is less elaborate and more scholarly than that of his rival, Adam, deriving partly from the French neoclassical tradition of Ledoux. The fine white brick façade to Brooks's, with its giant Corinthian pilasters and cornice, is scraped of any embroidery or illusion and decidedly anti-Adam. The interior is similarly restrained, the remodelled stone staircase leading, under a glass dome, to two superb rooms on the first floor and the subscription room with a coved ceiling and Venetian window. Next door, in the room with the second Venetian window, are busts of Fox and Pitt (by Nollekens), a reminder of Holland's successful association with members of the Whig hierarchy, and particularly Charles James Fox, whose career coincided with his own.

White's Club 1787–8   K64e
37–8 St James's Street SW1
James Wyatt
⊖ Green Park

The most memorable feature of Lockyer's façade to this famous club, added in 1852, is the large, round-headed central window. The banded rustication in the upper floor and oval relief panels in the garlands show French influence.

Theatre Royal 1810–12,   K65c
porch 1821, colonnade 1831
Drury Lane WC2
Benjamin Wyatt and others
⊖ Covent Garden

The London theatres of the eighteenth century regularly burned down – the present Theatre Royal is the fourth on the site. Its brick box is decorated with classical low relief. The porch and Ionic colonnade were added ten years after Wyatt's building, and the present painting scheme might be improved. The interior spaces are a rarity in London theatres: spacious, large, and with their original early nineteenth-century decoration.

Imperial War Museum   K66p
1812–15, 1839, 1989
Lambeth Road SE1
J Lewis, Sidney Smirke, Arup Associates
⊖ Lambeth North, Elephant & Castle

Ironically this building was originally the Royal Bethlehem for the Care of the Insane, or 'Bedlam', until the institution moved to Shirley in 1931. The Ionic portico and dome were added in 1838 by Sidney Smirke, the younger brother of Sir Robert. The Imperial War Museum was established by an Act of Parliament in 1920 and was to remain a rather lugubrious affair until its successful renovation by Arup & Associates in 1989. Built within the old courtyard, the new top-lit exhibition hall forms a dramatic spectacle for the arriving visitor of suspended aeroplanes and other large objects. This space also forms a focus for the four new exhi-

bition levels that surround it. The diagonal-latticed barrel-vault roof is supported by a light steel structure and contrasts convincingly with the restored heavy masonry walls of the original hospital.

If some relief is required from the military achievements of a warlike race, the museum also contains the second largest collection of twentieth-century British art in the country (some 10,000 works). This extensive collection of war artists like Stanley Spencer, Augustus John, Paul Nash, Wyndham Lewis and Eric Kennington makes a compelling and poetic statement against war. It cannot go unmentioned that the funding for this renovation was the only effective contribution made by the government to a national museum in the whole of the 1980s.

Sir John Soane's Museum   K67c
1812–34
13 Lincoln's Inn Fields WC2; 12 (1792–4) and 14 (1823–4) Lincoln's Inn Fields WC2
Sir John Soane
⊖ Holborn

A brief account of these three houses is necessary in order to understand the layout of the Museum at number 13. Number 12 was built first by Soane for himself and includes a particularly fine breakfast room with a star-shaped ceiling. It is to be opened to the public (1992) and will extend the present Museum. Number 14 was built and sold off immediately by Soane. The back half was retained, however, to be incorporated into the principal residence at number 13.

The present museum was the residence, studio and private museum of the architect Soane until his death in 1837. It is a complex and highly personal building and within its standard London house dimensions the eclectic, experimental, whimsical and, above all, illusionist preoccupations of its designer are immediately apparent: Soane was not as straight a neoclassicist as is commonly believed.

The model room has recently been reorganized and is open to the public on request. There are over one hundred architectural models, from reconstructions of sites from classical antiquity to working models for the Bank of England. The Museum also has more than 30,000 architectural drawings, some (designs for Tudor and Jacobean houses) by John Thorpe, others by Robert Adam, and a collection of etchings by contemporaries of Soane, including Piranesi. The house is

lovingly and authentically maintained, to the extent that you feel that Soane has just retired for the moment.

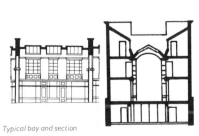

Typical bay and section

Burlington Arcade 1815–19   K68e
between Piccadilly and
Burlington Gardens W1
Samuel Ware
⊖ Green Park

This arcade, built on a narrow strip of the garden of Burlington House in the years after Waterloo, is the archetype of London's arcades, and one of the few to have remained fashionable over the years. Copied from earlier continental models (as was Nash's near-contemporary Royal Opera Arcade K69) it has a glass roof and very small, delicately detailed shops. The gross façades at the ends were added by E Beresford Pite in 1911.

Royal Opera Arcade   K69f
1816–18
connecting Charles II Street and
Pall Mall SW1
John Nash and G S Repton
⊖ Piccadilly Circus

This beautiful and modestly scaled arcade is one of London's earliest (following the French invention of the type at the end of the eighteenth century) and was once part of Nash's grand Royal Opera House on the Haymarket, which burned down in 1867. Because it was next to the opera, which needed secondary entrances, the arcade had shops on the west side only – in this it was unique. The perspective from either end conceals this imbalance: it is achieved by a series of simple vaulted bays with glass domes, which contain the bow-fronted shops. The gentle slope of the ground is also absorbed by minute adjustments between the bays.

 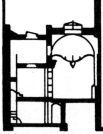

Typical bay and section

Trafalgar Square WC2 and   K70f
SW1 started 1820
⊖ Charing Cross

Nash suggested that a square should be made where the east-west route between Buckingham Palace and St Paul's crossed the top of Whitehall; he also proposed that the north-south route should be extended to the British Museum. But he designed only the east side, the West Strand Improvements (now Coutts Bank K173), behind St Martin's K40. The rest of the buildings which enclose this far from satisfactory space were built over the following century. Smirke's Royal College of Physicians (now Canada House K74), on the west side, was built of Bath stone in 1824–7, and was followed by William Wilkins' unsuccessful National Gallery K88 on the north side. Barry's granite terrace and steps in front of the Gallery were built in 1840. The Corinthian column supporting Nelson's statue was designed by William Railton and erected in 1842. The lions by Sir Edwin Landseer

and the reliefs were finished in 1867. Nash's proposed route north from the square was built as Charing Cross Road K113, to the west of St Martin's Lane. On the south side, the two huge Victorian former hotels by F and H Furness have been converted for use as offices. The magnificent view down Whitehall is framed by these and, on the south-west side, by George Aitchison's Royal Bank of Scotland (1885). Sir Herbert Baker's South Africa House K152 filled in the east side of the square in 1935, and Lutyens' fountains K153 were added in 1939. On the south-east corner with Northumberland Avenue, the late Victorian Grand Buildings was finished in 1990, the result of an architectural competition held in 1985. This was won, in a spectacular failure of patronage, by a design which proposed this replica of what already occupied the site. The most recent addition to the Square is the ingratiating Sainsbury wing K177 of the National Gallery in the north-west corner.

Suffolk Street and   K71f
Suffolk Place SW1 1820
John Nash and others
⊖Charing Cross

Nash's great 'Improvement' from Carlton House to Regent's Park was a strip of development which included not only the buildings along the route but also some of the side streets. These two are all that remain to give an indication of their quality. The north side of Suffolk Place and numbers 7–11 Suffolk Street are by Nash, and the style is Greek for all but number 7, which is in Roman Doric. All are stuccoed and have fine iron balconies. Numbers 18 and 19 are the back of the Theatre Royal K85.

St John 1822–4   K72l
Waterloo Road SE1
F O Bedford
⊖Waterloo

One of many 'Waterloo churches' built by the Church Commissioners to commemorate the battle. The Greek portico and three-stage tower with an obelisk-like spire form a dignified landmark at what is now a major traffic intersection. Originally there were iron railings between the fine pairs of stone gateposts; these were unfortunately removed in the Second World War (along with many others) to be melted down for raw materials. The interior has also been mostly destroyed.

Richmond Terrace 1822–5   K73j
Whitehall SW1
Henry Harrison
⊖Westminster

A strange domestic relic in the now pompous setting of Whitehall, formerly threatened with demolition by the grandiose plans of Sir Leslie Martin for the redevelopment of the area in the 1960s. The rebuilding of the interiors of this stone and brick terrace was finally begun in 1982. The jazzy neo-Perpendicular entrance from Whitehall was added in 1987 by William Whitfield and Partners. The building is now occupied by the Department of Health.

Canada House   K74f
ex Union Club and
Royal College of Physicians 1824–7
Trafalgar Square WC2
Sir Robert Smirke
⊖Charing Cross

With this block, Smirke successfully resolved the triangular wedge formed by Pall Mall and Nash's plan for Trafalgar Square K70 (1820). When built it was a dignified composition in Bath stone, with a recessed portico to the square and projecting porticoes to the side streets north and south. Only the building for the Royal College of Physicians remains unchanged, following the disastrous conversion and extension of the upper parts. Its particularly fine interiors, notably the staircase and library, remain intact.

Lancaster House 1825–9   K75i
Stable Yard Road SW1
Benjamin Wyatt
⊖ Green Park

Robert Smirke's foundations for this house for the Duke of York had already been built when Wyatt replaced him. Smirke returned to the job after Wyatt's death, adding the attic in 1841. The grand exterior (with *three* Corinthian porticoes) is in the fashionable Bath stone of the 1820s (see also Nash's Buckingham Palace K76 and Apsley House J13). The interior has a central hall and stair by Barry (1843) and is occasionally open to the public during the summer. The house is now used as a government conference centre.

Buckingham Palace   K76i
1825–1913
The Mall SW1
John Nash 1825–30, Edward Blore 1830–47, Sir Aston Webb 1912–13
⊖ St James's Park, Green Park

As Pevsner has observed, 'Buckingham Palace is in two ways supremely English.' Firstly, it was not originally intended as the monarch's official London residence: its faltering development over the years demonstrates a typically English empiricism. Secondly, the present building (despite Webb's *rond point* and radiating avenues) conveys the image of a large and rather stiff country house set in its own parkland, 'so the English delight in the country house and a humanized countryside triumphs in the Royal palace'.

The Palace takes its name from Buckingham House, a country house on the same site, built in 1715 by John Sheffield, Duke of Buckingham. In 1762 it was bought by George III and became known as 'The Queen's Palace' but remained a country house until the Prince Regent became George IV in 1820. The absence of an appropriate permanent residence for royalty was beginning to prove a national embarrassment, and the elderly John Nash was commissioned to transform Buckingham House into a royal palace. Despite great expenditure and Nash's involvement, the result retained much of its country house origins.

Of Nash's work, the west façade facing the garden is relatively intact. The large bow window at the centre is the only concession to a rather pedestrian elevation of Bath stone. The east front was formed by a grand deep forecourt, which in 1847 was built over by Edward Blore in order to provide extra accommodation for Queen Victoria and Prince Albert. Nash's north and south ranges, both modified by Blore,

are of little architectural interest.

The unexpected treasure of Buckingham Palace is to be found to the south-west, facing Buckingham Palace Road – the **Royal Mews**, entered through a giant archway with magnificent Roman columns on either side. The clock tower above was added in 1824. Inside, the Riding House (1764) has a fine acanthus frieze and a pediment depicting Hercules and the Thracian Horses, both commissioned by Pennethorne from William Theed Junior in 1859.

With Admiralty Arch K127, the Queen Victoria Memorial K119 and Webb's new façade (completed, astonishingly, in three months, in time for George V's coronation) London finally, in 1913, acquired a royal processional route. Webb's neoclassical front is in fact a recasing of Blore's east façade of 1847 – it remains a feeble and run-of-the-mill pastiche, and the design is popular more for what it represents than for any architectural merit. However, the work is significant, both as a conclusion to the Mall, and as the most recent building in London under royal patronage.

Carlton House Terrace K77f

SWI 1827–32
John Nash
⊖ Charing Cross

The terraces were built on the site of Carlton House, George IV's residence before the building of Buckingham Palace, and were Nash's last design before his death in 1835. They consist of two very long ranges, each of 140 m (460 ft), mounted on platforms overlooking the Mall, and framing the magnificent granite Duke of York's Steps K86. While they exhibit some eccentricities, such as the two-storey attics at the ends, the buildings have always received more favourable architectural criticism than Nash's other large-scale works. The squat Doric columns of the platforms are made of cast iron, an early use of the material for decoration. The buildings now house a variety of professional and artistic bodies, including the Institute of Contemporary Arts, the Society of Industrial Artists, and the Institute of Landscape Architects.

Numbers 7–9 contain the only London work of Albert Speer, the interiors of the pre-war German Embassy. At the southern end stands 4 Carlton House Gardens, by Sir Reginald Blomfield – unfortunately it is built in stone, and out of scale with the terraces.

Institute of Directors K78f

ex United Services Club
1827, 1842
Pall Mall and Waterloo Place SWI
John Nash, Decimus Burton
⊖ Charing Cross

Nash planned two clubs to face each other across Waterloo Place. Decimus Burton designed the Athenaeum K80 and although Nash designed the United Services, Burton was commissioned in 1842 to remodel his work. It is this later design which we now see: Victorian Italianate, mixing orders (but still using Roman Doric for the porch), and laboured in comparison with the lucid Athenaeum opposite. The grand internal arrangements are splendid but cannot be visited.

Waterloo Place WI c1828 K79f

John Nash
⊖ Piccadilly Circus

The beginning of Nash's triumphal way from Carlton House Terrace to Regent's Park, Waterloo Place is one of the most impressive pieces of town planning in London. Following the demolition of Carlton House in 1829, Carlton House Terrace was built with at its centre the Duke of York's column K86 and a broad flight of steps down to St James's Park. The simple and symmetrical composition of Waterloo Place is formed by the back of Carlton House Terrace (an extraordinary change in scale from the monumental front addressing St James's Park), the Institute of Directors K78 and the Athenaeum K80 on the intersection with Pall Mall, which form two pavilions.

The Athenaeum 1828–30   K80f
Pall Mall and
Waterloo Place SW1
Decimus Burton
⊖ Piccadilly Circus
This elegant stuccoed block, with its
large-scale porch of paired Doric columns
to Waterloo Place, is one of the most
distinguished buildings of the classical
revival in London and has similarities with
the work of Schinkel in Berlin. It has a
first-floor continuous balcony on finely
detailed brackets, a large gilded figure of
Pallas Athene by Baily above the porch, a
frieze above the main windows, and a
cornice and balustrade. Much of the
furniture was also designed by Burton.
The unfortunate attic storey was added in
1899. See also Burton's Grove House F17.

The Market Covent Garden   K81c
WC2 1828–31
Charles Fowler; restored 1975–80 by
GLC Architects Department, Historic
Buildings Division, B Ashley-Barker,
Surveyor of Historic Buildings
⊖ Covent Garden
The Earl of Bedford, having commissioned
Inigo Jones's Piazza K14, exploited his
invention by starting a market there in
1671. This grew, until 200 years later it
was rehoused in these buildings. In 1974
the market was moved out to a new site at
Nine Elms, and the Greater London
Council lovingly and expensively cleaned
and restored Fowler's building and the
surrounding cobbled streets and pavements. It was reopened in 1980 for use as
high-rent shops and restaurants.
The building has three routes running
east-west: an elegant central arcade is
flanked by two large market halls, roofed
with iron arches in the 1880s and '90s and
lit with patent glazing. The whole is
surrounded by a delicate Tuscan
colonnade of Aberdeen granite mono-

liths, with little square pavilions at the
corners, also faced in granite. The upper
parts are of sandstone.
The sculptures on the gable ends of the
central arcade are by R W Sievier; above
the entrances on the cross-axis are the
Bedford arms and motto, *Che sara sara*.

Travellers' Club 1829–32   K82f
Pall Mall SW1
Sir Charles Barry
⊖ Charing Cross
The Travellers' Club stands between
Burton's Athenaeum K80 and Barry's
later Reform Club K91. Together, these
clubs make a collection of neo-classical
buildings of a quality to equal Schinkel's
Berlin or von Klenze's Munich. Like those
architects, Barry was to extend his repertoire from strict ancient classical models
to include Italianate and, later, Gothic.
The plan is that of a *cortile*, the plain
stuccoed façade that of a *palazzo*.

King's College 1829–35 K83c
Strand WC2
Sir Robert Smirke
⊖ Aldwych

Founded as the Church of England's answer to the establishment of the non-religious University College (although both are now part of London University), King's forms the final, eastern section of Chambers' plan for the river frontage of Somerset House K62. Although contemporary with his early work on the British Museum G25, King's shows none of Smirke's usual elegant restraint, appearing merely dull. The smallness of the gateway from the Strand to the narrow courtyard provided the young Pugin with ammunition for an unfavourable comparison with the medieval colleges of Oxford and Cambridge.

West Strand K84f
Improvements
Adelaide Street WC2 1830
John Nash
⊖ Charing Cross

Immediately behind St Martin-in-the-Fields K40, the triangular block described by Adelaide Street, King William Street and the Strand is known as Nash's West Strand Improvements. The pepper pots at the corners and the stuccoed façades are characteristic of Nash, but the block has recently been totally refurbished by Sir Frederick Gibberd for the expanded premises of Coutts Bank K173. See also Charing Cross Hospital K87.

Theatre Royal 1831 K85f
Haymarket SW1
John Nash
⊖ Piccadilly Circus

The Theatre Royal and the houses behind it in Suffolk Street K71 are surviving fragments of Nash's ambitious triumphal way from Carlton House Terrace to Regent's Park. The theatre has a grand portico of six Corinthian columns built over the pavement, and above that a row of nine decorated circular windows. Facing the end of Charles II Street and closing St James's Square to the west, the portico is particularly monumental when viewed down Haymarket from the north. The interior has been much altered, but a lot of the stage machinery is original.

Duke of York's Column K86f
1831–4
Waterloo Place W1
Benjamin Wyatt
⊖ Piccadilly Circus

The Duke of York's Column marks the southern end of Nash's triumphal way from Carlton House Terrace K77 to Regent's Park. Set in Waterloo Place K79 above an impressive flight of steps down to St James's Park, it dominates one of the most dramatic spaces in London. Wyatt's memorial is a giant Tuscan column, carrying above its capital a dome bearing Westmacott's statue of the Duke of York, surrounded by a square balcony.

ex **Charing Cross Hospital** K87f
1831–4
Agar Street and William IV Street WC2
Decimus Burton, altered by J Thompson
1877
⊖ Charing Cross

Part of Nash's plan for the west Strand, this hospital (one of several built and rebuilt in this decade) has now ended its useful life, and the institution has moved to Fulham. Unused, the architecture – decent stuccoed Corinthian for the rounded corner, Doric for the entrance – looks wan.

National Gallery 1832–8 K88f
Trafalgar Square W1
William Wilkins
⊖ Charing Cross

Buildings appropriate to grand processional routes or very large public spaces are not as common in London as in other European cities. When the occasion has presented itself architects have often failed to rise to it, either because they are more used to domestic building (as with Chambers' Somerset House K62) or because their nerve failed, like Wilkins at the National Gallery. As the climax to Nash's newly formed Trafalgar Square K70, gently sloping to the north, Wilkins' façade is inadequate. It is, as Sir John Summerson observed, 'divided into no fewer than thirteen sections, six on either side of the central portico. Unfortunately all the subsidiary sections have approx-

imately equal value, and the two sorts of pavilions are so similar in height that one is inclined to evaluate them as alternative suggestions rather than complementary parts of a single design.'

The interiors are mainly by E M Barry (1867–76) and the central hall is by Sir J Taylor (1885). The gallery holds one of the world's greatest collections of paintings: begun in 1832 with thirty-eight pictures bought by the government from the Angerstein collection, it now has forty-six rooms covering the development of European painting from the mid-thirteenth century to the French Impressionists. The fine collection of early Renaissance paintings is now on display to the public in the recently completed Sainsbury wing K177.

Wellington Barracks 1833 K89m
Birdcage Walk SW1
Philip Hardwick
⊖ St James's Park

All European capitals built barracks at about this time: we are fortunate that such good neo-classical taste then reigned. This 120 m (394 ft) and pleasantly dull three-storey building, fronting its parade ground, has small accents of Greek Doric ornamentation. It was reconstructed in 1979–82, and now looks particularly good when floodlit.

Houses of Parliament   K90o
1835–60
Palace of Westminster SW1
Sir Charles Barry, Augustus Welby Pugin
⊖Westminster

Approached from Westminster Bridge to the east, the profile of the Houses of Parliament is immediately familiar, culminating with the clock tower containing Big Ben, 98 m (320 ft) high, in the north and the taller Victoria Tower, 103 m (336 ft), in the south. Approached from the west, the group of buildings known as the Palace of Westminster (including the Houses of Parliament) is a confusion of styles, including the authentic Gothic of Westminster Hall K5, and the excellent neo-Gothic of the Houses of Parliament.
The present Parliament building is on the site of Edward the Confessor's original Royal Palace of Westminster, but in 1834 a

fire destroyed everything but Westminster Hall, the Law Courts to the west and the Cloister of St Stephen. The following year it was decided to build new and enlarged Houses of Parliament on the same site, and a competition was announced for a building in either Gothic or Tudor style. The Houses of Parliament, with their exuberant neo-Gothic interiors, are the result of the collaboration of two architects, Barry for the general arrangements and Pugin for the meticulously detailed Gothic design. Their appearance prompted Pugin's famous comment from a boat on the Thames, 'All Grecian, sir; Tudor details on a classic body.'
The buildings have a simple axial plan, the principal rooms being arranged along a north-south spine in a progression befitting the hierarchic nature of British

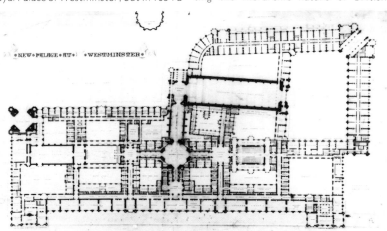

Barry's original plan

society (House of Commons, Commons Lobby, Central Lobby, Lords Lobby, House of Lords, Princes Chamber and Royal Gallery).

If the grand and eloquent exterior can be attributed principally to Barry, the interiors were exclusively Pugin's. From the public entrance, the visitor proceeds up a flight of stairs to the great octagonal lobby; in front lie the reception rooms, to the left the House of Commons and to the right the House of Lords. The interior of the House of Commons was completely redesigned and rebuilt by Sir Giles Gilbert Scott after bombing in the Second World War. Fortunately the House of Lords remains intact, and its very rich decoration is Pugin's London masterpiece. The mural paintings in the Palace of Westminster should also be noted: the most impressive is *The Death of Nelson and the Meeting of Wellington and Blucher* by Daniel Maclise in the Royal Gallery. As a result of the fresco technique many of the other patriotic murals are in a poor state of repair.

The principal dates of building activity were as follows: the river wall was started in 1837, and the building in 1840; the House of Lords was opened in 1847 and the other main buildings in 1852; the clock tower housing Big Ben (the bell) was completed in 1858 and the Victoria Tower in 1860, the year of Barry's death. E M Barry, his son, supervised the final stages.

It is sad that architects involved in large-scale public works are often inadequately appreciated and badly paid: Barry and Pugin were no exception to this general rule. Pugin died in Bedlam (the Bethlehem Hospital for the care of the insane) in 1852, the year of the official opening of the Houses of Parliament, and Barry died worn out by the worry of his massive undertaking.

Reform Club 1841   K91f
Pall Mall SW1
Sir Charles Barry
⊖ Piccadilly Circus, Charing Cross

The successor to Barry's Travellers' Club K82, next door to the east, the Reform is a grand two-storey *palazzo* in smooth Portland stone ashlar, raised half a storey above the pavement. Inside, the main rooms are grouped round a glazed, cloistered courtyard.

Offices ex Conservative Club   K92i
1843
74 St James's Street SW1
George Basevi and Sydney Smirke
⊖ Green Park

A grand Italianate effort which shows how quickly neo-classicism became pompous and decorated: the contrast between the Athenaeum K80 and United Services K78 is another example. Basevi seems to have been better at laying out houses, as in Pelham Crescent N11.

All Saints 1849–59   K93a
Margaret Street W1
William Butterfield
⊖Oxford Circus

A remarkable early High Victorian design
to the programme of the Cambridge
Camden Society, a reform group determined to reinstate the Liturgy and its
equipment in the Church of England. Two
houses for clergy and choir school frame a
small courtyard and expose the south wall
of the church, with its very un-English
tower and steeple. The highly decorated
interior was an inspiration for the Arts
and Crafts movement. The altarpiece is by
William Dyce. See also St Augustine,
Queens Gate N19.

Warehouses c1850   K94b
Neal Street, Earlham Street
and Shelton Street WC2
⊖Covent Garden

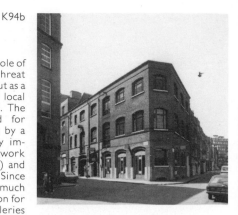

At the beginning of the 1970s the whole of
the Covent Garden area was under threat
of demolition and redevelopment, but as a
result of a successful campaign by local
residents this disaster was avoided. The
Earlham Street warehouse, used for
storage first by a brewer and then by a
paper manufacturer, is particularly impressive for its mid-Victorian brickwork
(in the style of the London Docks) and
simple segmental-arched windows. Since
the early 1970s it has fulfilled a much
needed role as rented accommodation for
local community groups, shops, galleries
and studios. With the other warehouses in
Neal Street and Shelton Street, it was the
focus for the renewal of the Covent
Garden area.

Victoria Street SW1   K95m
laid out 1850s
⊖St James's Park, Victoria

Victoria Street was one of the series of
'Improvements' carried out in the
nineteenth century, designed to alleviate
traffic congestion, remove slums and
develop land by speculation. This street
connected the southern end of Whitehall
to the top end of Vauxhall Bridge Road,
just south-west of Buckingham Palace, and
swept through notorious slums round
Tothill Street. Its line was later extended
north through Grosvenor Gardens J46 to
Hyde Park Corner. Most of the original
street of regular six-storey Italianate
shops, offices and 'mansion' flats has now
been destroyed and redeveloped as a
catalogue of the half-baked architectural
fashions of the last twenty-five years. New
Scotland Yard K167 and the recent development in front of Westminster Cathedral partly restore the Victorian cornice
line.

St Mary-at-Lambeth   K96o
nave 1851–2
Lambeth Road SE1
P C Hardwick
⊖Lambeth North

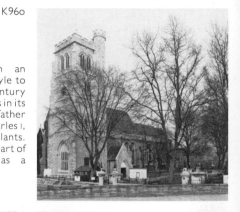

Hardwick rebuilt the nave in an
unremarkable Decorated Gothic style to
match the existing fourteenth-century
tower. The interest of the church lies in its
associations with the Tradescants, father
and son, who were gardeners to Charles I,
and travelled abroad collecting plants.
They are buried in the churchyard, part of
which is now being planted as a
seventeenth-century garden.

Public Record Office   K97d
1851–66 and 1891–6
Chancery Lane WC2
James Pennethorne, Sir John Taylor
⊖Chancery Lane

Pennethorne was architect and surveyor
to the Office of Works, but the Victorian
state built few public buildings.
Pennethorne's functional Gothic design
for the archive faces Fetter Lane, and
Taylor's later extension is to Chancery
Lane. Most Public Records are now
housed in a new building at Kew.

Swiss Protestant Church   K98b

1853
Endell Street WC2
George Vulliamy
⊖ Covent Garden

Strangely, the Swiss Protestants did not demand the Gothic that the period required for English Protestants: instead they were provided with this very late, clumsy Palladian.

Royal Opera House   K99c

1857–8, 1982
Bow Street WC2
E M Barry; Gollins Melvin Ward Partnership
⊖ Covent Garden

The casual siting of important institutions was not unusual in London at this time (see also the British Museum G25) but it has been said that the Royal Opera House was built in a Covent Garden back street because of public disapproval of the theatre. Garnier's near-contemporary Paris Opéra, on its prominent site, offers a pertinent contrast. The building replaced Sir Robert Smirke's neo-classical theatre (1809) burnt down in 1856, and was completed in six months.

Compared with the Paris Opéra this is not an imaginative building in either plan or style. Barry's giant Corinthian six-column portico above the rusticated ground floor conveys an image of great size with none of his father's invention. Behind the portico is a long frieze by Flaxman showing Tragedy and Comedy; this and the statues in the niches either side of the front are from Smirke's original theatre. The auditorium, however, is very good indeed. Despite its size, it manages to maintain the intimacy of the theatre and a festive atmosphere; a giant shallow saucer dome (an idea borrowed from Soane) unifies the space, and the balcony fronts are richly decorated with gilded angels and garlands.

At the same time Barry also built the **Floral Hall** next door, for selling flowers to opera-goers. It occupies the site of Smirke's auditorium, which ran parallel to Bow Street (as opposed to Barry's, which is at right angles to it). At present it is used for storing scenery. The westerly expansion was completed in 1982, thereby extending the 'back of house' accommodation to James Street. By replicating a further five bays of Barry's façade, the Floral Street frontage has been successfully completed. As a result it appears as if the Opera House has always inhabited this inevitable shoebox. At the time of writing there are further initiatives to extend the Opera House to the south, completing the north-east corner of the Covent Garden piazza, to designs by Jeremy Dixon Building Design Partnership with Edward Jones. Planning permission for these proposals was obtained in 1990.

Westminster Bridge   K100k

SW1 and SE1 1862
Thomas Page
⊖ Westminster

An unremarkable design replacing that of a century earlier, Westminster Bridge predates the development of the Embankment K103 by two years. With Waterloo Bridge K154 and Blackfriars Bridge L82, it is one of the trio which provide Thames crossings for routes north through Lambeth from the Elephant and Castle. While it seems too wide, it does give good views of the Houses of Parliament K90.

Hungerford Bridge

K101g

WC2 and SE1 1863
John Hawkshaw
⊖ Embankment

The bridge and Charing Cross Station were both built during the spate of terminus construction in the 1860s: until then trains serving London's south-eastern suburbs and Kent had terminated at London Bridge. The trussed iron bridge (replacing a footbridge by Brunel of the 1840s) is the only one in central London to combine train and pedestrian crossings. The views from it towards the City and Waterloo Bridge are spectacular, and the noise and rattle of the trains adds a metropolitan spice. In the GLC's repainting of London's bridges it has acquired a cheerful red livery.

Charing Cross Station and Hotel 1863–4

K102f

Strand WC2
John Hawkshaw (station), E M Barry (hotel)
⊖ Charing Cross

Charing Cross Station is another example of the architect using the railway hotel as the decorated front to the engineer's utilitarian train shed. The present station was built on the site of Hungerford Market and its massive railway bridge required the demolition of Brunel's Hungerford suspension footbridge (1841–5). Barry's hotel façade to the Strand, richly decorated with mixed Renaissance motifs, has been altered by the addition of two upper storeys; it was reputedly one of the first façades in England to use reconstituted stone. The **Eleanor Cross**, a stone spire in the station's forecourt designed by Barry and carved by T Earp, is near the site of the last of the thirteen crosses built by Edward I along the processional route from Nottinghamshire to Westminster Abbey for the funeral of his queen. It is also the point from which all distances to London are measured. The station has recently been transformed by building over the platforms K176.

Victoria Embankment

K103k, g, h

1864–70
SW1, WC2 and EC4
Sir Joseph Bazalgette
⊖ Westminster, Embankment, Temple, Blackfriars

Extending in a gentle curve from the Houses of Parliament K90 and Westminster Bridge K100 in the south-west to Blackfriars Bridge L82 in the north-east, the Victoria Embankment is a large-scale metropolitan 'Improvement'. It was also central London's first formal public Thames frontage.

In the most ambitious engineering scheme ever seen in London, a complex section was constructed simultaneously to contain a road bypass for the hopeless congestion of the Strand, an embankment as a defence against the disease-carrying Thames mud, a new trunk sewer and an underground railway. Above ground, the Victoria Embankment is memorable for its street furniture, bridges, granite wall and monuments, rather than for particular buildings. The cast iron lamp standards by Timothy Butler (1870), with dolphins twined around the columns, and the iron benches decorated with camels and sphinxes are particularly good. The many monuments randomly commemorate British imperialism and national heroes: for example, Boadicea by Thomas Thornycroft (1850), the Gilbert Memorial by George Frampton (1914), and a bronze of Isambard Kingdom Brunel by Marochetti (c1877) appropriately commemorating the great Victorian engineer.

Hungerford Bridge K101 (1863) was contemporary with the Embankment, and replaced Brunel's elegant suspension bridge (1841–5), and Waterloo Bridge K154 (1939–45) by Sir Giles Gilbert Scott replaced Rennie's famous classical bridge.

Cleopatra's Needle, dating from 1500BC, is London's oldest outdoor architecture, imported in 1877 from Egypt. The heroic operation of shipping and erecting its 177 tonnes (180 tons) of pink Aswan granite is well described in a display at the Museum of London. Since the obelisk's original function was to celebrate the sun it seems wan under our skies. Its twin is in Central Park, New York. The Victorian sphinxes are by George Vulliamy.

Museum of Mankind   K104e
ex University of London
1866–9
Burlington Gardens W1
Sir James Pennethorne
⊖ Piccadilly Circus
Whereas the Italianate style was successfully incorporated into English domestic architecture, its monumental equivalent in public buildings always looks lifeless (see Scott's contemporary Government Offices K105, and the additions to Burlington House K36). Pennethorne had started as a correct neo classical architect, but his attempt here to do cheerful *cinquecento*, with worthy statuary (spot the intellectual), merely looks crowded.

Home Office and   K105j
Foreign Office 1868–73
Whitehall SW1
Sir George Gilbert Scott
⊖ Westminster
Scott had publicly proposed Gothic as the only style appropriate for all buildings, and was proving his faith at St Pancras Station G38. However, the 'Battle of the Styles' (Gothic versus classical, inaugurated by Pugin's *Contrasts*, 1836) seems here to have become a personal battle between Scott and Lord Palmerston, his patron. Scott made two designs before the present Italianate one was accepted. The very large five-storey building, planned around five courtyards, is symmetrical, save for the picturesque excursion with two corner towers on the elevation facing the park. The elevations are erudite but (in spite of their extensive sculpture)

quite unlikeable, except when seen from across the park.

Royal Courts of Justice   K106d
1874–82
Strand WC2
George Edmund Street
⊖ Chancery Lane
The last great Gothic public building in London, known by its detractors as 'the grave of modern Gothic', although the Great Hall and the Strand façade are triumphs in anyone's terms.
The competition announced in 1866 to replace Kent and Soane's old Law Courts at Westminster was a farce, with an abortive change of site to the new

Embankment at the last moment. Although the style was not specified, it was assumed to be Gothic, and the well known Gothic revival architects entered. In the event the architect-judges put E M Barry first and George Gilbert Scott second; the lawyers put Scott first and Waterhouse second. Street and Scott were then recommended as joint architects, and when Scott resigned in 1868 Street was made sole architect.

In the centre of the building is the Great Hall, one of the most authoritative examples of English thirteenth-century Gothic revival, 70 m (230 ft) long, 15 m (48 ft) wide and 25 m (82 ft) high. With its ecclesiastical associations, it is suitably awe-inspiring for innocent and guilty alike. It also connects Lincoln's Inn to the Temple, thus completing the continuous walk which we have called Legal London, from Gray's Inn Fields to the Temple on the Embankment (see Lincoln's Inn K16). The Strand façade is a *tour de force*. The apparent symmetry of the plan is modified by the employment of repeating and overlapping elements, principally the bays of turrets and the position of the east tower. It has been said that Street intentionally put his staircases on the exterior to enliven the elevation.

Street died in 1881, just before the completion of the Great Hall. Like others employed on large public commissions, he was worn out by the Herculean task, made no easier by constant demands for economy and the growing critical reaction against the Gothic Revival. A monument to Street by Armstead was placed against the east side of the Hall in 1886: holding a pair of metal dividers, he is seated above a frieze of artists and craftsmen (this is not without irony, for Street could never delegate work).

Shaftesbury Avenue   K107b
W1 and WC2 1877–86

⊖ Leicester Square, Piccadilly Circus

Shaftesbury Avenue connects Piccadilly Circus in the south-west to New Oxford Street. Like the contemporary Charing Cross Road K113, it was one of the series of 'Improvements', starting with New Oxford Street and Holborn Viaduct, which cut through slum areas in order to move their inhabitants elsewhere and improve the circulation of traffic. Now it is a street of theatres, and many of the buildings date from its original setting out: see Collcutt's Palace Theatre K115 and the Shaftesbury, ex-French, Hospital in red terracotta by Thomas Verity (1899). The theatre built most recently was the Savile, by T P Bennett in 1931, with its Thespian frieze by Gilbert Bayes. It is now the ABC Cinema.

Royal Arcade 1879   K108e
connecting 28 Old Bond Street
to 12 Albemarle Street W1

⊖ Green Park

London's most elegant surviving High Victorian arcade, the Royal Arcade was built to form a direct shopping perambulation between the fashionable Brown's Hotel and Bond Street. It was originally called simply 'The Arcade' (see the entrance pediment) but was ennobled in 1882 as a result of its royal patronage – Queen Victoria bought her riding skirts and wool from H W Brettel's. The arcade is 40 m (132 ft) long with nine shops on either side. Each shop has a bay through the full height of the building; the bays are then separated by arches with an open pediment above, and the glass roof runs the full length of the arcade. The balance between decoration and structural elements is perfectly controlled, as is the play of light and shadow. The glass of the shop fronts is faceted at the corners, and the window frames, painted black with columns of gold piping, give the sense of a black reflective plinth to the lighter structures above. The street façade is reminiscent of Burlington Arcade K68; the four columns were originally crowned with urns. The proportions of the entrances have been ruined, however, by a new shop front.

James Smith and Sons c1880　K109b
53 New Oxford Street WC1
⊖Tottenham Court Road
An intact nineteenth-century shop front,
retaining its highly graphic Victorian
typography. Increased sales of umbrellas
in the nineteenth century coincided with
the popular introduction of window
shopping and promenades. Birch canes are
also still on sale!

The Red Lion c1880　K110e
Duke of York Street SW1
⊖Piccadilly Circus
One of the finest surviving small Victorian
pubs in London: the intimate interior of
cut, bevelled and mirrored glass set in
dark mahogany frames is magical.

Offices 1882　K111i
1 and 2 St James's Street SW1
R Norman Shaw
⊖Green Park
Built at the peak of Shaw's influential and
much-copied brick and gabled style, these
offices successfully turn the corner of Pall
Mall and St James's Street. See also Shaw's
later number 88 opposite, K121.

ex **New Scotland Yard**　K112k
1886–90 **south wing** 1906
Victoria Embankment SW1
R Norman Shaw
⊖Westminster
The first of these very large offices was
built when Shaw's style was turning away
from the domestic and towards the
baroque of his contemporaries. In Scotland Yard he incorporated the round
corner tower of the Scottish castle, and
the later south wing has a Scottish tower
on one corner and a baroque gable on the
other. The stone base surmounted by
stripes of red brick and stone, and the
grandly punctuated skyline set off the
procession of large buildings of character
– best viewed from the South Bank –
which continues along the Embankment
to Blackfriars Bridge.

Charing Cross Road WC2   K113b
1887
⊖Tottenham Court Road, Leicester
Square
Charing Cross Road is a Victorian
'Improvement' and companion of Shaftesbury Avenue, which crosses it at Cambridge Circus. It was the outcome of fifty
years of discussion, started by Nash, of a
north-south route which would clear
some of the slums of east Soho. (Nash had
proposed a route to the east joining
Trafalgar Square to the British Museum.)
Like Shaftesbury Avenue, it is now a
street of theatres, none of them architecturally noteworthy, and bookshops.
Number 109 is **St Martin's School of
Art** (1937–9), a good, large building for a
type now usually consigned to island sites
in the suburbs, designed for the LCC by
E P Wheeler.

St Martin's School of Art

Savoy Hotel 1889 and 1903–4   K114g
Strand and Victoria
Embankment WC2
Arthur Mackmurdo, Thomas Collcutt
⊖Charing Cross
The Savoy has two buildings: that on the
Strand is by Collcutt in his very mixed
style (see also his Palace Theatre K115),
unified here by the exclusive use of white
glazed terracotta. Mackmurdo's bedroom
wing overlooking the Thames looks curiously commercial; it might be a Chicago
office building of the period, and lacks any
art nouveau features.
In 1929 the entrance court to the Strand
was restyled by Easton and Robertson,
who introduced the stylish art deco
stainless steel fascia. Some of Basil Ionides'
interiors of the same time survive.

Palace Theatre 1890   K115b
Cambridge Circus WC2
Thomas Collcutt
⊖Leicester Square
This huge theatre (none larger has since
been built in London) was originally
constructed as an opera house for the
impresario D'Oyly Carte. The grand exterior is in Colcutt's mixed and striped
style, mingling bands of red brick and
impervious cream faience to disturbing
effect, made even more pungent by the
thorough cleaning and refurbishment of
the 1980s.

National Portrait Gallery   K116f
1890–5
Charing Cross Road WC2
Ewan Christian, J K Colling
⊖Charing Cross
Indistinguishable from the National
Gallery K88, of which it forms the east
flank to Charing Cross Road, the National
Portrait Gallery has an equally undistin-
guished entrance. The main building is in
the Italian Renaissance style, with Early
English detailing in its round-headed
windows, attributed to Colling. Like the
Houses of Parliament K90 and the Royal
Courts of Justice K106, it attempts to
apply an 'organic' English style of crafts-
manship to a national building.

St Patrick 1891–3
Roman Catholic ~~K117b~~

Soho Square W1
Kelly and Birchall
⊖ Tottenham Court Road

Italian on the inside, red-brick Italianate on the outside, St Patrick's is one of the many churches in Soho which have served various waves of settlers. See also the terracotta French Protestant Church in the north-west corner of the Square K24.

Cathedral of the Most Precious Blood of our Lord and Saviour Jesus Christ

Westminster Cathedral, Archbishop's House and Clergy House
K118m

1895–1903
Victoria Street SW1
John Francis Bentley
⊖ Victoria

Henry

A convert to Roman Catholicism, Bentley had done most of his church work in Gothic, but was asked by Cardinal Vaughan to build the new Roman Catholic Cathedral in Byzantine style, perhaps to avoid stylistic competition with the Abbey. He accordingly visited Italy, Greece and Constantinople, and designed quite the best modern church in London, in a mixture of Byzantine and Romanesque styles. The plan has a three-bay nave, each bay covered with a concrete dome, a crossing marked by a raised dome and transepts, and a semicircular apse, all held together by bridges supported on delicate Ravennesque columns. Bentley's designs for the marble and mosaic cladding to the stock brick structure have been only half carried out, but the result is impressive. For a suggestion of how it might look were the money ever to be found to finish it, see the Lady Chapel with its gold mosaic. The fine Stations of the

Cross, mounted on the main piers of the nave, are by Eric Gill and were done during the First World War (see also his later sculpture for Broadcasting House F41).

The exterior, with its off-centre tower, is less startling than the interior but is well done, and the recent redevelopment of Victoria Street has allowed for a little piazza in front of the narthex, whose decoration can now be seen properly for the first time.

Queen Victoria Memorial and Rond Point 1901–13
K119i

opposite Buckingham Palace SW1
Sir Aston Webb and Sir Thomas Brock
⊖ Green Park, St James's Park

In 1901, Webb and the sculptor Brock won a limited competition for the design of the Memorial. Over the next ten years, Webb laid out the Mall and designed Admiralty Arch K127 and the new front for Buckingham Palace K76, which was completed in time for George v's coronation in 1911. Webb's original design for the *rond point*, the symbolic hub of the Empire, had elaborate colonnades. As built, it is more modest, with formal gardens as the settings for Brock's Victoria Memorial, a gilded statue of Victory surrounded by allegorical groups. The monument stands on a marble base circled by solid granite paving.

Law Society Library 1902 K120d
Chancery Lane and
Carey Street WC2
H Percy Adams, designed by Charles
Holden
⊖Chancery Lane

Holden was twenty-seven and working in
Adams' office when this first example of
his stripped classicism was built. The
horizontal lines of the cornice and
window heads are continued from
L Vulliamy's offices next door, but the
Venetian windows in a crude Tuscan
order arranged symmetrically across the
corner are Holden's own. This could be
seen as a stage in his one-man evolution of
English modernism, which had started
with his training with C R Ashbee, and
was to finish with his Underground
Stations R23, T25 and Senate House G62.

Offices 1903 K121i
88 St James's Street SW1
R Norman Shaw with Ernest Newton
⊖Green Park

This building, which closes the west end of
Pall Mall – Wilkins' National Gallery K88
slews across the eastern end – is in Shaw's
late stone baroque style, but with one
large, symmetrical and very un-baroque
gable. See also Shaw's earlier 1 and 2 Pall
Mall K111 opposite.

ex **Country Life Offices** 1904 K122g
2–10 Tavistock Street WC2
Sir Edwin Lutyens
⊖Covent Garden

Recently restored, this was Lutyens' first
building in London, a large house or small
palace in a transitional style. It is a mixture
of what was later to become his complete
domestic 'Wrenaissance' and of the current Edwardian baroque. Those who like
complexity and contradiction will be
charmed by the window caught inside the
segmental entrance pediment.

Piccadilly Hotel 1905–8 K123e
Piccadilly W1
R Norman Shaw
⊖Piccadilly Circus

A contemporary of the Ritz K125, Shaw's
last big building is in his late heavy
baroque style. It was the only part built of
his larger scheme for the redevelopment
of Piccadilly Circus (see Blomfield's work
K135). The bedrooms are recessed from
Piccadilly behind a screen of triple-height
Ionic columns, but this arrangement has
been muddled by the later addition of the
glazed restaurant on the terrace. The
composition is framed at the west end by a
floridly pedimented gable, intended to be
one of a symmetrical pair. The Ionic
columns on the Regent Street façade are
engaged.

Methodist Central Hall K124n

1905–11
Storey's Gate SW1
Lanchester and Rickards
⊖ St James's Park

A huge hall for Methodist assemblies (although much used for secular meetings), sited appropriately near other national religious buildings, but built in a sumptuous, worldly style inappropriate to non-conformism. While other Edwardian architects were ransacking Wren for their baroque, Lanchester and Rickards used French and German models. The result is what might be, in Pevsner's words, 'a substantially-built *Kursaal*' or a casino. See also their Third Church of Christ Scientist, Curzon Street.

Ritz Hotel 1906 K125e

Piccadilly W1
Mewès and Davis
⊖ Green Park

This was the first steel-framed building in London. It has a redundant self-supporting skin of Norwegian granite on the ground floor and of Portland stone above. Note the very French two-storey roof. The grand arcade to Piccadilly (modelled, like Nash's plan for Regent Street, on Percier and Fontaine's rue de Rivoli in Paris) is the finest in London, where its scale and detailing have never been bettered. For a treat, and to relish the Edwardian elegance which the Ritz celebrated, take afternoon tea in the Winter Garden.

Inveresk House 1906–7 K126g

south-west corner of Aldwych
WC2
Mewès and Davis
⊖ Aldwych, Temple

The Norwegian granite facings to this suave Parisian façade conceal one of London's earliest steel-frame structures. This is one of many examples by these architects of the 'French' manner which they had introduced to Edwardian London with the Ritz Hotel K125. The style is normally associated with hotels, but Inveresk House was built to house the *Morning Post* newspaper. The later addition of the top two storeys diluted the original design.

Admiralty Arch 1906–11 K127f

between the Mall and
Trafalgar Square SW1
Sir Aston Webb
⊖ Charing Cross

The Arch terminates the grand axis leading from Buckingham Palace K76 and Webb's Queen Victoria Memorial K119 (completed in the same year), and skilfully straddles the obtuse angle formed by the axes of the Mall and the Strand. Constructed in Portland stone, it has a giant Corinthian order with heavy, characteristically Edwardian, classical decorative motifs, especially in the huge attic. The Latin inscription, Edward VII's tribute to his mother, is unique in London in its size and length. The completion of the Arch accomplished the transformation of the Mall, from its beginnings in the 1660s when it was laid out with St James's Park, to its present role as the first part of the royal route from Buckingham Palace to St Paul's Cathedral.

Zimbabwe House K128g

ex Rhodesia House, originally
the British Medical Association
1907–8
429 Strand WC2
Charles Holden
Θ Charing Cross

Holden is remembered principally for his services to London Transport and the stripped classicism of his Senate House G62, but the earlier buildings were more inventive within the same genre. With its complex system of narrow bays, 429 Strand suggested an alternative to the Free Style of the Arts and Crafts – in this case an example of Free Style classicism. The ground and first two floors (built in Cornish granite) use a remarkable number of classical devices, the blank and restrained detail to the entrance from Agar Street being particularly impressive. The mutilated and melted figures between the second-floor windows are by Jacob Epstein, who was a friend of Holden. This was his first major commission in England, and caused a scandal at the opening of the building, resulting in the disfigurement of the naked figures.

Royal Automobile Club K129i

1908–11
Pall Mall SW1
Mewès and Davis, with E Keynes
Purchase
Θ Green Park

With a current membership of 11,000, the RAC is much bigger than the earlier clubs in the district (such as the Reform K91 and Boodles K57): an opulent Edwardian celebration of the advent of the motorcar, and an expression of the cosmopolitan character of Edward VII's London. Mewès was a Frenchman and, apart from his earlier Ritz Hotel K125, most of his other commissions were for the fashionable *demi-monde* who frequented the spas of Le Touquet and Deauville.

The Portland stone façade to Pall Mall is large-scale and unexceptional, but it conceals the large double-height oval entrance hall leading to the grand club rooms, both in the Louis XVI style. The principal interest of the building, however, is below ground. Because of its modern steel and concrete construction, the basement houses extensive spaces, which are now used as squash courts, Turkish baths, a solarium and a swimming pool. The latter, a long green rectangle carved out of the marble floor, is truly spectacular. Its Doric columns are faced in fish-scale mosaic which is matched in the pattern of the large window panes (lit from a two-storey area). The whole shows a degree of Edwardian luxury and hedonism not to be found in contemporary chlorinated public baths.

Kingsway and Aldwych K130c

WC2, opened 1909
various architects
Θ Holborn

Kingsway was the last of the series of streets – the first was Nash's Regent Street – which wiped away slums and low-rent areas by driving new thoroughfares through them, usually on the seam between neighbouring estates: Kingsway is on the boundary between the Bedford Estate to the west and Lincoln's Inn Fields to the east. The street is 30 m (100 ft) wide, and mostly lined with unebullient Edwardian commercial buildings, from which the Gallaher Building K133 by Burnet and Tait, Holy Trinity Church K132, and Bush House K142 stand out.

In an early example of multi-level engineering, a subway for trams was built under the street: it left the surface at the north end (in Southampton Row, where the ramp can still be seen) and travelled south the full length of Kingsway, emerging at the Embankment under the abutment of Waterloo Bridge K154. In 1961 the southern end was converted to take ordinary traffic, bypassing the Aldwych.

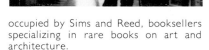

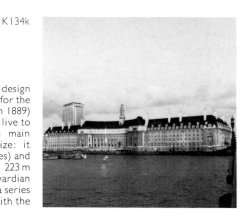

Piccadilly Arcade 1909–10   K131e
connecting 174 Piccadilly W1
to 52 Jermyn Street SW1
Thrale Jell
Θ Green Park, Piccadilly Circus
London's last real arcade, Piccadilly
Arcade was built (a century later) as an
extension to Burlington Arcade K68.
Unlike its predecessor it is not an independent piece, but more of a passageway
under a building, lined by shops and
insufficiently lit by occasional circular roof
lights. It is more like the arcades at
entrances to the London Underground.
However, the glazed bow-fronted shops
(twenty-six in all) were extremely elegant, stepping gently and almost im-
perceptibly down the slope to Jermyn
Street. Seen in perspective the little steel
balconies act as 'capitals' to the 'columns'
of the shop windows. Number 5 is
occupied by Sims and Reed, booksellers
specializing in rare books on art and
architecture.

Holy Trinity 1910–12   K132c
Kingsway WC2
Belcher and Joass
Θ Holborn
The church's beautiful and unexpected
stone façade describes a shallow concave
curve facing Kingsway. Pevsner attributes
this Roman baroque manner to Pietro da
Cortona's Santa Maria della Pace; the
influence of Nicholas Hawksmoor's
English baroque is also important. By
comparison the interior, with its white
plastered walls and exposed brick above,
is very simple.

Gallaher Building   K133c
ex Kodak House 1911
65 Kingsway WC2
Sir John Burnet
Θ Holborn
Most of the architecture of Kingsway
K130 was provided by Trehearne and
Norman. Burnet's classicism (see also the
contemporary Edward VII Galleries G49)
was here stripped, leaving a freestanding
six-storey commercial office building. It is
elegantly articulated, with a base, middle
and cornice in fine materials: Portland
stone and decorated bronze. The standard
architectural histories describe this building as proto-modern. This is not helpful,
for its traditions are much older, and its
successors are more like the Smithsons'
Economist Building K170 than the continental modern of the 1930s.

ex **County Hall**   K134k
1911–22 and 1931–3
east end of Westminster
Bridge SE1
Ralph Knott
Θ Westminster, Waterloo
Knott won the competition for the design
of the administrative headquarters for the
London County Council (formed in 1889)
at the age of thirty, but he did not live to
see the building completed. Its main
characteristic is its enormous size: it
occupies a rectangle of 2 ha (5 acres) and
the main façade to the river is 223 m
(730 ft) long. Like any thick Edwardian
office building it is planned round a series
of white glazed-tiled light wells, with the

important rooms, the Council Chamber and the Members' suites, in the middle. These are marked on the river side by the segmental niche (*not* a portico or pediment), which, within Knott's already out-of-date baroque, is the only original feature of the design. This is as it should be, as the entrance is on the side away from the river on Belvedere Road. An integral part of the design was the start of the embankment of the south side of the river at this point, and Londoners gained a

well-engineered granite traffic-free walk next to the Thames, as well as an only-too-large symbol of their local government. Sixty years later the walk is still being extended.

County Hall was last inhabited by London's elected city-wide strategic authority, the Greater London Council. This institution was abolished in 1985, since when proposals for the building's redevelopment have been sought from commercial developers.

County Fire Office and   K135e
Department Store ex Swan
and Edgar 1913–30
north and west sides Piccadilly
Circus W1
Exteriors by Sir Reginald Blomfield
⊖Piccadilly Circus
The destruction of Nash's great work began in 1848, when the colonnades were removed from his Quadrant. It continued with the rebuilding of the Swan and Edgar block (including Shaw's Piccadilly Hotel K123) and continued up Regent Street over the next thirty years. Blomfield, using the new French (rather than English) baroque style, had the grace to repeat Nash's County Fire Office dome to close the view up Lower Regent Street. It is perhaps a pity that Blomfield's grandiose plan was not realized round the north and east sides, but the circus's present irregular shape is wonderfully character-

istic of London, and Blomfield's stiff façades might not easily have accommodated neon advertising signs.

Oxford Circus W1 1913–28   K136a
Sir Henry Tanner
⊖Oxford Circus
The demolition of Nash's Regent Street continued with the rebuilding of the western side of Piccadilly Circus by Shaw (Piccadilly Hotel K123) and Blomfield (Swan and Edgar K135) from 1905. Tanner redesigned Oxford Circus, where stucco was felt to be inappropriate to the intersection of London's two most important shopping streets. His façades are neat if uninspired, and now frame a hopeless confusion of traffic and people.

The Cenotaph 1919–20   K137j
Whitehall SW1
Sir Edwin Lutyens
⊖Westminster
In 1917 Lutyens was among those established architects asked by the Imperial War Graves Commission to advise on the design of memorials to the dead in both Britain and France: his pre-war work in India at New Delhi had already made him the country's 'imperial' architect *par excellence*. The Cenotaph was the national memorial, first erected in temporary form in 1919. The design was felt to be so appropriate that it was rebuilt in stone by November 1920, when the tomb of the Unknown Soldier was established in Westminster Abbey.
Lutyens' design commemorates the dead without Christian imagery, using instead purely architectural means, classically derived and of extreme delicacy and refinement: tapering planes and minute

articulations of the Portland stone courses. The monument is the centrepiece of the national rituals of Armistice Day on 11 November.

Westmorland House 1920–5   K138e
117–27 Regent Street W1
Sir John Burnet, Thomas Tait
⊖ Piccadilly Circus

After the interruption of the First World War, the rebuilding of Nash's Regent Street and Quadrant continued in earnest in the 1920s. Westmorland House, immediately north of Blomfield's contemporary Quadrant, was Burnet and Tait's contribution to the redevelopment and their first post-war commission. A comparison with their other work of the early 1920s (for example Adelaide House L107) suggests that although the firm could work in several styles at once, their buildings nevertheless exhibit the common feature of end pavilions enclosing a plain range, the centre of which is scarcely emphasized. This was the same scheme as Burnet's pre-war Edward VII Galleries G49, and one which later proved very popular for the fronts of factories (for example the Hoover factory T26). The style of Westmorland House is con- tinental stripped classical. The ends are circular to accommodate the acute corner at Vigo Street, decorated with columns, and crowned with copper-covered domes; they enclose six storeys of shops and offices, without columns, but topped with a cornice.

Midland Bank 1922   K139e
196a Piccadilly W1
Sir Edwin Lutyens
⊖ Piccadilly Circus

A charming confection in red brick and Portland stone, owing as much to Verona's Sanmicheli as to Wren, but a fitting neighbour for St James's Church K21. Inside, the original single volume of the banking hall is spoilt only by the modern security screens.

National Westminster Bank

Barclays Bank

National Westminster   K140e
Bank 1922–3
63–5 Piccadilly W1
Barclays Bank, Wolsey Buildings 1926
157–60 Piccadilly W1
W Curtis Green
⊖ Green Park

Only four years separate Curtis Green's designs for these two large bank branches, yet they are remarkably different. The elevations of the National Westminster on the corner of Piccadilly and Albemarle Street are original, lively compositions. There are arches on the ground floor, more arches spanning the next three floors, and at the top, under the green slate roof, a loggia of two storeys behind slender Ionic columns.

Barclays Bank, on the south side of Piccadilly (at the corner of Arlington Street) is by contrast heavy and conventional. The large arches on the ground floor, decorated with magnificent iron- work, support a giant Corinthian order with coupled columns. This motif later became one of the clichés of bank design: see for example Sir Edwin Cooper's National Westminster (formerly National Provincial) Bank, Poultry L115.

Liberty's Department   K141a
Store 1924, 1926
Great Marlborough Street and
Regent Street W1
E T and E S Hall
⊖ Oxford Circus
Before the First World War, Liberty's
were among the advanced proponents and
sellers of art nouveau, but their first post-
war store changed direction towards
selling a regressive 'Tudor' dream. The
store is a perfect example of the type
developed in Paris (for example
Samaritaine): a central rooflit well is
surrounded by galleries over the edges of
which merchandise is displayed. The
Tudor style is carried through consistently, producing a building of great
character, with hand-made roof tiles,
leaded lights, and linen-fold panelled lift
doors. The timbers are of oak recycled
from two nineteenth-century battleships.
In contrast to the earlier Tudor-style
building, Liberty's on Regent Street by

the same architects (1926) is neo-classical,
with a massive concave screen of columns
above the rectangular base at street level,
topped with an impressive group of
figures flanking Britannia. Note the ob-
servant figures looking over the parapet.

Bush House 1925–35   K142c
Aldwych WC2
Hemle and Corbett
⊖ Holborn
Kingsway K130 was opened in 1905, but
lining it and Aldwych with buildings took
many years. The architects here were
American, and there is certainly no other
street termination in London to compare
with Bush House's vulgar but grand
exedra and the heap of masonry on top of
it, which bring a welcome flourish of
American Corinthian to London. It looks
very good floodlit: the effect is pagan. The
building is the home of the BBC's
Overseas Service.

Broadway House 1927–9   K143n
55 Broadway SW1
Charles Holden
⊖ St James's Park
When built, the new headquarters of
London Transport was one of the capital's
tallest (53 m/175 ft) and most 'modern'
buildings, but it is now difficult to be very
enthusiastic. The composition is similar to
Holden's later Senate House G62, but
here the cruciform tower and wings sit on
a low two-storey podium, seriously
damaging the integrity of the Broadway
and Petty France street façades. The end
of one wing, however, marks the entrance
and dominates the corner appropriately.
The sculptures (art for those of the
travelling masses who notice it) are by
Jacob Epstein (*Day* and *Night*), Eric Gill,
Henry Moore and others.

Freemasons Hall 1927–33   K144c
Great Queen Street WC2
Ashley and Newman
⊖ Holborn

A very large building with assembly
rooms and offices addresses the corner to
Wild Street with a magnificent door and
tower: its Edwardian confidence was
already twenty years out of fashion. See
also Port of London Authority L100.

ex **Daily Telegraph Building**   K145d
1928
135 Fleet Street EC4
Elcock and Sutcliffe, with Tait
⊖ Blackfriars

It is ironic that the down-to-earth *Daily
Telegraph* should have provided itself with
this modernistic delight. Only three years
later, the popularist *Daily Express*
occupied Owen Williams' orthodox
modern palace L117 in the same street.
London has so few examples of jazz
modern that this one should be relished
for its façade and entrance hall.

The Daily Telegraph moved its printing
works and offices to the Isle of Dogs in
1989, leaving their Fleet Street headquarters for development. A huge extension
designed by Kohn Pedersen Fox was built
on the north of the site. The expensive
detailing and many setbacks cannot disguise its enormous bulk.

Palladium House   K146a
ex Ideal House 1928
Great Marlborough Street and
Argyll Street W1
Raymond Hood, G Jeeves
⊖ Oxford Circus

Palladium House is a notable exception to
the lamentably unimaginative architecture which, justified by morality,
theory or expediency, is all too common
in England. The American architect,
Raymond Hood, had won first prize with a
neo-Gothic design in the famous *Chicago
Tribune* Building competition of 1923.
Later in the 1930s his designs for the *Daily
News* Building (which anticipated the
abstract verticality of the Rockefeller
Center and the McGraw-Hill Building
acquired him a reputation as one of the
pioneer architects of the New York
skyscraper.

The severity of the sheer, polished, black
granite cube with simple window openings is tempered by an Egyptian cornice,
the slightly battered inclination of the
walls, decorative floral tiles, and a piping
of inlaid gilt. The whole combines the
suave urbanity of 1930s New York with a
nostalgia for the florid decoration of the
1925 Paris Exhibition.

Bank and **flats** 1929   K147i
67–8 Pall Mall SW1
Sir Edwin Lutyens with W H Romaine-
Walker and Jenkins
⊖ Green Park

A corner building to Marlborough Gate,
incorporating a bank on the ground floor
and flats above. As with many of his
London buildings, Lutyens was responsible only for the design of the
elevations. The windows on each floor are
different (not unlike his Reuters and Press
Association Headquarters L118), showing
'how to get up a building without repeating yourself'.

New Victoria Theatre   K148m
1929–30
Wilton Road SW1
E Walmsley Lewis
⊖ Victoria

This very large theatre has fronts to both
Vauxhall Bridge Road and Wilton Road.
Both confidently exhibit, for the first time
in London, the continental *moderne* styling of alternate horizontal bands of
windows and striped spandrels. The style
is developed in the splendidly decorated
garish interiors.

YWCA Hostel 1930–2   K149b
16 Great Russell Street WC1
Sir Edwin Lutyens
⊖ Tottenham Court Road

One of Lutyens' later works, the hostel is
planned round a doughnut round very mean
light wells, producing unpleasant interiors. Outside, it uses the domestic neo-
Georgian language of red brick with
Portland stone dressings: very dead-pan.
The Post Office successfully used exactly
the same style for telephone exchanges.

Shell-Mex House 1931   K150g
Strand and
Victoria Embankment WC2
Messrs Joseph
⊖ Embankment, Charing Cross

Shell-Mex House, occupying an entire
block from the Strand to the Embankment, was originally the Cecil Hotel,
which with 800 bedrooms was the largest
hotel in Europe when it was opened in
1886. The riverside façade, characterized
by the giant and eccentric clock face, was
remodelled in 1931. Looking like a giant
mantelpiece ornament, or the top of a
much taller building, it is positively suave
(almost a New Yorker) when compared
with the lugubrious tower which Howard
Robertson built across the river for the
same company.

Simpson's Department Store 1935   K151e
Piccadilly W1
Joseph Emberton
⊖Piccadilly Circus

One of the great pioneering works of 'rational' store design, Simpson's was the result of collaboration between Emberton, the engineer Felix Samuely and the designer Laszlo Moholy-Nagy. The façade to Piccadilly, with horizontal strip windows and a canopy to the top storey, is reminiscent of tough European modernism (particularly Eric Mendelsohn's Hirpich Fur Store in Berlin, 1924) rather than the decorative *moderne* style of much British shop design in this period. The structure of Simpson's followed Samuely's first all-welded steel frame in England, for Mendelsohn's De La Warr Pavilion, Bexhill (1934). The welded steel structure with massive *vierendeel* girders above the first floor was thought by the LCC to be too unconventional, and modifications were required. The detailing of the external metalwork and the illumination of the façade (incorporating the sign) at night are particularly impressive. Unlike the 'warehouse' planning of most department stores, Simpson's is arranged like a large house, with a sequence of rooms. As a result the interiors have been subject to relatively little change over the years. These 'rooms' and the central staircase have a spaciousness and generosity which are emphasized by the luxurious use of materials: glass lifts, travertine floors and walls, and the original rugs. The ground floor can be used as a shortcut from Piccadilly to Jermyn Street. The top two storeys, added in the 1960s by the Architects' Co-Partnership, are unfortunate.

South Africa House 1935   K152f
Trafalgar Square WC2
Sir Herbert Baker
⊖Charing Cross

The latest significant addition to Trafalgar Square shows the prolific Baker not quite rising to the occasion. The massing of his large white building provides, with Wilkins' unsatisfactory National Gallery K88, another sound edge to help hold the square together, but the rhyming of his new porticoes with that of St Martin's is too obvious.

Pools and **fountains** 1939   K153f
Trafalgar Square WC2 and
SW1
Sir Edwin Lutyens
⊖Charing Cross
The pools, used traditionally by revellers
on New Year's Eve and General Election
nights, look as if they had always been
there. They are in fact Lutyens' last
London work, and mark the end of the
Imperial works by other designers which
started with Kingsway K130, the Queen
Victoria Memorial K119, and Admiralty
Arch K127. The edges of the pools are
large blocks of granite – now polished by
millions of visitors – set in a splendid
pavement of granite slabs. Public furniture, now usually designed by engineers, has never since achieved such
excellence (compare with the recently
pedestrianized Leicester Square K19).

Waterloo Bridge   K154g
WC2 and SE1 1939–45
Sir Giles Gilbert Scott
⊖Waterloo
The view from the bridge is one of
London's best: a good place from which to
get one's bearings in the city – upstream
to the Houses of Parliament K90 on the
right, and the Royal Festival Hall K157 on
the left, downstream to Somerset House
K62 on the left and the new National
Theatre K172 on the right. The Embank-
ment sweeps round to the towers of the
City (now a poor copy of, say, Houston or
Pittsburgh) which rear over St Paul's.
From the bridge, London still looks
surprisingly like a white city: most of the
buildings in sight are built of or covered in
Portland stone. The present bridge, which
replaces that designed in the Greek style
by Rennie, has five spans of 76 m (250 ft).
Built in concrete, it is clad in Portland
stone which has weathered to a beautiful
crusty white, exposing some of the fossils
of which it is composed. The abutments
and details are elegantly and tactfully
designed: note particularly the junction
with the Duchy of Lancaster building of
1930-2 on the north-east side, and the
steps next to Somerset House on the
north-west. The bridge was the last big
engineering structure in London to be
integrated successfully into the fabric of
the city, enhancing rather than destroying
its surroundings. See also Holborn
Viaduct H27.

The Citadel 1940   K155j
The Mall SW1
W A Forsyth
⊖Charing Cross
A curiously expressionist and enigmatic
cube on the north-west corner of Horse
Guards Parade, the Citadel is one of the
few remains in London of the architecture
of the Second World War. The building
contains approaches to a subterranean
shelter, six floors below, for the country's
leaders during the Blitz, and the observation slits were for gun emplacements
with the Mall as their arc of fire. The
massive compressed pebble and flint walls
are formed into black and beige strips, and
the building is now almost totally concealed by Virginia creeper, resembling in
summer a large work of topiary.

Parliament Square SW1 K156j

1945–60
Ministry of Works
⊖Westminster

Laid out originally by Barry, but now not so much a square as a lawn surrounded by statues of parliamentarians and national heroes, this is insufficiently defined by ordinary buildings to warrant being called a square. The thunderous, dangerous traffic makes it hard to contemplate the Palace of Westminster K90, St Margaret's K7 and the Abbey K3. The government buildings on the north side (1898–1912) are by J M Brydon, completed by Sir Henry Tanner. The **Middlesex Guildhall** (1905) on the west side is by Gibson and Russell.

River façade

Foyer

Restaurant

Royal Festival Hall K157k

1951, extended 1962
South Bank SE1
LCC Architects Department; Robert Matthew, J Leslie Martin, Edwin Williams and Peter Moro
⊖Waterloo, or Embankment and walk over Hungerford Bridge.

The large 2600–seat concert hall was the only permanent building of those erected for the 1951 Festival of Britain. London acquired a modern acoustically-designed hall to replace the Queen's Hall (destroyed in the Second World War) and to supersede the Albert Hall J45, with its huge capacity and uncertain acoustics. For Londoners this building was an introduction to the marvels of Modern Architecture, used confidently and consistently in a non-utilitarian public building. The 'egg' of the auditorium nests high in a forest of columns, among galleries and huge glazed screens, recalling Le Corbusier's unbuilt Palace of the Soviets. The scale and detailing of the interiors are just right for what passes for social display in England. Thirty years on, it is possible to relish the decoration of the Hall itself (the curly fronts to the boxes, the obsessive use of enclosing frames), and to admire its excellent lighting. The Hall's present management is, however, conducting what appears to be a determined war of attrition against the original integrity of the open foyers and circulation spaces. These have gradually been filled with kiosks and concessions, and many original features are being unnecessarily replaced with feeble inappropriate essays in 'interior design'. The exterior, clad largely in Portland stone, had already lost much of its decorative character when the building was extended and recased in the 1960s.

Offices and **showrooms**   K158e
1953–8
45–6 Albemarle Street W1
Ernö Goldfinger
⊖ Green Park

This six-storey office building with a four-bay structural frame and projecting two-bay oriel windows on the third and fifth floors has a European toughness, unlike its post-Festival of Britain contemporaries. It derives from the work of Auguste Perret in whose atelier Goldfinger spent a year of his apprenticeship in 1924. Goldfinger later used the same approach less successfully in his massive Elephant and Castle offices L124.

Congress House 1953–60   K159b
Great Russell Street WC1
David du R Aberdeen
⊖ Tottenham Court Road

Aberdeen's winning entry in the competition for the TUC is stylistically a lone voice of pre-war modernism. Maintaining the continuity of the street while at the same time giving expression to its role as a public building, it is a rare and stylish instance of the language of modern architecture successfully rebuilding the city within its own traditions. The extensive use of bronze window frames and large areas of plate glass, marble and mosaic gives the building durability and an appropriately monumental air. However, the central court proves to be more of a light well than the grand memorial public space anticipated from the street.

Lloyds Bank and   K160e
British Aerospace 1956–8
100 Pall Mall SW1
D Armstrong Smith and Donald
McMorran
⊖ Piccadilly Circus

After the Second World War, when classical forms had become associated with totalitarianism, the Swedish modern style was generally adopted in England as the 'architecture of democracy'. For this reason McMorran's London buildings (see also Wood Street police station L123 and the Old Bailey extension L97) are particularly interesting.

In this ambitious building, which replaced Sydney Smirke's Carlton Club (1847), a number of overlapping influences can be detected. The general proportions of the six storeys are neo-Georgian; the window openings, apparently carved out of a giant cube of Portland stone with occasional segmental arches, recall the Italian Rationalists of the late 1930s; the symmetrical roof pavilions refer back to Lutyens (see Aldford House J67); and the thick teak window frames and spindly ironwork of the street railings are of the Festival of Britain era.

Orion House, ex Thorn House K161b

1957–9
Upper St Martin's Lane WC2
Sir Basil Spence and Partners,
designed by Andrew Renton;
renovated by Renton Howard Wood
Levin 1988–90
⊖ Leicester Square

After only twenty years many of the office buildings of the 1960s were found to be unsatisfactory, having been built to standards lower than those subsequently required for easy letting. Some were demolished and rebuilt. Others like Thorn House were stripped, refitted and recased. The original composition had been, with New Zealand House K165, one of London's earliest efforts at the tower-on-a-podium format: a low, two-storey podium on St Martin's Lane appeared to pass independently through the base of the tower. In the alterations, the amount of accommodation on the site has been increased, an undistinguished street frontage has been restored to St Martin's Lane, and the original curiously tentative architecture of the slab has been replaced by crude metal panelling with pink-painted window frames, with a new projecting services stack at the back. Originally placed on the east side of the building, the spiky sculpture on the north side of the slab is by Geoffrey Clarke.

The startlingly stylish restaurant **Now and Zen** now housed in the foot of the tower is by Rick Mather.

New South Wales House K162g

ex Peter Robinson
Department Store 1958
65 Strand WC2
Sir Denys Lasdun
⊖ Charing Cross

In his only commercial building Lasdun, unlike most of his contemporaries, avoided the tower and podium format. The shop windows on the ground floor are separated by a projecting canopy from the blank stonework of the first floor. A continuous recessed clerestory separates this from the three floors of offices with their bronze window frames above. It is surprising, then, that the side façade in Durham House Street should ram so ignominiously into the very fine, blank, pilastered rear elevation of the Royal Society of Arts.

ex **Old Vic Theatre Workshop** K163l

1958
83–101 The Cut SE1
Lyons Israel and Ellis, designed by John Miller
⊖ Waterloo

A very early example of English Brutalism – the style is here used appropriately for a semi-industrial building, with a large double-height scene-painting workshop on top.

Flats 1958–60   K164i
26 St James's Place SW1
Sir Denys Lasdun
⊖Green Park

The first architecturally respectable luxury flats to be built in London after 1945, this small eight-storey block, on a very privileged site next to Vardy's Spencer House K51 and overlooking Green Park, signalled Lasdun's later concern with horizontal banding. Here the bands mark the floor levels, establish a grand scale, and demonstrate the split-level section: three storeys of smaller rooms to the north are set against two floors of generously high-ceilinged living rooms on the corner overlooking the park. The arrangement is like those of Wells Coates' Palace Gate flats 124 and Tecton's Highpoint 2 R26 (Lasdun had worked for both), and was probably derived from Le Corbusier's work. The block is still remarkable for its fine, impervious materials: granite facings for the horizontal bands, and bronze for the heavy window frames – both, as the Victorians knew, well suited to London's atmosphere.

New Zealand House 1960   K165f
Haymarket and Pall Mall SW1
Sir Robert Matthew, Johnson-Marshall
⊖Charing Cross

This is London's archetype of the slab-on-a-podium form of redevelopment, derived from Le Corbusier and from Skidmore Owings and Merrill's Lever House in New York. Although it is a good example of its kind, it nevertheless now seems more destructive than constructive, and remains isolated in a predominantly eighteenth- and nineteenth-century part of London. The podium breaks Haymarket's cornice-line at an important corner where it would be better strengthened, and the tower acquires an unwarranted importance in views, especially from Trafalgar Square. It was one of the first fully air-conditioned office buildings in London, and this was exploited in the design by using large sheets of glass. Subsequent appreciation of the strength of the sun led to extensive screening measures, and the design now consists of opaque pleated curtains separated by thin horizontal strips of stone. See also the delightful Royal Opera Arcade K69, which was restored when New Zealand House was built.

Offices 1960   K166d
Greystoke Place EC4
YRM Architects and Planners
⊖Chancery Lane

YRM built these offices for their own occupation, but the firm has now moved on to Britton Street H43. The style is an intermediate stage between their routine European modern and the full embrace of the Chicago style. The white tiles (used here as they were by the Victorians on restricted city sites) were employed extensively in YRM's late '60s buildings, for example Warwick University.

New Scotland Yard 1962–6 K167n
Victoria Street and
Broadway SW1
Chapman Taylor Partners, façades
designed by Adrian Gale
⊖St James's Park
As a part of the general redevelopment of
Victoria Street started in the late 1950s,
these offices were built speculatively and
only later occupied by the Metropolitan
Police. The two slabs occupy a triangular
site. The lower one on Victoria Street
continues the street line, though without
enough shops on the ground floor; however, the arrangement of the rear block
creates nasty pockets of residual space
which are useful only for parking police
vehicles. Given these reservations about
the composition, the granite and aluminium façades are smart and the planning
rational, and both show evidence of well
digested Chicago examples.

St Thomas's Hospital K168o
started 1963
Lambeth Palace Road SE1
Yorke Rosenberg Mardall
⊖Westminster
Established in Southwark 800 years ago,
the hospital was moved to this site in the
1860s. Of the nineteenth-century hospital, built to Florence Nightingale's
specification in the Italianate-hygienic
style, only the southernmost wards
remain. The rest has been rebuilt, most of
it to YRM's master plan. This proposed
an open 'campus' layout of rectangular
buildings at right angles to each other, and
parallel to the Houses of Parliament K90
opposite, and to YRM's Beckett House on
the other side of Lambeth Palace Road. A
sizeable part of London thereby acquired
the rudimentary geometrical order which
exists in Mayfair and in many North
American cities. YRM here employed the
tile style both for the huge cubic ward
block and for the linear nurses' homes on
the north-east corner of the site.
Good views of the Houses of Parliament
can be had from the public walk along the
Thames in front of the hospital.

Centre Point 1963–7 K169b
101 New Oxford Street WC1
Richard Seifert and Partners
⊖Tottenham Court Road
The position of Centre Point marks St
Giles Circus, conforming to a fashion in
the early 1960s for placing tall buildings at
principal traffic intersections. The
elephantine structure allows a bridge of
first-floor accommodation to span the
newly formed roundabout; the pathetic
pond and fountains which further incon-
venience the pedestrian on the already
inadequate pavements are only some of
the building's many drawbacks. The 121 m
(398 ft) tower of thirty-five storeys has
remained empty for over a decade. Land
speculation has been central to the
development of London since the seventeenth century, and the private development of the Great Estates endowed the
city with much of its character. However,
when private speculation is not constrained by consensus on desirable forms
of development it contains the seeds of

destruction for the city. Centre Point is
London's most conspicuous monument to
this fatality.
Construction is soon to begin on Allies
and Morrison's new square and canopy. It
is hoped that these will moderate some of
the building's shortcomings.

The Economist Building K170e
1964
25 St James's Street SW1
Alison and Peter Smithson
⊖ Green Park

Offices for *The Economist* newspaper, a bank and flats are each accommodated in separate buildings on a slightly raised plaza at the south end of a block in St James's. The architects' objectives were to make a group of buildings compatible with the eighteenth-century scale of St James's Street; to provide public open space and through views, possibly beginning a wider system of separate routes for traffic and pedestrians; and to tidy up the backs or 'inside' of the block. The buildings have reinforced concrete frames clad with roach-bed Portland stone spandrels and pilasters. Window frames and water-channelling trim are of aluminium painted light grey. The exposed flank wall of Boodles Club K57 is faced in yellow stock brick, and its new bay window in precast concrete is painted to match the rest of the Club's stucco. The design is remarkable for having largely achieved the architects' intentions; for its intelligent approach to the rebuilding of a vulnerable part of the city; and for having successfully extended the idea of a building standing free in its plaza. The group treats St James's Street civilly and, even if the tower is too tall, the effect of this is far less damaging than that produced by the directional slabs which had been the model for this kind of development (see New Zealand House K165). The architects have controlled the weathering of Portland stone, and thus have prevented the formation of the black and white 'moustaches' which ruin the appearance of other modern London buildings without classical ledges and copings.

The buildings were refurbished by Skidmore Owings Merrill in 1990, when the glazed lobby to the tower was enlarged and conventionally Americanized, and the inconsequential glazed canopy added.

Queen Elizabeth Hall, K171g
Purcell Room and **Hayward Gallery** 1964
South Bank SE1
LCC/GLC Architects Department; Sir Hubert Bennett and Jack Whittle
⊖ Waterloo

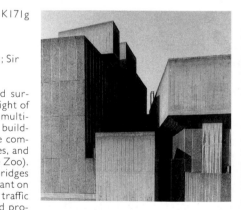

These buildings and their terraced surroundings were designed at the height of two fashions: first, for creating the 'multi-level city', and second, for making buildings look like something else (here comparisons were made with landscapes, and the craggy Mappin's Terraces at the Zoo). The raised pedestrian decks and bridges seem both inconvenient and irrelevant on this quiet site, with no through traffic from which pedestrians might need protection. The decks are windy, offering no shelter from the weather, and are difficult for the frail or disabled to negotiate. Neither they, nor the buildings' other forms, mark or indicate the entrances for the intending visitor: there are no 'front doors'. The ground on which the buildings stand has been degraded to a shabby undercroft, used only by skateboarders and rollerskaters. The construction – of exposed rough-shuttered reinforced concrete with some areas of exposed aggregate concrete cladding panels – has weathered badly. The concert hall, seating just over 1000, is an ugly room: more concrete, no decoration and unsympathetic lighting. The Purcell Room, for recitals, seats 368. The lobby common to both halls works badly, and shuffling queues always form at the entrances to the auditoria. This is particularly strange, as part of the rationale of 'organic' architecture of this sort is that each space or form should be tailored specifically to suit its function. The Hayward Gallery, home of the Arts Council's exhibitions, has five galleries of different shapes and lighting methods, most of them inconvenient.

The South Bank Board, present management of these buildings and of the Royal Festival Hall K157, wishing to remedy some of the inconveniences and to speculate on the value of the site, in 1987 commissioned an improvement scheme from Terry Farrell and Co. This proposed demolishing many of the raised pedestrian decks, bringing the entrances of the buildings back to ground level, and coating the concrete of the Queen Elizabeth Hall and Hayward Gallery in decorative architecture. Fortunately the scheme has not yet proved financially viable, and this pungent reminder of a very particular period in

London's architecture remains, with all its faults.

The space now known as 'Cardboard City' under the roundabout at the southern end of Waterloo Bridge was built at the same time as the Queen Elizabeth Hall and now provides shelter to about 1000 of London's homeless, who sleep there in cardboard boxes.

Royal National Theatre K172h
1967–77
Sir Denys Lasdun and Partners
Θ Waterloo

The National Theatre's opening was the culmination of a long campaign, by George Bernard Shaw among others, to establish such an institution. Many sites were considered, and Lasdun's first commission was for a building between the Royal Festival Hall and County Hall. The present building contains three separate auditoria: the Olivier, with an open stage and seating 1160: the Lyttelton, a smaller conventional proscenium 890-seater theatre; and, with its own separate entrance at the back, the Cottesloe, a black-painted 'shed' with movable seating, for experimental productions. The Olivier is a huge success, perhaps at its best with epic productions and a full house: the combination of the audience's proximity to the acting and the very sophisticated stage machinery and lighting is unique. In plan, the main axis of the Olivier is set at forty-five degrees to that of the Lyttelton. This, together with the insistent but broken-up horizontal layers which Lasdun has wrapped around the theatres, provides a series of highly differentiated foyers and terraces, with

good views both of each other and across the Thames to Somerset House.

Immediately to the east of the Royal National Theatre is the **IBM Central London Marketing Centre** of 1978–84. It houses offices, suites for conferences and seminars, and computers, and was also designed by Sir Denys Lasdun, Peter Softley and Partners. The architectural language is similar to that of the National Theatre, with strong continuous horizontals, of concrete panels pre-cast rather than cast *in situ*.

Coutts Bank 1973–9 K173f
Strand WC2
Sir Frederick Gibberd and Partners
Θ Charing Cross

The prominent position of this triangular block to the east of Trafalgar Square and directly north of Charing Cross Station has resulted in a series of speculations over the last 150 years. First it was the site of John Nash's West Strand Improvements of 1830–2 K84 (by William Herbert to Nash's plans); then in 1875 the Lowther Arcade was built through the centre of the block, a shorter but grander version of the Royal Opera Arcade K69. The arcade was unfortunately demolished in 1903 and a building for Coutts Bank was erected by J MacVicar Anderson on the site. More recently the entire block was threatened with either total demolition or subdivision by a new road proposal, but in the event the original Nash stucco façades and corner pepper pots were preserved (like the Regent's Park façades). The interior of the block was demolished and replaced by enlarged premises for Coutts Bank. The four-storey glazed entrance façade to Coutts is sliced into the Strand elevation, the tall triangular central hall is visible from the street, and Nash's façades are correspondingly diminished. The luxurious materials of the interior are in the contemporary American banking hall mode: bronze, travertine, acoustic plaster, frameless plate glass and an abundance of plants.

Queen Elizabeth II   K174n
Conference Centre 1979–86
Broad Sanctuary SW1
Powell Moya and Partners
⊖ St James's Park

The site opposite Westminster Abbey had been empty for forty years. Proposals for a purpose-built official conference centre here originated in Sir Leslie Martin's plan of the 1960s for the redevelopment of Whitehall: conferences had previously been held in, for example, Lancaster House K75. The present building provides four large conference rooms on the third floor: these are signalled on the outside by the projecting glazed foyers visibly hanging from beams. Below this floor is accommodation for the press, and above it, recessed, a further conference room and offices. The external composition is additive – it has no strong corners or edges – but it respects its neighbours in height, if not in its materials of bush-hammered white concrete and lead.

Comyn Ching Triangle   K175b
started 1984
between Monmouth Street, Mercer Street and Shelton Street WC2
conversion by Terry Farrell and Co.
⊖ Leicester Square

Named after the firm of architectural ironmongers who had occupied much of the site, this block of late seventeenth and early eighteenth-century houses which forms an important part of the area of Seven Dials K25 might have been demolished had the more grandiose plans for Covent Garden been realized. It was, however, spared, and Farrell tactfully consolidated the original work, supplied a taller new building in inoffensive pastiche to each of the three corners, and opened up the interior of the block for public use. This last is the only questionable aspect of the scheme: unlike the nearby Neal's Yard, there are no frontages on the inside and it is unclear what the space is for.

Charing Cross 1990   K176f
Strand WC2
Terry Farrell and Co.
⊖ Charing Cross

The overbuilding of Charing Cross Station is a dilemma. On the one hand the project continues the unfortunate fashion for dismantling London's fine nineteenth-century railway sheds and replacing them with commercial offices built over the existing platforms, thus sacrificing the public realm for private profit. On the other hand it can be argued that, unlike London's other railway termini, Charing Cross is double-fronted and is therefore a special case. Although rather oversized and formally diagrammatic when viewed from Waterloo Bridge, Farrell's building contributes a new and monumental profile to the Embankment.

Sainsbury Wing 1990   K177f
National Gallery
Trafalgar Square W1
Venturi, Rauch, Scott Brown Architects;
Executive architects Shepherd Robson
and Partners
⊖ Charing Cross

The Sainsbury Wing stands to the west of
the National Gallery. There have been
three competitions for its rebuilding, the
penultimate one prompting the royal rebuke 'a monstrous carbuncle on the face of
a much-loved and elegant friend' for the
winning design by Ahrends Burton and
Koralek in mid-1984. The combination of
lack of funds, royal interference and a
protracted row meant that the project
was shelved. In 1985 the National Gallery
accepted an offer from the Sainsbury brothers to fund the present building. A final
limited competition was embarked upon,
the results of which were unpublicized in
order to avoid acrimony.

After all the fuss Venturi's building is a
rather pedestrian affair. As an addition to
Trafalgar Square it is not unlike the replacement of Grand Buildings diagonally
opposite. (Also the subject of a controversial competition in 1985.) It neither
threatens nor directly enhances the
square, and is most prominent in the
rather casual display of its rooflights. The
discontinuous treatment of the various
elevations is by now a well-tried 'post-
modern' reaction to the varying importance of city streets. The result is not
altogether successful: a part-decorated
and part-melted classical billboard.

Inside, the galleries compensate to some
extent for the failings of the exterior. The
enfilade grid of lofty galleries (inspired in
section by Soane's Dulwich Picture Gallery W3) forms an appropriate permanent
home for the gallery's magnificent collection of early Renaissance paintings – both
Italian and Northern European works are
housed, including such masterpieces as
Uccello's *Battle of San Romano* and Jan van
Eyck's *Arnolfini Marriage*. The muted greys
of the galleries combine well with the
gilded detail of the paintings.

Venturi has always expressed a fondness
for an English interpretation of classicism
– from the mannerism of Hawksmoor and
Vanbrugh to the playfulness of Lutyens. It
is in the more detailed resolution of
aspects of this building that we see his
hand to best effect. The slicing and recom-
position of classical mouldings at the head
of the main stair are to be noted.

Section L: City of London/Whitechapel South/The Borough/ Bermondsey

The Thames, from Blackfriars Bridge in the west to Tower Bridge in the east, is a convenient north-south dividing line for this area. Embedded in the north is the historic City of London, and to the south are the Borough and Bermondsey. The Roman wall, built at the beginning of the third century AD, stretched from the Tower of London to Blackfriars, enclosing a total area of 134 ha (330 acres). The smallness of this area was to encourage early settlements outside the wall, and the City quickly became scattered rather than concentrated in form. Watling Street, Ermine Street, London Bridge (the only permanent crossing until 1729) and the great wall are the Roman legacy to London; their other buildings have disappeared, and are now the study of archaeologists.

Following the Romans' withdrawal in the fifth century the Saxons invaded, but very little remains of anything that they might have built in London. The Norman city has all but vanished under later rebuilding, the White Tower L3 and St Bartholomew the Great H1 being conspicuous exceptions. By the early thirteenth century Royal Charters had established London's independence by granting the trading privileges still enjoyed by the City, and the markets of Eastcheap, Leadenhall, Billingsgate and Smithfield were established within its dense fabric. Urban medieval London imposed its patterns on manorial London: inns and religious foundations are now buried in urban blocks, indicated only by a gate and an alley.

By the middle of the seventeenth century London was an extraordinarily dense and labyrinthine timber-built city, an easy prey to the Great Plague of 1665 (killing at least 100,000 inhabitants) and the Great Fire the next year, which laid waste 136 ha (436 acres) and destroyed 13,200 houses (virtually all the City's domestic buildings). London as a brick city emerges from this time. Plans for the reconstruction of the City were immediately put forward by Christopher Wren, Robert Hooke and Richard Newcourt. Despite these ambitious proposals, inspired by the regular grids and *rond points* of the continental city, pressing needs for housing and business premises meant that London's reconstruction actually took place on its medieval foundations.

This pattern still remains, giving the City today its special feel of being a City within the city. When the Great Estates to the west were developed into coherent new sections of London (Bloomsbury, Belgravia and so on) the City stubbornly resisted. The small patterns of land ownership established by guilds, trading companies and parks were permanently to frustrate any large-scale re-ordering.

The most impressive and significant architectural remains of the seventeenth and early eighteenth centuries are Wren's City churches, built after the Great Fire, of which only 23 of the original 51 remain (19 were destroyed in the Second World War). In 1672 Wren also began the designs for rebuilding St Paul's Cathedral L27, which was complete by 1711.

At the turn of the century a few squares, crescents and some fine houses on a par with the more elegant developments in the West End were introduced (Devonshire Square L56 and the Minories L59). The most important single building of this period was the Mansion House L55 (the official residence of the Lord Mayor, designed by George Dance the Elder). In 1760 the City gates were demolished and the houses removed from London Bridge under the supervision of George Dance the Younger, architect to the Corporation. In the eighteenth and early nineteenth centuries the City gained a hospital (James Gibbs' St Bartholomew's) and a bank (the Bank of England, designed by George Sampson).

As part of the metropolitan 'Improvements' carried out at the beginning of the nineteenth century, Southwark Bridge was built in 1815 and in 1823–31 London Bridge was rebuilt. In 1830 King William Street was cut through to connect the new bridge with the Bank of England, and in 1841 the Royal Exchange L74 was built to mark the Bank crossing and to celebrate the new focal point of the City. In 1801 the City had a population of 128,000, but by

1881 it had fallen to 50,000 (by 1951 there were only 5,000 residents).

The railways made an early appearance, connecting the commercial and trading centre with the expanding suburbs: London Bridge Station L72, in Bermondsey, was London's first railway station. Next was Fenchurch Street L76, to the north of the Tower of London, built in 1836 to serve the London and Blackwall Railway; Cannon Street L78 and Blackfriars Stations followed in 1865 and 1880, providing more bridges across the Thames to connect the City to the expanding southern suburbs; and Liverpool Street Station (1870) made nationwide connections to the north and east. In 1863 the first Underground line opened from Paddington to Farringdon. There were now six railway stations within the boundaries of the Roman City Wall.

The contemporary City gives no visible clues to its rich and complex past, apart from a few distinguished Victorian office buildings, Wren's City churches, and fragments of the medieval pattern of courts and alleys. Before the Great Fire (1666) London had been destroyed by invading armies several times; since then its architecture has suffered one great misfortune and two disasters. The misfortune was that none of the plans put forward for rebuilding after the Great Fire could be fully realized; the disasters were, first, Second World War bombing and, second, the completely inept efforts at reconstruction which ensued (the Holden-Holford plan for St Paul's Precinct is outstanding in this respect). In the 1960s and '70s the City acquired a skyline of ugly towers and slabs which are at variance with the medieval pattern of streets from which they rise. Some have since been refaced, but there have been two proposals for the replacement of the Holden-Holford buildings to the north of St Paul's, the first a modern scheme by Arup Associates, the second a 'neo-classical' *mélange*.

The history of Southwark, across the Thames to the south, is inextricably bound up with the City of London. With the bend of the river to the west, the area forms the hinge point between the Cities of Westminster and London, and as a result was the focal point of roads converging on London from the south and south-east (including the Roman Watling Street). It also formed a bridgehead for London Bridge, the sole Thames crossing until the eighteenth century. The evidence of its colourful past as a place of theatres, inns and bearbaiting rings, and of the less colourful history of its prisons has all but disappeared. However, the borough possesses the most important medieval monument south of the river apart from Lambeth Palace: the Augustinian Priory of St Mary Overie (now Southwark Cathedral) L4, founded in 1106, and with much remaining thirteenth- and fourteenth-century work.

By the middle of the eighteenth century Southwark was bounded by Bankside along the river and by the High Street from London Bridge. The possibilities of its position between Westminster and the City were opened up with the building of Westminster Bridge (1739–50) and Blackfriars Bridge (1760–9). George Dance the Younger, Clerk of Works to the City, realized this potential with his master plan of 1769, which extended the line of Blackfriars Bridge due south in a wide avenue to meet the road from Westminster Bridge at the *rond point* of St George's Circus. Dance's was the boldest plan to be carried out in eighteenth-century London and opened up more land for development: St George's Road and the New Kent Road quickly followed and by 1815 Great Dover Street had been cut through to the east. Southwark Street (1864) and Tower Bridge Road (1900) followed Haussmann's example in Paris, cutting through decayed and congested areas. Dance's work and the improvements of the nineteenth century are now only lines on the ground: Southwark was badly bombed in the Second World War, and its recent housing gives little care to making good streets – a familiar and depressing spectacle. To the east lies Bermondsey (the north-west corner in this section, the remainder in section U). The northern limits were densely built over by 1750, but the only relics of its medieval past are fragments of a gatehouse to the Priory. Bermondsey suffered the same fate as Southwark during and after the Second World War: unfortunately the good intentions of post-war local authority housing policies have damaged parts of London even more permanently and extensively than the Blitz.

Roman Wall LIh
3rd and 4th centuries
Tower of London, Tower Hill EC3
☉ Tower Hill
The early third-century Roman wall terminated at the Thames where the Tower now stands. A short stretch with part of a mid-fourth-century bastion is visible to the east of the White Tower. See also Barbican H40.

Roman Wall L2h
3rd and 4th centuries
Trinity Square EC3
☉ Tower Hill
One of the largest fragments of the wall still visible, over 7 m (24 ft) high. On it can be seen the courses of flat red Roman brick separating and binding layers of masonry rubble. Above these is the ashlar facing of medieval rebuilding.

Roman wall, Trinity Square

White Tower and L3h
Chapel of St John
11th century
Tower of London, Tower Hill EC3
☉ Tower Hill
The Tower was begun by William the Conqueror twelve years after his invasion of England in 1066: the White Tower stood alone when finished in 1097, and was a defence against attacks from the continent via the Thames estuary. While much altered (the corner cupolas which give the Tower its toy-like silhouette were added in the fourteenth century), it remains one of the most important examples of Norman military architecture in the country. Built of Caen stone (like Canterbury Cathedral) with walls 3.7m (12 ft) thick at the base, the keep's square plan is divided into three rooms on each floor; the rooms have been converted to more ceremonial uses over 900 years, and the lower floors now contain the Tower's collection of armour.
The inner curtain wall was started under Henry III and completed under Edward I, who began work on the outer curtain

wall. The two large circular bastions on the north of this outer wall were remodelled by Henry VIII. Much of this original work survives in spite of four centuries of alterations and additions.
The Chapel of St John is London's Norman church masterpiece – tiny, but massive and primitive, yet with more than adequate lighting through its two arcades.

Southwark Cathedral 1106 L4f
Borough High Street SE1
☉ London Bridge
Once the Augustinian Priory of St Mary Overie, founded in 1106, this subdued Gothic church became a cathedral in 1905 and is one of the few tangible reminders of Southwark's Norman and medieval past.
In the thirteenth century the Priory was burned down and in 1303 it was declared a ruin. As a result the dates of some of the original parts of the building are in doubt, but from the fourteenth century the general arrangement of the cathedral is well documented. There were significant renovations in the nineteenth century: in 1822 the tower and retrochoir were restored, and in 1838 the nave was demolished and rebuilt, to be further replaced by Sir Arthur Blomfield's nave of 1890–7. This is a rather feeble imitation of the existing thirteenth-century chancel, and detracts significantly from the whole.

Pevsner has observed that the Gothic style and detail of the building are part French and part English. The proportions of the chancel are English, but the arcaded first-floor wall passage was found only in

John Harvard, after whom Harvard College is named, was baptized here. Rev. John Harvard, was "The Teacher" of the First church of Charlestown who left his books and his death to the new college at New Towne (Cambridge).

cathedrals like Chartres and Reims. The capitals are puritanically undecorated, but the vaulting shafts are taken to the ground in the French manner. The clerestory is typically English with an exclusive use of lancet windows, while the vaults of the aisles, chancel and retrochoir are quadripartite, following French precedent.

The dates of the individual parts of the building are equally varied: the crossing tower is fourteenth-century in its lower stages, early fifteenth-century in the top two stages, and the parapet and pinnacles date from 1689. The north and west walls of the north transept are Norman, while the south transept is exclusively fourteenth-century. The elaborate south window is nineteenth-century. The interior of the Harvard Memorial Chapel, east of the north transept, dates from 1907, while the walls are of the twelfth century. Today it is marooned and almost engulfed by the upper-level railway tracks from Cannon Street to London Bridge.

To the west, between the railway and the river, lies an atmospheric area of nineteenth-century warehouses, still giving the impression of London as a working port. On **Clink Street** (site of the famous Clink prison) is an unexpected fourteenth-century rose window in a freestanding wall – all that remains of the Bishop of Winchester's medieval palace.

St Olave 15th century L5h
Hart Street and Seething Lane
EC3
⊖ Tower Hill

One of the City's few remaining Gothic parish churches, St Olave's is best approached through the churchyard from Seething Lane. The gateway, of 1658, has a pediment decorated with skulls and bones. The nave and aisles, of three bays, have quatrefoil piers of Purbeck marble: it has been suggested that much of the building material was re-used from the original thirteenth-century church. The Interior was gutted in the Second World War and rebuilt by E B Glanfield; however, many of the original furnishings were saved, notably the pulpit, communion rail, main door, and the panelling and stucco ceiling of the vestry.

St Helen, Bishopsgate L6c
started 15th century
Great St Helen's EC3
⊖ Liverpool Street

St Helen's is the largest medieval London church to have survived both the Great Fire and Second World War. A convent church was added to the earlier parish church, their two naves standing side by side (in what looks like an early and knowing example of duality) and finishing in a common west front with two doors. The northern nave was for the nuns, the southern for the laity, and they were originally separated by a screen. The bulk of the interior is of the fifteenth century, with some seventeenth-century work – the south door dates from 1633 – and nineteenth-century rearrangement by J L Pearson. There is an extensive collection of monumental brasses from 1470 on, and

some very fine Elizabethan and Jacobean tombs, the gaudiest of which is that of the Spencers (1609).

Guildhall 1411–40 L7b
front 1788–9
Guildhall Yard EC2
John Croxton, front by George Dance the Younger
⊖ Bank

Built only a few years after Westminster Hall, the Guildhall, while more extensively altered, still retains its medieval outlines. It is the City's largest secular room and, with the Mansion House, is still used for formal civic occasions. The roof is modern, but the eighteenth-century front to the Yard is an extraordinary and delicate mixture of Greek, Gothic and Indian (the cusped windows) motifs.

St Michael Cornhill 1421,   L8c
rebuilt 1670–2, 1715–22,
1856–60
Cornhill EC3
Sir Christopher Wren, Nicholas
Hawksmoor, Sir George Gilbert Scott
⊖ Bank

The lower parts of the tower to the
original church, built in 1421, survived the
Great Fire. Following Wren's rebuilding
of the nave, his office rebuilt the rest of
the tower to Nicholas Hawskmoor's
Gothic design (1715–22). In 1856–60 Scott
added the north entrance porch and the
Venetian tracery to the windows, best
viewed from the former churchyard to
the south.

Like St Peter's L33, St Michael's is connected by its side passage to a complex
system of medieval alleys behind, a pattern which characterized most of the City
up to this century (note Bengal Court,
only 1 m/3 ft wide).

Holy Sepulchre without   L9a
Newgate mid-15th century,
1666–70
Holborn Viaduct EC1
⊖ Chancery Lane

The church was considerably rebuilt in
1666–70 following the Great Fire, but the
fine west tower belongs to the fifteenth
century and is a proud reminder of the
Gothic parish church, first mentioned in
1137. The interior has seven bays and is
surprisingly spacious, with no division
between the nave and chancel.

St Andrew Undershaft   L10c
1520–32
Leadenhall Street and St Mary Axe
EC3
⊖ Bank

Though dull and much restored, St
Andrew's is remarkable for being one of
the few medieval churches to have survived both the Great Fire and the bombs
of the Second World War, even to the
seventeenth-century stained glass of the
west windows. However, any atmosphere
it might have had is now dispelled by its
use as a centre for the Christian teaching
and training of businessmen and young
people.

St Katherine Cree 1628–31,   L11d
tower 1504
Leadenhall Street EC3
⊖ Aldgate

Saved from the Great Fire, St Katherine's
is an important survival from a transitional period in English architecture. Its
interior has a vaulted plaster ceiling with
bosses at the intersections, but this is
supported on arches carried on the very
primitive-looking Tuscan order of nave
columns. The church was restored in 1962
when the aisles were closed off. The
cupola was added to the tower in the
eighteenth century.

Dean's Court 1670   L12a
Deanery, St Paul's Churchyard
EC4
Sir Christopher Wren(?)
⊖St Paul's
With its very large windows and slightly incompetent-looking decoration the house looks more Dutch than English, and is an important domestic survival from the post-Fire seventeenth century. The attribution to Wren is dubious. No longer the Dean's house, it is being restored and developed as luxury offices by Haslemere Estates.

St Vedast-alias-Foster   L13b
1670–3 tower 1697
Foster Lane EC2
Sir Christopher Wren
⊖St Paul's
The attraction of this church is the tower – late Wren, with the last memory of English Gothic and its steeples gone. The baroque is Italian, at least for the upper stages, where convexity, concavity and transparency are combined. The interior is a plain flat-ceilinged box.

St Mary-at-Hill 1670–6   L14g
St Mary at Hill EC3
Sir Christopher Wren
⊖Monument
St Mary's is reached through the narrow doorway of Peek House L84, and across a typical City courtyard – a tiny paved garden in the centre of the block. The interior is one of Wren's most extreme centralized compositions: a central dome, supported at the four corners by Corinthian columns, from which four 'transepts' emerge. Much of the woodwork is original, and was repaired in the general overhaul of the church in 1848–9. The façade to the street is best ignored.

St Edmund the King 1670–9   L15c
Lombard Street EC3
Sir Christopher Wren(?), Robert Hooke(?)
⊖Bank
The vertical street façade (of three bays with arched windows incorporating the octagonal lantern) and the curved sides to the short black spire are the main points of interest in this church. The interior, reorganized by Butterfield in 1864, has some excellent woodwork and panelling.

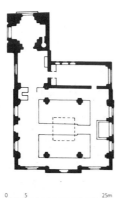

St Mary-le-Bow 1670–83   L16b
Cheapside EC2
Sir Christopher Wren
⊖St Paul's

St Mary's is distinguished by its magnificent tower and steeple. The tower was set forward from the body of the church and separated from it by a lobby to dominate the huddled houses of Cheapside. It is now splendidly isolated, the plain upper stages

contrasting with the elaborate doorway recessed into a rusticated opening.

The interior, restored since bombing, is now bourgeois: the trim modern pulpits and harshly coloured modern glass have reduced the plain white and gold of the architecture to calendar prettiness. In the crypt, however, some original Norman columns can still be seen.

St Bride 1670–84,   L17a
tower 1701–3
Bride Street, off Fleet Street EC4
Sir Christopher Wren
⊖Blackfriars

St Bride is one of the grander churches of Wren's series after the Great Fire of 1666. It nestles in its small yard, entirely surrounded by newspaper offices: a plain box of a nave, to which is attached the tallest of all Wren's steeples – 68 m (226 ft) high. His fully fledged baroque starts at the foot of the west door with a segmental pediment. which is repeated across the full width of the second stage. Above this starts the succession of octagonal arcades, pulled out 'like a telescope', as Pevsner says, and surmounted by a vestigial steeple.

Inside, the five-bay nave and aisles are separated by the Tuscan arcade which supports the tunnel-vault ceiling. The woodwork is new (restored after bombing) and although the original galleries

have not been restored, a good sense is conveyed of the original seventeenth-century church where the wooden fittings were independent of the brick or stone shell of the architecture. Note the permanent exhibition in the crypt.

St Lawrence Jewry 1670–87   L18b
Gresham Street EC2
Sir Christopher Wren
⊖St Paul's

A big church, whose uninterrupted nave is separated from a small screened chapel (all restored after bombing, when coloured modern glass was inserted). The magnificent Corinthian east front, facing the entrance of Guildhall Yard, is based on Wren's model design for St Paul's Cathedral L27. The plain projecting tower at the east end has a fine lead-covered baroque steeple.

The east front

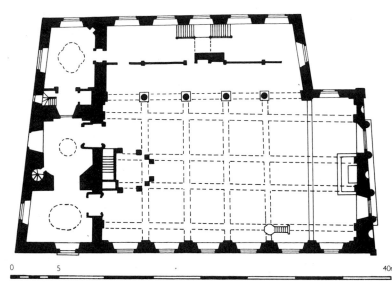

St Lawrence Jewry

0   5   40m

Innholders Hall c1670,   L19f
façade 1886
College Street EC4
J Douglass Mathews
⊖Cannon Street
The façade's interest lies in the early
eighteenth-century doorway, with a dec-
orated scroll pediment and coat of arms.
The hall was badly damaged in the Second
World War and uninterestingly restored
in 1950.

Vintners Hall 1671, 1870,   L20f
1909–10
Upper Thames Street EC4
Edward Jarman and others
⊖Mansion House
The original brick hall, marked by a
nineteenth-century Coade stone statue,
can be seen in Vintners Place. The squat
front which shields it from Upper Thames
Street is of the late nineteenth and early
twentieth centuries.

College of Arms 1671–7   L21a
Queen Victoria Street EC4
⊖St Paul's
The design of the College of Arms was the
responsibility of a master bricklayer, not
an architect, and the result is a good
example of the 'artisan style' (see also
Cromwell House R4). The simple brick
façade forms three sides of a shallow open
court, closed to Queen Victoria Street by
magnificent black and gilded iron gates,
transferred to the College in 1956 from
Goodrich Court, Hertfordshire. The first
floor has an external stone gallery, from
which the view to the river – with Wren's
St Benet's in the foreground – is a vignette
of seventeenth-century London.

Monument 1671–7   L22g
Pudding Lane EC3
Sir Christopher Wren, Robert Hooke
⊖ Monument

The site of the outbreak of the Great Fire of 1666 is marked by this robust Roman Doric column 62 m (202 ft) high. Of fine white Portland stone, it stands on a square pedestal, on which the wings of the City's griffins act as acroteria at the corners. Wren's original design was decorated with gilded flames and crowned with a statue – replaced by Robert Hooke with the present spiky ball. One can climb to the top, and while the panorama is not particularly spectacular, it does afford a rare aerial view of the City. For a vivid description of the Fire based on Samuel Pepys' account see the 'Fire Experience' at the Museum of London H42.

St Nicholas Cole Abbey   L23b
1671–7
Queen Victoria Street EC4
Sir Christopher Wren
⊖ St Paul's

Wren's church, which replaced the original dating back to 1144 and destroyed in the Great Fire, was itself burnt out in the Second World War. Unfortunately, the restoration by Arthur Bailey is undistinguished, and the approaches have fallen victim to 'traffic improvements' and pedestrian precinct planning of the mid-1950s.

St Magnus 1671–85,   L24g
tower 1705
Lower Thames Street EC3
Sir Christopher Wren
⊖ Monument

Now in an extraordinary position almost underneath London Bridge, St Magnus has one of Wren's more conventional plans: aisles flank a straight nave, whose tunnel vaulting – punctuated by oval windows – is supported by Ionic colonnades. The original reredos and west gallery, restored in the 1920s, are among the best surviving. The exterior was cleaned and partly refaced in 1980–1.

St Stephen Walbrook L25b

1672–7, spire 1717
Walbrook EC4
Sir Christopher Wren
Bank, Cannon Street

The site of St Stephen's is typically dense and irregular. The tower and spire look up to the Mansion House L55 from the corner of Walbrook, and the main body of the church and its small garden were buried in the interior of the block, with a narrow passageway on one side. The entrance is by a stairway leading from Walbrook into an apsidal lobby, from which the church appears, ambiguously, to be a longitudinal space with a centralized plan. St Stephen's demonstrated better than his later churches Wren's preoccupation with centralized plans (a means of providing a closer connection between the service and the congregation) as opposed to the traditional longitudinal east-west orientation. Simultaneously, he was working on the same combination of nave, aisles and transepts with a central dome space at St Paul's Cathedral.

The beautiful coffered dome is carried on eight arches and freestanding columns, giving the sense of a building within a building. Four arches determine the nave, chancel and transepts and another arch is thrown across each corner; the resulting half-groin vaults, each supported on a column, describe a triangular space. This aspect of the design is very much in the spirit of St Paul's.

At the time of writing St Stephen's is undergoing extensive renovation work; this and infrequent opening times make it difficult to appreciate the majestic interior.

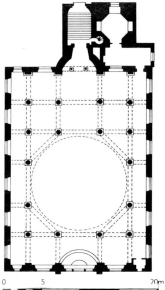

St James Garlickhithe L26f

1674–87, steeple 1713
Garlick Hill EC4
Sir Christopher Wren
Mansion House

St James, one of Wren's more accessible works, is a contemporary of St Stephen Walbrook L25; the brightly lit interior shows Wren exploring the theme of centrality versus the east-west liturgical axis (which later exercised Hawksmoor). Centrality wins in the open central bay of the nave, but the liturgical axis is emphasized by the window at the east end, unfortunately now obscured. There is much good original woodwork in the interior, which is one of the few among Wren's churches to have retained some of the atmosphere of late seventeenth-century Protestantism. The spire is one of Wren's more delicate baroque inventions, marking the entrance through the pedimented door.

St Paul's Cathedral

L27a

1675–1711
Ludgate Hill EC4
Sir Christopher Wren

⊖ St Paul's, but the best approach is on foot from Ludgate Circus

The present building replaces the Norman and Gothic cathedral destroyed in the Great Fire of 1666. The previous building was itself a replacement of one destroyed by fire in 1087. The pre-Fire building had fallen into decay, having lost its pointed spire in 1561, and in 1634 Inigo Jones refaced some of the walls and added a giant portico to the west end. After Jones's death, but before the Fire, Wren was appointed to report on the fabric. He suggested recasing the nave 'after a good Roman Manner'.

In 1669 Wren, aged thirty-seven, was appointed Surveyor-General. He produced two designs, the first a domed Greek cross (the enormous model of which is in the Library, visits by arrangement). The second, an elongated plan with a spire over a domed crossing, received royal approval in 1675. The foundation ·stone was laid at the east end on 21 June 1675, and the building finished in 1711, when Wren was seventy-nine.

The design is an arrangement of four volumes: the dome and crossing, nave and choir of medieval section (nave with two lower aisles, the nave vaulting supported by flying buttresses), the transepts, and the west end. Externally, all the lower parts are clothed with a two-storey screen, the upper storey is blind, and the two storeys are carried across the west front in a double portico which can be read as two superimposed temple fronts. The relief in the pediment, including a pyramid, shows the Conversion of St Paul. Two very complex towers flank the portico. The dome above the drum is constructed in three parts: an inner dome of brick, an intermediate cone of brick, and an outer casing of wood, without ribs, covered in lead. The clear separation of drum and dome is made by a projecting circle of attached columns, of which every fourth one engages a structural pier.

The interior, in grey and white, is one of the coolest in Europe (try to see it without too many other visitors). A single Corinthian order supports round ribs and saucer domes; the only original decorations are the frescoes in the dome by Sir John Thornhill (see also the Painted Hall, Greenwich U3) done in 1716–19. The baroque complications at the crossing arise from making the dome as wide as nave and aisles combined; where these pierce the piers supporting the drum, they are roofed with segmental arches.

Climb the dome (entrance and ticket from south-west corner), walk round the Whispering Gallery and climb to the lantern, ball and cross, for a fine view of the Cathedral and of the City, largely and ineptly rebuilt since 1945. The crypt (entrance from the south transept), although utilitarian and architecturally unremarkable, contains Wren's Great Model of 1674, the final design from which the Cathedral was built. Among the many tombs and monuments is that of Wren himself (*lector, si monumentum requiris, circumspice*) as well as those of British celebrities from Ivor Novello to Horatio Nelson. The Cathedral is floodlit up to midnight during the summer: the symmetrical composition of the south side can then clearly be seen.

The George Inn started 1676   L28j
71 Borough High Street SE1
⊖London Bridge

The George is London's only remaining working example of the inn type, predecessor of both the motel and the theatre (although it is now missing the northern side of the galleried courtyard). The interiors, their style now more of the eighteenth century than of the seventeenth, still provide a plausible impression of an inn's hospitality; generations of brewers' improvements have been accomplished discreetly. It is owned by the National Trust.

St Anne and St Agnes   L29b
1677–80
Gresham Street EC2
Sir Christopher Wren, restored by Braddock and Martin Smith 1966
⊖St Paul's

First mentioned in about 1200, rebuilt by Wren following the Great Fire, and very well restored after the Blitz, St Anne and St Agnes has one of Wren's purest centralized plans. The exterior is of pink brick, the three bays, with arched windows and a central 'Dutch' pediment, accurately expressing the interior volume. The tower and end bay are rendered and the curiously squat spire was added in 1714. The interior space, deriving from the early Christian plan of a Greek cross, is very fine indeed. In the centre is a large dome supported on four columns: the arms are vaulted and at the corners are four smaller domes. The Lutherans, the present occupants, keep the church locked most of the time – otherwise it would (and should) be better known.

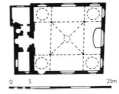

0   5   25m

St Benet, Paul's Wharf   L30a
1677–83
Upper Thames Street EC4
Sir Christopher Wren
⊖Blackfriars, Mansion House

Replacing an earlier church (c1111) St Benet's is a delightfully simple brick cube of red and blue chequerwork, with a hipped roof, and garlands above the three windows on the west and south sides. The tower has a simple short lead spire on a lead dome. Like many of Wren's churches, it now stands marooned by municipal open-space 'improvements' of the worst kind. The interior, lit by large, clear windows, has great charm.

Christ Church 1677–87   L31a
Newgate Street EC1
Sir Christopher Wren
⊖ St Paul's
All that remains is the tower, one of the most elegant in London. It is in three stages: the bell stage is crowned by segmental pediments; the next stage is recessed with a freestanding colonnade; and above this is a miniature spire topped with a vase. The tower is best seen as the conclusion to an avenue of trees in the garden to the west.

St Martin 1677–87   L32a
Ludgate Hill EC4
Sir Christopher Wren
⊖ Blackfriars, St Paul's
Wren here used one of his centralized plans, a cross inside a square (see also St Anne and St Agnes L29 and St Mary-at-Hill L14). The cross is defined by columns which support two intersecting barrel vaults. There were originally wooden galleries in three of the arms of the cross, but now only that on the west remains, supporting the organ. The symmetrical street façade has the entrance under the tower.

St Peter upon Cornhill   L33c
1677–87
Cornhill, via St Peter's Alley and Gracechurch Street EC3
Sir Christopher Wren
⊖ Bank
As its extended address implies, this church is buried in a labyrinth of medieval passageways and courtyards. The most comprehensive view of it is from the churchyard to the south: a stuccoed exterior with a simple brick tower capped by an obelisk on a dome. From Gracechurch Street to the east, the façade is impressively Palladian: the ground floor has five uniform arched windows separated by pilasters, and the upper floor has one arched and two semicircular windows, completed by a pediment and two curved side-pieces.

Gateways c1680   L34b
21–22a College Hill EC4
⊖ Cannon Street
A typical piece of historical transformation on a small scale. These two magnificent late seventeenth-century stone gateways, both with broken and richly decorated pediments, were originally part of Whittington's College, which itself was part of St Michael Paternoster Royal L42 on College Street. With their bull's-eye windows they form a symmetrical group. Behind number 21 is a delightful small courtyard.

St Augustine 1680–3   L35b
Watling Street EC4
✸ Sir Christopher Wren
⊖ St Paul's, Mansion House
The tower, all that remains of the church
after the Blitz, has been incorporated into
the post-war Choir School of the Cathedral. It is not one of Wren's more
exuberant designs, and only the graceful
steeple suggests his hand.

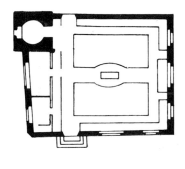

0   5   25m

St Mary Abchurch 1681–6   L36c
Abchurch Lane EC4
✸ Sir Christopher Wren
⊖ Bank, Monument
If the interior of this seemingly modest
church were more publicly accessible it
would be well known. Hidden away down
Abchurch Lane, the church (which replaced the twelfth-century original)
addresses a tiny square, once its
graveyard. The restrained exterior has
three-bayed south and east elevations, all
in brick with stone dressings, and a tower
in the north-west corner. The interior is a
surprise and deeply impressive: the
dome, supported by eight arches, stands
free of the outer walls and conveys an
impression of great spaciousness in a very
small building. It was painted by William
Snow in 1708–14, and the superbly designed altarpiece is by Grinling Gibbons.

St Mary Aldermary 1682   L37b
Queen Victoria Street EC4
✸ Sir Christopher Wren(?)
⊖ Blackfriars
This is a Gothic copy, possibly by Wren, of
the sixteenth- and seventeenth-century
church destroyed in the Fire. The problem of whether it is correct or a pastiche
still exercises art historians. The details –
the fan vaulting and pinnacled spire – can
be matched in earlier English
Perpendicular churches, but our guess is
that the design is a free reinterpretation.
The strange bald tower looks like an
essay in Perpendicular Expressionism.
The setting of the church is not its
original one; Queen Victoria Street was
cut through the City in 1867-71 as a
Victorian Improvement, an extension
of the Embankment's east-west traffic
route.

St Clement Eastcheap   L38c
1683–7
Clements Lane and
King William Street EC4
Sir Christopher Wren
⊖Bank, Monument

A simple little church, with a pedimented and stuccoed exterior, and exposed brickwork in the top parts of the tower. The interior is equally plain; the south aisle was much altered by Butterfield (1870–89) and has since been further modified.

St Margaret Pattens 1684–9   L39g
Eastcheap EC3
Sir Christopher Wren
⊖Monument

There are two noteworthy features to this otherwise plain church: the entrance, flanked by a good early nineteenth-century house and shop, and the tower, set back from Eastcheap and crowned with a tall, spiky, and very un-baroque spire. The interior has good original joinery, including the excellent churchwardens' pews, dated 1686.

St Andrew-by-the-Wardrobe 1685–95   L40a
Queen Victoria Street EC4
Sir Christopher Wren
⊖Blackfriars

A brick church, its interior now largely without character. It was rebuilt after bombing, when the aisles under the galleries were enclosed behind panelling. For contrast, see St James Garlickhithe L26, an un-bombed church which has retained both its parish church flavour and some of the strange rigour of English Protestantism.

St Margaret Lothbury   L41b
1686–90
Lothbury EC2
Sir Christopher Wren
⊖Bank

The present church (the original dated from about 1200) has a simple, nearly rectangular plan, with the tower rising in the south-west corner. The delicate lead spire of the square and undecorated tower is an obelisk on a domed base. Particularly interesting are the furnishings, many of which originate from St Olave Jewry.

St Michael Paternoster Royal 1686–94   L42j
College Street EC4
Sir Christopher Wren
⊖Cannon Street, Mansion House

The old church of St Michael, which dated back to 1219 and in which Dick Whittington established a college before his death, was destroyed in the Great Fire. Wren's replacement – one of his last City churches – was further damaged in the Second World War and restored by E Davies. The spire, surmounted by a delicately recessed and transparent octagonal lantern in three stages, is particularly fine and was completed in 1713. The church itself is a plain brick parallelogram with a stone-faced front executed by Wren's master mason, Edward Strong. The renovated interior is of no great interest apart from a pulpit attributed to Grinling Gibbons.

St Mary Somerset 1686–95   L43b
Upper Thames Street EC4
Sir Christopher Wren
⊖Blackfriars

The body of the church was demolished in 1871. The plain tower which remains finds itself in a sad little garden typical of the City's absent-minded approach to the design of its outdoor spaces.

St Dunstan-in-the-East 1697   L44g
St Dunstan's Hill EC3
Sir Christopher Wren
⊖Monument

Only Wren's tower remains after bombing – the body of the church had in any case been rebuilt in 1817. The four-stage tower is seventeenth-century Gothic, distinguishable from the real thing in its occasional continuous horizontals – compare with Hawskmoor's west towers K48 at Westminster Abbey.

The Anchor and houses early 18th century   L45j
1, 49, 50 and 52 Bankside SE1
⊖London Bridge

These surprising fragments are all that remain of eighteenth-century Bankside. The Anchor pub, number 1, and its setting against the abutment of Cannon Street railway bridge are picturesque, but the inside has been redone in all-purpose brewer's Dickensian. Number 49, 'Cardinal's Wharf', is the house on which a confident plaque claims (although there is no evidence) that Wren lived in it while designing St Paul's on the opposite side of the river. Numbers 50–2, 'Provost's Lodgings', were restored after being gutted in the Second World War.

49 Bankside

Spanish and Portuguese   L46d
Synagogue 1700–1
Bevis Marks EC3
Joseph Avis
⊖Aldgate

A routine Georgian place of worship, indistinguishable from contemporary buildings of other religions. Built by a Quaker master-builder, this early and well preserved synagogue, complete with many contemporary furnishings, is now a unique survival.

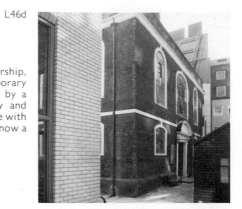

Chapter House   L47k
Southwark Cathedral 1702–3
St Thomas Street SE1
⊖London Bridge

The square brick chapel tower projecting into the street and the fine house with giant pilasters to the east formed the nucleus of the original St Thomas's Hospital, before it moved to its present site in 1868. In the eighteenth century the group was extended with a terrace of houses (numbers 11–15), and set back from the line of St Thomas Street.

Houses 1703, rebuilt 1976   L48f
1–2 Laurence Pountney Hill
⊖Monument

These grand houses and the small street in which they stand convey very well the red-brick, domestic matrix of the rebuilt City, within which stood Wren's white churches and Cathedral. They are sumptuously but innocently decorated, the work of master-builders rather than architects. See also Queen Anne's Gate K31 of the same date.

Wardrobe Place c1710   L49a
off Carter Lane EC4
⊖Blackfriars, St Paul's

This contained and tranquil close is a good surviving example of the medieval City's pattern of courts. Of the buildings, numbers 3–5 date from about 1710 and the remainder are more recent. The name derives from the Great Wardrobe, or royal storehouse, moved here from the Tower L3 in the fourteenth century and destroyed in the Great Fire of 1666.

Chapter House L50a
St Paul's Cathedral 1712–14
St Paul's Churchyard EC4
Sir Christopher Wren
⊖St Paul's

The Chapter House was gutted in the Second World War and has since been restored. A modest cube-like building of seven bays, with quoins at the corners and angles of the central three bays, it now stands alone in Lord Holford's inadequate precinct design of 1961, marooned in a sea of inept modern buildings.

St Mary Woolnoth 1716–27 L51c
Lombard Street and
King William Street EC4
Nicholas Hawksmoor
⊖Bank

The elements of this exquisite composition are the square of the plan and the clusters of Corinthian columns inset from the corners. The columns support a clerestory which supplies light through huge semicircular windows. The galleries previously occupying the north and south sides have been dismantled and the woodwork placed against the walls. The exterior is quite different from those of Hawksmoor's other churches: the 'tower' has become so broad as to occupy almost the full width of the west front. Hawksmoor's rustication and the intensely decorated blind niches of the south side seem more Mannerist than either antique or baroque. The church was cleaned in 1980 – but its present sand colour will probably turn to black and white again (see for example St Paul's Cathedral L27).

Guy's Hospital 1722–80 L52k
St Thomas Street SE1
W Jupp
⊖London Bridge

Guy's Hospital was founded by Thomas Guy to deal with the overcrowding at St Thomas's Hospital across the street. The original building (1722) forms a magnificent *cour d'honneur* set back behind iron gates and railings. In 1774 the centre bay was improved by Jupp in the Palladian manner, and the ground floor is rusticated and arcaded, as were the wings originally. The eighteenth-century courts beyond are unexceptional (although an alcove from the London Bridge of 1758–62 is preserved in one of them), as are the extensive additions from the nineteenth and twentieth centuries.

St Botolph 1725–9 L53c
Bishopsgate EC2
James Gold, George Dance the Elder
⊖Liverpool Street

A decent uninspired design which has been much altered and added to (the interior in 1821 and 1878). Notice the Parish Hall with its touching wooden statues of charity children.

St George Southwark L54j
1734–6
Borough High Street SE1
John Price
⊖ Borough
A grand but provincial-looking affair, St George's has a plain nave, a solid tower and a giant, if squashed, open segmental pediment to the west end. The tower and spire are almost completely solid: they have none of the baroque playfulness of the contemporary St Giles-in-the-Fields K45.

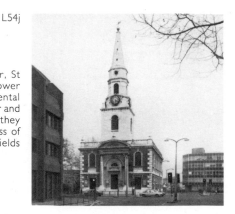

Mansion House 1739–52 L55b
Mansion House Place EC4
George Dance the Elder
⊖ Bank
Official residence of the Lord Mayor of London, the building displays a porticoed front and side, Palladian as the date would suggest, but both ungainly and provincial. The original unlikely double attics have been reduced in height. The allegorical sculpture in the pediment of 1744 is by the young Robert Taylor, and shows London defeating Envy and bringing Plenty. The building's main interest lies in its axially-arranged sequence of state rooms, entered originally via a vestibule from the portico. The sequence ends in the extraordinary Egyptian Hall, a Vitruvian idea which interested Palladio and was revived by Burlington.

Devonshire Square EC2 L56c
c1740
⊖ Liverpool Street
Only just a square – the open south side provides a view of the City at its most unprepossessing. The earliest remaining houses are numbers 12 and 13, both of four bays, in the north-east corner. On the east side is part of the New Street warehouse H23, refurbished as offices in 1982.

St Botolph 1741–4 L57d
Aldgate EC3
George Dance the Elder
⊖ Aldgate
Built while Dance was constructing the Mansion House L55, this church suffers from the same clumsiness. The Venetian windows are merely the tired remnants of earlier Palladianism; the interior is remarkable for Bentley's 1889 redecoration, especially the ceiling and very bold balustrade.

Hopton Almshouses 1752   L58e
Hopton Street SE1
⊖ Blackfriars
A bizarre survival, this group of little
houses now faces one of the large clearing
banks' computer centres. The houses are
grouped in U-shapes round three sides of a
square courtyard, at the end of which is
the double-height pedimented committee
room.

The Crescent, America   L59d
Square and **Vine Street** EC3
1760–70
George Dance the Younger
⊖ Tower Hill
Of the original scheme planned by Dance –
from north to south, a square, a crescent
and a circus – only a small group of five-
storey houses in the crescent remains,
numbers 7 and 8 in stock brick, and
number 9 in brick with red dressings. See
also Seven Dials K25 and Alfred Place G13.

All Hallows 1765–7   L60c
London Wall EC2
George Dance the Younger
⊖ Liverpool Street
Dance was twenty-four when he designed
this, his London masterpiece. It combines
rudimentary forms (the tunnel vault lit by
three semicircular windows on each side,
and the segmental apse) with spare linear
decoration like that of the Adams. The
engaged Ionic columns carry only a frieze
before supporting the springing of the
vaults to the windows. (Dance's pupil
Soane later extended the use of primitive
forms and developed the use of arches
unsupported by impost mouldings.) Bomb
damage and road-widening have removed
the church's original huddled setting to
reveal its brick flanks, which, refaced after
bomb damage, now have a rationalist
severity.

Skinners' Hall 1770–90   L61f
Dowgate Hill EC4
W Jupp
⊖ Cannon Street
One of three surviving Livery Companies'
halls in Dowgate Hill, Skinners' Hall is
(typically) set back from the street. The
five-bay façade is reminiscent of designs by
the Adam brothers in Portland Place F3,
and the Coade stone pediment above the
two-storey pilasters was modelled by John
Bacon in 1770. The arched passage in the
left-hand bay leads to a delightful small
court, beyond which is the Hall (c1670).
Rebuilt in 1850, it is decorated with
paintings depicting the history of the
skinners and the fur trade from the Middle
Ages to the end of the seventeenth
century. The court room (c1670) has fine
detailed woodwork.

Frederick's Place 1776   L62b
off Old Jewry EC2
Adam Brothers
Θ Bank
An unexpected close of relatively intact Georgian houses, Frederick's Place was a speculative venture by the Adam brothers. Although the individual houses are not particularly special, they have some good external details, and the formal composition of the space is a relief from the ugly and anarchic surroundings of the contemporary city.

Watermen's Hall 1778–80   L63g
St Mary at Hill EC3
William Blackburn
Θ Monument
A sober stone Ionic front to the headquarters of the Honourable Company of Watermen, originally the oarsmen of boat traffic on the Thames.

Trinity House front 1792–4   L64h
Tower Hill EC3
Samuel Wyatt
Θ Tower Hill
Next to and crushed by Cooper's Port of London Authority building L100, Trinity House is the headquarters of the corporation which organizes the country's harbour pilots and lighthouses. It has a robust Ionic façade, and some good interiors, both restored by Albert Richardson after war damage.

Warehouses 19th century   L65 l
Shad Thames SE1
reconstruction Conran Roche
Θ Tower Hill, London Bridge
The reconstruction in the 1980s of the magnificent warehouses on both sides of Shad Thames and of the bridges connecting them obliterated the decayed charm of the narrow street, but was as well done as possible and as archaeologically correct as modern building codes allow. The ground floors of the buildings were converted for shops and small offices, and the upper parts into flats.

Life Association of Scotland

L66a

ex Bridewell Hospital Offices
c1805
14 New Bridge Street EC2
James Lewis
⊖ Blackfriars

Bridewell was one of Henry VIII's many palaces, and from the late sixteenth century was used as a prison. It was demolished in 1863, but these offices remain, their chaste architecture – a very flat, giant pilastered order supporting a pediment, all in good ashlar – giving no hint of their former functions.

Royal Mint 1807–9

L67h

Mansell Street E1
Sir Robert Smirke
⊖ Tower Hill

In 1809 the Mint was moved from the neighbouring Tower of London to this dull if dignified classical stone factory. Smirke completed work already in hand by James Johnson, and only the two lodges are his own. In 1986–9 the Mint was 'decentralized' to Wales, and the buildings were renovated as offices by Sheppard Robson, who also designed the over-excited paraphrase of the Lloyd's building to the south.

Custom House 1813–17,

L68g

river façade 1825
Lower Thames Street EC3
D Laing, river façade Sir Robert Smirke
⊖ Tower Hill

Laing's undistinguished building was much improved by the rebuilding of the 148 m (488 ft) river façade. Behind Smirke's porticoed Portland stone elevation is the Long Room with a magnificent carved ceiling and Tuscan pilasters.

Holy Trinity 1823–4

L69n

Trinity Church Square SE1
F O Bedford
⊖ Borough

One of the innovations in urban form in the early nineteenth century was the placing of objects, usually churches, in the middle of squares which the earlier Georgians would have left empty. Here is a very successful example: a regular square of houses with two closed corners and Bedford's church set to the south. The north face of the church, acting as the south side of the square, was given monumental width by placing the Corinthian entrance portico *alongside* the nave, and putting the tower above it. Although this arrangement is wildly unorthodox, there are parallels: for instance, in the original arrangement of Hawksmoor's St George, Bloomsbury G8. Holy Trinity shows the church architects of this period re-exploring the classical repertoire, finding still new combinations. See also Porden's St Matthew, Brixton W5.

Fishmongers Hall 1831–4　　　　L70g
London Bridge Approach EC4
Henry Roberts
⊖Monument

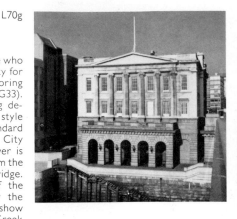

Henry Roberts was a pupil of Smirke who later became architect to the Society for Improving the Condition of the Laboring Classes (see Streatham Street G33). However, this competition-winning design is in impeccable Greek Revival style with two elevations of very high standard – with interiors to match – for a City Company. The elevation to the river is very grand, especially when seen from the river walk passing under London Bridge. It is reminiscent of the work of the Palladians a century earlier; only the battered surrounds to the windows show evidence of Stuart and Revett's Greek researches. The entrance front of the Approach is quite different: it could happily find itself in Berlin (note the flat square pilasters at the corners).

City Club　　　　L71c
1833–4 restored 1980
19 Old Broad Street EC2
Philip Hardwick
⊖Liverpool Street

Following the destruction of his slightly later Euston Arch G67, only this club remains as an indication of the quality of Hardwick's work. The style is more plain Italianate than neo-classical. The interiors of the ground and first floors were restored in 1980, after the building was saved from engulfment by the neighbouring development of the National Westminster Bank's offices.

London Bridge Station SE1　　　　L72k
1836–51
G Smith, S Beazley
⊖London Bridge

London Bridge Station is the earliest railway terminus in London, but approached by road it appears to be one of the most recent. The public concourse has been 'comprehensively redeveloped' in a mindless speculators' recipe of a twenty-storey tower and supermarket-type low building. The original building lies behind, and the simple elegance of the fine and slender cast iron trusses (painted white), over the platforms to the right, is a rebuke to the crass and lurid space-frames of the concourse outside.

Dyer's Hall 1839–40　　　　L73b
10 Dowgate Hill EC4
Charles Dyer
⊖Cannon Street

The entrance, set asymmetrically in the classical brick and stucco façade, leads to a long and beautiful glass-vaulted corridor. At the end is the dignified committee room, whose principal feature, apart from its fine embossed art nouveau wallpaper, is the curved east wall with a magnificent window.

Royal Exchange 1841–4   L74c
Threadneedle Street and
Cornhill EC3
Sir William Tite, war memorials Sir
Aston Webb
⊖ Bank

The massive Corinthian portico, with Roman lettering and sculpture in the pediment by Westmacott the Younger, dominates the space between Baker's Bank of England L104 and Dance's Mansion House L55. At the east end is a fine baroque spire, reminiscent of a City church. The interior arcaded courtyard accommodates offices; until 1880 it was open to the sky, like a large external room. The original Exchange was burnt down in 1838, and the competition for a replacement was even more ludicrous than most nineteenth-century competitions: the designs of C R Cockerell (one of the most distinguished early nineteenth-century classical architects) were widely regarded as far superior to Tite's, and in a subsequent muddle

London lost a truly remarkable and monumental building. This is doubly unfortunate as all Cockerell's London commercial buildings have since been demolished: the magnificent Sun Assurance Offices of 1841 were criminally destroyed in 1971.

Banco Commerciale   L75b
Italiana 1850
44 Gresham Street EC2
Sancton Wood
⊖ Bank

Built originally for an insurance company, this corner building is important in the nineteenth-century development of a style appropriate for commercial premises. Sancton Wood is better known for his railway stations (Shoreditch, for example, now replaced) but here he uses the language of the *palazzo*, extending it in three ways: firstly, by opening up the ground floor, using Tuscan columns to support segmental arches; secondly, in putting the upper-floor windows so close together that they begin to take over the wall surface; and thirdly, in attempting to find motifs to treat the important corner. In the last he cannot be said to have been successful, but was saved by his own Italianate cornice which unites the two street façades.

Fenchurch Street Station   L76d
EC3
1853, 1881–3
George Berkeley, engineer
⊖ Tower Hill

Fenchurch Street was originally the terminus of the London and Blackwall Railway and the first terminus of the North London Railway, which now stops at Broad Street. It was the completion of this line to Willesden Junction which put the Victorian suburb developments of Hackney, Highgate and even Kilburn within commuting distance of the City. The station is undistinguished architecturally, but the form is clever: the bow-arched shape of the elevated train shed roof is continued over the Italianate brick offices at the front, where it forms a pediment.

National Westminster   L77c
Bank
ex National Provincial Bank
1865
15 Bishopsgate EC2
John Gibson
⊖ Liverpool Street

We may smile at the earnest pretensions of Victorian bankers, but there were few architectural models for the new institution of the branch bank, and finding an appropriate image was important. They were well served by Gibson, who designed many banks across England. This richly decorated single-storey Corinthian pavilion, ornamented with sky-puncturing statuary and 'improving' panels (showing Industry, Agriculture, Education and so on), has survived. It was thoroughly refurbished in 1981.

Cannon Street Station   L78f
1865–6
Cannon Street EC4
J Hawkshaw and J W Barry, engineers
⊖ Cannon Street

Two splendid triumphal towers on the river, and the massive flank walls of stock brick, are all that remain of the original station built for the South Eastern Railway. The overall roof has been removed, as has E M Barry's hotel front. Their replacement is a sub-standard curtain wall of offices and shops by Poulson (1961).

Central Buildings   L79j
ex Hop Exchange 1866
Southwark Street SE1
R H Moore
⊖ London Bridge

Few of London's great Victorian exchanges survive, and this one does so only through its use as a warehouse, and through its fortunate position on a site as yet resistible to developers. It is an important survival, largely for the iron columns on the face and an internal iron structure which supports the galleries running round the central, glass-roofed exchange space.

Offices 1866   L80b
103 Cannon Street EC4
Frederick Jameson
⊖ Cannon Street

This inventive mid-Victorian street façade of four bays, with arched Venetian windows retreating in size to the top, is exceptional in contrast with the mediocrity of its recent neighbours. This is now a familiar story in the City, where relatively ordinary Victorian buildings have acquired architectural status by virtue of their increasing rarity.

Albert Buildings 1869   L81b
Queen Victoria Street EC4
Frederick J Ward
⊖ Bank

One of the few buildings remaining of those that originally lined the newly created 'Improvement' of Queen Victoria Street, this recently restored speculative office block has pretensions to French Gothic art. Like Bucklersbury to the north, it is an excellent example of the final form of the Victorian City, devoted to commerce.

Blackfriars Bridge EC4 and   L82e
SE1 1869
James Cubitt
⊖ Blackfriars

Until Westminster Bridge was built in 1738, London Bridge was the only river crossing. The original Blackfriars Bridge followed in 1760–9, opening the way for the eighteenth-century development of Southwark. As a result of the sharp bend in the river at King's Reach the two bridges and their approach roads form a triangle, with the cities of London and Westminster at the northern and western points: a further connection between London's financial and administrative centres was thus established. The present bridge is unremarkable.

Mappin and Webb 1870   L83b
Poultry and
Queen Victoria Street EC2
J and J Belcher
⊖ Bank

A high-Victorian lesson in how to go round a (pointed) corner: use a circular feature, here topped by a spiky turret. The commercial Gothic façades in Bath stone are competent. Mies van der Rohe's scheme for a twenty-storey fully glazed tower on the site, commissioned by developer Peter Palumbo in 1968, met with strong opposition, both official and amateur. Having become a legal and architectural *cause célèbre* it was eventually rejected. Stirling and Wilford were asked to produce a new design, which after further legal proceedings was accepted. This proposes a solid building filling the site to its edges, with offices arranged round a circular well. At the time of writing it is likely that this will be built.

Peek House 1873   L84g
6–7 St Mary at Hill EC3
Ernest George and Vaughan
⊖Monument

While visitors are looking for the entrance to the church of St Mary-at-Hill L14, they might admire this mannered High Victorian façade, cleaned in 1981. It is an extraordinarily 'artistic' composition, using very carefully placed decorated openings in what seems to remain an almost solid wall. The entrance to the church is through the open arch to the small court beyond.

Offices ex Billingsgate Market   L85
1875, 1990
Lower Thames Street EC3
Sir Horace Jones; Richard Rogers and Partners
⊖ Monument

Since the time of the Roman occupation there has been a fish market on the site of Billingsgate, a tradition broken when the market moved to the Isle of Dogs in 1982. Behind the arcaded ground floor, where once were two large halls filled with the bustle and noise of the market, there is now the silence of unoccupied space dedicated to another market. The well-designed *burolandschaft* of Richard Rogers' dealing floors hardly compensates for the lost drama of Billingsgate porters carrying fish in towers of baskets on their heads, now remembered only in the weathervanes of gilded fish on the roof pavilions.

Youth Hostel ex St Paul's   L86a
Choir School 1875
36 Carter Lane EC4
F C Penrose
⊖St Paul's

The Venetian windows and continuous panels of Renaissance sgraffito decoration of the former choir school are in what Pevsner calls the South Kensington Style. This highly decorated façade recalls the Royal College of Organists J49 of the same date.

Royal Bank of Scotland 1877   L87c
3–5 Bishopsgate EC2
Thomas Chatfield Clarke
⊖Bank, Liverpool Street

A classical façade is successfully reconciled with an extensive commercial frontage in this fine building. From the outside, the banking hall on the ground floor is clearly visible through large windows set between substantial Ionic columns (the base). The two storeys of offices above are separated by Corinthian pilasters (the *piano nobile*), and topped by the principal cornice and dormer windows (the attic). The façade is of Portland stone, while the rest of the structure is wrought iron.

Shops and **offices** 1877   L88g
33–5 Eastcheap EC3
R L Roumieu
⊖Monument
An extraordinary survival: Gothic elements are used for a secular building in an
expressionist manner more appropriate
to high religious fervour than to the trade
and banking of the City, which earlier in
the century had found its style in Italianate
palaces. The building has worn as well as
its designer must have intended.

Minor Canons' House 1879   L89a
Amen Court EC4
Ewan Christian
⊖St Paul's
The court is a mixture of architecture, the
earliest being fragments of Roman wall
tucked away behind the shrubbery at the
far end. To the south, and facing the back
of St Martin's, Ludgate Hill, is a short row
of modest seventeenth-century houses
equipped with later torch snuffers. To the
north, Christian's Canons' residence is in
a watered-down Shavian style. The whole
quiet ensemble is a remarkable survival.
Ewan Christian is better known as the
architect of the National Portrait Gallery
K116.

Leadenhall Market 1881   L90c
Gracechurch Street EC3
Sir Horace Jones
⊖Bank
The market is on the site of the large
Basilica of Roman London, and there has
been a poultry market here since the
fourteenth century. The present design
has iron and glazed arcades which curve
up and give access to the centre of a tight
City block, surrounded by financial
institutions like Lloyd's Exchange.

Tower Bridge   L91h
E1 and SE1 1886–94
J Wolfe Barry, engineer; Sir Horace Jones
⊖Tower Hill
One of the most potent tourist images of
London, Tower Bridge is, like most great
British traditions, a Victorian invention.
There are two levels: the lower one which
opens to allow for the passage of tall
ships, and the upper one for pedestrians.
Architecture (Sir Horace Jones was City
Architect) and engineering are integrated
in the massive steel-framed towers. These
house the lifting machinery (originally
steam-driven, now electric) and the stairs
to the upper levels. The bridge was
restored in 1982.

Institute of Chartered   L92b
Accountants 1889–93
Great Swan Alley,
off Moorgate EC2
John Belcher
⊖Moorgate

Twenty years on from the High Gothic of Mappin and Webb L83, Belcher fully developed his extraordinary free English baroque style in this building. Belcher was a founder of the Art Workers' Guild, and felt that this loose baroque afforded the best opportunity for the incorporation of sculpture. Here it is by Thorneycroft and Stevenson, with that on the first-floor string-course and above the door drifting towards art nouveau (ladies turning into leaves). It is surprising that this building is not better known among those at present trying to re-invent and then distort the classical language; Belcher has almost certainly done it already, even to the keystones.

The Black Friar 1875, 1904   L93a
Queen Victoria Street EC4
H Fuller Clark
⊖Blackfriars

An unexpected survival – a full Arts and Crafts pub, its finely built stone exterior suggesting an important house. The interior exhibits a jolly religiosity very different from the touristic picture of the Victorian pub or gin palace; this was presumably for the City gent rather than the labouring classes.

Courage's Brewery 1891   L94 I
Shad Thames SE1
⊖Tower Hill

From the river the distinctive profile of the brewery and its cupola and galleries forms a picturesque group with Tower Bridge L91. From the interior of Shad Thames the brewery and other warehouses are very Piranesian, with various bridges spanning the narrow, canyon-like street at different levels. The buildings were mostly rebuilt after a fire in 1891, and remain one of London's few working breweries.

St Olave's Grammar   L95 I
School 1893
Tooley Street SE1
E W Mountford
⊖London Bridge

Brick with stone trimmings, the so-called Hampton Court style, was the usual treatment for Victorian institutions. The red brick and white stone dressings are astonishingly fresh-looking in this school building by the architect of the Old Bailey L97 and the Northampton Institute H35. The hall, with a high Georgian lantern, forms the centre of the composition. The school was founded in 1561, and a statue of Elizabeth I from the original building is preserved in the gymnasium.

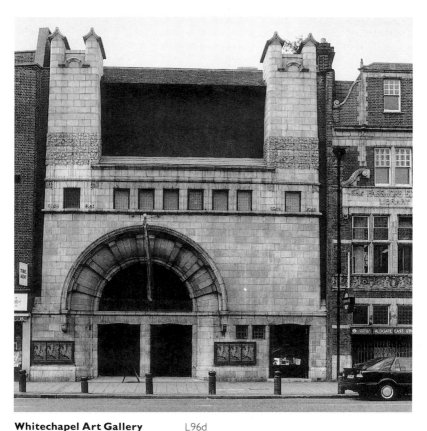

Whitechapel Art Gallery L96d
ex East London Art Gallery
1897–9
Whitechapel Road E1
C H Townsend
⊖ Aldgate East

With square corner towers, high strip windows and a massive asymmetrically placed arched doorway in a windowless wall, Townsend's East London Art Gallery marks a decisive break with tradition. An active member of the Art Workers' Guild and follower of the American architect H H Richardson, Townsend (with Lethaby, Shaw, Ashbee and others) was a prime exponent of the English Arts and Crafts style at the turn of the century. The building's monumental mass has characteristic Arts and Crafts foliage decoration, but a great mosaic designed for the central panel by Walter Crane was never executed owing to lack of funds. The gallery was completely and beautifully refurbished to designs by Colquhoun and Miller in 1984, when the upper gallery was reopened and new accomodation including a restaurant was built at the back.

Central Criminal Court L97a
1900–7
Old Bailey EC4
E W Mountford
⊖ St Paul's

Mountford, ransacking Wren's baroque for motifs, produced an appropriately grand Edwardian composition on the site of Dance's famous Newgate Prison. The courts are tightly planned on the first floor. The statue of Justice on top of the Greenwich-inspired dome U3 has become famous from countless scenes in films. The extension to the south is by Donald McMorran, 1972.

St Anne's Vestry Hall 1905   L98a
Church Entry,
off Carter Lane EC4
Banister Fletcher and Sons
Θ Blackfriars
Carter Lane survives between Ludgate
Hill and Queen Victoria Street, its
seventeenth- and eighteenth-century
scale in strong contrast with that of the
nineteenth- and twentieth-century commercial development in which it is embedded. The hall is in a typical City passage off
the lane, its tiny façade a gem of baroque
from the firm which brought us *A History
of Architecture by the Comparative Method*,
first published 1896.

Thames House 1911   L99f
Queen Street and
Upper Thames Street EC4
Collcutt and Hamp
Θ Mansion House
It would be easy to overlook the virtues of
these cheerful Edwardian baroque offices
were it not for the post-war reconstruction of Upper Thames Street. This
has destroyed the form of the street,
especially the corners at which this
building excels, without offering a satisfactory new alternative.

Willis Faber ex Port of   L100h
London Authority 1912
10 Trinity Square EC3
Sir Edwin Cooper
Θ Tower Hill
A fitting monument to the London Docks
as the Edwardian capital of the mercantile
world, Cooper's building dominates
Trinity Square just as its giant expressive
tower still dominates the approach across
Tower Bridge. The building occupies a
city block, with a vast circular hall 34 m
(110 ft) in diameter and 20 m (67 ft) high at
its centre. The winning entry in a competition, it was criticized at the time for
its extravagant architecture: colossal
columns, domes, towers, and groups of
sculpture. (Cooper's later designs for the
St Marylebone Town Hall F39 show a
greatly simplified use of classicism.) With
internal renovations by Michael Hopkins
it is now occupied by Willis Faber, a major
insurance company, who in 1967 commissioned Norman Foster to design their

headquarters in Ipswich. Foster's Ipswich
building enjoys an international reputation, but unfortunately the patronage of
City institutions remains conservative in
the worst sense.

Blackfriars House 1913   L101a
New Bridge Street EC4
F W Troup
Θ Blackfriars
The fine pioneering design of these offices
has been spoilt by the insertion of modern
aluminium windows. However, the un-
blemished and delicately decorated white
faience facing and the proportions of
frame to opening are both admirable,
reminiscent of Otto Wagner's Vienna and
of Chicago. See also Gallaher Building,
Kingsway K133.

National Employers' House L102c

ex Holland House 1914
1–4 and 32 Bury Street EC3
H P Berlage
⊖ Liverpool Street

This decorative and idiosyncratic City office building was commissioned by a Dutch shipping company, and marks a departure by Berlage, the eminent Dutch expressionist, from the style of his Amsterdam Exchange (1896–1903). On its complex City site, with two frontages at the corner of Bury Street, the design speculates on the architectural possibilities of the steel frame. The structural steel mullions are closely spaced at 1.3 m (4 ft 6 in) and clad in greenish glazed tiles. They sit on a polished black granite plinth, which also forms surrounds to the principal entrances and rises the full height of the building at each end, forming five-storey pilasters. Seen in perspective, the mullions give the illusion of a solid masonry wall. The ornamental detail of the spandrel panels, the faceted connections between the mullions and the plinth, and Joseph Mendès da Costa's large, stylized nautical sculpture on the building's acute corner are some of Berlage's devices to temper the geometric tendencies of the steel frame. The recent extension to the east, supposedly built in the spirit of the original but without its inventive detail, shows depressingly the lack of self-confidence in much recent architecture: here the frame is not an end in itself but only one of the means to architectural expression.

Christ's Hospital Offices L103g

1915
26 Great Tower Street EC3
Sir Reginald Blomfield
⊖ Tower Hill

A good example of 'Wrenaissance' from someone other than Lutyens, who coined the term: calm, restrained, and with excellently crafted brickwork.

Bank of England 1921–37 L104b

Threadneedle Street EC2
Sir Herbert Baker
⊖ Bank

In the early eighteenth century the Bank was housed on this site in the mansion of one of its founders. The wonderful banking halls built by Soane between 1788 and 1808 were additions to this house. Soane's work was scandalously demolished to make way for Baker's huge enlargement of the Bank's offices and only the screen walls to the surrounding streets remain. Although Baker, with Lutyens, was entrusted with the Imperial work in New Delhi, this design, like most of his London work (for example South Africa House K152), lacks distinction and in no way compensates for the loss of Soane's masterpiece.

In 1988, when the Bank converted part of its accommodation to a museum (entered from Bartholomew Lane), some of Baker's work was undone and Soane's original Bank Stock Office of 1793 was re-created.

Although brand new, this now provides an impression of the spatial novelty, the manipulation of light and aggressively primitive styling of Soane's work. Baker's dull rotunda houses another part of the museum.

National Westminster L105c
Bank 1922–31 extended 1936
51 Threadneedle Street EC2
Mewès and Davis
⊖Bank

Here Mewès and Davis digressed from their customary French style. The handling of the softly curved frontage of Threadneedle Street is a knowing parody of Peruzzi's Palazzo Massimi in Rome (1535). However, the plan lacks the elegant internal displacements of the original.

Mercantile Marine L106h
Memorial 1922–52
Trinity Square EC3
Sir Edwin Lutyens; additions by E Maufe 1952
⊖Tower Hill

Maufe's work is of no interest, but Lutyens' memorial shows him operating in two modes. The first is the 'representational' Tuscan barrel-vaulted temple below, where the piers are covered in panels of bronze, imitating ashlar and bearing the names of the dead. The second is above, in the extraordinary abstract arrangement of white oblongs topped by a low drum in the middle of the Portland stone roof.

Adelaide House 1924–5 L107g
King William Street EC4
Sir John Burnet Tait and Partners
⊖Monument

Adelaide House and Fishmongers' Hall L70 opposite form the bridgehead to London Bridge, which ambitiously spans Lower Thames Street. Although it was one of the earliest City office buildings to abandon the classical style, some style was still felt necessary and the Egyptian was adopted. Gavin Stamp has pointed out that 'Egyptian was fashionable in the 1920s by virtue of being exotic and excessively monumental'. The building is notable for its massive curved cornices, the regularity of its vertical system of bays and the four exaggeratedly squat black marble Doric columns at the entrance (the only lapse into the classical).

Midland Bank Head Office   L108b
1924–39
Poultry and Princes Street EC3
Sir Edwin Lutyens; executive architects
Gotch and Saunders
⊖ Bank

Lutyens started this, his biggest building in England, at the height of his career. All his experience in the use of classicism shows in the way he composed and inflected the surfaces of the massive building: note for example the re-entrant corners of the fifteen-bay elevation to Poultry, and the way in which the two axes extending from Poultry and Princes Street are united on the skyline by the shallow dome. Despite its bulk, the building does no damage to the delicate structure of the tight City streets. The grand public ground-floor interiors, clad in black and white marble, are worthy of inspection.

London Life Association   L109c
1925–7
King William Street EC4
W Curtis Green
⊖ Bank, Monument

A monumental *palazzo* façade with a screen of recessed columns in the centre, all in stone, gives the intended image of permanence and reliability.

Hasilwood House LI10c
ex Hudson's Bay House 1928
52–68 Bishopsgate and
St Helen's Place EC2
Mewès and Davis
⊖ Liverpool Street

The massive symmetrical stone façade
with a mansard roof has a central double-
height gateway supported by Tuscan
columns. This leads to St Helen's Place, in
plan a typical City close, angled to the line
of Bishopsgate. In section, however, it is
seven storeys high: the close is really
more of a *cour d'honneur* with another
'French' façade by Mewès and Davis at the
end. This is an exemplary type for the City
of London, and a rebuke to the tower
forms that have generally replaced it. The
builders were Dove Brothers, who are
one of the very few firms of builders still
to maintain a high standard of
craftsmanship.

Midland Bank 1929 LI11c
140–4 Leadenhall Street EC3
Sir Edwin Lutyens, Whinney and A Hall
⊖ Bank

Completed while Lutyens' Midland Bank
headquarters LI08 was still being built,
this branch of the same bank shows him
working with a straightforward street
infill façade. One of the neighbouring
buildings has since been removed in the
development of the P&O building LI25
next door, revealing the elaborate towers
above an otherwise strangely flat and
cramped façade, in which the seven bays of
the office floors are supported on five bays
of grand arches at street level. Also
revealed is the utilitarian back of the
building: white glazed brick and big
'factory' windows.

Cunard House 1930 LI12c
88 Leadenhall Street EC3
Mewès and Davis
⊖ Bank

A competent but unmemorable large
building, designed when the inspiration
was deserting this once urbane London
practice. Mewès died in 1914, and his
partner Davis was unable to make the
transition from Edwardian baroque to
modernism. His contemporary, John
Burnet, managed to achieve this with the
help of younger partners, moving easily
from Gallaher Building (ex Kodak House)
K133 to the Royal Masonic Hospital T24.

Unilever House 1930–1 LI13e
New Bridge Street and
Victoria Embankment EC4
J Lomax-Simpson with Sir John Burnet,
Tait and Lorne
⊖ Blackfriars

The last independent work by Burnet
before the practice went modern,
Unilever House is a massive baroque
urban design, marking the emerging
conflict between the use of historical
styles (including the classical) and the
need for more spacious buildings. The
stone quadrant, with a huge rusticated
base and giant screen of columns above,
seems to anticipate an extension of the
same scale along New Bridge Street and

the Embankment, making Unilever House a fragment of a much larger scheme. The sculpted groups at either end are by William Read Dick. Note also the splendid art deco interiors renovated by Theo Crosby in 1982.

National Westminster Bank L114b
ex National Provincial Bank 1930–2
Poultry and Princes Street EC2
Sir Edwin Cooper
⊖Bank

Cooper, faced with the difficulties of building next to Lutyens' magnificent bank in Poultry L108, and of getting round the Princes Street corner – one of the City's most important street crossings – resorted to well-mannered blandness. Only the giant recessed columns and the sculpture show any spirit.

Hay's Wharf and
St Olave House 1931–2
L115g
Tooley Street SE1
H S Goodhart-Rendel
⊖London Bridge

The warehouse fronting the river and St Olave House, the office building facing Tooley Street, are gems of lively *moderne*. The buildings stand on columns above the ground to allow access for traffic to the river, and their composition contrasts the vertical lift-tower against the horizontal projecting 'bulkhead' bronze-framed windows. The steel frame is clad in Portland stone, and both buildings are decorated inside and out with jazz modern works of art. The river façade boasts sculptured panels by Frank Dobson, and the splendid big triangular-sectioned wooden letters of the name. The buildings are listed, and will be spared in the present redevelopment of the river front between London Bridge and Tower Bridge.

ex **Daily Express Building** 1932   L116a
Fleet Street EC4
Ellis Clarke and Atkinson with Sir Owen
Williams
⊖Chancery Lane

In the middle of London's newspaper-
land, this building is a glazed envelope of
black and transparent glass with curved
corners. The rails for the cleaning gantry
form a cornice, as in Williams' warehouse
(1934) for J Sainsbury in Southwark (now
demolished). The top three floors retreat
behind the gantry to allow daylight to
reach the street and adjacent buildings. A
comparison with the same architect's
building for the *Daily Mirror* at Holborn
Circus, completed thirty years later,
shows the sad decline of the new architecture in the service of land speculation
in the 1950s and '60s. Despite this Sir
Owen Williams remains probably the
most original and enigmatic architect-
engineer of his generation.

Ronald Atkinson's entrance hall with its
elaborate metal decoration is a fabulous
moderne extravaganza. To left and right
are metal relief wall sculptures depicting
colonial enterprise past and present. The
central approach to the beautiful cantilevered staircase is in the spirit of the
entrance to Cleopatra's tomb, complete
with chromium twisted snakes as handrails. The lighting is incorporated in
metallic stalactites suspended from the
ceiling. With the removal of the interiors
of the Strand Palace Hotel to the Victoria
and Albert Museum, the *Daily Express*
entrance hall is now almost unique as a
working art deco interior.
In 1989, as part of the general exodus of
newspapers from Fleet Street, the *Daily
Express* moved to new offices on the south
side of Blackfriar's Bridge.

Reuters and Press Association Headquarters
L117a

1935
85 Fleet Street EC4
Sir Edwin Lutyens with Smee and Houchin
⊖ Chancery Lane

Lutyens' handling of the Reuters site and of the architectural masses and complex geometrics of the building is character-istically masterful. Immediately next to Wren's beautiful St Bride's L17, its L-shaped plan acts as a backdrop to the church. The west door of St Bride's is ingeniously linked to Salisbury Square by a double-height vaulted passageway (St Bride's Avenue) through the centre of the building - a modest but thoughtful ad-dition to the labyrinth of passages and courts of this historic area of London.

The building's steel frame is clad in Portland stone – the upper walls are battered and the windows decrease in width vertically. The independent roof pavilion is another typical Lutyens device – a concave-fronted structure crowned by a large drum. The double-height entrance

hall gives the impression of having been carved out of solid marble – its approach is crowned by a deep and massive circular window with a bronze figure of Fame at the centre. The series of long, low window openings, with shallow reveals and standard metal window frames, is as close as Lutyens comes to 'modern' in this, his last commercial building in London.

Ibex House 1937
L118d

42 Minories EC3
Fuller, Hall and Foulsham
⊖ Tower Hill

A spirited, large, horizontal office build-ing clad in beige faience with nicely rounded corners. The unbroken stretch of continuous strip-windows (21 m/70 ft) was the longest in London.

Chamber of Shipping 1939
L119c

Bury Court, off St Mary Axe EC3
Sir John Burnet, Tait and Lorne
⊖ Aldgate

Completed a year after Burnet's death, the Chamber of Shipping is a rather pathetic and fumbling four-storey office building. The best thing about it is the *moderne* sign above the entrance.

Bankside Power Station   L120e
1955
Bankside SE1
Sir Giles Gilbert Scott
⊖ London Bridge

In comparison with Battersea Power Station N29 and the Guinness Brewery T27 and despite the use of the same monumental brickwork, Scott's design for Bankside is more a municipal building than a cathedral of power. It faces St Paul's across the river, but curiously nothing has been made of this relationship.

Bracken House   L121b
ex *Financial Times* building 1956–9.
1988–90
Cannon Street, Friday Street
and Distaff Lane EC4
Sir Albert Richardson;
Michael Hopkins and Partners
⊖ Mansion House

It is to the credit of the recent reconstruction that Richardson's orginal *Financial Times* building and the Hopkins' alteration gain mutually from their conjunction. The seven-storey walls to Cannon Street and Queen Victoria Street have been retained. The two-storey octagonal central hall has been replaced by a seven-storey circular atrium providing additional offices. The glass and steel crenellations of Hopkins' new perimeter sit convincingly between the heavy abutments of the original building.
Richardson has usually been associated with neo-Georgian. Here the architecture is less easily categorized. A plinth of red sandstone is surmounted by four-storey piers of dark-red brickwork and topped by an attic cornice of copper set back on miniature glass-brick piers: a

combination of a classical formula with Milanese Liberty detail.
The new elevations, by contrast, do not distinguish so emphatically between tops, middles and bottoms. Each floor is treated equally, with the emphasis being placed on maximum transparency. There are echoes here of another heroic enterprise – Owen Williams' Pioneer Health Centre in Peckham of 1934–6 X10.

Police Station 1962–6   L122b
Wood Street EC2
Donald McMorran and George Whitby
⊖ Moorgate

Historically, this is a very important building, representing a reworking of classicism during one of its most neglected periods. The square plan of three storeys surrounding a courtyard, with a twelve-storey campanile of offices to one side, makes a very strong composition. Its cool and abstracted forms connect with Lutyens' later City buildings, and stand out from the banal designs surrounding them. Among its formal inventions are the screen walls marking the basement entrance and the two large rusticated chimneys projecting through the pitched roof. However, in the detail the architects have misplaced some of their classical aspirations. There are no parapets to the pediments, and the lack of sills to the windows has resulted in streaking of the stonework. The 'abstract' pattern-making

of the ground-floor rustication and the 'Swedish' window frames place the building historically in the post-Festival of Britain era, from which it is simultaneously dissociated by its general forms.

Department of Health and Social Security Offices 1963 L123m
Newington Causeway
Ernö Goldfinger
⊖ Elephant and Castle

Following Abercrombie's planning proposals, one of the methods of 'improving' London from 1945 on was to enlarge traffic intersections. The left-over spaces round the new engineering works were then available for 'comprehensive' redevelopment (usually, as here, with results inferior to those envisaged by Abercrombie). These offices were built as part of that process. There are two seven-storey blocks which enclose a third block of thirteen storeys, a small piazza and a cinema. Goldfinger's concern for modelling is well demonstrated in the apparently arbitrary setting in and out of the façades, and in the use of the (now grubby) exposed concrete of the frame. We do not know whether concrete can be cleaned as successfully as Portland stone.

Offices: Commercial Union Assurance and ex P&O Group 1968–9 L124c
Leadenhall Street and
St Mary Axe EC3
Gollins Melvin Ward Partnership
⊖ Aldgate

The two freestanding buildings, one continuing the Leadenhall Street frontage, the other taller and set back from the street, loosely address a large piazza. The sureness of style and the technology of the Commercial Union tower (its floors are suspended from cantilevers from the central core) easily match those of its models in the United States, particularly those in Chicago. But it is doubtful whether the open space is appropriate among the tight streets and narrow alleys of the City, and whether, if it is offered in contrast to these, it is done sufficiently well. The squat, horizontally banded P&O building, different from the tower at the request of a client seeking a separate 'identity', is less successful, perhaps because there was no model to follow. The curiously empty and open first floor of the tower and the elaborate stairs leading to it are remnants of a largely abandoned planning requirement which proposed an alternative and continuous system of first-floor pedestrian circulation throughout the City (see the Barbican H40 and London Wall H41).

London Bridge in 1749

London Bridge L125g
EC4 and SE1 1968–72
Harold King (engineer) and Sir Robert Bellinger
⊖ London Bridge

As the first Thames crossing, London Bridge has a long and rich history going back to the first century and has been rebuilt many times. Debate about the original position of the Roman crossing was resolved in 1981, when remains of its abutments were found under Billingsgate Market L85. The narrow picturesque houses of the famous inhabited medieval bridge (about 1200) were removed when it was widened in 1758–62. Fragments of the replacement by Robert Taylor and George Dance the Younger can be seen in Guy's Hospital L52 and Victoria Park. The bridge was rebuilt by Rennie (1823–31) and can now be seen crossing Lake Havasu, Arizona, where it has been since 1971. The present bridge is the least distinguished structure in this long history.

Offices 1973

L126c

36–8 Leadenhall Street EC3
YRM Architects and Planners
⊖ Aldgate

The tradition of good proportions and fine materials which seemed to have died with Lutyens is revived (via the Chicago School) in this excellent commercial building. The deceptively simple frame, covered with travertine as a change from Portland stone, is a reproach to the oriels, bizarre facing-bricks and absurd mansards which are the City's going style.

Bush Lane House 1976

L127b

80 Cannon Street EC4
Arup Associates
⊖ Cannon Street

An extraordinarily complicated little office building, and the only example in London of a tubular stainless steel, diagonal external structure, filled with water as fire-protection. The ground floor, where some commercial activity might be expected, is empty.

Lloyd's 1978–86

L128c

Leadenhall Street EC3
Richard Rogers and Partners
⊖ Bank, Monument

The present Lloyd's building stands on the site previously occupied by Sir Edwin Cooper's neo-Roman building for Lloyd's of 1928. Of all the buildings built in London since the first publication of this book, Lloyd's has to be the most celebrated and the most controversial.

Despite its agitated profile, Lloyd's is a simple rectangle in plan. It reverses the conventional core arrangement for office buildings, moving lifts, fire stairs and lavatories to the exterior wall in order to make way for a dramatic twelve-storey-high barrel-vaulted atrium at the centre. This arrangement of 'servant and served' spaces is a tribute to Louis Kahn (Richards Laboratories, University of Pennsylvania 1961) and more distantly to medieval castles.

Although some find the appropriateness of such a defensive idea for a city building is questionable, for others this is the most important building of the century, courageously keeping faith with modern architecture during one of its more vulnerable periods. For one of Britain's more conservative institutions to have commissioned such a building is doubly remarkable. The detailing of the exterior is magnificently obsessive and contributes to the overall impression of a remarkable stainless steel sculpture, which is particularly dramatic when floodlit. In the context of the limp contemporary architectural debate in Britain, Lloyd's stands as a heroic and magnificently fallible building.

Photograph 1981

National Westminster   L129c
Tower 1981
25 Old Broad Street EC2
Richard Seifert and Partners
⊖ Bank
The tower is 183 m (600 ft) high and is
Britain's second tallest building, Europe's
third tallest, and the world's tallest canti-
levered building.

Offices 1983   L130x
68 Cornhill EC3
Rolfe Judd; design by Richard Dickinson
⊖ Bank

Despite the acknowledged importance of
considered new façades for repairing gaps
in the street wall, there have been few
good examples since earlier in the century. Here we have a well-composed and
substantial façade in Portland stone on a
granite base which sits well between its
more elderly neighbours. This is achieved
without imitation or pastiche and, to
quote Lutyens' phrase, the architect
knows in this instance 'how to get up a
building without repeating himself'. See
too the corner offices of 1989 at **62–64
Cornhill**, also by Rolfe Judd.

Offices 1985   L131b
36 Queen Street EC4
Terry Farrell and Co.
⊖ Mansion House

A speculative office block in the form of a
small palazzo makes good decorated
street architecture. Its seven storeys are
successfully disguised with set-backs, and
exuberance is confined to the attic, where
the keystones and curved shapes first
popularized by Michael Graves are
celebrated. See also Farrell's L133.

Horselydown Square 1986–91   L132I
Gainsford Street, Copper Row,
Horselydown Lane, Shad Thames SE1
Wickham and Associates
⊖ London Bridge, Tower Hill
This mixed development of 76 flats with
offices and shops on the ground floor
forms a pedestrian close diagonally opposite to the drama of Tower Bridge. Stylistically the development is a joker in the
pack of the well-mannered rehabilitation
of Butler's Wharf to the north. The project challenges comfortable ideas of housing typology. The five- and seven-storey
façades are both complex and picturesque
recalling the European new town in general and the Dutch contribution in
particular.

Offices 1987   L133d
69 Leadenhall Street, 95–7 Fenchurch
Street EC3
Terry Farrell and Co.
⊖ Aldgate
The most comprehensive homage in London to Michael Graves' style of the 1970s,
these offices successfully fill out their
triangular site on the prominent corner of
Leadenhall and Fenchurch Streets. The
cladding, a mixture of granite, stainless
steel and painted aluminium, is well and
expensively detailed, and its variations are
designed to emphasize the traditional
horizontal division of base, middle and
top.

The Circle 1987–9   L134I
Queen Elizabeth Street SE1
CZWG Architects (Campbell,
Zogolovitch, Wilkinson and Gough) with
executive architects Robinson Keefe and
Devane
⊖ London Bridge, Tower Hill
The project provides 302 flats, eight office
suites, twelve shops, one restaurant and a
swimming pool/health club. In plan it
maintains a conventional relationship to
the street, with a circular forecourt to
serve the entrance halls to the flats. In its
vertical surface, however, the scheme is
less conventional. The circular forecourt
is finished in deep-blue glazed bricks, and
with its owl-like profile to the parapet, its
diagonal window mullions and its stepped
balcony, the project takes on a curiously
menacing quality. By contrast the street
elevations are built in London stock

bricks, with an undulating parapet and
louvred balustrades to the balconies,
which appear to be supported by brackets
of pine logs.

Hall of Residence 1987–9   L135I
11 Gainsford Street SE1
Conran Roche
⊖ London Bridge, Tower Hill
Part of the redevelopment of the area
between Shad Thames and Tooley Street,
these study bedrooms are for students at
the London School of Economics. They are
arranged as four 'houses' marked by front
doors and central balconies, and are notable for their simple street architecture
and good finishes.

Shop and **offices** 1987–91   L136I
24 Shad Thames SE1
Michael Hopkins and Partners with David Mellor Design
⊖ London Bridge, Tower Hill

A small building with frontages both to Shad Thames and to the dock beyond provides a new headquarters for the designer David Mellor. Although as utilitarian as the warehouses it replaced, the building fits beautifully into the site and the street. Its detailing is robust, and parts of it, including the lead panelling to the flanks and the shuttering to the carefully-made concrete frame, were made by the client. The office building immediately to the south, **Saffron Wharf**, finished in 1990, was designed by Conran Roche.

Design Museum 1989   L137I
Butler's Wharf
Shad Thames SE1
Conran Roche
⊖ London Bridge, Tower Hill

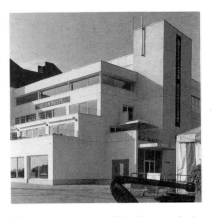

First impressions of a new '1930s' building are misleading, as The Design Museum is the result of an extensive renovation and transformation of an undistinguished warehouse. As a result the building is architecturally inconsequential, and regrettably its 'cool' stuccoed surfaces are cracking as quickly as those of the 1930s buildings that inspired it. The Museum is more important, however, for what it represents, for two reasons: firstly it provides much-needed public focus for the emerging 'Docklands' community, and secondly, as a museum of twentieth century design it fills a conspicuous gap in the otherwise broad range of London's museums.

Inside there is an atmosphere of quiet decorum. The galleries on the top two floors work well, and their calm manner is further enhanced by the exhibition display system by Stanton Williams. The Blueprint Café provides well-designed food and makes good use of the building's extensive balconies overlooking the Thames.

Directly to the south of the Museum is the **Clove building**, refurbished by Allies and Morrison in 1987, containing flats, offices and shops (sooner or later). This is another transformation of an existing warehouse using the language of 1930s modernism. However in this case the black window frames and 'heroic' projecting balconies contrast more convincingly with the white stucco.

Vogan's Mill 1989   L138I
St Saviour's Dock and Mill Street SE1
Michael Squire Associates
⊖ London Bridge, Tower Hill

The replacement of an existing grain mill with a seventeen-storey tower, and the renovation of listed warehousing to provide sixty-five luxury flats, might read as a pretty routine Docklands development. However the project makes two significant contributions. Firstly, when viewed from the river the slim proportions of the tower and its conspicuous modernity stand as a spirited rebuke to the creeping pestilence of 'pixie' vernacular housing which has contaminated the optimism of Docklands. Secondly, the residents are offered the luxury of one flat per floor.

continu

Olympia

4

5

a

b

Cadby Hall
(Factory)

West Kensington

WEST CROMWELL ROAD

e

f

Hammersmith Cemetery

The Queen's

Hostel

Empress St
Building

Roof Car Park

continued section T

Normand Park

Recreation
Ground

i

j

Chapel

Cemetery

Baths

m

h

Fulham

Parsons
Green

Parson
Green

contin

School

The Warren
Allotment Gardens

Fulham Palace

Imperial College

British Museum

c

d

South Kensington

g

h

West Brompton

BROMPTON CEMETERY

k

l

COLLEGE

Stamford Bridge Stadium

Walham Green

Kensington Boro Wharf

Durham Wharf

Chelsea Wharf

Cremorne Wharf

Eel Brook Common

o

p

Chelsea Creek

Flour Mills

Battersea Reach

Wharves

Sands End

Regent Wharf

Lensbury Wharf

Dock

Shell Wharf

Section M: West Kensington/Fulham/Parson's Green/ Earl's Court/West Brompton/South Kensington (west)

Old Brompton Road, winding like a lane, runs from west to east passing through the mid-Victorian developments of South Kensington (The Boltons M2 in stucco, for example, and Bolton Gardens in red brick). To its north, Cromwell Road, once a genteel street of mansions, carries thunderous traffic to and from Heathrow Airport and South Wales. Brompton Cemetery M1, one of the series of cemeteries built outside the city in the mid-nineteenth century, now lies alongside the District Underground line. Parallel to the railway is Earl's Court Road, now colourfully devoted to the needs of the district's mainly transient population (see also Queensway, section I).

There are two huge exhibition halls: Olympia M5 to the north, built in the 1880s, and Earl's Court, 1937. Since the building of the National Exhibition Centre at Birmingham, both have tried to find new roles, Olympia as a conference centre and retail furniture warehouse, and Earl's Court as a venue for rock concerts.

To the south of the District Line lie Fulham and West Kensington, huge tracts of late nineteenth-century two-storey housing for workers. Dull but still serviceable, these houses are preferable both to Peabody dwellings and to their municipal successors, high-rise flats.

Brompton Cemetery

Brompton Cemetery 1840 M1g
Old Brompton Road and
Fulham Road SW10
⊖West Brompton

Founded in 1831 as the West of London
and Westminster Cemetery and con-
secrated in 1840, Brompton Cemetery is
one of the earliest of the seven large
cemeteries initiated by the period of
Sanitary Reform in the 1820s. Unlike the
more romantic Highgate R7, which was
built on the southerly slopes of the north
London ridge, Brompton Cemetery is
large and rectangular, planned symmetrically on flat ground. The principal architectural feature is the octagonal chapel
with its extensive and impressive arcad-
ing. The mausolea are a mixture of late
classical, Gothic and Egyptian, with
humorous touches such as the upturned
skiff to commemorate Coombes, the
champion rower, and the large lion with a
portrait of John Jackson, the famous
boxer.

The Boltons SW10 1850–60 M2h
⊖Gloucester Road
A unique form in the westward expansion
of London between the Fulham and Old
Brompton Roads, the Boltons has very big
semi-detached stuccoed villas arranged
around a mandala-shaped garden. The
Italianate details are of a coarseness
characteristic of the time. The church in
the middle is by George Godwin, 1850.

St Paul's Studios c1870 M3e
135–49 Talgarth Road W14
⊖Barons Court

These eight astonishingly ornate studio
houses used to look north across their
own quiet residential street to the
massive ranges of Waterhouse's equally
ornate St Paul's School (1881–5). Sadly,
the school was demolished in 1970, the
traffic has increased in density on Talgarth
Road, now London's principal western
exit, and the Studios show signs of
deterioration. There are two house types
forming a system of pairs at entrance
level: one doorway is arched and frontal,
and the other is approached diagonally.
Both have seats in the doorway (like
Baillie Scott's work) for waiting clients or
models, and on each side there is a bay
window of lead lights. The double-height
studio windows are magnificent, and
beside them are tall narrow windows for
the removal of finished canvases.

Pembroke Studios 1890   M4b
Pembroke Gardens W8
⊖West Kensington
The group of thirteen studios in two rows,
to the south-west of Edwardes Square 13,
is approached through a single-arched
entrance (like alms-houses), and focuses
on a long rectangular garden. The glazed
studios face north and the supporting
rooms south, giving the façades on
asymmetrical composition. Unlike the
more affluent studios of fashionable portrait painters (see Leighton House 19)
Pembroke Studios are a modest conversion of an existing mews, given impetus
and patronage (for the residents) by the
Great Exhibition of 1851.

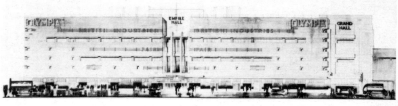

Olympia Exhibition Hall   M5a
façade 1930
Hammersmith Road W14
Joseph Emberton
⊖Olympia, Earl's Court
The distinguished entrance elevation,
with deep window reveals and cast
lettering, forms a façade to the original
exhibition hall (1884) which lies behind.
Although the appearance is of white
painted concrete, the construction is of
brick and steel. The four-storey garage
(1937) in Maclise Road to the north is also
by Emberton.

Bousfield School 1955   M6h
Old Brompton Road
and Boltons SW10
Chamberlin, Powell and Bon
⊖Gloucester Road
The school and the housing estate, as
types, were the architectural manifestos
of post-war socialism. In housing, Alton
East Estate V8 signified the triumph of
'people's detailing', and Bousfield is its
equivalent in school buildings. There is
intentionally no overall coherence of plan.
The details – spindly steelwork, randomly
placed coloured spandrel panels, a water-
jump (instead of a fence) to the main
entrance, an external amphitheatre, and
viewing slots in the extensive boundary
walls – confirm the 'democratic' intent.
However, rather than standing in the
espace et verdure of the *Ville Radieuse*,
Bousfield School sits ambiguously in a
large garden of the fashionable Boltons.

East Stand Chelsea   M7k
Football Club 1975
Stamford Bridge, Fulham Road
SW6
Darbourne and Darke; Felix Samuely and
Partners, engineers
⊖ Fulham Broadway

London has few sports buildings of any
distinction; here is an exception. It is the
first part of a grandiose plan to cover all
the spectators' seating and provide a
gallery, all under a stylish exposed cantilevered Cor-ten steel canopy which hangs
down over the seating. Its front edge
collects rainwater which is pumped back
up to be discharged in the usual way.

Brompton

South Kensington

a

b

e

Chelsea

f

continued section M

i

j

THAMES

Battersea
Bridge

RIVER

Albert Bridge
Suspension

Cadogan Pier

m

h

19
37
11
28
18
15
31
33
14
6
27
5
1
5
20
38
4

continued

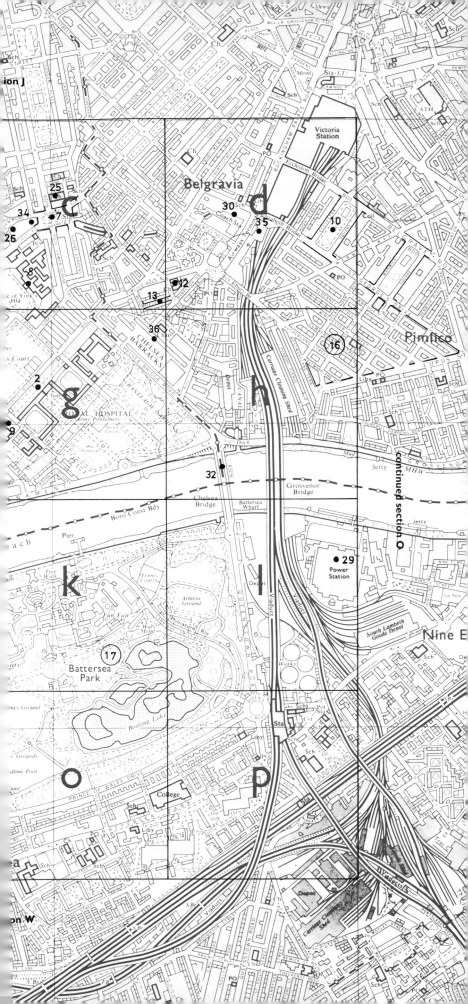

Section N: Battersea/Chelsea/West Pimlico/South Belgravia/ South Kensington (east)

The Thames – from Chelsea Reach in the west to the contemporary Chelsea Bridge in the east – separates Chelsea in the north from Battersea in the south. It was not until the second half of the nineteenth century that the north and south were linked by permanent bridges – Albert Bridge (1873) and Battersea Bridge (1890): as a result their early development was quite separate, despite their geographical proximity.

Chelsea was a riverside fishing village until the late eighteenth century: Old Church Street and King's Road were its high streets, and it was separated from the City of London by open countryside. The Royal Hospital N2, founded in 1681, was the nearest building of consequence, and was itself built outside the City for the treatment and convalescence of war veterans. Wren's palatial building of 1689 was to have been part of a grand axial relationship with Kensington Palace to the north-west – connected by a royal avenue set in open countryside. Royal Avenue N3 was all that was ever constructed of this ambitious scheme (in 1692–4), reaching only as far as King's Road.

The eighteenth-century expansion of Chelsea took the form of piecemeal developments of brick terrace housing close to the parish church. With Henry Holland's development of Hans Place in 1777 the village became less concentric in plan, and began to be drawn into the western expansion of the City of Westminster initiated by developments in Mayfair (see sections J and K). This took the form of spontaneous and progressive overlays. First to be built were the streets and squares either side of King's Road, at the beginning of the nineteenth century, then from the north came the encroaching stucco terraces of South Kensington (for example Pelham Crescent N11 and the tall red-brick houses of the Cadogan Estate, in a style loosely termed 'Pont Street Dutch' (Cadogan Square N24, for example); and finally, by the turn of the century, the eighteenth-century houses of Cheyne Walk, Tite Street and New Chelsea Embankment were replaced by architects of the Arts and Crafts Movement, such as Norman Shaw and C R Ashbee. London's westerly expansion in this period consolidated Old Brompton Road, Fulham Road and King's Road: the three radial routes converging from the west on the City of Westminster.

To the east of the Royal Hospital, and now divided by the mainline rail link from the south to Victoria Station, is the western section of Pimlico (see also section O). Like Battersea to the south, Pimlico was an area of market gardens at the beginning of the nineteenth century; but it was rapidly developed by Thomas Cubitt as an extension of his enterprise in Belgravia (see section J). By the middle of the century it had a consistent pattern of stuccoed streets, terraces and squares, for example Eccleston Square and Warwick Square N10.

Unlike Chelsea, the medieval village of Battersea is now hardly decipherable. In Elizabethan times a marsh wall was built along the Thames, forming an embankment to the south, and the reclaimed marshland was used for market gardening. As there was no bridge across the Thames to it, Battersea enjoyed a relatively remote and agrarian existence until the advent of the railways in the 1830s. In 1838 the Southampton Railway opened its London depot at Nine Elms and in 1845 Battersea Station (later called Clapham Junction) was built. With the building of Grosvenor Bridge and Victoria Station in 1862, a permanent connection with central London was finally established.

Albert Bridge (1873), Battersea Bridge (1890) and Chelsea Bridge (1934) were constructed surprisingly late, as was Battersea's chief monument, Battersea Power Station N29, completed in 1955. Probably as a result of its remoteness from the western expansion of London in the eighteenth and nineteenth centuries, Battersea is architecturally almost unendowed.

Lindsey House c1674   N1i
95–100 Cheyne Walk SW3
⊖Sloane Square, then bus down King's Road
A large comfortable country residence, defended by its boundary walls from the menace of the twentieth-century traffic outside, Lindsey House is the only surviving house of its date and scale in Chelsea. Originally it was a simple, three-storey house of eleven bays, with a pedimented centre and two corner pavilions. In 1775 it was divided into separate dwellings. The engineers Sir Marc Isambard Brunel and his more famous son, Isambard Kingdom, both lived in Lindsey House, and Whistler lived in number 96 from 1866–79. The gardens to numbers 99 and 100 were remodelled to designs by Lutyens.

Royal Hospital 1681–91   N2g
Royal Hospital Road SW3
Sir Christopher Wren, Nicholas Hawksmoor, John Vanbrugh
⊖Sloane Square
The hospital was established to house army veterans, imitating Louis XIV's building of Les Invalides. It gave Wren one of his largest 'domestic' jobs, and while the planning is that of the traditional closed squares of Oxford colleges, the courts are *open*, the largest looking outwards to the river. The style, in brick, is more Dutch than French, although each façade is equipped with a triple-height Tuscan portico or centrepiece in stone. Those on the wings are freer, with broken pediments. The hall and chapel are incorporated in the main east-west wing, and share with a modern ease the same roofline as the four-storey ward wings – only the taller arched windows distinguish the special rooms inside. The hall is gaunt, the chapel very grand. In introducing an institution and inventing a style for it, Charles II and Wren provided a model for institutional and collegiate architecture which has proved workable for three centuries in all the English-speaking countries. See also Soane's Stables N9.

Royal Avenue SW3 1692–4   N3f
⊖Sloane Square

The Royal Avenue, planted with four rows of plane trees and connecting Wren's Royal Hospital N2 to King's Road, is all that was built of William III's more ambitious triumphal way to connect the Hospital with Kensington Palace 12. Such dynastic assertion was possible on the agrarian land from Bushy Park to Hampton Court VI, but was to be largely frustrated in London. The contemporary Avenue, with its gravel surface lined by nineteenth-century terraces, is one in a series of open-ended squares along the King's Road.

Old Battersea House 1699   N4m
Westbridge Road SW11
⇌Clapham Junction

A reminder that Battersea was once a village along the banks of the Thames, with a history predating the now conspicuous presence of industry. Set behind a high wall, the house has nine bays, a hipped roof and a pedimented door. Until recently it was a museum housing the outstanding pottery collection of William de Morgan.

Cheyne Walk SW3   N5i, j
c1700–1880
⊖Sloane Square, then bus down King's Road

From Lindsey House N1 in the west to the beginning of Chelsea Embankment in the east, Cheyne Walk was the focus of the quiet riverside village of eighteenth-century Chelsea. It now boasts 300 years of the finest domestic architecture, and a long list of famous artistic residents.

The most continuous surviving stretch of eighteenth-century buildings is between Oakley Street and the beginning of Royal Hospital Road. In section it rises in layers from the river to the front of the houses, making an excellent model for building alongside rivers: the houses are separated from the river by a row of common gardens 6 m (20 ft) wide, a pavement planted with plane trees and, finally, their own walled and gated gardens. Many of the gates have fine decorated gateposts and ironwork.

From east to west, numbers 3–6 are examples of the original early Georgian style dating from about 1717, characterized by their segmental headed windows. The painter William Dyce and the novelist George Eliot lived in number 2. Numbers 7–12 (particularly number 9) are in Shaw's style of the 1880s, and numbers 15 and 16, the Queen's House or Tudor House, are further survivors of the early Georgian period. The Queen's House is the largest in the terrace and is well preserved, apart from the nineteenth-century bay window rammed into the centre bay. The ironwork to the entrance court is excellent. Dante Gabriel Rossetti, A C Swinburne and George Meredith were among those who lived here. Numbers 19–26 form a fairly complete terrace, built in 1760 on the site of Henry VII's manor house (demolished in 1753). To the other side of Oakley Street the buildings are less distinguished, apart from C R Ashbee's remarkable group at numbers 38–9 N27, and numbers 95–100 (Lindsey House) N1.

Houses started 1708   N6j
16–34 Cheyne Row SW3
⊖Sloane Square and bus down King's
Road
Contemporary with Queen Anne's Gate
K31 but much altered, this terrace retains
only numbers 26 and 34 in a nearly original
state. Thomas Carlyle lived in number 24,
now owned by the National Trust and
maintained as a domestic museum in
Carlyle's memory. The collections of
furniture and memorabilia (not all belonging to the Carlyles) give the visitor the feel
of a nineteenth-century writer's house.
The garden is delightful.

Sloane Square SW1   N7c
laid out c1780
Henry Holland(?)
⊖Sloane Square
This square is now surrounded by undistinguished commercial buildings, with
the notable exception of the Peter Jones
department store N33 of 1936. Nevertheless the ensemble is coherent, showing
how resilient the format of the London
square can be. At night the young plane
trees in the central paved space are
decorated with coloured fairy lights.

Duke of York's   N8c
Headquarters 1801
King's Road SW3
J Saunders
⊖Sloane Square
The long and dignified west façade, of
stock brick with a central Tuscan portico
of stone and Palladian curved screens at
either end, is best appreciated from
Cheltenham Terrace.

Stables, Royal Hospital   N9g
1814
Royal Hospital Road SW3
Sir John Soane
⊖Sloane Square
Soane was Clerk of Works to the Hospital
from 1807. The stables exhibit many of the
features characteristic of his work. The
large yellow stock brick wall is modulated
with arches, with up to four layers of
recesses; there are no mouldings, except
for the thin Portland stone plinth, and no
decoration other than the delicate octagonal chimneys with their toadstools at the
corners. Soane also designed the house
(now much altered) on the other side of
the hospital's axis, east along Royal
Hospital Road.

Eccleston Square SW1 1835 N10d
Thomas Cubitt
⊖Victoria

Before the intervention of Victoria Station, Pimlico and Belgravia were less separate than they are today, though the stuccoed façades in Pimlico are more uniform. Nineteenth-century squares generally differed from those of the two previous centuries in accepting through traffic as an inevitable ingredient of the plan. The large houses of Eccleston Square, now subdivided into either flats or bed and breakfast establishments, are a reminder of a more opulent past. **Warwick Square** (1843) next door is also by Cubitt and is almost identical.

Pelham Crescent

Pelham Place

Pelham Place and N11a
Pelham Crescent SW3 c1840
George Basevi
⊖South Kensington

Pelham Place and Crescent form an ingenious planning set-piece in the triangle formed by Pelham Street, Fulham Road and Onslow Square. The houses are regular, three-storeyed, with an attic and basement, and (in Pelham Place) individual, almost suburban, front gardens. The Crescent is large in plan, 149 m (491 ft) in diameter, with houses of the same type except for the projecting porches (note the open niche device to the balconies). Despite the grandeur of the plan, the result is domestic.

St Barnabas 1847–50 N12d
St Barnabas Street, Pimlico
SW1
Thomas Cundy III; schools and house by William Butterfield
⊖Sloane Square

Although this was a pioneering Anglo-Catholic church, and is still 'High', much of the original decoration of the tall interior was removed in various refits. The grand exterior composition remains, all of Kentish ragstone. Cundy was surveyor to the Grosvenor Estate and this church is one of his best works and also one of the finest of the period. Butterfield's charming clergy house, less brutal than his usual style, has pointed windows set flush in the stone on either side of the artistic chimney.

Bloomfield Terrace SW1 N13c
c1850
⊖ Sloane Square
A complete street of simply decorated semi-detached houses, mostly now joined up, with a little grandeur added to number 39 by Oliver Hill (1930).

53–8 Glebe Place

35 Glebe Place

Glebe Place SW3 c1850 N14f
⊖ Sloane Square, then bus
down King's Road
Chelsea was an artists' colony in the nineteenth century, as is apparent in Glebe Place, whose east and south sides consist almost exclusively of nineteenth-century studios. Numbers 66–70 form a symmetrical terrace; numbers 60–1, Glebe Studios, are in red brick with two fully glazed, north-facing lantern studios projecting above the eaves. Numbers 53–8 make another symmetrical group of two pavilions in blank red brick with

Norman Shaw chimneys. Number 48 was Charles Rennie Mackintosh's studio house during the last years of his life. The land behind numbers 43 and 44 is almost totally built over by studios – numbers 1 and 2 Hans Studios were reputedly used by the suffragette movement for their meetings. Number 35 (1869), by Philip Webb, is an early experiment in the Queen Anne domestic style, using red brick instead of the Georgians' yellow stock and the Gothicists' stone or terracotta, and wooden windows. Many of the studios are still used by artists.

Sidney Close c1850 N15a
off Fulham Road SW3
built by Smith Charities
⊖ South Kensington
These fifteen magnificent studios between Onslow Square and Fulham Road were built on the original mews by Henry Smith, a local landowner, for artists involved in the Great Exhibition of 1851. There are two entrances from Fulham Road: the one to the west (under number 74 Fulham Road) is formal, for visitors and models; to the east is the working entrance, giving direct access to all studios from Sidney Mews. The studios are planned linearly either side of a generous and top-lit vaulted corridor 3m × 61 m (10 ft × 200 ft) entered from Sidney Close. The cross-section is asymmetrical, with two storeys to the north and three to the south, so that all the studios receive north light. Sargent was a resident of number 12, and it is said that Baroness Orczy wrote *The Scarlet Pimpernel* in number 10.

West Pimlico c1850   N16h
Cambridge Street,
Sutherland Street, Alderney Street,
Westmorland Street, Winchester Street,
Cumberland Street and Gloucester
Street SW1
✦Pimlico

A triangular area of late nineteenth-century housing in west Pimlico bounded by St George's Drive to the east, Lupus Street to the south and Clarendon Street to the west. It is remarkable for its regular and uncharacteristically small urban blocks, generous streets and decent building, and makes a salutary contrast to the more recent Churchill Gardens O13.

Battersea Park 1853–8   N17
Albert Bridge Road SW11 and
Queenstown Road SW8
Sir James Pennethorne and John Gibson
⇌ Battersea Park, Queenstown Road,
Battersea

Following the lead of Victoria Park, Hackney (also by Pennethorne), Battersea Park is London's second significant Victorian park. Its long and protracted conception was frustrated by grudging government support, and the park is more exceptional for its Victorian engineering than for its landscape design. The level had to be raised above the low-lying marshlands of Battersea and a new embankment built: this was achieved with the spoil from the recently excavated London Docks (transported up the river by barge) and additional earth from Thomas Cubitt's development of the surrounding roads (Albert Bridge Road and Prince of Wales Drive). The serpentine lake and paths (8.5 km/5 miles in extent) and the central avenue (12 m × 800 m/40 ft × half a mile) were by now standard park ingredients. John Gibson (the gardener of Victoria Park) was responsible for the detailed distribution of the 40,000 trees and 45,000 shrubs within the framework of Pennethorne's

plan. Battersea Park was a serious contender for the site of the Great Exhibition (1851) and also for Sir Edward Watkin's abortive counterpart to the Eiffel Tower eventually started at Wembley in the 1890s. A century later it became the Festival of Britain pleasure gardens (1951). At the time of writing a further initiative is under discussion – for London's Disneyland. Today it is a strange and uncertain mixture of Victorian pleasure ground and Festival of Britain whimsy, with sculpture by Henry Moore.

Onslow Square SW7 1860   N18a
✦South Kensington

From London's last great square-building phase, Onslow Square is representative of the area between Old Brompton and Fulham Roads, to the west of Basevi's earlier Pelham Place and Crescent N11. The square is fine, but the houses are enormous and grossly Italianate, and were probably always too large for the single-family occupation intended by their builders. The numerous Lutyens family (Edwin, his parents, and twelve siblings) lived in number 16 and managed to fill it.

St Augustine 1870–7 N19a
Queen's Gate SW7
William Butterfield
⊖South Kensington

In the twenty years between his All Saints, Margaret Street K93 and this church, Butterfield lost none of his obsession with colour: every part of the simple interior of St Augustine's is brightly patterned and decorated. The restoration of 1970 removed the whitewash applied in 1928, when the reredos covering the west window was erected. With its multi-coloured and diaper-patterned brickwork, the façade is in violent contrast to the Italianate stucco of the rest of Queen's Gate.

Albert Bridge N20j
SW3 and SW11 1873
R W Ordish
⊖Sloane Square

Albert Bridge connects Chelsea and Battersea and was the first river crossing to incorporate suspended central and side spans – other single-span suspension bridges had been built earlier, for example Brunel's Hungerford Bridge, now demolished. It is a straightforward engineering design with just enough architectural decoration on the piers and spandrels to be delightful: recently re-painted, it is now spoilt only by its undignified later central support. At night there is a marvellous view of the illuminated bridge from Oakley Street.

Swan House 1876 N21g
17 Chelsea Embankment SW3
R Norman Shaw
⊖Sloane Square

The finest Queen Anne Revival domestic building in London, Shaw's Swan House has three first-floor caged and fully glazed oriel windows. Above these the second floor projects with three high narrow oriel windows, alternating with flat, narrow Queen Anne windows. The effect is remarkably original, light and graceful.

Houses 1878–9   N22g
44 and 46 Tite Street SW3
Edward Godwin
⊖ Sloane Square

As the rue Malet Stevens in Paris commemorates the studio apartment production of Michel Malet Stevens in the 1930s,
so Tite Street might have been called
Godwin Street by the end of the 1880s. In
the event the street was (ironically)
named after the odious Sir William Tite,
architect and chairman of the Metropolitan Board of Works – responsible for
censoring Godwin's many designs for Tite
Street.

Numbers 4, 5 and 6 Chelsea Embankment
(1876–8), on the corner of Tite Street, and
numbers 44 and 46 Tite Street are the
remains of Godwin's many houses for its
emerging avant garde artistic community.
They probably survived as a result of their
relatively conventional Queen Anne style.
Number 46, known as the Tower House,
is distinguished by its multi-storey studio
windows. Number 44 was designed for
Frank Miles, one of the prominent Aesthetic Movement artists. The design was
initially rejected by the Metropolitan
Board of Works for being too radical, and
its scraped and abstracted forms in white

brickwork were revised to give the high
gabled elevation of the present building.
Number 35, the 'White House', built for
James McNeill Whistler, suffered a similar
transformation, and was senselessly demolished in the 1960s. Godwin remains an
enigma, but was one of the most respected
architects of his generation, responsible
for encouraging the emergence of a new
'modern' English architecture, free of
historical styles.

Houses 1885–6   N23c
63–73 Cadogan Square SW1
J J Stevenson
⊖ Knightsbridge, Sloane Square

Stevenson, the leading light of the Queen
Anne Revival, was here trying the impossible: to design a terrace of houses while
drawing attention to their individuality.
As a result the façades are a mess of motifs.

Houses 1887   N24b
60a, 62, 68 and 72 Cadogan
Square SW1
R Norman Shaw
⊖ Knightsbridge, Sloane Square

These four houses in 'Pont Street Dutch'
style show Shaw working happily in the
mode which he and Webb had helped to
make fashionable: red brick, gables, white
painted sashes and occasional leaded
lights. The façades are always carefully
asymmetrical and 'artistic' compared with
the more routine development of the rest
of the square. See also Street's 4 Cadogan
Square J51.

Holy Trinity 1888–90　　　　N25c
Sloane Street SW1
J D Sedding
⊖ Sloane Square

This is London's Arts and Crafts church *par excellence*. It was bombed in the Second World War and the vault over the nave destroyed, but it remains a treasure-house of decoration in a mixture of Italian and Gothic styles. The stained glass of the east windows was made by Morris and Company to designs by Burne Jones; the altar rails, the grille behind the altar in the north aisle and the railings to Sloane Street are by Henry Wilson; and the woodwork of the chancel is by Harry Bates. Other work is by Nelson Dawson, F W Pomeroy and Bainbridge Reynolds.

Studio house 1893–4　　　　N26c
25 Cadogan Gardens SW1
A H Mackmurdo
⊖ Sloane Square

This corner studio house, in the Anglo-Dutch tradition established by Norman Shaw, was designed for the artist Mortimer Mempes. Its principal interest lies in the windows, which are used to indicate the relative importance of the two façades. The three richly decorated double-height oriel windows on the principal façade are replaced on the side elevation by flat, recessed windows of identical dimensions.

Houses 1904   N27j
38–9 Cheyne Walk SW3
C R Ashbee
⊖ Sloane Square, then bus down King's
Road

Charles Robert Ashbee was one of the more important architects working at the turn of the century. Apart from his active involvement in the Arts and Crafts movement, he was also influential in the creation of the *Survey of London*. Of the eight houses he designed for Cheyne Walk only two remain; a third, his Magpie and Stump house of 1894, was demolished quite recently. Of the two, 39 was only a speculative development, but 38 was built as a studio house for the artist C L Christran. The studio occupies the top two floors behind the gabled façade with a porthole window, the gable adjusting to buildings of different height on either side. The tall windows to the lower floors, and the street railings of black ironwork with ornamental gold balls (no doubt made at Ashbee's Guild of Handicraft), help to make this a particularly fine example of Arts and Crafts work.

Michelin building 1905–11   N28b
91 Fulham Road SW3
F Espinasse; rebuilding and restoration
by Conran Roche, YRM 1984–8
⊖ South Kensington

An exuberant and delightful freak of a building, faced in white faience, decorated with tyres and celebrating the pleasures and early history of motoring in a series of panels on the ground floor. If only young designers attempting to break away from routine modern could match it for style, verve and craftsmanship!

The building was completey overhauled in 1984–8 when the illuminated corner turrets in the forms of stacks of tyres were restored, two more set-back office floors were added, and part of the less distinguished side to Sloane Avenue was replaced with the sleek glass skin of the Conran Shop.

Michelin building

Battersea Power Station

N29 1

1929–55
Queenstown Road and
Battersea Park Road SW8
Halliday and Agate with Sir Giles Gilbert
Scott; S L Pearce, engineer
⇌ Battersea Park

Battersea Power Station was a symbol of 1930s industrial power and progress. The power station occupies a 6 ha (15 acre) site and is divided internally into two sections, A and B.

The construction of section A began in 1929 to the designs of the engineer Dr S L Pearce and quickly ran into controversy. It was completed in 1935 by the London Power Company. Section B was commissioned in 1944, to be completed in 1955 by the Central Electricity Authority.

The architectural background is complex and Scott, as consultant architect to the exterior, was called in to improve on the 'pedestrian brick elevations'. Scott made his final design in 1931 and even then the result was a compromise: he had preferred red square-section chimneys to the final fluted columns. The station provided heating for the Churchill Gardens Housing Estate O13 on the north bank until 1983, when the station was closed down. There have since been various unsuccessful initiatives for its reuse. At the time of writing it is regrettable to report that the future of this extraordinary example of twentieth-century industrial architecture is uncertain, and large portions of it have been senselessly demolished.

Victoria Coach Station N30d
1931–2
Buckingham Palace Road SW1
Wallis Gilbert and Partners
⊖Victoria
London's only *moderne* transport terminal. The new style suited the up-to-date
function, but the arrangement follows the
nineteenth-century pattern: 'architecture', including the cheerfully decorated traditional tower, encloses and
provides a façade to the 'engineering' of
the coach shed.

Houses 1934 N31e
40 and 41 Chelsea Square SW3
Oliver Hill
⊖South Kensington
Hill was capable of doing quite serious
modern architecture (for example his
house in Redington Road A6), but these
houses, white stucco in a square of neo-
Georgian brick terraces, are in a fey and
imaginary neo-Georgian style. The surrounding houses by Darcy Braddell are
well-mannered, with only the occasional
green pantiles to betray their actual date
(1930).

Chelsea Bridge 1934 N32h
SW1 and SW8
G Topham Forrest and
E P Wheeler
⊖Battersea Park
This fine suspension bridge replaced the
original of 1858 and, like Albert Bridge
N20, its illumination is spectacular.

Houses 1936   N33e
64 Old Church Street SW3
Mendelsohn and Chermayeff
66 Old Church Street SW3
Walter Gropius and Maxwell Fry
⊖ Sloane Square

Gropius and Mendelsohn were émigrés from Germany, and this pair of houses, together with the contemporary High-point I R26, seemed to bring authentic continental modernism to London for the first time. They are not, however, among their architects' better work – Fry and Gropius's Impington Village College, Cambridgeshire, is much more assured. Originally stuccoed, they were refaced by Crosby Fletcher Forbes in 1968.

Peter Jones Department   N34c
Store 1936–8
Sloane Square SW1
W Crabtree with Slater, Moberly and
C H Reilly as consultants
⊖ Sloane Square

One of the finest buildings of the decade in London, and a rare example of a modern (semi-engineering) building solving the complex urban problem of relating both to existing street and square frontages, and to a corner. In this respect it is clearly influenced by Eric Mendelsohn's Schocken store (1927) and Columbus House, Berlin (1931). Although it was not London's first curtain wall, the façade remains one of its finest examples. Its secret lies in the glazing bars, which adjust to the gentle curve of King's Road, avoiding any sense of mechanical repetition. The continuous and apparently unsupported ground-floor display windows are elegant as well as technically innovative; the top floor is set back, like an ocean liner. The interior has a large glazed spiral staircase and triple-height spaces, and maintains the pleasurable promenade and fantasy elements of shopping.

British Airways Terminal   N35d
1939
Buckingham Palace Road SW1
A Lakeman
⊖Victoria
A pompous stone affair, one of the series
of transport buildings in the district (see
Victoria Station J42 and Victoria Coach
Station N30). This one is the most recent
and most self-important, representing
flying as an important imperial activity –
the first national airline was called
Imperial Airways. This it does both by the
shape of the building, with its symmetrical
outstretched wings, and in the splendid
sculpture by E R Broadbent over the
entrance.

Chelsea Barracks 1960–2   N36g
Chelsea Bridge Road SW1
Tripe and Wakeham
⊖Sloane Square
Low, dull and repetitive as barracks
should be (compare Knightsbridge Bar-
racks J76), by a long-established firm
better known for its commercial work.

Issey Miyake 1990   N37b
270 Brompton Road SW3
Stanton Williams
⊖ South Kensington
The recent shops by Stanton Williams for
Issey Miyake have interestingly inverted
the normal conventions for retailing display. Here the ground floor is enigmati-
cally calm and empty, the sale and display
of clothes being relegated to the basement. The staircase forms an important
double-height volume connecting the
spare entrance hall to the 'gallery' of
clothes below. The use of natural

materials (oak, limestone, raw silk, marmorino, etc.) gives a tactile sensuality reminiscent simultaneously of traditional Japanese architecture, and the modern interior surfaces of Adolf Loos and Louis Khan. This simple but beautiful interior stands as a rebuke to the crass fetishism of much contemporary shop design. It is regrettable that the other Issey Miyake shop opposite at number 311 Brompton Road (1987) has recently closed and the future of its beautiful vaulted interior is now uncertain.

Offices and flats 1990   N38j
Hester Road SW11
Foster Associates
⊖ Sloane Square, ⇌ Clapham Junction
Another example of a practice building its own offices (see Hopkins' Broadley Street offices F58, and Richard Rogers' riverside offices T39). Although in all these instances the obvious message might be self-promotion, they also express a private utopia. When seen from across the river the eight-storey matter-of-fact glass-clad building is conspicuously positioned between Battersea and Albert Bridges. On closer examination the building conveys a nostalgia for the 'medium cool' forms of the 1960s , with occasional more distant references to Owen Williams in the window-cleaning 'cornices'. The layered sectional composition of residential penthouses above four floors of flats above three floors of studios, connected by a grand staircase to the entrance lodge and courtyard, proposes a self-contained world.

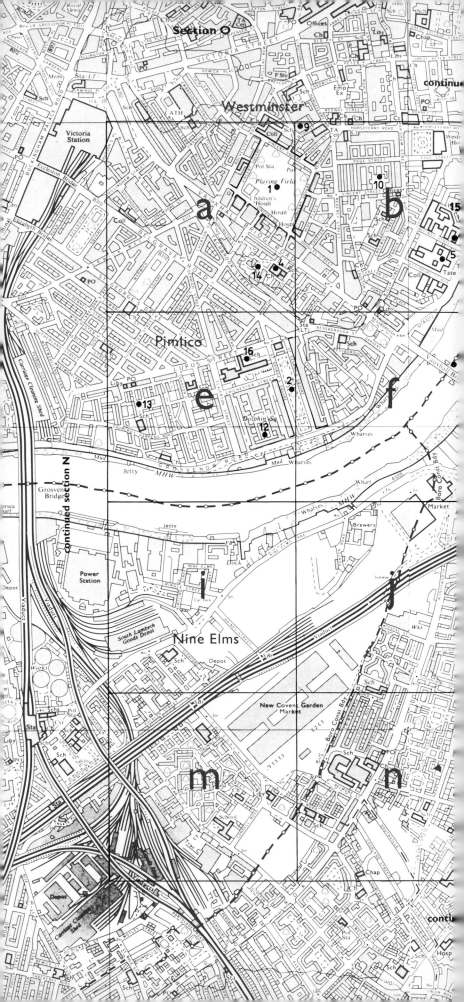

Section O: Westminster (south)/Pimlico/Nine Elms/
South Lambeth/Vauxhall/Kennington

North of the River

Until 1816, with the construction of Vauxhall Bridge and the octagonal penitentiary on the site now occupied by the Tate Gallery, only the northern part of this section had been built on. There were good houses round Smith Square and slums round Vincent Square. The slums were the target for nineteenth-century reformers, religious and social (Baroness Burdett-Coutts, for example, was a benefactor to the poor and built churches such as St Stephen with St John, Rochester Row). The twentieth century has continued the process: the Millbank Estate by the LCC's young architects provided an alternative housing model to the Italianate barracks of the Peabody Trust; and in the 1920s Lutyens was employed to lay out the large area of slum-clearance housing on either side of Page Street O10. An unfortunate result of a century of improvement is the architectural incoherence of the district; even the huge Vincent Square O1 seems inconsequential.

To the south of Vauxhall Bridge Road lies the large residential area of Pimlico, developed from 1835 on flat marshy land which had been used for market gardens and the pleasure gardens of Ranelagh. Thomas Cubitt, the builder of Belgravia, laid it out as streets and squares on two grids, one parallel to Belgrave Road, the other parallel to the river. The grids meet at Lupus Street, giving rise to wide, splayed junctions unusual in London. The houses are in a reduced version of the Italianate stucco of Belgravia. The squares are large; and St George's Square O2, the last to be built, with one end open to the river, is enormous. The twentieth-century Dolphin Square O12 remains England's answer to the *unité d'habitation*, and Churchill Gardens O13 and Pimlico School O16, part of the post-war redevelopment of the area south of Lupus Street, demonstrate the architecture of the Welfare State.

South of the River

This flat area is marked by routes running south-west to north-east: first the Roman road (now Clapham Road), and most recently the London and South Western Railway, which terminated originally at Nine Elms and was extended to its present terminus at Waterloo (section K) in 1848. The eighteenth century left only ribbons of fine Georgian houses, for example, along Kennington Road. The Industrial Revolution set up factories along the Thames to serve the city north of the river: glassworks, potteries and mills. The area became the home of the desperately poor, but nevertheless did not attract the attention of the Victorian improvers, with the exception of the brave speculation of Lansdowne Gardens, the establishment of the Oval cricket ground in 1846, and the construction of Henry Roberts' exhibition houses for the poor on the edge of Kennington Park. The twentieth century's slum clearance programme has left Lambeth and Kennington in a state of urban incoherence from which they may never recover.

In 1974 Covent Garden Market was moved to a new building at Nine Elms, encouraging the commercial redevelopment of the riverside west of Vauxhall Bridge.

Lambeth Bridge O11

Vincent Square SW1 c1780   O1a
⊖Pimlico, Victoria
Surrounded by a medley of buildings, this
is now more of a large open space than a
characteristic London square. The garden
is currently used as playing fields by
Westminster School. Numbers 84, 85 and
the detached 86 are all that remain of the
original houses. The square is the address
of the Royal Horticultural Society; the
main building (1904) is by E J Stebbs, and
the hall O9 (1923–8) is by Easton and
Robertson. In the north corner of the
square is the Westminster Technical
College (1893) by Blashill, with a particularly fine extension (1937–52) by
H S Goodhard-Rendel. The great width of
the square gives prominence to the
nearby high-rise buildings, notably Hide
Tower, 64 m (212 ft) high, by Stillman and
Eastwick Field (1957–62).

St George's Square

St Saviour

St George's Square SW1   O2e
1844
⊖Pimlico
A deep, rectangular riverside square, its
south side giving the bay-windowed
houses long diagonal views of the river. St
George's Square is appropriate for its site,
and a model from which neighbouring
Churchill Gardens O13 could have prof-
ited. The Perseverance pub at the north-
east corner dates from 1840, the rest of
the houses from 1850. The square is a

fitting end to a Belgravia/Pimlico promenade, beginning at Wilton Place, immediately south of Hyde Park.
At the north end is **St Saviour** (1863–4)
by Thomas Cundy III. This neo-Gothic
church's traditional east-west alignment
creates an ambiguous relationship with
the orientation of the classical square. The
major features of the church – the west
front, spire and east window – face the
sides of the square, ignoring its formal
north-south axis.

Cottages 1851   O31
Kennington Park Road SE11
Henry Roberts
⊖Oval
Now serving as the lodge for Kennington
Park, these little Tudor-style flats (two
dwellings on each floor) were re-erected
after being shown at the 1851 Great
Exhibition as examples of Reformist housing. With their multi-coloured brickwork
and feeble decoration they lack the
robustness of Roberts' earlier work (for
example the Streatham Street flats G33).

St James-the-Less, Parish Hall and Infant School
O4a

1860–1
Vauxhall Bridge Road SW1
George Edmund Street
⊖Pimlico

One of the best Victorian Gothic churches in London, St James-the-Less is now ignominiously embedded in the Lillington Gardens housing estate O14. The composition of church, hall and school is elemental and formally excellent, with the detached tower marking the entrance from Vauxhall Bridge Road. All the buildings are in red brick with black brick enrichment. The interior of the church, with three wide bays on broad circular columns, is spatially generous and richly decorated with black brick and red and yellow diagonal wall tiles. The fresco above the chancel arch is by G F Watts.

Tate Gallery
O5b

1897–1979
Millbank SW1
Sidney Smith 1897; additions WH Romaine Walker 1909; new sculpture gallery J Russell Pope 1937; extension J Llewelyn Davies, Weeks Forestier-Walker Bor and I 1971–9
⊖ Pimlico

Millbank, on which the Tate now stands, was in the nineteenth century the site of Jeremy Bentham's massive model penitentiary (1812–21) which covered 7 hectares (18 acres). Its octagonal plan can still be traced in the street pattern around the present gallery.

The Tate might appear from the outside to have been conceived integrally, but in fact there have been six additions, with a seventh presently planned (1991) for museums of new art and sculpture by James Stirling and Michael Wilford. It is surprising that the impressive central cupola and sculpture galleries were contributed by the Tate's second patron, Lord Duveen, as late as 1937.

Three recent initiatives have significantly altered the Tate, two by the ex-Director, Sir Alan Bowness, and the third by his successor Nicholas Serota. First, Stirling and Wilford's Clore Gallery completed in 1985 to house the Turner Collection. Second, Jeremy and Fenella Dixon's transformation of catering in the form of the new Coffee Shop (1982) and the Whistler Restaurant (1983). The interpretation of Whistler's mural as an ideal landscape seen from under a canopied restaurant terrace is particularly memorable. Third, Colquhoun and Miller's renovation and rehang of the collection in 1989, which has achieved a didactic circuit, thereby making sense of the building's plan and the chronology of its collection.

At the time of writing the Nomura Gallery and a new bookshop are under construction on the opposite side of the Duveen Gallery axis, to the designs of John Miller and Partners. See also the Clore Gallery O17.

Belgrave Hospital for Children
1900–3
O61

Clapham Road SW9
H Percy Adams, designed by Charles Holden
⊖Oval

Holden was twenty-five when he designed this, his first executed building. He had worked for C R Ashbee for a year, and the hospital combines a rational plan with simple Arts and Crafts details such as the fine panel of lettering over the front door. His taste for pyramidal massing is exhibited in both the corner towers and the high stepped and pointed gable of the entrance.

Vauxhall Bridge SW1 and   O7f
SE1 1906
Sir Maurice Fitzmaurice, W E Riley
✆Vauxhall, Pimlico
The wide five-span bridge gives good views downstream towards the Palace of Westminster and the City beyond; the south is unfortunately marred by the grotesquely oversized traffic arrangements of Vauxhall Cross. The piers are decorated with big statues of the Arts and Sciences by F W Pomeroy and Alfred Drury. *Architecture* faces upstream and carries a model of St Paul's Cathedral.

Courtenay Square SE11   O8h
1914
Adshead and Ramsay
✆Oval
Part of a slum clearance scheme on the Duchy of Cornwall Estate, Courtenay square, together with houses in Courtenay Street, and Cardigan Street and the Old Tenants' Hostel (1913–14) in Newburn Street, is a fragment of a model estate. The two-storey terraced houses follow the Regency model, built in stock bricks with timber trellis porches. They remain a salutary and convincingly modest example of how to reconstruct a city within its own traditions, without recourse to the mindless pursuit of new types.

Royal Horticultural   O9b
Society Hall 1923–8
Vincent Square SW1
Easton and Robertson
✆Pimlico, St James's Park
The roof of this exhibition hall introduced to England the reinforced concrete catenary-shaped arches already in use on the continent. The hall is lit for its full length by stepped-back patent glazing between the arches.

Housing 1928–30   O10b
Page Street and Vincent Street
SW1
Sir Edwin Lutyens
✆Pimlico
Designed for the LCC while Lutyens was continuing his brilliant work for the Midland Bank L108, L112, this scheme suggests that the master of classicism was, like other twentieth-century architects, at a loss with public housing. Blocks of flats are arranged round courts at right angles to the street, and covered in an arbitrary chequerboard pattern of alternating windows and brick and stucco panels. Facing the street between the blocks are shops in the form of classical pavilions.

Lambeth Bridge SWI and   OIIc
SEI 1932
LCC Architects Department; G Topham
Forrest and Sir Reginald Blomfield
⊖Westminster

The bridge has five spans, its shallow steel arches springing from massive masonry bases topped by obelisks supporting lamps, with further pairs of giant obelisks topped by pineapples at each end. It replaced the original bridge of 1862 and forms part of an ambitious composition completed by the broad granite staircase leading to the riverside gardens and the monumental Thames House (1931) on the north bank; this was one of the last urban designs for London as an imperial capital.

Flats, Dolphin Square 1937   OI2e
Grosvenor Road SWI
Gordon Jeeves
⊖Pimlico

1236 corridor-access flats are arranged in a doughnut around a central garden on a 3.1 ha (7.6 acre) site. In the middle there is a sports building with courts for tennis and squash, a public restaurant, recently refurbished in the *moderne* style of the 1930s, and an underground car park for 200 cars. The style is a dull neo-Georgian for the base and upper storeys, with a modern striped top floor. The proposed landing stage for tenants on the cleared waterfront was never built. Dolphin Square is more dense than Churchill Gardens OI3 along Grosvenor Road, but while only twenty-five years separate their design, the two schemes make a telling urban contrast: one the space-making 'block', the other isolated slabs standing on lawns.

Churchill Gardens Estate   OI3e
1946–62
Grosvenor Road, Lupus Street
and Claverton Street SWI
Powell and Moya
⊖Pimlico

Approached via the particularly fine nineteenth-century terraces and squares of Victoria and Pimlico, Churchill Gardens suggests a totally new form of urban life. This particularly massive and bleak housing estate is one of London's first significant post-war comprehensive redevelopments. The open competition for the design was won by its young architects, Powell and Moya, when they were still in their final year at the Architectural Association school, and the scheme has always been praised as exemplary. Pevsner, for example, recently wrote, 'The aesthetic significance of Churchill Gardens is that even now, after twenty-five years, it has remained one of the best estates of this type'. If the type referred to is Le Corbusier's *Ville Radieuse*, the thirty-six blocks built in four sections have always seemed too close together, conveying an image of overcrowding rather than the *espace, verdure et soleil* (space, greenery and sun)

of its continental inspiration. At the same time it conjures up the now familiar and haunting spectre of urban alienation. Estates like Churchill Gardens have been excused as the result of high density

building, but this is a popular myth – as is revealed when its 1661 flats on 12 ha (30 acres) are compared with Dolphin Square O12 next door, of 1236 flats on 3.1 ha (7.6 acres).

Lillington Gardens Estate O14a
1961–71
Vauxhall Bridge Road SW1
Darbourne and Darke
⊖Victoria, Pimlico

The first appearance of what was later termed loosely 'the new vernacular', Lillington Gardens Estate occupies the area between Vauxhall Bridge Road, Charlwood Street and Tachbrook Street. One of the largest comprehensive redevelopments of the decade, the planning brief required housing for 2000 people, shops, pubs, surgeries, a community hall and a library. The development was planned in three phases, phase one being the subject of an open competition in 1961. This large complex red-brick building, with cantilevered balconies, 'streets in the air', irregular profile and ample external planting, offered a popular and expressive alternative to the drab postwar tradition of mixed development.

Phase one established for its architects a lasting popular reputation. Phases two and three proved less exceptional and expressed a more rigorous economic housing climate.

Millbank Tower O15b
ex Vickers Tower 1963
Millbank SW1
Ronald Ward and Partners
⊖Pimlico

At the time of its completion – when tower building was fashionable – this thirty-two-storey tower, marking the bend of the river between Vauxhall and Lambeth and dwarfing the Tate O5 next door, received popular approval. With hindsight it is clear that there were certain preferred positions for towers in the city: a) as a focus at large-scale traffic intersections, notably Seifert's Centre Point K169 and Goldfinger's Elephant and Castle L124; b) at the edge of a park (after Le Corbusier's *Ville Radieuse*), as at Roehampton V9 and the new hotels and barracks surrounding Hyde Park; and c) at the edge of water (after Mies van der Rohe's Lakeshore Drive apartments in Chicago), as at Millbank. The preferred architecture was a shiny glass envelope; but the Millbank Tower's irregular plan form stands awkwardly on its podium, and its great mass has no positive order, either vertically or horizontally. It is not surprising that the profile of London, constructed from such disparate and arbitrary sets of references, should have degenerated so rapidly during the 1960s.

Pimlico School 1966–70   O16e
St George's Square and
Lupus Street SW1
GLC Architects Department;
John Bancroft
⊖ Pimlico

In the wake of the 'route building'
proposals of the late 1950s, this four-
storey comprehensive school for 1725
pupils, with a long internal 'street' and
glazed exterior, has all the disadvantages
of an over-extended organization with
none of the advantages. The internal route
merely duplicates the streets on either
side, whereas nineteenth-century arcades
were generally at right angles and sup-
plementary to existing streets. The glazed
façades to the classrooms, apart from
offering tropical conditions to the children, reverse the basic front/back,
public/private logic of street architecture.

The building received an RIBA award in
1972.

Clore Gallery 1979–85   O17b
Tate Gallery, Millbank SW1
Stirling and Wilford
⊖ Pimlico

The Clore Gallery largely realized the
architect's intentions. These were firstly
that the building might be read as a garden
pavilion attached to a large house, an
impression reinforced by the pergola, lily
pond and general informality of the entrance sequence (designed with Janet Jack
of BDP); and secondly that the façades
might be seen as heterogeneous, thereby
deferring to the various adjacent buildings. The empty entrance pediment and
string courses refer to the classical parent

building and the free-style composition of
the corner refers to the Queen Alexandra
Military Hospital.

Inside, as in other museums by Stirling and
Wilford, (notably the Staatsgalerie in
Stuttgart), the eventful promenade to the
galleries contrasts with the conventional
enfilade of the galleries themselves. The
main stair leads away from the galleries in
a compressed top-lit space. The visitor is
then presented with a large window acting as a proscenium to the works beyond.
The eight principal top-lit galleries were
designed to restore some of the liveliness
of natural light while meeting the requirements of conservation.

Lambeth Community Care O18d
Centre 1985
Monkton Street, SE11
Edward Cullinan Architects
⊖ Elephant & Castle

The familiar paradigm of house and garden is used to draw together an ambitious social and medical programme. The building combines a day care centre with physio- and occupational therapy, dentistry and social work as well as short-stay accommodation for twenty patients. This building reasserts the role of modern architecture as a principal participant in social innovation and change. The inclusive and democratic nature of Cullinan's architecture is here a key to the building's success which stands as a rebuke to the alienating tendencies of the large hospitals.

continued section

contin

conti

NEWINGTON

KENNINGTON

CAMB

MYATT'S FIELDS

Kennington Park

Imperial War Museum

LAMBETH HOSPL

a

b

e

f

i

j

m

n

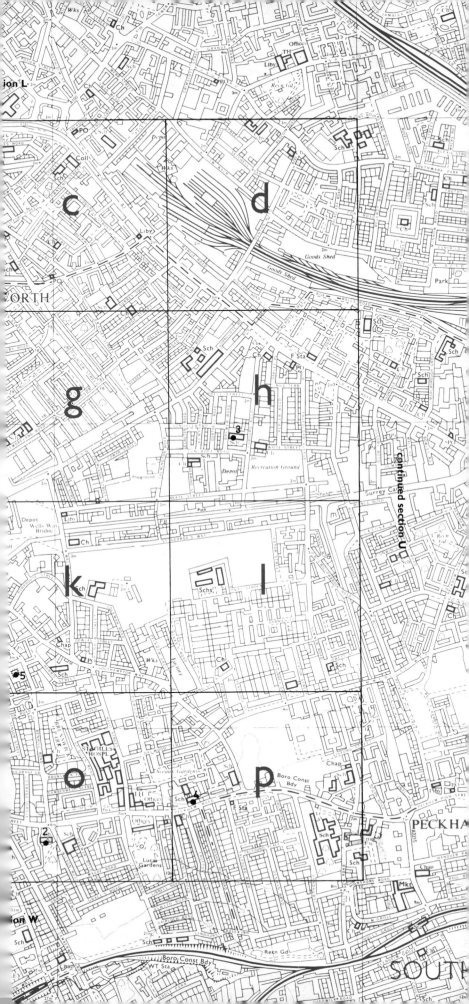

Section P: Camberwell/Kennington/Walworth

The earliest construction in this architecturally undistinguished area is the Old Kent Road, following the line of the Roman Watling Street, which ran from Southwark and London Bridge to the north-west of England. To the south the majority of the area was open countryside until the late eighteenth century, with the village of Camberwell separated from the nearby villages of Peckham and Dulwich by fields which supplied produce to the markets of London. There is now very little evidence of these village nuclei.

The urban development of the area took place in the second half of the nineteenth century, with a framework formed by the Old Kent Road, Walworth Road, Peckham Road and Camberwell New Road. When the Surrey Canal was built to the east in 1807–9 it passed through open fields Camberwell New Road, laid out in 1815, connected the village of Camberwel' to Kennington and then to Westminster. As in much of nineteenth-century suburban London, ribbons of speculatively built brick terraces followed, leaving between them empty areas which were developed later.

In this century, as a result of heavy bombing in the Second World War, the LCC and the more recently formed London Borough of Southwark have replaced much of this nineteenth-century housing stock. The resulting urban picture is sad – at best a piecemeal catalogue of local authority housing fashions. The most unfortunate developments are to be found south of the Elephant and Castle: the Heygate Estate and the Aylesbury Estate, north of Peckham Road. The unremittingly regimented and public nature of this heavily vandalized estate was used by the American critic Oscar Neuman to support his thesis that private or 'defensible' space is necessary in housing design, a theory which has since been extended and endorsed by many other critics. London has its own housing types developed over the centuries, and to attempt to replace them with other models is to court disaster.

The Heygate Estate

St Peter Walworth 1823–5   P1f
Liverpool Grove SE17
Sir John Soane
⊖ Elephant and Castle

An astonishing work and the best remaining of Soane's churches in London, St Peter's is a compendium of the architect's concerns: geometry, layered and detached planes, and the invention of extensions of the classical language. The flat front has an Ionic portico recessed by exactly the depth of the columns. These support a frieze with incised Greek key decoration running the full width of the façade. The arched windows to the sides of the portico show the same two layers – a motif continued down the flanks of the church. At the back there is a very dense plastic composition of arched windows and brick arches. The two-stage tower which rises from a plinth the width of the portico is extremely elongated in contrast to the horizontality of the front. The interior, while now decorated in unappetizing colours, shows Soane's use of thin screens to define the adjoining spaces. The chancel is marked by two full-width segmental arches, echoing another that defines the organ loft at the west end, and these are joined to the galleries by round-arched moulding-free screens. See also Marylebone Road F22 and Bethnal Green U18.

St Giles 1844   P2o
Camberwell Church Street SE5
Sir George Gilbert Scott; west front Sir Arthur Blomfield
⇌ Denmark Hill

Because it has been so much copied – no English town is without its St Giles – the strength of Scott's design, though innovatory at the time, is not evident today. It embodies the prescriptions of those campaigners for Anglican correctness, the Camden Society – considerable length (47 m/153 ft) and use of the Gothic style. Scott won the competition for the design, and with the £14,500 insurance money from the fire which destroyed the old church, was able to erect this very large replacement. The style is roughly English Gothic but with continental details, all well built in Kentish ragstone.

St Mark 1887–94   P3h
Cobourg Road SE5
R Norman Shaw
⊖Elephant and Castle, then bus
Not a very good church, and now derelict, but a relief perhaps from the Kentish ragstone or papery ashlar of the standard product of the period: strictly for Shaw admirers.

Camberwell School of Arts   P4p
and Crafts and
South London Art Gallery
1896–8
Peckham Road SE5
Maurice B Adams
⇌Peckham Rye
Fussy 'Jacobethan' and baroque in red brick, stone and slate.

Brunswick Park Junior   P5k
School 1958–61
Bantry Street and
Picton Street SE5
Stirling and Gowan
⊖Oval, then bus to Camberwell Green
In this small school building there are many stylistic references to Stirling and Gowan's regrettably unbuilt competition entry for Churchill College, Cambridge (1958), termed by Colin Rowe 'the Blenheim of the Welfare State'. This is its microcosm, and despite its physical neglect, buried in the particularly bleak housing estate behind Camberwell Road,

it has worn very well architecturally. The modest school hall, like Churchill College, uses a square plan divided into four smaller equal squares. Above three of these are steep monopitched rooflights with exposed trusses, rotated swastika fashion. The brick chimney completes the corner of the fourth square. The walls are built of white brickwork with occasional red-brick banding, and the building is connected to the ground by large grassy banks extending its geometry. This early use of decorative brick banding considerably predates the current fashion for its use by the 'post modernists'.

Outer London

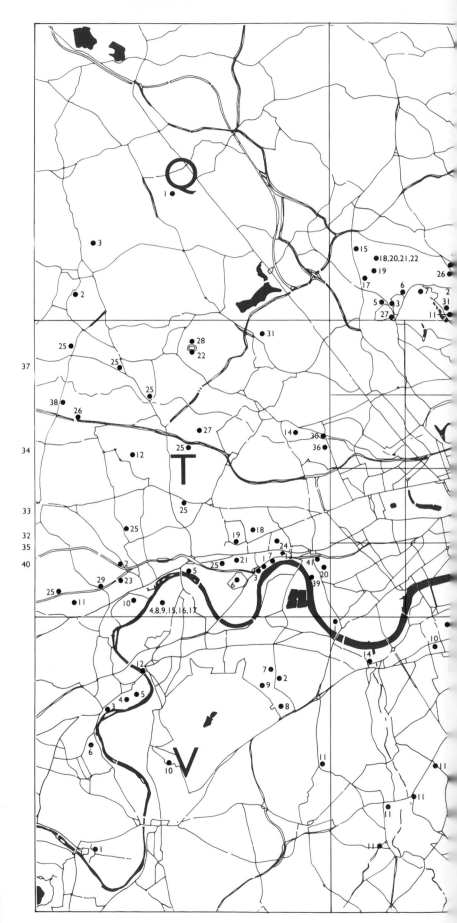

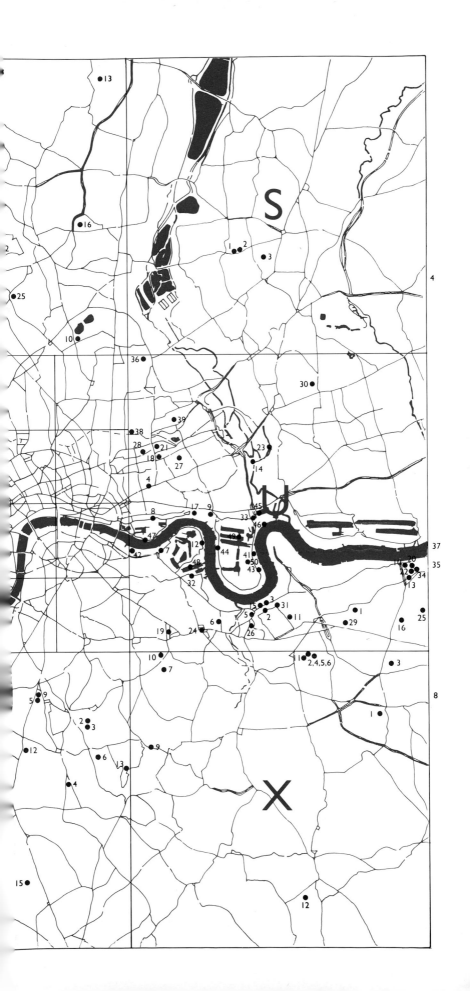

Section Q: Outer London, north-west

This section's villages and the small town of Harrow are still discernible, though now engulfed in the suburban development between the wars, which stops at the Green Belt running in an arc from Harrow Weald in the west to Totteridge Park in the east. The land rises from the plain of the Thames, and the low hills are dominated by the spire of Harrow's parish church, St Mary. Transport routes divide up the area: the Roman Watling Street runs straight from Marble Arch to St Albans, bending at Brockley Hill and Elstree. The nineteenth-century railway builders followed its track north from St Pancras. Britain's first motorway, the M1, built in the 1950s, follows the railway before turning north-west for Birmingham.

Most of the villages had a sprinkling of Georgian additions to their High Streets (see for example Stanmore's Broadway) but it was the extension of the underground railway after the First World War which led to the suburbanization of the entire area. To the south, the Metropolitan Line runs through Northwick Park and Harrow to Amersham in Buckinghamshire; the Bakerloo Line follows the main line via Harrow and Wealdstone to Watford, the Jubilee Line to Stanmore; and the Northern Line connects both the West End and the City to Edgware and Mill Hill. These routes were the single cause and means of London's expansion between the wars. The name Metroland, lovingly revived by Sir John Betjeman, was coined to describe the suburbs springing up around the new lines, and London Transport helped the developers sell their product with posters illustrating seductively the new life they offered. High fares for commuters may by now have dulled the promise, but the pattern of outer London – now so suitable for those with cars – was established by its public transport.

The section has few architectural gems, although Harrow School Q2 has character, and the huge sheds of Elstree Studios are interesting; they are all that remain of Britain's film industry, established in the 1930s at Borehamwood, and are now used mostly to make Hollywood blockbusters.

Cinema, Rayners Lane ('Metroland')

St Lawrence rebuilt 1715   Q1
Whitchurch Lane, Edgware
⊖Canons Park
The Duke of Chandos, Paymaster-General to the Duke of Marlborough, lived nearby in the now-demolished Canons, and was responsible for rebuilding and decorating the interior of this parish church. It is a unique, if failed, attempt to bring Roman baroque to London: the interior is painted all over (by Laguerre), like the attached Chandos mausoleum.

Harrow School c1818–1921   Q2
Harrow-on-the-Hill
C R Cockerell, Charles Foster Hayward, George Gilbert Scott, William Burges, Basil Champneys, Herbert Baker and others
⊖Harrow-on-the-Hill
The public school was principally an invention of the nineteenth century, given impetus by the needs of Empire. Although the school was founded in 1571, the majority of the buildings date from 1845–84, the period of its greatest expansion. Most of them were designed by Hayward in an unfortunate gloomy red brickwork, but a number of eminent architects designed individual buildings.

Cockerell's chapel (1838) was replaced in 1854–7 by Scott's flint and stone New Chapel in his preferred Decorated Gothic style, anticipating St Mary Abbots 111. The Vaughan Library is also in Scott's Gothic style, but built in brick. The Speech Room (1874–7) is by Burges, and with its Greek theatre plan and arcaded façade is the most formally ambitious building at Harrow (see also his Tower House 114). In contrast, the Butler Museum (1884–6) by Champneys is in the late Victorian Queen Anne style, with high Dutch gables, oriel windows and skilful asymmetries. The open staircase running the height of the building is particularly good. Finally, Baker's classical War Memorial Building (1921) deals skilfully with a difficult site.

Grims Dyke 1870–2   Q3
Wealdwood Road, Harrow
R Norman Shaw
⊖Harrow and Wealdstone
Near the Saxon earthwork after which it is named, this excellent example of Shaw's Domestic Revival shows two typical features of his 'Old English' style: the asymmetrical plan and the Great Hall. It was built for a painter, and was later occupied by W S Gilbert (of Gilbert and Sullivan). In the garden are the statues of English river gods from Soho Square K24.

Section R: Outer London, north

Highgate Village and the hamlet of North End, the earliest surviving developments in this area, were quite separate from London until the late nineteenth century. From the sixteenth century Highgate was a favourite spot for the wealthy to build their country retreats: Kenwood R7 is the most conspicuous example. The Grove and Pond Square R2 are among the best surviving seventeenth- and eighteenth-century village nuclei in London, as Waterlow Park and Highgate Cemetery R9 are the most characteristically Victorian examples of their type.

For the rest, the urban development is exclusively twentieth-century, consisting typically of the speculative dormitory suburbs of the inter-war years. This recent northerly expansion of London was given added impetus by the extension of the Northern Line underground. At the beginning of the century Golders Green was a country crossroads with signposts to London; its rapid development began in 1906 with the arrival of the Northern Line, as did Hendon's in 1926.

Apart from isolated parks and buildings – for example Repton's Trent Park in Enfield or Charles Holden's Arnos Grove Station R23 at Southgate – the suburbs of north London are architecturally uninteresting. There are two key exceptions: the first is Hampstead Garden Suburb R18, founded in 1906 by Dame Henrietta Barnett, and laid out in 1907–15 by Sir Raymond Unwin, with significant contributions from Sir Edwin Lutyens and Baillie Scott. The second, in contrast, is a heroic fragment of Le Corbusier's *Ville Radieuse*: Tecton and Berthold Lubetkin's Highpoints 1 and 2 R26 of the late 1930s.

Highgate West Hill

Lauderdale House 1580 R1
Highgate Hill N19
⊖ Archway

Built for John Maitland, Earl of Lauderdale and a City merchant, on the traditional exit route from London up Highgate Hill, Lauderdale House had a part in the rich social history of the Restoration – it is believed that Nell Gwynn and her baby son by Charles II were residents in 1670. The story of its renovation is as complex as its social history. Of the sixteenth-century house only the masonry and south-east room remain; two notable eighteenth-century features are the lantern on the seventeenth-century staircase, and the entrance hall with a fine recess and Corinthian columns; and the exterior is late Georgian, plastered and rather modest. In 1889 the house with its 12 ha (29 acres) of grounds was given to the LCC by Sir Sidney Waterlow. A fire

gutted it in 1963, but it is now enjoyed by the public as a tea room and small cultural centre. The magnificent first-floor gallery remains to be restored.

Pond Square

The Grove

Highgate N6 R2
17th and 18th century
⊖ Highgate

The nucleus of Highgate village is on top of Highgate Hill, and its earliest houses are round the Grove, to the west, and in Pond Square to the east. These loose spaces are joined by South Grove, with grander detached houses. The High Street has a pleasant collection of modest Georgian shops. In spite of the torrents of rush-hour traffic it is still possible to see **The Grove**, a marvellous group of houses, as a seventeenth-century village well outside London: they overlook a small green, and have most uncharacteristic gravelled sidewalks sheltered by trees. Numbers 1 and 2, of the late seventeenth century, have a cornice but no parapet, and the broad sash-window frames are flush with the outside. Number 5 has a fine Doric

porch, number 6 a good iron gate and Coleridge lived at number 3.

In **South Grove** number 17, Old Hall, is a fine four-bay house of the 1690s. Opposite stands an extraordinary survival: numbers 25 and 26, two tiny pantiled cottages for the servants of the grander houses like Moreton House, number 14, and Church House, number 10, both of five bays and three storeys. The stuccoed Literary Institute was founded in 1839.

Pond Square cries out for a reticent re-paving to replace the inappropriate asphalt. Numbers 1–6 are a noteworthy group of tiny cottages.

In the **High Street** numbers 17–21, 23 and 42 are good and well preserved eighteenth-century houses.

More Georgian houses are to be found at West Hill (45–7) and on Highgate Hill (106–8).

Wyldes Farm 17th century   R3
North End NW3
⊖ Golders Green, Hampstead
The only surviving farmhouse in Hampstead, Wyldes Farm sits in its own fenced grounds, having lost its farmland to the Heath extension between North End R5 and the Garden Suburb R18. Its residents have not always been farmers, however: John Linnell the painter lived here from 1792 to 1882, with William Blake his frequent visitor. Sir Raymond Unwin, the architect and planner of Hampstead Garden Suburb, also lived at Wyldes and was responsible for converting the large barn into living quarters.

Cromwell House 1637–40   R4
104 Highgate Hill N6
⊖ Archway
Cromwell House was built for Richard Springwell, and is one of the few remaining large houses in London of its date. It is an example of what Summerson calls the 'artisan style', built as a joint production by skilled craftsmen (probably co-ordinated by the bricklayer) without the controlling influence of an architect. The street façade, with its richly moulded cornices, carved *in situ* at first and second floor levels, is a *tour de force* by the bricklayer-contractor. The regularity of the seven window bays is a testament to the growing influence of Inigo Jones. A range of dormer windows and a central cupola complete the top of the house. Inside, the staircase is the earliest in London to have a handrail formed by pierced decorative panels instead of balustrades. Later the staircase would have terminated at the *piano nobile* but here it

rises the full height of the building. The house was considerably restored in 1865 by Thomas Harris and is now occupied by a missionary society. (For the artisan style see also College of Arms L21.)

North End NW3 c1700   R5
⊖ Golders Green, Hampstead
Like the Vale of Health B10, North End is a surviving hamlet which can still be appreciated as an entity, although Golders Green encroaches on it via North End Road. The Old Bull and Bush pub, Wyldes Farm R3, Byron Cottage, and the site of Pitt's House (residence of Pitt the Elder in 1776) are its oldest remaining features. As a hamlet, North End is best appreciated when approached along the bridle paths from Golders Hill Park to the east, or from the Heath extension to the north and west.

The Old Bull and Bush

The Spaniards 18th century   R6
Spaniards Road NW3
⊖ Hampstead
A group of 'country' buildings halfway to Highgate along Spaniards Road: on one side the whitewashed public house and its outbuildings, and on the other side a small lodge, once a toll-house. The interior of the pub, with its sequence of small rooms, is a fairly well preserved example of an eighteenth-century coaching inn.

Kenwood House I /54, 1764–9, 1793–6
Hampstead Lane NW3
Robert Adam

R7

⊖ Hampstead, then walk across the Heath; or bus to Highgate

Kenwood is the first example of Adam's mature style applied to an exterior. Built at the beginning of the seventeenth century, the house was acquired by the first Earl of Mansfield in 1754 and re-modelled as a holiday retreat by Adam in 1764. In 1780 it became a permanent residence.

The Hampstead-Highgate road ran much closer to the house in 1754, and it was the second Earl who in 1793 set the public road back to its present line, allowing the house to stand free in its park. The house is now approached by two serpentine drives through dense woodlands, from which the grand Adam entrance front with its full-height portico and pediment (1769) is suddenly revealed. The white-brick wings are by George Saunders (1793–6).

In contrast with the closed north approach the south front lies open to extensive parkland. The long classical façade confronting a contrived but 'natural' world is quintessential of English house and park design in the eighteenth century. It has been suggested that

Humphrey Repton was consulted by the architect, because the serpentine drives and the gardens adjacent to the house are characteristic of his work. The sham bridge at the east end of the lakes was introduced by the first Earl.

The symmetrical arrangement of the south front was prompted by the existing orangery on the left, suggesting the building of the library on the right to balance it. Adam refronted the centre block and raised it a storey with slim pilasters of his own invention. Although much of Adam's enriched original stucco has disappeared with time, the capitals and principal mouldings were restored in 1955–9.

Of the interiors, the sequence from the hall to the main staircase and the marble hall (on the first floor) is all by Adam. It culminates in the library, perhaps one of the finest Adam rooms in existence. Although much of the original Adam furniture has been removed, Kenwood has a very fine collection of paintings, contributed by Lord Iveagh when he bought the house in 1925. The second Earl of Iveagh opened the house to the public in 1928 and it is now run by English Heritage. The concerts by the lake on summer evenings are highly recommended.

St John the Evangelist 1826 R8
Holloway Road N19
Sir Charles Barry
⊖ Archway

One of a pair of nearly identical churches (the other is St Paul's, Balls Pond Road), this undistinguished work is in thin Perpendicular Gothic. Barry is famous as the designer of the Travellers' Club K82 and the Houses of Parliament K90. This church should be compared with the contemporary and much better work of Bedford and the Inwoods, for example St John, Waterloo Road K72 and St Pancras G21.

Mausoleum of Julius Beer

Highgate Cemetery R9
started 1838
Swains Lane N6
Stephen Geary, J B Bunning and
J Oldred Scott
⊖ Archway

The British cemetery is a product of the great period of Sanitary Reform that began in 1820. By the beginning of the nineteenth century the rapid growth of population had made the reform of burials long overdue, and seven commercial cemeteries were laid out around London, including Kensal Green T14 (1833), Brompton M1 (1831), Nunhead X7 (1840) and Tower Hamlets (1841). Laid out in the tradition of eighteenth-century landscape gardening, Highgate Old Cemetery epitomizes the High Victorian preoccupation with death and its drama. In 1838 Stephen Geary (owner and architect of the London Cemetery Company) planned the first Highgate Cemetery to the west of Swains Lane. (Ironically, Geary is reputed to be the architect of London's earliest gin palaces.)

As a result of its architecture, its ingenious layout of paths and magnificent views over London, it soon became popular, and favourable comparisons were made with Père Lachaise, built outside Paris in 1804. In 1854 the cemetery was extended to the east of Swains Lane and now contains approximately 51,000 graves with about 166,000 bodies buried in them. As opposed to the classical mausolea of Kensal Green, Geary wanted the architecture of Highgate to be a mixture of Gothic and Egyptian (the latter was fashionable in mortuary art in the early nineteenth century). Two chapels were provided at the entrance to the west cemetery, and both were in use up to 1956. Their details – stairs set in octagonal buttresses, coloured glass set directly into the masonry, and superimposed bays of lancet windows – show the originality of Geary's architecture. The bier at the southern end displays ingenuity *par excellence*, with a hydraulic system to lower the coffins through a deep tunnel under Swains Lane to the new cemetery to the east. To the west a fine arcaded retaining wall forms a large, curved assembly area for mourners and a turning point for hearses. Up the hill to the north are the Egyptian Avenue and the Cedar of Lebanon Catacombs, formed around a tree from the original estate. The site planning uses the levels skilfully in a series of circuitously connecting paths. In the northern part of the cemetery, abutting the churchyard of St Michael's, are the Gothic Catacombs (1842), attributed to J B Bunning, who relieved Geary as surveyor to the London Cemetery Company in 1839. At the north of the Lebanon Circle is the mausoleum to Julius Beer, the most ambitious architectural work in the cemetery, designed by J Oldred Scott. The stepped pyramidal roof, derived from the tomb of the Greek King Mausolus at Halicarnassus, is two storeys high and magnificent.

Among a host of eminent Victorians interred at Highgate are George Eliot, Dante Gabriel Rossetti, Michael Faraday, Henry Crabb Robinson, Carl Rosa, John Galsworthy, Herbert Spencer and Karl Marx.

Waterworks Pumping Station 1854–6   R10
Green Lanes N16
Chadwell Mylne
⊖ Manor House

One of London's most remarkable working follies, its muscular and castellated forms lend credence to the claim that it pumps a million gallons of water a day to Crouch Hill and Maiden Lane. At one corner of the 'castle keep' is a large, angled tower. At the opposite corner is a turret with a conical top. The buttressing to the keep is exaggerated, and the chimney is a very tall polygonal tower.

Holly Village 1865   R11
Swains Lane N6
H A Darbishire
⊖ Archway

Perhaps the most ludicrous architecture in this book, this group of highly wrought and decorated houses was erected by Baroness Burdett Coutts. As campaigner and benefactor of the East End poor she was also responsible with Darbishire for Bethnal Green's Columbia Market (now demolished) and for the first of the Peabody Trust's five-storey housing blocks H26. At Holly Village, a group of eight buildings placed about a green, Darbishire was in rustic mood to provide fitting dwellings for the Baroness's servants. He allowed his lust for detail to exercise itself on every feature: even the apparently symmetrical gatehouse's bay windows are different.

Alexandra Palace 1875   R12
Alexandra Park N10
J Johnson
⇌ Alexandra Palace

An attempt to build a north London equivalent of Sydenham's Crystal Palace, the Alexandra Palace (named after the Princess of Wales) was ill-fated. Despite its concert hall for 14,000 people and one of the largest organs in the world, its large, melancholy spaces have never caught the imagination as a 'people's palace'. It was totally gutted by fire a few days after it opened and completely rebuilt the same year. The central section was again destroyed by fire in 1980 and was completely rebuilt and reopened to the public in 1988.

Brooklyn 1886–7   R13
8 Private Road, Enfield
A H Mackmurdo and H P Horne
⇌ Bush Hill Park

An astonishingly modern house for its time. The flat roof, very restrained classical detail, and the six bays of the ground floor suggest an early pioneering work of modern architecture, and the design may also be seen as 'an idiosyncratic interpretation of neo-classicism' (Gavin Stamp). It is more like Edward Godwin's work (before its revision) in Tite Street N22 than Mackmurdo's later 25 Cadogan Gardens N26. See also Mackmurdo's first house at 6 Private Road (1873), in the tile-hung style of Norman Shaw.

Archway 1900   R14
Hornsey Lane and Archway
Road N6
Sir Alexander Binnie
⊖ Archway

Archway Road was cut through in the nineteenth century in order to bypass Highgate Hill. The original Archway bridge spanning the cutting was by John Nash; the replacement is a fine cast iron construction, and apart from its view of the City (a reminder that north London is built on a ridge), also serves as a symbolic gate to it, and a boundary to nineteenth-century London.

Shops and **Flats** 1900   R15
Temple Fortune, Hampstead
Garden Suburb NW11
Barry Parker and Raymond Unwin,
designed by A J Penty
⊖ Golders Green

Two almost identical large blocks of redbrick flats, with shops on the ground floor, stand either side of the junction of Finchley Road and Hampstead Way, acting as a pavilioned western gateway to Hampstead Garden Suburb R18. The flats are approached along timber arcaded galleries from the staircase pavilions at either end. The large pitched roofs with dormer windows are particularly inventive.

White Hart Lane Estate   R16
1904–12, 1921–8
Risley Avenue N17
LCC Architects Department; W E Riley
(1904–12) and G Topham Forrest (1921–8)
⊖ Wood Green

This estate was the largest cottage development undertaken by the LCC (71 ha/177 acres) before the First World War. The first stage (1904–12) was laid out in parallel rows of two-storey cottages between Lordship Lane and Risley Avenue, with the Arcadian square of Tower Garden (turfed for tennis and bowls) at the centre. The architects complied as far as possible with the highest ideals of the Garden City movement. The inventive detailing of porches and the two-storey projecting bays were attempts to relieve the flat street frontage – features recommended by Parker and Unwin, who designed Hampstead Garden Suburb R18. The second stage, north of Risley Avenue, was completed after the war. Its curvilinear streets mark a romantic development in suburban layout.

Golders Green Crematorium 1905–38

Hoop Lane NW11
Sir Ernest George and Yates
⊖ Golders Green

Sir Henry Thompson, Professor of Clinical Surgery at University College Hospital from 1865 to 1875, founded the secular Cremation Society whose reforming agitation eventually led to the adoption of cremation as an alternative to burial. The society built Golders Green Crematorium and the group of chapels in good red-brick Romanesque make it a handsome place from which to depart. Behind them is a very large pleasant un-mown meadow for the scattering of ashes, where Lutyens' Philipson Mausoleum (1914) stands.

Free Church, Central Square

Hampstead Garden Suburb

NW11 started 1906
Parker and Unwin, Sir Edwin Lutyens, Baillie Scott and others
⊖ Golders Green

Founded largely as a result of the reformist zeal of Dame Henrietta Barnett, Hampstead Garden Suburb was an attempt to realize a fragment of Ebenezer Howard's grand prescription for London in his influential book *Tomorrow* (1898). Howard pointed to the Garden City as the solution to all our economic and social ills, an argument that was to be misunderstood by the suburban and new town lobby in England and abroad in the twentieth century. Raymond Unwin deepened the misunderstanding with his book *Nothing Gained by Overcrowding* (1918), and Howard's prophecy does not find its embodiment at Hampstead Garden Suburb.

At the turn of the century, Golders Green was a country crossroads complete with cows and signposts to London; in the following decade, largely as a result of the development of the Underground, it was transformed into an urban intersection. Parker and Unwin were appointed as planners of the new suburb as a result of their successful plans for Letchworth a few years earlier. Sir Raymond Unwin remained in charge from 1907–15. The original sections were the west fringe of the Hampstead Heath extension on both sides of Hampstead Way and Wellgarth Road; this land, owned by the original trust, is approximately 128 ha (317 acres)

and constitutes the Garden Suburb proper. It has expanded over the years to 324 ha (800 acres) and is now less easily identified demographically or architecturally.

The layout is a mixture of residential closes and gently curving principal roads, lined with well established privet hedges and flowering cherry trees, with a secondary pattern of pedestrian paths. All houses have private gardens divided by the ever-present hedges and are freestanding, semi-detached or terraced, either in country vernacular styles or in Lutyens' new Georgian (see for example Erskine Hill R20). The zoned density of eight houses to the acre (about twenty houses to the hectare) and the absence of other uses gives the Garden Suburb the impression of being a benign sanatorium. Only in the central square can any urban formality be detected, and this is due mainly to Lutyens. However, many distinguished domestic architects have made contributions to the Suburb – among them Baillie Scott (Waterlow Court R19), Curtis Green, Guy Dawber and Geoffrey Lucas.

The tendency for the Suburb to devolve into a one-class area (as opposed to its original mixed social idealism), the absence of commercial uses as a result of the zoning and the inability of public transport to serve such low densities have justified the now familiar criticisms of Hampstead Garden Suburb and, by extension, of Unwin's misappropriation of the Garden City ideal.

Waterlow Court 1908–9   R19
Heath Close,
off Hampstead Way NW11
M H Baillie Scott
⊖ Golders Green

Of all Baillie Scott's enlightened designs for multiple housing groups in the Suburb this was the only one to be built. It was designed to contain fifty flats for single working women.

Within the general 'Arcadian' context of Hampstead Garden Suburb R18 the fully enclosed courtyard of Waterlow Court is quite surreal. The court as a type normally suggests an oasis of calm in a hostile world, and in this case it is approached by a timber-covered way at the end of the leafy close. Inside the two-storey court the white-painted brickwork, arcades with fine semicircular arches on all four sides, and central pavilion with a bellcote opposite the entrance give the impression of a Spanish colonial college somewhere in

rural California. The 'back garden' is approached through the corners of the court, and its potting sheds and orderly flower beds call to mind the world of Beatrix Potter.

Houses 1908–10   R20
Erskine Hill,
Hampstead Garden Suburb NW11
Sir Edwin Lutyens
⊖ Golders Green

Only the west is by Lutyens but both sides form a symmetrical composition treated in Lutyens' magnificent 'Wrenaissance' style, in grey brick with some stone, and white-painted wood windows. The balance between motifs from high architecture and those from domestic, like the dormers, is exquisite. For the essence of the Suburb R18, walk up Erskine Hill across Central Square and along Heathgate, apparently a cul-de-sac. Go to the end where, leaving the town behind, you are in the country. No, it is Hampstead Heath – but what an illusion!

St Jude and **Parsonage**   R21
1909–14 **Free Church** and
Manse c1910 **Institute** 1909–20s
Central Square, Hampstead
Garden Suburb NW11
Sir Edwin Lutyens
⊖ Golders Green

It fell to Lutyens to give Unwin and Baillie Scott's domestic matrix its symbolic non-commercial centre. This group of buildings, set inside a loosely defined square of low two-storey houses on the highest part of the Suburb, is probably the most recent example of successful town planning in London. Lutyens was forty when work started, and, while his earlier 'Wrenaissance' style was already developed (see his houses in Erskine Hill R20), these buildings include new motifs and ideas.

In the most important position, on the main axis, is the Institute, built of small grey bricks with red dressings and stone trim. It is so successful a pastiche of a late seventeenth-century public building that the magnificent courtyard which terminates the axis looks more Colonial-American than English. To the south of the square, to one side of the axis, lies St Jude, which has one of the 'nicest' accessible Lutyens interiors in London. It has a three-bay tunnel-vaulted nave, a domed crossing, and an apsed end. The arches and piers are of red brick, the piers meeting the floor with characteristic semicircular splays. The bizarre con-

The Institute

sequences of bringing an Arts and Crafts roof through brick classical arches and introducing square-headed dormers are startlingly revealed in the aisles. The ceiling and dome are decorated with delightful frescoes by Walter Starmer which are continued in the Lady Chapel, where they celebrate as a war memorial a wild collection of ladies, including Harriet Beecher Stowe, Christina Rossetti, Joan of Arc and a Girl Guide.

The Free Church to the north of the square is, rightly, much plainer than St Jude's, with a central dome instead of a spire. The sides are good, but the front is unattractive.

Houses c1910 R22
6–10 Meadway, 22 Hampstead
Way NW11
Baillie Scott
⊖ Golders Green
Baillie Scott's only group of street houses
in Hampstead Garden Suburb (but see
Waterlow Court R19). After seventy
years it is possible to imagine these tiny
pebble-dashed cottages with shallow-
arched windows and steeply pitched roofs
as remnants of an Arcadian village.

22 Hampstead Way

Arnos Grove

Southgate

Piccadilly Line R23
Underground Stations
1932–3
Arnos Grove and Southgate, Charles
Holden; Oakwood, Charles Holden with
C H James
Arnos Grove Station has its place in the
histories of modern architecture: it was
used at the time as proof of the moral
fitness of the style for a modern transport
system, and, by extension, for modern
life. It is now clear that Holden's concerns
were always with abstract geometrical
combinations, produced by the elemental
forms which he gave to the various
functions of an Underground station: the
canopy, booking hall and covered platforms. See also the stations at the western
end of the line T25.

Cholmeley Lodge 1934 R24
Cholmeley Lane, Highgate Hill
N6
Guy Morgan
⊖ Archway
These well maintained flats present a non-
revolutionary alternative to the modern
style of Highpoint I R26. They have an
artistic front and a utilitarian back. The
front is scalloped to face the view, with
red-brick bands alternating with the
window-strips and continuous balconies;
the back is of stock brick with the
plumbing exposed.

Hornsey Town Hall 1934–5

R25

The Broadway, Crouch End N8
R H Uren
⇄ Hornsey

The tall brick tower and the principal entrance façade of the Town Hall form an asymmetrical composition set back from the busy Broadway behind a 'planned' town square. On either side of the square are further municipal buildings in the same brick style, their ground floors occupied by the Gas and Electricity Boards. If the buildings pay mute homage to Dudok's Town Hall in Hilversum (1928), there is more than a hint of neo-Georgian in the disposition of windows in the principal elevation. The public foyers, detailed in marble and bronze, express the optimism of the period; however, there are now signs of disrepair and neglect, despite its London Architectural Medal of 1935.

Highpoint I

Highpoint I and 2 1936 and 1938

R26

North Hill N7
Lubetkin and Tecton
⊖ Highgate

These two apartment buildings are the closest we have to Le Corbusier's ideas. As the name implies they are positioned on the top of Highgate ridge, commanding magnificent views of the City to the southeast and of the extensive suburbs of Hendon to the west. During a rare visit to London Le Corbusier congratulated Lubetkin on producing 'a vertical garden city'. Highpoint I is the more didactic of the two, representing fully Le Corbusier's *Five Points of Modern Architecture* – *pilotis*, roof garden, liberated plan and long windows. The plan is double cruciform with eight flats on each floor. The white rendered façade has recently been re-painted and, like Nash's terraces in Regent's Park, looks new again. The building is intentionally detached from its immediate surroundings, anticipating the new millennium of *La Ville Radieuse*.

Highpoint 2, on the other hand, attempts to fit in with its surroundings in both general form and facing materials. The building runs parallel to the street, and its façade is composed of a mixture of tiles, bricks and glazed bricks, a change of style caused by public reaction to Highpoint I. However, in section the building exhibits further debts to Le Corbusier in its use of double-height 'studio' apartments, and externally it is reminiscent of Le Corbusier's own apartments at Porte Molitor in Paris. In the *porte cochère* Lubetkin incorporated reproductions of two of the Erechtheum caryatids as a humorous rebuke to his stylistic critics, who complained of the absence of historical references in Highpoint I.

The buildings share a garden, with swimming pool, tennis courts and tea room. They confirm the idea that this particular model of living can be successful when inhabited by the middle-class intelligentsia, but that it can be a wholesale prescription neither for the Welfare State nor for the renewal of the traditional city – as the recent past has disastrously demonstrated.

Highpoint 2

Jack Straw's Castle 1964   R27
North End Way NW3
Raymond Erith and Quinlan Terry
⊖ Hampstead

The brick south wall is all that remains of this famous eighteenth-century pub with its romantic associations with highwaymen. Its replacement by Erith and Terry has nothing to do with its previous style, but is one of the few large timber-frame structures to have been built in London since the Great Fire. The cream-painted timber sidings, projecting windows and castellated cornice give the building a festive quality.

Highgate New Town   R28
Stages I and 2 1965–80
Dartmouth Park Hill and
Chester Road N19
London Borough of Camden Architects Department; Peter Tabori (Stage I) and William Forest (Stage 2)
⊖ Archway

Built in stages over fifteen years, Highgate New Town is situated immediately to the east of Highgate Cemetery on the steep southern approaches to Highgate Village. It is a case-study in shifts of taste and ideology in public housing in this reactionary period. Stage I displays a belief both in repetitive and rational precast systems of construction and in the open row model layout. This results in confusion between fronts and backs, exaggerated by its relationship to the existing street pattern. Stage 2, on the other hand, is quaint, with hipped pitched roofs and small windows in decorated brick façades. It pays earnest lip service to the nineteenth-century urban forms that were swept away in the mid-1960s in the name of comprehensive redevelopment.

Stage I

Stage 2

Houses 1966–8　　　　　　　　R29
24–32 Winscombe Street N19
Neave Brown
⊖Archway

Neave Brown went on to design the huge Alexandra Road scheme E7 for the London Borough of Camden, and this little row of houses shows some of the concerns which there acquired monumental significance. Their chief interest lies in the manipulation and insistent zoning of the section: the top floor contains a main bedroom on the street side and a living room with a view of the garden; the middle and main entrance floor a dining-kitchen and a large terrace; and the ground floor, sunk slightly below the street, a divisible children's bedroom. Externally, they are less successful: the individual houses are at odds with the terrace, and the top and bottom of each house conflict with each other.

House 1969　　　　　　　　R30
81 Swains Lane N6
John Winter
⊖Archway

Overlooking Highgate Cemetery like a lodge, this three-storey Cor-ten steel-framed house was designed by John Winter for himself. The frame is extended on either side of large sheets of fixed glass in order to accommodate vertical steel louvres for ventilation. Cor-ten steel was an American invention of the early 1960s to allow exposed structural steelwork simply to rust in a controlled manner as a permanent finish, thereby avoiding costly maintenance and giving the building the patina of age. This is the only example in London of the domestic use of the material. The absence of opening windows gives the building a very abstract image, recalling the hermetic and 'cool' buildings in Chicago by Skidmore, Owings and Merrill, in whose offices Winter worked as an assistant in the 1950s.

Houses 1970–2　　　　　　　　R31
91–103 Swains Lane N6
Haxworth and Kasabov
⊖Archway

A row of seven houses with wide (6 m/20 ft) frontages is set on a sloping site overlooking Highgate Cemetery and the City. The living rooms are on the top floor on the road side, at the middle level are dining-kitchens giving directly onto the gardens at the back, and the lowest floor houses the entrance and garage. See also Winscombe Street R29 and South Hill Park B32.

Flats 1980   R32
119 Hornsey Lane N6
Colquhoun and Miller
⊖ Archway

Sited on a narrow plot between two
existing blocks, these flats for single
people were commissioned by the London
Borough of Haringey. The planning is
straightforwardly modern, and their remarkably suave and carefully proportioned façade demonstrates the form of
construction: a frame of load-bearing
brick walls and concrete floors. The apertures in the frame are filled with spandrels
of glass blocks and simple timber-framed
windows.

Highgate Group Practice 1986   R33
Health Centre
North Hill N7
Douglas Stephen and Partners
⊖ Highgate

On its narrow and deep site, the atrium
house plan provides a surprisingly generous and welcoming interior for this small
medical building. The two levels of consulting rooms are skilfully planned around
a central double-height waiting and reception room. Intimations of this interior's
order are given in the simple gabled street
façade of glass and brick. In its unpreten-
tious way the building re-establishes a
connection with a more caring and heroic
tradition of medical/welfare building in
London. (Finsbury Health Centre G64,
Kentish Town Health Centre C13), a
tradition almost eclipsed in the 1980s.

Section S: Outer London, north-east

There is little significant architecture in this section. It is dominated by the valleys of two rivers running north-south. To the east the River Lea, now mostly tamed by reservoirs, runs towards the Thames: its undeveloped marshes and abandoned watercress farms are now being planned as a regional park for recreation on the drained land. To the west lies the Roding Valley, reaching the Thames just to the east of Beckton sewage works. On a ridge between the two valleys is Woodford, the most prosperous of the suburbs which now cover the land on which building is possible. Its development was prompted by the extension in the 1940s of the underground Central Line, running along the west side of the Roding Valley to Epping and Ongar. The motorway to Cambridge and East Anglia (the M11, opened in the 1970s) runs down the middle of the valley, stopping at the A12 but poised to continue south.

To the north is Epping Forest: originally royal hunting grounds (see Queen Elizabeth's Hunting Lodge just north of Chingford Green), it became available to the public with the building of the railway from Liverpool Street to Chingford. Bought by the City of London in 1878, it became east London's equivalent of Hampstead Heath: a resort for the crowded poor of Whitechapel and Bethnal Green. It is wilder than the Heath, and has cattle grids on its approach roads.

Walthamstow Civic Centre

William Morris Gallery 1762   SI
Lloyd Park, Forest Road, Walthamstow
EI7
⊖ Walthamstow Central

Morris was born in Walthamstow in 1834 and between 1847 and 1856 his family lived in this large, three-storeyed and double fronted Georgian house which was built in 1762. Now used as a gallery but with very little disturbance to its original domesticity, it contains a marvellous collection of many of the fabrics, carpets, wallpapers, fittings, furniture, stained glass and books produced by his firm Morris and Company, together with drawings and sketches of the designs for them. Furniture and designs by Arthur Mackmurdo and members of the Century Guild, and books designed by Frank Brangwyn form related displays.

Walthamstow Civic Centre   S2
1937–42
P D Hepworth
Forest Road, Walthamstow EI7
⊖ Walthamstow Central

The importance of London's local government has declined over the twentieth century, but the town halls which the various boroughs built usually attempted architectural significance and were built in the progressive style of the day. Walthamstow's is a very late example, and its date suggests that it might have been built in the neo-Georgian or even modern style. But although the layout is classical, the first two buildings of the intended group of three were carried out in a rare and late version of a style derived from the comfortable official architecture of Scandinavia.

Housing 1990   S3
20b Bisterne Avenue EI7
Wickham and Associates
⇌ Wood Street Walthamstow

This modest housing development for the London Borough of Waltham Forest caused much commotion when built on account of the strong colour scheme for its exterior rendered walls—a vibrant blue and burnt sienna. The arrangement of six flats planned on three floors either side of a glass-canopied external stair is eminently sane, and no doubt the colours will eventually be accepted.

South West Essex Reform Synagogue 1990–1   S4
Oakes Lane
Newbury Park, Ilford
Michael Gold Architects
⊖ Newbury Park

The winning entry in an RIBA competition in 1988, this synagogue is impressive for its cool and spartan interior. The circular prayer hall is effectively lit by a series of small luminaries set in deep conical reveals at a high level in the external wall. The play of light emphasizing the building's pure geometry as a setting for the liturgical ritual is free of sentimentality and recalls Gold's theoretical preoccupation with 'people' in architecture from the early 1980s.

Section T: Outer London, west

Enlarged arterial roads going west to Heathrow Airport and beyond overshadow this part of London: the tail of Westway (London's only urban motorway) connecting to Western Avenue, and Chiswick Flyover connecting the Great West Road and the M4 motorway. From sections of elevated carriageway the motorist can see the dormitory suburbs of Ealing, Acton and Uxbridge stretching loosely to the horizon in either direction, unceremoniously absorbing the historic houses and parks of Syon T10, Osterley T11, Chiswick T6 and Kew T4. Until the mid-nineteenth century the area was predominantly rural, sprinkled with country houses and their attendant villages close to the Thames, and with the Grand Union Canal passing through open fields on its way to Paddington.

The most significant remains of this more privileged past are to be found in two large houses: Syon and Osterley. They mark the step from early to late Tudor, and both were later successfully converted by Robert Adam. While Syon and Osterley are now embedded in between-the-wars suburbia, Chiswick retains much of its eighteenth-century character, with a large house (Lord Burlington's Chiswick House) supported by a village (the relatively intact Chiswick Mall and Lower Mall).

To the south, held in the bend of the Thames, are the Royal Botanic Gardens at Kew, laid out by Sir William Chambers in 1758–63. Chambers' ten-tiered Pagoda, his variety of small temples, and Decimus Burton and Turner's later Palm House, all set in beautiful gardens, are together one of London's main architectural treasures.

Notable late Georgian architecture includes Uxbridge Town Hall (1789) and a small number of private houses, particularly Sir John Soane's own house at Pitshanger T12 (now a public library), built in 1801–3 overlooking Walpole Park in Ealing, and Berrymead Priory in Acton.

Hammersmith has some good early nineteenth-century streets and squares (for example St Peter's Square T13) but the most important development was in the mid-nineteenth century when the Victorian suburb was given one of its chief models in the curved and tree-lined streets of Norman Shaw's Bedford Park, Acton T18, the earliest garden suburb in London. As with north and south London, the initiative for twentieth-century suburban expansion came from the London Underground (here the Piccadilly and District Lines). Charles Holden's many stations built in the 1930s (T25) are consistently excellent, unlike later stations on the lines at Hatton Cross and Heathrow.

The 1930s produced the architecture of transport, recreation and work places, and its white factories are remarkable – notably the strip of industrial palaces lining the Great West Road T23, and the Hoover Factory T26 by Wallis Gilbert and Partners on Western Avenue. The Guinness Brewery T27 at Park Royal by Sir Giles Gilbert Scott and Banister Fletcher's Gillette Building T29 at Boston Manor are more architecturally conservative, but still notable. Further to the north is Wembley Stadium T22, with Sir Owen Williams' structurally expressive Empire Pool T28 of 1934 marking the end of the era's optimism about mass society and its institutions. Heathrow Airport T32 shows the grim reality . As the London docks had given impetus to the expansion of London's East End in the nineteenth century, so London Airport has extended the westerly limits of London 32 km (20 miles) from the centre.

Wembley Stadium T20

St Nicholas T1
started 15th century
Church Street W4
nave rebuilt by Pearson, 1882
⊖ Turnham Green

The church forms the charming nucleus of Chiswick village, now passed by, sandwiched between the Thames and the torrential traffic of the Great West Road. The tower is of the fifteenth century, but the body of the church was rebuilt by Pearson in 1882. There is a monument to William Hogarth in the churchyard, and Lord Burlington and his protégé William Kent are buried here. See also Chiswick Mall T7, Chiswick Square T3 and Strand on the Green T5.

Boston Manor 1622 T2
Boston Manor Park, Brentford
⊖ Boston Manor

Originally the property of the wife of Sir William Reade, this large and simple three-storey manor house stands in its own grounds behind a high boundary wall. The Jacobean exterior is brick, with three plain gables on the front and two on the sides, and a surprising mixture of Italian motifs which may have been added later — segmental pediments, niches in the gables and a modillion cornice above the second storey. As Pevsner notes, only Inigo Jones would have used such devices so early in England.

The view from the south-west shows the intrusion of the outside world: the M4 motorway bisects the grounds, and the industrial strip of the Great West Road forms the skyline. Nevertheless, with its attractive small lake full of geese and wild fowl, the park is good for Sunday walks.

Chiswick Square 1680 and T3
forecourt to **Boston House**
1740
Burlington Lane W4
⊖ Stamford Brook

Two- and three-storey cottages flank Boston House, forming a picturesque forecourt. The tranquillity of this once secluded enclave off the Great West Road is now shattered by the motorway flyover opposite.

Royal Botanic Gardens, Kew T4
1696
⊖ Kew Gardens

The Royal Botanic Gardens have three principal origins: Kew Palace, its gardens planted in 1696 by Sir Henry and Lady Capel, and the park of Richmond Palace to the north. George II lived at Richmond Lodge, with his son Frederick and daughter-in-law Princess Augusta nearby at Kew House. All that now remains of this Hanoverian retreat is Kew House, renamed Kew Palace. It was here that the Capel family planted the first specimen trees in the late seventeenth century.

Kew Gardens now cover 121 ha (300 acres), forming an extensive park held by the bends of the river Thames. The river also gives views to Syon Park T10 in the west. As a museum of landscape and botanical specimens Kew is unsurpassed, containing specimens collected over two centuries.

In the mid nineteenth century Princess Augusta's eighteenth-century gardens at Kew (derived from the work of William Chambers) and Queen Charlotte's gardens at Richmond Lodge (by Capability Brown) passed to the state, under the charge of the great botanist Sir William Hooker (1841–65) and his son Joseph (1865–85).

In the first five years of Sir William's directorship the gardens expanded from 4.5 to 31 ha (11 to 76 acres), and W A Nesfield (father of W E Nesfield) later laid out the four major vistas (Pagoda Vista, Broad Walk, Holly Walk and Cedar Vista)

Temperate House

Temperate House interior

and designed the picturesque lake (1845) and the pond in front of the Palm House (1847). The gardens now became a repository of the world's botanical species, with a research laboratory and separate houses for orchids, alpine plants, ferns, cacti and so on. The cataloguing spirit of the Victorian age is exemplified by the Palm House, containing every known variety of palm. An excellent map and guidebook are available at the entrance.

The architecture of Kew Gardens is the subject of separate entries: Chambers' Pagoda T9, Orangery T8, Nash's Aroid House T15, Nesfield's Temperate House Lodge T17 and Turner and Decimus Burton's Palm House T16. Note also Turner and Decimus Burton's magnificent Temperate House (1862–98), newly restored to its former glory by Manning and Clamp and reopened in 1982.

Strand on the Green W4   T5
18th century
⊖Gunnersbury

A companion to Chiswick Mall T7, but even less urban — only a footpath here separates the modest eighteenth-century houses from the river.

Chiswick House 1725–9   T6
Hogarth Lane and
Burlington Lane W4
Lord Burlington
⊖Turnham Green

Erect new wonders and the old repair;
Jones and Palladio to themselves restore
And be whate'er Vitruvius was before.

Alexander Pope

Burlington's public career as an architect started with Westminster School K41 and continued with the building of this, his country villa, to be used for entertaining, and as a library and art gallery. He had already designed and built the Summer Parlour building (next to the villa) as an extension to the old Jacobean family house (largely demolished in 1788). Work on the new house started in 1725, when Burlington was twenty-nine. The design is based on Palladio's Villa Capra ('Rotonda') at Vicenza (its 21 m/68 ft square plan is the same dimension as that published for Capra) but it also borrows from Scamozzi (Rocca Pisana) and, in the details of the

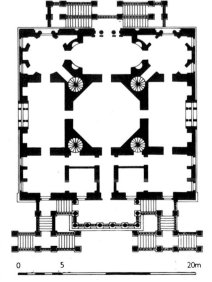

0   5   20m

interior, from Inigo Jones. The vermiculated Portland stone ground floor originally housed Burlington's library in the long room facing the garden. The stuccoed first floor has a suite of state rooms arranged round a central domed saloon, reached from a hall via the portico. The character of the outside resides in the way the octagonal drum of the dome pushes through the pyramidal roof, improving on Scamozzi by replacing the oculus with 'thermal' windows more appropriate to the English climate, and in the quirky chimneys housed in obelisks at the perimeter. The fussy arrangement of steps up to the portico, with statues by Rysbrack of Palladio (left) and Jones (right), derives from Palladio's drawings.

The *en suite* arrangement of the first-floor rooms was to be fully developed by Adam and is now a cliché, but was then new to England. The design of the interior was under the general direction of Burlington, but his protégé William Kent did much of the detailed design of ceilings and chimney-pieces, borrowing many of them directly from Jones. In the 1950s the rooms were restored and furnished

where possible with original items. They have not been lived in since this restoration, and have a curiously cold quality which, however, is probably appropriate to the designers' didactic intentions. The gallery, facing the gardens, is a suite of circular, apsed double-square and octagonal rooms, each lit with a Venetian window. On a summer afternoon it seems a wonderfully evocative and idealized synthesis of English and Italian country living.

Burlington remodelled the grounds, using as landscape architect William Kent, who here developed the 'natural' style to complement the architecture. They are now a public park, with restoration proceeding piecemeal, and Kent's intentions are therefore hard to read. The Obelisk to the west, the Doric column and Deer House to the east and the Temple belong to his original decorative scheme. The Inigo Jones gateway, north-west of the house, was brought from Beaufort House, Chelsea, in 1736; and the classic bridge over the canal was built by Wyatt in 1788.

Houses c1730   T7
Chiswick Mall W4
⊖ Stamford Brook
A short walk from Chiswick House T6, the Mall, despite much development, preserves the waterfront of a Georgian village, the street separating the houses from their front gardens on the unembanked river. The best eighteenth-century buildings are Walpole House, Strawberry House and Morton House.

Orangery 1761   T8
Royal Botanical Gardens, Kew
Sir William Chambers
⊖ Kew Gardens
The Orangery was for a long time England's largest hothouse. It has seven bays, rusticated walls and arched openings.

Pagoda 1761   T9
Royal Botanical Gardens, Kew
Sir William Chambers
⊖ Kew Gardens

One of London's great eccentric and eclectic structures, the Pagoda is a vivid reminder that there were other influences at work in the period besides Palladianism. Standing in the south-west corner of Kew Gardens T4, at the end of Pagoda Vista, the ten-storey structure of stock brick rises to a height of 50 m (163 ft). Unfortunately, the eighty enamelled dragons which were originally positioned at the corners of its Chippendale balustrades have been removed. The building is now unsafe and the magnificent views over the gardens are closed to the public.

Although Chambers is remembered principally as a classical architect, he travelled extensively in China, and as a result of this interest in the exotic he also built a Chinese Temple (1760), a Turkish mosque (1761), and a Moorish Alhambra at Kew. None of these structures remain today.

Syon House 1761–8   T10
London Road, Brentford
Robert Adam
⇌ Brentford Central

In 1761, at the same time as he started work at Osterley, Adam was commissioned by Sir Hugh Smithson, first Duke of Northumberland, to remodel the state rooms of Syon 'entirely in the Antique style'. The house, built in the fifteenth century as a convent, was altered to its present form – 30 m (100 ft) square with corner towers – in the mid-sixteenth century. Adam proposed a huge dome filling the central courtyard of the existing house. The rotunda was not built, but the perimeter rooms are his grandest in London: the ceilings are higher than those of Osterley, and the sequence more extensive than at Kenwood. Adam here combines classical plan forms with a range of very different decorative schemes. The white entrance hall, apsed at the north end, screened at the south, has the authentic chilly grandeur of English neoclassicism at its best. Nevertheless it is quite small: 11 m × 9 m × 6 m (36 ft × 30 ft × 21 ft). The steps behind the screen lead to the anteroom, green and gold, with projecting green marble columns. Some of these are recycled from Rome,

and all carry a piece of projecting entablature and a gilded statue, a motif used here for the first time in England. The well preserved scagliola-work floor is part of the original decoration. The dining room is more bittily decorated – only the ceiling unites the two apsed and screened ends. The drawing room separates the dining room (for men) from the gallery (for women). Its walls are covered in red Spitalfields silk, and the ceiling and fine Adam-designed carpet compensate for their sparseness. The door-cases exhibit another of Adam's decorative sources: *cinquecento* Italy. Adam inherited the long thin shape of the gallery from the Jacobean house. The bays are divided and subdivided with low-relief pilasters, and the intervening spaces are covered with arabesque plaster work of extreme delicacy.

The screen and lodges to London Road, by which the grounds are entered, were built in 1773. The screen is of insubstantial delicacy and transparency, the heaviest element being the Northumberland lion over the gate. The grounds were laid out by Capability Brown, who gave the house its present view down the Thames. See also Osterley T11 and Kenwood R7.

Osterley Park 1763–7
Isleworth
Robert Adam
⊖Osterley

TII

Adam's three greatest works extant in London – Osterley, Syon T10 and Kenwood R7 – are remodellings of existing houses; all belong to the early years of his practice and were started in the 1760s. Of the original house built by Sir Thomas Gresham, a successful Elizabethan businessman, only the corner towers remain. In 1711 the house was bought by Francis Child, goldsmith and banker, whose grandson commissioned Adam to restyle it.

Adam's first work was the grand Ionic double portico across one face of the original courtyard, raising its level to that of the main rooms on the first floor. Then, in the 1770s, he began to decorate and furnish seven of the nine rooms on the ground floor. The entrance hall is double-apsed, white and boldly decorated. The segmental arches show Adam's use of archaeologically correct Roman motifs and his departure from Palladianism. The library ceiling is flat, not coffered, and decorated in Roman low relief. The bookcases are exquisite. The drawing room completes the rooms finished in 1773; the walls are plain, but the ceiling, the design derived from Palmyra, is one of Adam's most successful experiments with colour - gold, pink and green. The decoration here is thinner, but the furniture is still sumptuous and elegant. The Etruscan room is the only one remaining of the four Adam designed in London; the painted decoration and matching furniture are freely derived from Greek pottery, which was wrongly thought by both Adam and his contemporary Wedgwood to be Etruscan. The remaining rooms are not by Adam: the gallery may have been restyled by Chambers, and the breakfast room was completed before Adam started. In the attractive grounds, the lakes and stables (now tea-rooms) belong to the original house, and the ruined bridge and conservatory are by Adam. The house is owned by the National Trust.

Pitshanger Place 1801–3 T12
High Street, Ealing W5
Sir John Soane; restoration by John
Wibberley and Ian Bristow 1986.
⊖ Ealing Broadway

Soane rebuilt this house for himself,
leaving only the south wing of the earlier
house by his teacher George Dance the
Younger. Although it is small, the front is
particularly grand. Soane used the triumphal arch motif of Ionic columns, set
forward from the façade and surmounted
by statues. Robert Adam had reintro-
duced this usage at Kedleston Hall in
Derbyshire, and in the south-east anteroom at Syon T10. The back of the house is
quite different. Horizontal bands of alternate brick and stucco and vertical ashlar
strips divide the façade into nine parts,
each containing a window.

Soane sold the house in 1811 when he
moved to Lincoln's Inn Fields. Following a
succession of owners the house was
bought by the council in 1900 and used as a
public library. In 1980 the library moved

out and some of the building's long-
neglected interiors were restored. These
include Soane's magnificent library and
breakfast room. The dark-red porphyry
and grey marbling in the breakfast room
are particularly dramatic.

St Peter's Square

St Peter

St Peter's Square and T13
Black Lion Lane W6 1825–30
⊖ Stamford Brook

St Peter's Square is the very successful
result of a single plan by an anonymous
designer. Although not formally complete
and dilapidated in places, it is particularly
fine. The three-storey houses on the east
and west sides give the impression of large
semi-detached villas, while actually forming unusual groupings of three houses.
The villas are connected by single-storey
walls, giving access to garages or garden
studios behind, which have large scrolls at
the centre; eagles and sleeping lions adorn
the doors, and the gateposts are topped by
pineapples. The houses, which are faced
with sandy stucco and have white-painted

doors, window frames and central balconies, act as a background to this exuberant decoration. On the north side of the
square are two-storey versions of the
same theme. The result is pleasant and
relaxed, conveying, as Pevsner has observed, 'the flavour of a suburban
Belgravia'. The church of **St Peter**
(1827–9), by Edward Lapidge, closes the
view to the east. Hammersmith's oldest
and most elegant church, its attached
Ionic portico and the octagonal west
tower are reminiscent of Soane, and can
be seen in deep perspective from the
square. The interior is very simple, with
the gallery on three sides carried by
Tuscan columns, and columns and pews
painted in Pompeian red.

Kensal Green Cemetery   T14
opened 1833
Harrow Road W10
⊖Kensal Green
The hygienic, out-of-town cemetery is, like the museum, the railway station and the zoo, among the building types invented in Europe in the early nineteenth century and built for the first time in London in the 1830s and '40s. Kensal Green was the largest of the new suburban cemeteries, laid out by private companies to provide better conditions than those available in the scandalously crowded graveyards of central London. Its architectural fittings are in the correct taste of the time. although (unlike Highgate R9) not particularly funereal; the entrance screen to the road is in Doric, the Anglican chapel is in Greek Doric and the Nonconformist in Ionic. Architectural burials include Sir Robert

Smirke and the Brunels, father and son. See also Nunhead X7 and Brompton M1 Cemeteries.

Aroid House 1836   T15
Royal Botanic Gardens, Kew
John Nash
⊖Kew Gardens
Originally designed as one of the two garden pavilions for Buckingham Palace, the Aroid House was moved to Kew Gardens T4 in 1836, its twin remaining at the Palace. The building has six Ionic columns in antis and pediments, and was subsequently glazed in order to house plants from the tropical rainforests.

Palm House 1844–8   T16
Royal Botanic Gardens, Kew
Decimus Burton, Richard Turner
⊖Kew Gardens
The finest existing glass and iron structure in England, Burton and Turner's sensuously curved giant conservatory predated Paxton's Crystal Palace by three years. The fine, slender cast iron work, the complex intersecting geometries, and the sheer size of the glass envelope establish the Palm House as a truly innovative building. All the known species of palm can be viewed from delicate cast iron galleries, which in turn are decorated with cast iron insignia of palm leaves, painted white. The combination of delicate structures, both living and man-made, their white and green tracery filling the warm damp spaces, is magical.

Although the building was restored in the 1950s, by the late 1970s it was apparent that despite regular maintenance the high temperatures and humidity had severely degraded the original cast-iron structure. In 1985 the entire building was dismantled down to the main frames, and stainless steel components substituted for those beyond repair. The 5500 components and 16,000 panes of glass were reassembled in 1988.

The engineer Richard Turner was also responsible for the particularly fine botanical gardens in both Dublin and Belfast. See also Burton and Turner's recently renovated Temperate House (1862–98).

Palm House

Temperate House Lodge 1866–7   T17
Royal Botanic Gardens, Kew
William Eden Nesfield
⊖ Kew Gardens

This sophisticated small building was as influential in its way as Burton's more famous Palm House. Designed by R Norman Shaw's partner, it is said to be one of the first buildings in the Queen Anne style. The central chimney, coved cornice and roof are exaggerated in their proportions, suggesting a top to a much larger building. The detailing of the windows is particularly fine. Nesfield was in partnership with Shaw from 1866–9 only, and there are no buildings in their joint names. Unfortunately the talented Nesfield died prematurely.

Bedford Park W4   T18
started 1875
R Norman Shaw, Maurice B Adams,
E W Godwin, E J May and others
⊖ Turnham Green

Only five years after it was started, Bedford Park, the suburb which set the pattern for English low density development for the following century, had gained a reputation as a colony of the artistic, bohemian and progressive middle classes. The loose Queen Anne style of the earliest houses, built from prototypes by Godwin, became identified with bohemianism. This does not seem to have been the intention of Jonathan T Carr, the young developer of the 46 ha (113 acre) estate, who merely undertook a routine speculation.

The layout is pleasant if unremarkable, consisting of curved streets with T-junctions, aligned to preserve the existing trees. It is this very vagueness, like that of the earlier and equally influential Ladbroke Estate I 7, which made it so easy to copy. While Godwin provided the first models, however, it was Shaw's work which set the style in the houses listed below. His group of non-domestic buildings from 1880 (St Michael and All Angels, Tabard Inn and Bank) shows him at his most picturesque, the church exhibiting an extraordinary mixture of late English Gothic, Dutch and Georgian features. Houses by Shaw are: 24–34 Woodstock Road; 5–7 Blenheim Road; 6 Bedford Road; 3 and 5 Blenheim Road; 19–22 The Avenue; 3–5 Queen Anne's Gardens. See also Voysey's Houses T19, T20.

Studio House 1889–94   T19
14 South Parade W4
C F A Voysey
⊖ Turnham Green
One of London's outstanding Arts and Crafts houses, Studio House is an early work and, unusually for Voysey, a tall one. Set in Shaw's suburban cosiness its style – white rough cast and stone trim with banded windows – looks chaste and brittle.

Studio house 1891   T20
17 St Dunstan's Road W6
C F A Voysey
⊖ Barons Court
Set back from the corner of St Dunstan's Road behind its Arts and Crafts iron railings, this house is deceptively small. The low, horizontal forms of the projecting eaves and the asymmetrically composed chimney, doors and windows are unmistakable signs of its architect. See also 14 South Parade, Bedford Park T19 and Annesley Lodge, Platts Lane A3.

Voysey House   T21
ex Sandersons wallpaper
factory 1902–3
Barley Mow Passage W4
C F A Voysey
⊖ Chiswick Park
One of Voysey's few non-domestic buildings, this was originally built for Sandersons, for whom he had designed wallpapers. The unashamed 'factory' language of the outside – big bays, large windows, white and blue glazed brick – is moderated delightfully by the soft but assured curves of the segmental arches over the windows, and the irregularly drooping high parapet.

Wembley Stadium 1924   T22
Stadium Way, Wembley
J W Simpson
⊖ Wembley Park, ⇌ Wembley Complex
The 1924 British Empire Exhibition was staged at Wembley: the stadium, on the highest part of the site, is the only building now intact. The last international event held there was the 1948 Olympic Games. The design is not radical, and the interior has no architectural quality whatever. The roof was added in 1963 to celebrate the 100th anniversary of the Football League. The prominent twin domes of the exterior (derived from Lutyens' New Delhi?) provide a long-distance landmark from the North Circular Road in an area dominated by squat semi-detached houses. See also Owen Williams' Wembley Arena T28.

Factories Great West Road   T23
1929–32
Firestone Factory 1929 and
BMW Warehouse (ex Pyrene)
1930 Wallis Gilbert and
Partners; Coty Factory c1932;
Trico Factory c1932
Great West Road between Syon Lane and
Boston Manor Road W6
⊖ Osterley

This section of the Great West Road, with its dual carriageways lined with buildings, is a fragment of a triumphal entrance to London which was superseded by the M4 motorway. Taken as a whole, the factories are a unique aspect of twentieth-century industrial archaeology: a series of buildings dedicated to the new industries, now eclipsed by recent economic events. Following the criminal destruction (1980) of the central pavilion of Wallis Gilbert's listed and magnificent Firestone building, the future of the other factories is uneasy. (Ironically Wallis is recorded as saying that when his factories had outlived their usefulness they should indeed be demolished!) Their Pyrene (now BMW) building opposite has a fine moated entrance and characteristic rounded corner windows, and the Coty Factory next door has a sensuously streamlined

BMW warehouse

entrance. Unlike the Hoover Factory T26 the majority of these buildings are decorated office fronts to utilitarian factory spaces, but they possess a formal inventiveness and humour sadly lacking in contemporary architecture. Note the sign on the Trico windscreen-wiper factory – a giant wiper revealing a picture of the world. To the east is the magnificently eccentric white Fiat clock tower (previously Martini tower), clearly visible from the M4.

Coty Factory

Fiat clock tower

Royal Masonic Hospital   T24
1930–4
Ravenscourt Park W6
Sir John Burnet, Tait and Lorne
⊖ Stamford Brook

The Royal Masonic Hospital marks the retirement both of Sir John Burnet and of his variety of scraped classicism from this famous London practice. The large hospital is laid out symmetrically, and pays homage to the brick style of the Dutch architect Dudok, in the handling of large masses and the raked-out brick detailing, and also to Eric Mendelsohn in the adoption of large curved corner balconies. The firm's extensive and consistent output during the 1930s, of which the hospital at Ravenscourt Park is the best and most ambitious example, was to derive much inspiration from these two continental influences.

Sudbury Town

Park Royal

Piccadilly Line Underground Stations
T25

1930–3

Acton Town, Ealing Common, Park Royal, Alperton, Sudbury Town and Sudbury Hill, Charles Holden; Northfields and Osterley, Charles Holden with S A Heaps

During the expansion of London's suburbs in the 1930s, encouraged by the extension of the Underground, the station was often the first building of the new suburb's nucleus, standing apart from the existing village (if there was one) and incorporating its own small parade of shops. It was the symbol of the suburb dweller's connection with the metropolis, and the architects used elemental modern language. The booking hall was usually identified by the single large volume, and sometimes there was a vertical marker as well, like the very tall decorated towers at Osterley and Park Royal (Day, Welch and Lander, 1935–6). The stripped classicism of the style, though sometimes brutal, has worn well and subsequent work for London Transport has not bettered it. See also Arnos Grove and Southgate R23.

Hoover Factory 1932–5
T26

Western Avenue W5

Wallis Gilbert and Partners

⊖ Perivale

The Hoover Factory is a *tour de force* expressing the 1930s preoccupation with representing the factory as a palace. (Wallis Gilbert's Firestone Building was another good example of the genre before it was scandalously demolished in 1980.) Unlike many of the other *moderne* factories of the period, the Hoover building is not just a façade but a serious attempt to dignify the workplace. The canteen block to the west, with its high, well-lit rooms and richly designed entrance, was exceptional for England at the time – reminiscent of Brinkman and van der Vlugt's Van Nelle Factory in Rotterdam (1927). The principal elevation to Western Avenue absorbs and digests a mixture of modernist influences – the corner windows to the towers at either end call to mind Eric Mendelsohn's famous Einstein Tower in Potsdam (1921), the decorative bands of red and blue tiles set into the white stuccoed surfaces are memories of Josef Hoffmann's Palais Stoclet in Brussels (1905), and the beautifully crafted iron gates are like Mackintosh's Glasgow School of Art. Pevsner describes the Hoover building as 'perhaps the most offensive of the modernistic atrocities along this road of typical bypass factories' – this is also a comment on the shift of taste over the last thirty years. At the time of writing, with mass redundancies at Hoover, the future of the building is uncertain.

Guinness Brewery 1933–6   T27
Park Royal Road NW10
Sir Giles Gilbert Scott, Sir Alexander
Gibb engineer
⊖ North Acton

Contemporary with Battersea Power Station N29, and in the same monumental brick industrial style, Guinness Brewery is a dignified and asymmetrical grouping of large cubic blocks connected by high *passerelles*. The composition is best appreciated from the south, and conveys the image of an industrial palace set in its own grounds. In the 1930s Scott, like Lutyens, acquired numerous consultancies to tidy up façades for buildings already worked out by less gifted designers. The Guinness Brewery is a clear example of this; Scott's monumental brick architecture has stood the test of time, though it remains unappreciated by the biographers of modernism.

Wembley Arena   T28
ex Empire Swimming Pool
1934
Empire Way, Wembley
Sir Owen Williams
⊖ Wembley Park, ⇄ Wembley Complex

Despite Owen Williams' claims to pure objectivity, this building has a romantic and expressive view of structure. At the time of its completion it was the largest covered pool in the world. The daring cantilevered concrete roof spans 72 m (236 ft), and is counterweighted by monolithic concrete seating and massive external piers. The external appearance of these piers, seen in perspective, is truly monumental, and further evidence that Williams was not just solving problems.

Factory ex Gillette 1936   T29
Syon Lane W5
Sir Banister Fletcher
⊖ Osterley

Designed by the author of *A History of Architecture on the Comparative Method* (mandatory reading for students of architecture twenty years ago), the green copper dome to the clock tower of the Gillette Factory acts as a landmark on the Great West Road. The three-storey red-brick façade (141 m/562 ft long) is less memorable: the fine detailing of the central clock tower, the expressive masonry and the entrance steps are not enough to hold the overall composition of Fletcher's principal London work together. See also St Anne's Vestry Hall L98.

Kensal House 1936   T30
Ladbroke Grove W10
Robert Atkinson, Maxwell Fry,
C H James, Grey Wornum; housing
consultant Elizabeth Denby
⊖ Kensal Green

The best example of pre-war workers' housing in London, Kensal House was sponsored by the Gas, Light and Coke Company, owner of this unpromising site next to the railway, with its derelict gasholder. It closely followed continental examples (such as May's Frankfurt and the Siemensstadt at Berlin) in both method and form. The method involved research into the ergonomic requirements of the minimum and efficient 'work unit' – the kitchen and bathroom – and the integration of gas-fired hot water and heating. The form is that of parallel blocks; there are two of six storeys running north-south to allow sunlight to reach both sides of the flats, one straight and the other curved with a returned north end. The curve of the western block derives from the circle of the gasholder on whose site stands the nursery school,

Dollis Hill Synagogue 1937   T31
Parkside and Clifford Way
NW2
Sir Owen Williams
⊖ Dollis Hill

Owen Williams, the architect of twentieth-century building types like newspaper offices L117, health centres X10 and covered stadia T28, had here to reconcile his 'new objectivity' with the archaic programme of the Jewish faith. The hexagonal windows of Dollis Hill recall the apertures in castellated beams (in particular the Findhorn Bridge in Perth, 1926), while the roof was an early example of the use of pre-stressed concrete.

Heathrow Airport   T32
1951 onwards
Frederick Gibberd and Partners and others
⊖ Heathrow Central

With approximately 1000 planes arriving and departing daily, Heathrow is one of the world's busiest airports. However, since its opening it has been a perpetual building site and an inauspicious point of arrival for visitors to London. This can be attributed to the shortsightedness of its plan, in which the demands of growth and change were not fully considered. Since the end of the Second World War (the era of its conception) air travel has developed from being the privilege of a few into a necessity of a mass society. The hexagonal plan is also extremely inhibiting to the rational layout of buildings.

Of the four Terminal buildings, three were designed by Frederick Gibberd and Partners. Terminal 2, the Queen's Building and the Control Tower were opened in 1955. These buildings can be identified by the extensive use of red facing bricks in the Swedish *moderne* style of the Festival of Britain. Terminal 3 was opened in 1961 — a large utilitarian structure of glass and spindly steel columns; It was the first terminal building in Europe to accommodate jumbo jets (Pier 7). The building was significantly refurbished by D Y Davies Associates in 1990. The undistinguished Terminal 1, with its integrated car park structure, was opened in 1969. Finally Terminal 4 was designed by Scott Brownrigg and Turner and was completed in 1985. A fifth terminal by Richard Rogers and Partners is presently at the planning stage. The design of the concourse was by the London Transport Architects, with super-graphics' by Minale Tattersfield.

much photographed for modern architectural histories. With its well maintained concrete, now painted eau-de-nil, and its assured, repetitive and un-fussy elevations, the scheme still looks good.

The remaining buildings at Heathrow are of little interest.

Beginning in 1978, all terminal buildings are now connected to the London Underground System. The design of the concourse was by the London Transport Architects, with 'super-graphics' by Minale Tattersfield. The remaining buildings at Heathrow are of little interest excepting the Sterling Hotel of 1990 by Manser Associates and Yorke Rosenberg and Mardall's black, steelframed Cargo Agents' building and white glazed tiled offices on the southern perimeter road. (YRM were also responsible for Gatwick, London's second airport.)

London's third airport at **Stansted** by Foster Associates opened in 1991. In contrast with Heathrow, Foster's Terminal at Stansted represents a major achievement for British architecture, regrettably not within the scope of this book.

Heinz Research and Administration Centre

T33

1965
Hayes Park, Hayes, Middlesex
Skidmore, Owings and Merrill with
Matthew Ryan and Partners
⊖⇄Hayes and Harlington

The industrial headquarters building formed in the image of a contemporary palace in its own park was, by 1965, a tradition of the famous American practice of Skidmore, Owings and Merrill — see the Connecticut General Life Insurance Company, Hartford, Connecticut (1954–7) and Reynolds Metal Company, Richmond, Virginia (1955–8). The Heinz building at Hayes was England's first taste of this 'well made' American tradition. But when built, the pair of two-storey court buildings, with their slightly tapered white concrete frames, proved to be banal. However, the extreme professionalism of their construction is undeniable.

Highgrove Housing 1972–7

T34

Eastcote Road, Ruislip
Edward Cullinan
⊖Pinner

The 113 houses built for the London Borough of Hillingdon, set in a sloping meadow in the suburb of Ruislip, are in the line of development which began with the architect's own house in Camden Mews C11 in the early 1960s, and continued with research at Cambridge in suburban forms and models in the mid-1960s. The back-to-back semi-detached houses at Highgrove have 9 m (30 ft) frontages to allow kitchen, dining and living rooms to be side by side, divided or open-plan, but all opening — suburban style — on to their own gardens. The houses are in groups of four (not unlike Frank Lloyd Wright's Broadacre City proposals) and the site is organized particularly around a network of paths at right angles to each other. The resulting 'molecular' structure of the site plan is reminiscent of recent work in Holland by Herman Hertzberger — characterized by planning ideas that are relatively exclusive to the project, making physical external connections (to ordinary city streets, avenues and so on) more or less difficult. The bright blue plastic-coated corrugated steel roofs give the buildings their distinctive appearance.

Cranford Court 1974–7

T35

53–9 Cranford Lane, Hounslow
Edward Jones
⊖Hounslow West

This small group of fourteen old people's dwellings forms a three-sided south-facing public court. The plan is symmetrical, partly inspired by the traditional almshouse, with two-storey 'lodge' houses on the street frontage. The single-storey façades to the court are stuccoed and collective in character, playing down the expression of the individual dwelling. The waist-high planting boxes, projecting porches and doorsteps are contained within a pergola. The private courts at the back of each dwelling are intended to be used by the residents as they wish.

Houses and **flats** for　　　　　T36
Kensington Housing Trust
1975–80
103–23 St Mark's Road W10
Jeremy Dixon
⊖Ladbroke Grove

This terrace of forty-four flats and houses
set out with the intention of fundament-
ally reinterpreting the tradition of the
London house – the principal relationship
to the street, arrangement of front façades
and back gardens, and so on. The scheme
resembles a terrace of large houses, each
subdivided into a pair of narrow-fronted
houses above a ground-floor flat. The
gabled façades absorb a number of influences: Queen Anne eclecticism, the English
Free Style of Norman Shaw and the
ubiquitous speculative builders' architecture of the turn of the century.

Civic Offices for London　　　　T37
Borough of Hillingdon 1977
High Street, Uxbridge
Robert Matthew, Johnson Marshall and
Partners
⊖Uxbridge

That the imagery of vernacular housing
should be applied to a large bureaucratic
institution (with its open-plan offices) is a
sad comment on the times and evidence of
an architectural loss of nerve. The adoption of 'friendly' forms is intended to
make unwieldy local government less
inaccessible. Architecturally the opposite
proves to be the case, for in a secular age
civic centres are one of the last institutions that can legitimately be distinguished from housing or commercial
building. But the building is very popular
and a relief from the banal office blocks
normally associated with local
authorities.

IBM Industrial Park 1979　　　T38
Greenford Road, Greenford
Foster Associates
⊖Greenford

The first phase of IBM's light-industrial
development on the site of an earlier
heavy industry factory is clad in very large
sheets of glass and corrugated siding. It
provides warehousing, research offices,
and large-installation computer showrooms under a single level roof. The car
park at the front has been planted as a
small forest of plane trees.

Offices, flats and **restaurant**　　T39
1984–7
Thames Wharf, Rainville Road W6
Richard Rogers Partnership
⊖ Hammersmith

A utopian development next to the river
(see Foster Associates' Hester Road offices N38) provides offices for the architects to the south of the site in a converted
factory with a new barrel-vaulted steel
roof, and a fine restaurant overlooking a
courtyard. To the north, at 1–25 Thames
Reach, are three new blocks of flats, their
planning a textbook example of the com-
positional methods of the 1960s in which
the individual elements are identified and
then arranged to make a picturesque
assemblage. Only the elaborately
wrought steel balconies between the
blocks provide a clue to their authorship.

Offices by Ian Ritchie

6 Furzeground Way

Stockley Park started 1985   T40

London Borough of Hillingdon. Master planners Arup Associates; Architects Arup Associates, Foster Associates, Ian Ritchie Architects, Troughton McAslan, Richard Rogers Partnership, Peter Foggo Architects, Eric Parry Associates, Lifschutz Davidson and others.
⊖ Uxbridge ⇄ West Drayton

It was only a matter of time before the north American business park made a significant appearance in London's outer boroughs. Stockley Park is the most ambitious of its type.

Built on former gravel pits and rubbish tips, it has convenient road (M4, M40 and M25), rail (British Rail to the west country) and air connections (Heathrow). Of its 150 hectares (350 acres), 100 are dedicated to parkland, lakes, playing fields and a golf course, part of a joint venture for the reclamation of land for a major public park, between the developer, Stockley plc, and the London Borough of Hillingdon. The remaining 36 hectares (90 acres) are planned for a commercial development devoted to the high technology business community. The Business Park is made of seven building zones designated for new office and workshop buildings, with an eighth zone reserved for the central amenities building. The new buildings are restricted to three storeys and are to provide 140,000 square metres (1,500 square feet) gross floor area.

Arup Associates, Troughton McAslan and Foster Associates have so far contributed office buildings. Arup have also been responsible for the central amenities building. Two other buildings are memorable. The first of these is the 8400 square metre (90,000 square feet) office building by Ian Ritchie. The double-glazed external wall advances the Pilkington 'planar glazing' system, with its use of clear, toughened, and in some cases low-energy-coated glass. The result is a building form of remarkable abstract purity. In contrast to the rather timid use of solar shades elsewhere at Stockley Park, here the building is animated by a monumental three-storey steel frame supporting large curved and perforated stainless-steel shades on the south, east, and west façades.

The second building of note is by Eric Parry Associates at 6 Furzeground Way. If earlier buildings were conceived in the spirit of abstract installations, Parry's building is the first to engage the possibilities of the site and to reaffirm the reciprocal relationship between architecture and landscape. While the earlier buildings eschewed hierarchy and representation, Parry's building is deliberately figurative. The exterior '*piano nobile*' wall is formed of panels of glass block and clear glass placed in a standard 'stick' system.

These two buildings demonstrate clear alternative architectural directions for Stockley Park, which do not nevertheless compromise its overall unity.

Offices 'The Ark' 1988–91   T41

Ralph Erskine, Rock Townsend, executive architects
⊖ Hammersmith

Erskine's first building in London recalls the sheltering of his Byker Wall housing in Newcastle (1969–80) and, more distantly, that of his 'Arctic City' project of the 1950s. It now stands as one of the series of monuments on the road between London and Heathrow, on a site lassooed by railway lines and the elevated road. The idiosyncratic design of the building attempts to provide a form appropriate to the scale of the super highway. Eight floors of offices, their shape reminiscent of a helmet or shield, are set against the road to defend the atrium to the south.

Section U: Outer London, east

The historical significance of this part of London is military and industrial: it forms a time corridor which has expanded from west to east along the Thames over 2,000 years. The Roman city of London is the western end of this axis, which continues through William the Conqueror's Tower (protecting the city from invasion by sea) to Henry VIII's naval yard at Deptford and the Royal Naval College and Hospital U3 at Greenwich, and finishes in the east with the eighteenth-century dockyards and military establishments at Woolwich U10, U13.

Industrial complexes are generally concentrated to the east of cities, and London is no exception: in the nineteenth century the East End became the city's principal dockland and manufacturing area. ('East End' and 'West End' derive from the eighteenth century when the areas actually marked the eastern and western limits of London.) A boat trip from Westminster pier to Greenwich shows the Thames as a 'working' river, with the magnificent exception of Wren's set-piece design for the Greenwich Hospital.

The docks were planned on the north banks of the Thames (with the exception of the Surrey Docks at Rotherhithe), taking advantage of the marshy ground, the River Lea and the serpentine curves of the Thames. The first were built by the West India Company in 1789–1802, to be followed in 1805 by the East India Docks at the mouth of the River Lea. The East India Dock Road and Commercial Road are built, making connections with the City, and this basic infrastructure was then expanded over the following century. Impressive for their sheer size and the zeal of their Victorian engineers, the docks are best appreciated from the air (see Cameron and Cooke's *Above London*). The docks have now moved to Tilbury, continuing London's easterly expansion.

The vast area of land vacated by the docks was put under the control of a public Development Corporation which proved incapable of planning much beyond a rudimentary new infrastructure — the Light Railway, the new City Airport and some very expensive stretches of road. The buildings are unsatisfactory in proportion to their size. Canary Wharf U47, the largest single development, built with north American investment on an island, remains severed from the rest of the city. More successful models are those where development has proceded incrementally, for example Butler's Wharf L65.

Hackney, Bethnal Green, Stepney and Poplar, to the north of the river, were villages in the Middle Ages, and the Isle of Dogs (the name deriving from the royal dogs, kennelled here out of the hearing of the royal palace at Greenwich) was pasture and marshland. Hackney has the most distinguished past, which today is hardly discernible. In 1750 the parish had twelve villages or hamlets, including Kingsland, Dalston, Hacklewell, Clapton and Homerton. By the mid-nineteenth century, these areas had lost their identity and were absorbed into the expanding East End of London. Bethnal Green, Stepney and Poplar went the same way, and by the end of the nineteenth century their names were synonymous with some of the worst slums and overcrowded conditions in the country. Their combined population in 1880 (working mostly in and around the docks) was over half a million, and Stepney alone had a larger population than Bristol. The area's chief architectural interest now lies in its philanthropically endowed workers' housing. In 1842, in the reformist climate which brought amenities to the working population of the East End, Pennethorne laid out Victoria Park (217 acres/87.8 ha). This was London's first Victorian park, and is the largest under the control of the GLC.

The medieval fishing villages of Rotherhithe, Deptford, Woolwich and Greenwich, to the south of the river, were relatively unchanged until they became caught up in nineteenth-century London's industrial sprawl. Further to the south and east the land rises in hills and bluffs to the plateau of Blackheath, where Wren's Morden College X2 and the elegant Paragon X5 testify to more gracious standards of living.

Charlton House 1607–12   UI
The Village SE7
⇌Charlton

Since the destruction of Holland House 11 by bombing, Charlton is the only complete Jacobean house in Greater London, and is a perfect example of the E-plan of the period. The hall is in the middle of the plan and is entered through the large-windowed porch on its long axis. To either side, in the wings, are the chapel and parlour, the kitchen and the pantry, with bay windows on the legs of the E.

Queen's House 1616–35   U2
Greenwich Park
Inigo Jones
⇌Greenwich, or boat from Westminster or Tower Bridge

England's first Palladian villa and Inigo Jones's earliest surviving work, the Queen's House has a long and complicated history. With its proximity to the naval dockyards, Greenwich was always favoured by royalty. In 1613, James I gave Greenwich Palace to his Queen, Anne of Denmark, who was dissatisfied with the large rambling building. Accordingly Inigo Jones, the King's Surveyor, was instructed to build a more modern house on the site of the palace's southern gatehouse.

Jones's original plan consisted of two parallel ranges, either side of the Dover Road, connected by a bridge at first floor. As well as allowing access on the north side to Greenwich Palace, this would also give the Queen unimpeded and dry-shod access to the park on the south. Anne of Denmark died in 1619, and the villa was left unfinished until Charles I decided to complete it for Henrietta Maria's occupation in 1637. Inigo Jones's son-in-law, John Webb, enlarged the house by adding further bridges along the east and west fronts, giving it the apparently square appearance we know today (actually it is 33 m × 36 m (110 ft × 120 ft). In 1690 the Queen's House became the official residence of the Ranger of Greenwich Park and Governor of the Naval Hospital, as William and Mary preferred the healthier air of Hampton Court.

Four years later Wren was instructed to prepare plans for a Naval Hospital on the site of Greenwich Palace. The Queen's House was now to form the rather modest focus of Wren's truly baroque and palatial design, the finest of its kind in England, best appreciated from the Isle of Dogs on the north of the river. The Queen's House remained the residence of the Governor of the Naval Hospital until in 1806 it was turned into a school for seamen's children. At the same time the Dover Road was moved to the north, where Romney Road now runs, and open colonnades were added in 1807–16 by David Alexander. These connect the house on both sides to a much larger composition. In 1933 the school moved out of the building and four years later the Queen's House was opened to the public as the National Maritime Museum.

The architecture is remarkable for its restraint and for the absence of contemporary Elizabethan elements (bay windows, turrets and gables). Among its innovations are the strict Vitruvian proportions, rusticated base, south-facing loggia with unfluted Palladian Ionic columns, and the double open staircase with symmetrical curves leading up to the terrace on the north side. The sills to the ground floor windows were dropped in 1770, destroying the primacy of the *piano nobile*.

The interior is as consistently Palladian as the exterior. The hall, 12 m (40 ft) square. unlike the traditional hall of the Elizabethan manor, is a grand vestibule with a fine marble floor. However, the gallery supported by brackets is a remnant of the Elizabethan minstrels' gallery, and Lord Burlington, despite his admiration for the house, observed that any room of this size required columns. The most impressive feature is the main staircase, known as the Tulip Staircase.

The interior of the house was restored in 1990 to its hypothetical appearance c1662. This controversial project has come close to undermining the buildings's architectural character.

Royal Naval Hospital   U3
1664, 1696–1702
Romney Road SE10
Sir Christopher Wren, Nicholas
Hawksmoor, Sir John Vanbrugh, John
Webb and others
⇄Greenwich

The country south-east of London was a favourite retreat for medieval royalty (see Eltham Palace X1), and in 1423 the Duke of Gloucester took over a Carthusian establishment at Greenwich. Later, Henry VII and Elizabeth I were born there, and Henry made the original manor into a palace. Inigo Jones built the Queen's House U2 for James I's queen, Anne of Denmark, and it was completed after her death by Jones's son-in-law, John Webb. No more building was done at Greenwich until after the Civil War, when Charles II determined to replace the old Tudor palace, using Webb as architect.

Webb planned three buildings arranged to form an open courtyard facing the river. This was started in 1664, but only the building nearest the river on the west was completed. The river façade consisted of three bays with a central pediment – the extension eastward is a later addition. When William and Mary came to the throne in 1688 they decided to live at Hampton Court VI, where Wren's State rooms in the east wing were just being finished. Greenwich was to be turned into a hospital for sailors, on the pattern of the earlier one for soldiers at Chelsea N2 but more magnificent; in 1695 Wren was appointed Surveyor-General for the Commission to build it. His first plan was for a series of buildings on either side of Webb's axis. These would have formed progressively narrowing courtyards, with a large domed building on the axis between the river and Queen's House (a scheme not adopted at Greenwich but useful for Vanbrugh at Castle Howard and Blenheim). Wren's second plan was the one we now see, continued for many years after his death: the completion of the first court by mirroring Webb's first building, and behind this, up a grand flight of steps, two U-shaped buildings facing each other across the axis. The northern legs of the Us contain on the east the chapel and on the west the hall, each marked with a dome at the corner. The spaces between the legs of the Us are closed with colonnades of paired columns (probably influenced by Perrault's Louvre); these form courtyards overlooked by the wards.

The **hall** is the grandest secular interior of the period in England – a baroque synthesis of Wren's spaces, Hawksmoor's architectural decoration and the painting of Thornhill (who painted the interior of the dome of St Paul's Cathedral L27). The ceiling (1707–26) shows William and Mary surrounded by the four cardinal virtues, while, under Apollo, Architecture makes a rare painted appearance carrying a drawing of the hospital. The hall is connected by flights of stairs to two more painted spaces: the entrance vestibule under the dome, and the tall room at the other end, which provides a ceremonial dais for the high table.

Wren's plan continued to be executed by his pupils – see Hawksmoor's extraordinary closing block to the westward courtyard behind the hall. Vanbrugh made plans reviving the idea of a central domed closure to the axis, but nothing came of them. In 1755 the hospital had over 1500 pensioners, and in 1769 Webb's original building was extended on the south side. In the 1780s the interior of the chapel U15 in the Queen Mary building was magnificently refitted by Stuart and Newton.

Almshouses U4
Trinity Hospital 1695
Mile End Road E1
⊖Whitechapel
Built by Trinity House for retired seamen
or their widows, here is a fine example of
seventeenth-century planning. Two rows
of houses face each other across an avenue
of trees, at the end of which is the chapel.

St Alfege 1712–18 U5
Greenwich High Road SE10
Nicholas Hawksmoor and John James
⇌Greenwich, or boat from Westminster
Pier
Of the fifty new churches commissioned in
1711, this was both the Commissioners'
and Hawksmoor's first. Developed from
his earlier theoretical studies, it set the
pattern for the later ones. To the biaxially
central space are added auxiliary spaces:
the richly decorated, segmentally-arched
chancel and small transepts. The identity
of the nave is emphasized by an oval
moulding occupying most of the flat
ceiling. The interior was rebuilt after
being gutted in the Second World War.
Outside, the portico is at the *east* end,
facing the main road. Its Roman arch rises
into the pediment and its Doric order
continues all round the church. Set between the pilasters, smooth, unmoulded,
round-headed windows contrast with the
heavily keystoned square ones. The nearly

freestanding tower at the west end was
finished by John James in 1730. See also St
George-in-the-East U8, St Anne,
Limehouse U9, and Christ Church, Spitalfields H6.

St Paul 1712–30 U6
Deptford High Street SE8
Thomas Archer
⊖New Cross, ⇌Deptford
Archer's two churches for the 1711
Commissioners, St Paul and the more
ebullient St John, Smith Square K35, are
the best example of the importation of
Roman baroque to early eighteenth-
century London. St Paul's plan is fluid and
derived from Rome's Sant'Agnese, the
flat-ceilinged space defined by a
Corinthian order. The exterior is more
stiff, but the arrangement of tower and
steeple (an amalgam of Borromini and
Wren) is a relatively early and successful
experiment in relating tower to nave
(compare with the later St Martin K40).
The drum of the tower continues down to
the ground as a vestibule, and is wrapped
in a semicircular Doric colonnade. Just to
the north is **St Nicholas**, Deptford
Green, in the style of Wren and worth
a short detour.

St Mary Rotherhithe 1714   U7
St Marychurch Street SE16
⊖Rotherhithe

A reminder of a once active shipbuilding village, St Mary Rotherhithe stands among trees' in its own railed and gated yard. Across the street is the Free School, founded in 1613, a simple three-storey house, with two charming painted sculptures of a boy and girl pupil on its first floor.

St George-in-the-East   U8
1714–29
Cannon Street Road E1
Nicholas Hawksmoor
⊖Shadwell

Started in the same year as St Anne U9 and Christ Church, Spitalfields H6, St George's is now only a bombed shell housing a sad new church structure. The plan has the two right-angled axes of the other churches. The cross-axis is marked with stair towers set towards the corners, not with projecting transepts as at St Alfege U5. These towers, together with the horizontal box of the nave and the wide main tower (now lacking its finial pepper pot), make one of the noblest compositions of English baroque. Decoration is restricted to the Corinthian order at the base of the tower, the open octagon with Roman altar finials at its top, and the famous keystoned doorways to the stair towers. The typical chalk-white and soot-black weathering of Portland stone is here shown particularly well. See also U5, U9 and H6.

St Anne 1714–30 U9
Commercial Road E14
Nicholas Hawksmoor
⇌Stepney East

The most obvious feature of the interior is the ceiling's great flat circle, edged by a Corinthian entablature moulding, which marks the junction of the two cross-axes. This and the Corinthian columns set in from the corners allow the plan to be read as a Greek cross. The interior was gutted by fire in about 1850, but was faithfully restored.

The external composition is not as 'elemental' as that of St George U8. The tower is more Gothic in spirit, and is joined to the body of the church with a wide blank stage against which rests the porch; the stage is echoed by the small attics at the east end.

Royal Arsenal 1717–20 U10
Beresford Square SE18
Sir John Vanbrugh (?)
⇌Woolwich Arsenal

Three buildings constitute the Royal Arsenal: the Brass Gun Foundry (1717), the Model Room (1719) and the Gun Bore Factory (c1720). The Model Room is the most distinguished and the most characteristic of Vanbrugh. The stock brick entrance is magnificently robust. On either side are rusticated piers, above which are cylindrical pedestals supporting lions. The high central semicircular arch is concluded by a dropped pediment.

Vanbrugh Castle 1717–26 U11
Westcombe Park Road SE3
Sir John Vanbrugh
⊖⇌ Maze Hill

Vanbrugh was appointed Surveyor to Greenwich Hospital as successor to Wren in 1716. Overlooking the Royal Hospital he built England's first sham castle, a building of seminal importance in the development of the Picturesque. Vanbrugh Castle was the first private house to be designed with conscious associations with the Middle Ages, a medieval fantasy rather than the scholarly reconstruction of the nineteenth century. As John Summerson has observed, 'the house is without a scrap of Gothic detail about it', but its steep proportions, narrow, heavy windows and round towers are Gothic in spirit. Vanbrugh's later additions gave the house its asymmetrical shape and plan.

Nelson Wharf c1770 U12
265 Rotherhithe Street SE16
⊖Rotherhithe

This fine five-bay house is the only surviving example of the eighteenth-century merchant ship owners' style. The separation of living and working accommodation, characteristic of the nineteenth-century city, was yet to take place. See also Shad Thames L65.

Royal Artillery Barracks U13
1775–1802
Grand Depot Road SE18
⮀ Woolwich Arsenal
The magnificent south elevation to the parade ground is the longest (323 m/1060 ft) continuous architectural composition in London. From a white triumphal arch in the centre spread ranges of two- and three-storey plain stock brick barracks, connected by lower white colonnades. Behind this façade the barracks were set out as a small town on a gridiron plan, but few of the original buildings now remain.

Tide Mill and U14
Distillery 1776, 1813
Three Mill Lane E3
⊖ Bromley-by-Bow
Of these two fine buildings the earlier, dating from the beginnings of the Industrial Revolution, spans Bow Creek, whose tide drove its machinery. The later, with its cupola and hoist, was a distillery and is still used by vintners for storage.

Chapel 1789 U15
Greenwich Hospital SE10
James 'Athenian' Stuart and William Newton
⮀ Greenwich
A fire in 1779 gutted the chapel, designed by Wren and finished after his death by Ripley. It was rebuilt by Stuart, Surveyor to the Hospital U3, and it remains his finest London work. With Nicholas Revett, Stuart had visited Greece, and on return had published *The Antiquities of Athens* (Vol 1, 1762). The chapel presents the fruits of their journey: exquisite, archaeologically correct neo-classical decoration laid over a broadly seventeenth-century scheme. The 3.6 m (12 ft) high doorway between the chapel and the octagonal vestibule is the finest marble carving in the Greek style produced in eighteenth-century England. The organ gallery, carried on marble Ionic columns, has workmanship which is almost equally refined.

Woolwich Garrison U16
ex Royal Military Academy
1805–8
Academy Road, Woolwich
Common SE18
J Wyatt
⮀ Woolwich Arsenal
Built to replace the original school within the Arsenal, this design presents a silly contrast to the classicism of the Royal Artillery Barracks U13. Wyatt's plan for the parade ground façade is the same, but carried out in brown and yellow brick in a thin Gothic style. The centrepiece is a parody of the Tower of London's White Tower L3, complete with corner turrets. The bright red-brick end pavilions are later.

Albert Gardens c1810 U17
Commercial Road E1
⊖Shadwell
Albert Gardens is a regular and completely preserved small-scale square. Laid out following the building of Commercial Road (1803–10) to link the docks to the City of London, it was rehabilitated in the late 1970s by Anthony Richardson and Partners.

St John 1825–8 U18
Cambridge Heath Road E1
Sir John Soane
⊖Bethnal Green
The conjunction of west front and tower is here resolved with great sophistication. There is no pediment and the square piers either side of the central bay continue past the cornice line so that the square stage of the tower is engaged. The piers continue to form the short tower, and in a manner typical of Soane are detached from the tower, revealing a tense slice of space between. The tower was apparently intended to be higher, with the result that the circular cupola looks rather squat. The interior was burnt out in 1870 and insensitively remodelled. The window tracery is also an uncharacteristic later addition. See also St Peter Walworth P1.

Licensed Victuallers' U19
Benevolent Institution
1827–8
Asylum Road SE15
Henry Rose
≹Queen's Road Peckham
Had they been built ten years later these almshouses would have been done in well-meaning Tudor; instead, the two extremely plain yellow-brick L-shaped domestic wings enclose an undecorated court. Architectural richness is reserved for the chapel in the centre, which has a handsome Doric portico and an elaborate sarcophagus on the roof, and the very fine iron railings and gates. It is now being surrounded with Southwark's Pixie-style housing which has replaced the towers of the previous decade.

St Peter 1843 U20
Woolwich New Road SE18
Augustus Welby Pugin
≹Woolwich Arsenal
It has been said that Pugin's zeal to provide places for Catholic worship often overcame his artistic judgement: St Peter's is a clear example. The exterior, with no tower and a chancel added later by another architect, is most uninteresting. The interior is decidedly mean, with cheap cruciform columns and no clerestory.

Museum of Childhood U21
ex Bethnal Green Museum
1855–6 and 1875
Cambridge Heath Road E1
J W Wild, C D Young and Company, Sir
William Cubitt
⊖ Bethnal Green

A philanthropic social experiment in its day, the Bethnal Green Museum was intended to bring Art to the East End, thereby civilizing the working population. Ironically, the three-bay red-brick façade seems more appropriate to a factory or railway station than to a museum, and the entrance is curiously understated. Nevertheless, when seen across Bethnal Green the regular bays of the façade, with a frieze of terracotta inlaid panels below the eaves, have a quiet dignity. Wild's exterior conceals the cast iron galleries of the original Iron Museum from South Kensington, designed and built by C D Young & Company. Having proved unpopular as the South Kensington Museum, the building was dis- mantled and moved to Bethnal Green under the supervision of Sir William Cubitt, in an early example of the economy and flexibility of prefabricated building. The museum is famous for its collection of dolls' houses.

Garrison Church of St U22
George 1863
Grand Depot Road SE18
T H Wyatt
⇌ Woolwich Arsenal

The church was badly damaged in the Second World War, and with the removal of the roof it has been interestingly transformed into a commemorative garden. The Villa Giulia in Rome is evoked by the combination of the 'external rooms' of the garden, the Lombard porch and the 'early Romanesque' basilica. This seems an excellent use for obsolete church buildings.

Abbey Mills Pumping U23
Station 1865–8
Abbey Lane E15
J Bazalgette and E Cooper
⊖ West Ham

Bazalgette and Cooper were engineer and architect to the Metropolitan Board of Works, established in 1855 to deal with London's sewage (see the Victoria Embankment K103). Designed to raise the level of the northern outfall sewer, this eccentric building is a good example of their collaboration, and of the split between Victorian engineering and architecture. The exterior is a well-mannered mixture of Byzantine and Gothic, complete with a mansard roof. The large, galleried machine hall – all in cast iron – originally accommodated the massive beam engines, replaced by electric motors in 1933.

Deptford Town Hall 1900–3   U24
New Cross Road SE14
Lanchester, Stewart and Rickards
⊖New Cross, New Cross Gate
Lanchester (brother of the car designer)
and Rickards, who won the competition
for the design of Cardiff City Hall and Law
Courts in 1897, were an influential force
both in the classical revival at the turn of
the century, and in the establishment of
the Edwardian baroque style. Deptford
Town Hall was the subject of a competition organized by the newly formed
Borough of Deptford, and remains one of
the most enjoyable Edwardian public
buildings. The seven-bay front elevation
has been variously described as playful,
nautical, florid and fanciful. It has a central
oriel window with statues in niches on
either side, and a set-back pediment
capped by a clock tower, in the style of
Hawksmoor's churches.

Houses 1935   U25
85–91 Genesta Road SE18
B Lubetkin and A V Pilichowski
⇥Woolwich Arsenal
Because they wished to transform the city
by the invention and superimposition of
new housing types, many modernists
overlooked the traditional terraced
house. These four houses are an exception. The rendered fronts and curved
second-floor balconies show that the
language of Highpoint I R26 is not
exclusive to the block of flats.

Greenwich Town Hall 1939   U26
Greenwich High Road and
Royal Hill SE10
E C Culpin and Bowers
⇥Greenwich
A rare example of successfully imported
and digested continental modern: the
style is from Dudok, carried out in yellow
stock brick. For once, the modern style
and programme – a public building to
house and represent a socialist administration – come together in a knowing
composition of carefully balanced vert-
icals and horizontals. The tower is as
stylish as that of an eighteenth-century
church, and serves the same symbolic
purpose. See also Hornsey Town Hall R25.

Housing 1952   U27
Usk Street E2
Sir Denys Lasdun
⊖Bethnal Green
To most people the cluster block represents just another version of the local
authority tower block with the lifts and
staircases exposed, but Lasdun's cluster
blocks in Bethnal Green were an early
realization of a mixture of contemporary
urban theories. 'Cluster' was a loaded
architectural/sociological word which
Peter Smithson defined as 'a specific
pattern of association ... introduced to
replace such group concepts as house,
street, district and city which are too
loaded with historical overtones. Any
coming together is "cluster".'

Lasdun's previous housing, with Tecton, had involved arbitrary pattern-making in the façades (see Priory Green Estate G66 and the Hallfield Estate I26); the style of the cluster block, on the other hand, derives from attempts to identify each dwelling, making a 'vertical street'. But its eight-storey tower, a composite of four smaller towers set at different angles to each other, is not a street. Architecture is a precise art and such imprecise images cannot be used as its justification. See also Claredale Street U28.

Housing, Keeling House   U28
1960
Claredale Street E2
Sir Denys Lasdun and Partners
⊖ Bethnal Green

Lasdun's second attempt at the articulated tower (the first was at Usk Street U27), Keeling House can be regarded either as an eccentric tower block or as a determined attempt to invent architectural alternatives both to the street and to the conventional mixed development of the previous decade. Lasdun hoped that the stacked maisonettes, separated by wide bands of concrete, might remind tenants of the two-storey houses in the district, and that the shared landings would foster sociability. The two six-storey blocks of maisonettes in dark brick are part of the same scheme.

This area, bounded by Hackney Road to the north, Cambridge Heath Road to the

east, Bethnal Green Road to the south and Shoreditch High Street to the west, contains an example of virtually every English experiment in public housing.

Old People's Home 1960   U29
Rectory Field Crescent,
off Marlborough Lane SE7
Stirling and Gowan
⇌ Charlton

The least well known building of this famous partnership. Accommodation for sixty-two people is planned around an internal courtyard, with the height of the building varying from one to three storeys to allow the maximum sunlight into the courtyard. The castellated, stepped engineering brickwork, the forty-five degree and ninety degree planning geometries and expressive boiler flue are unmistakable signs of its authorship. Quinlan Terry was an assistant on this building.

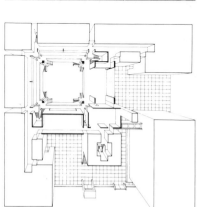

Forest Gate School 1963   U30
Forest Street E7
Colquhoun and Miller
⇌ Forest Gate, Wanstead Park

The school is a fine early example of this firm's departure from the rugged English Brutalism of Lyons Israel and Ellis, for whom the architects had worked, towards their later, cooler, more rational method. Influenced by the teaching of Colin Rowe, by Dutch examples, and by the many schemes originating in Cambridge about this time, the plan bisects a right angle by extending two wings of classrooms from a square, double-height assembly hall. The result looks as if it has been carved from shiny red brick.

Perspective plan

Trafalgar Road

Creek Road in 1981

Housing 1965–8   U31
Trafalgar Road SE10
James Gowan
⇌ Maze Hill

This handsome courtyard of four-storey maisonettes enclosing an internal court was designed by Gowan in the last years of his partnership with James Stirling. The buildings have a complex architectural lineage. Their red-brick façades and industrial metal windows are inspired by the 1930s; on the other hand, the second-floor access gallery cut into the surface of the block, with its corner bridges, refers back to the Preston Housing of the original partnership and recalls the Spangen flats in Rotterdam (1921) by Brinkman.

The reinterpretation of the nineteenth-century by-law street in the form of access galleries has been a central preoccupation of British architects since the war. Nevertheless access galleries can only form surrogate streets, having only one side and no common ground level. As a result the central space at Trafalgar Road is under-used. The same architecture is used in Gowan's contemporary and smaller **Creek Road** housing scheme down the road, which the housing authority subsequently 'normalized' with pitched roofs.

Sutton Dwellings 1967   U32
Plough Way SE16
Frederick MacManus and Partners,
designed by Jeremy Dixon
⊖ Surrey Docks

Although this building turns its back to the street, and as a result there is some confusion about the entrances, its virtues include forty-eight generously planned family flats (each pair being served by a small continental lift, avoiding the use of access galleries), a raised shared garden forming a roof to the parking area on the south side, and a workshop and crèche run by the Save the Children Fund. But it is a salutary lesson that much of the careful internal planning of the flats was misinterpreted by the tenants, and the generous collective ideas were misunderstood by the housing trust – the roof garden, for instance, now has restricted access. This is the first building credited to Jeremy Dixon, and a comparison with his more traditional housing at St Mark's Road T36 is illuminating.

Housing 1968–72   U33
Robin Hood Gardens, Cotton
Street and Robin Hood Lane E14
Alison and Peter Smithson
⇌ Bromley-by-Bow, then bus

At first sight just another large and dreary
GLC estate: two long cranked slab buildings of rather drab precast concrete
address each other across a no-man's-land
of common gardens, distinguished by a
large artificial mound.

However, the Smithsons' Robin Hood
Gardens is the final, built reality of nearly
twenty years of urban theory, beginning
with their competition entry for Golden
Lane (1953) in which a network of streets
in the air was projected. It was not a new
idea, but the reappraisal of the street and
its function was to characterize their
frequent writing and contributions to
Team X (the successor to *CIAM*) over the
years. Even if it can be justified as a
fragment of a larger piece or a city within
the city, Robin Hood Gardens must
nevertheless be a particularly depressing
place to live in, severed as it is from any
connections with the existing city by its
almost manic defence system of walls and
moats.

This scheme is an example of the late
modernist avant-garde determination to
realize a theoretical position at all costs. In
this the Smithsons are not alone.

Hostel Thames Polytechnic, 1971   U34
Thames Street SE18
Frederick Macmanus and Partners;
design by Edward Jones
⇌ Woolwich Arsenal

These 250 south-facing study bedrooms
positioned above a communal ground
floor took their inspiration in part from
Le Corbusier's Pavillon Suisse in Paris of
1927 and the 'social condenser' of Russian
constructivist architecture of the 1920s.
With Jeremy Dixon's housing in the Surrey Docks U32, Michael Gold's Clipstone
Street housing G70 and Christopher
Cross's housing for the GLC at Besson
Street, Lewisham of 1969 (all for Frederick Macmanus), the projects represented
a search for a lost objectivity.

Thamesmead started 1972   U35
Abbey Wood SE2
GLC Architects Department
⇌ Abbey Wood

Before shedding the responsibility of
being the biggest landlord in the world by
handing over its houses to the London
Boroughs, the GLC had a huge
programme of house building both in
London and in the 'expanded towns'
outside. By the middle of the 1960s the
supply of large sites was exhausted, and
the Erith marshes, with their sewage
works and disused ordnance range, were
identified as a possible site for the new
town that the GLC had long wanted to
build. Plans were made following up-to-
date models: low buildings which defined
routes, tower blocks for the childless, and
big roads, including a crossing of the
Thames to Barking. The first artists'
impressions showed canals weaving
through all this.

A factory was set up on site to produce
heavy precast concrete units, and the
earlier linear housing and towers were
built from these. This method has been
discontinued and the factory closed;
recent housing has reverted to the currently fashionable Pixie style, while re-
medial work goes on to improve the
spaces left over in the earlier phases, and
to waterproof the towers. The Thames
crossing has not yet been built, and the
area still suffers from the poor communi-
cations which prevented its earlier
development.

Ickburgh School U36
special care unit 1972–3
Ickburgh Road E5
Foster Associates for the Spastics Society
≹Clapton

Foster Associates' first non-commercial, non-industrial building, this little single-storey shed adapts the steel-framed structure of their IBM Cosham building to the particular requirements of severely handicapped children. The plan, with partitions that can be fully dismantled, places WCs in the centre, a ring of circulation round them, and two activity areas facing a small play court. The non-glazed parts of the exterior are faced with enamelled aluminium siding.

Warehouse and showroom U37
for Modern Art Glass Ltd
1973
Hailey Road, Thamesmead
Foster Associates
⊖≹Belvedere

The Modern Art Glass Warehouse, set in the wastes of an industrial estate in Thamesmead, is a prototype for Fosters' later and better known Sainsbury Centre at the University of East Anglia (1975–8). The skin to the building is a blue stove-enamelled corrugated steel sheet wrapped over a system of steel portal frames: by breaking with the traditional relationships of wall, eaves and roof the building manages to resemble an extremely large industrial product.

Unlike the majority of recent buildings in England it is meticulously detailed, emphasizing its industrial design lineage. Nevertheless, as with the Sainsbury Centre, it is still possible to appraise the architecture.

The end bay of an industrial hangar is functional, and that of a Greek temple is rhetorical or symbolic: by contrast, the gable ends of Modern Art Glass and the Sainsbury Centre do not play a part in an industrial process, nor do they mark a formal entry. The lines of the building could be endlessly extruded; its length is determined only by practical considerations, and the end walls simply mark off a length of an ideally limitless form.

Housing 1982–4 U38
10–12 Albion Drive, 15–37 and 28–30 Shrubland Road and 37–43 Brownlow Road E8
London Borough of Hackney; Colquhoun and Miller
≹ London Fields

Taking its cue from the neighbouring mid-nineteenth century semi-detached villas, this 'infill housing' goes some way to correcting the mistakes of previous generations of public housing. Instead of distinguishing between people with and without children or between houses and flats, the project proposes a more generous semi-detached villa. This can then be used either to infill small gaps without disruption to neighbouring houses, or to make terraces for the larger sites. The street is thus reconfirmed as an important space. The buildings have a desirably loose

fit between plan and elevation, though the central column has always appeared too spindly.

Housing 1984   U39
22–5 Church Crescent E9
London Borough of Hackney; Colquhoun
and Miller
⇌ London Fields
Here is further evidence of this firm's
commitment to an intelligent reworking
of London's house types. As at Caversham
Road C16, the overhanging hipped roof,
the second-floor loggia and the extensive
white-rendered blank panel to the first
floor give the buildings a generosity not
normally associated with public housing.
Although the brief called for only four
large houses, it is possible to imagine this
type forming the basis of a street or local
district.

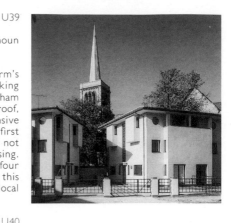

Docklands Light Railway   U40
1984–7
Architects: Atkins, Sheppard Fidler;
consulting engineers: W S Atkins
Although much of the new railway runs on
existing track, all the stations were new:
such a complete architectural programme
had not been attempted since the southern extension of the Northern Line in the
1920s W11. The 'kit-of-parts' used for
these stations gives them a provisional air:
the parts are neither substantial enough
nor well enough detailed to provide shelter or satisfaction. The 'cheerful' red,
white and blue colours of the railway's
livery, relentlessly applied to the architecture, have become an irritating cliché.
(Holden's work on the Northern Line by
contrast looks more mature: generally
neutral backgrounds were enlivened with
brightly enamelled signs.)
The original modest plans for the railway
were overtaken by the colossal scale of
some of the developments in Docklands,
and the platforms had to be lengthened to
take new, longer trains. The system is
being extended to Stratford, with new
stations designed by Ahrends Burton and
Koralek.

Pumping station 1985–8   U41
Stewart Street E14
John Outram Associates
DLR Blackwall
A shed for automatic pumping machinery
decorated in Outram's cheerful, eclectic
and thoughtfully detailed architecture, to
an allegorical programme which remains
obscure to the observer.

China Wharf 1986–8   U42
29 Mill Street SE1
CZWG Architects (Campbell,
Zogolovich, Wilkinson and Gough)
↔ Tower Bridge
China Wharf is not a Chinese dragon but a
housing building of seventeen flats with
offices on the ground and first floors. It has
three distinct and separate elevations.
The façade to Mill Street is clad in London
stock bricks with gault brick and blue
engineering brick details to match the
neighbouring warehouses. The courtyard
façade is stuccoed and painted white to
reflect light into the area. The river façade
is more fully glazed and its concrete frame
is painted red.

Housing 'Compass Point' 1987   U43
Manchester Road E14
Jeremy Dixon BDP
DLR Island Gardens

A further episode in Dixon's thoughtful programme to rework existing housing types and forms, the buildings are arranged on either side of an axis running at right angles to the Thames. The treatment of the frontages to the Thames is exemplary. The noticeably low floor-heights and the absence of chimneys are difficult to reconcile with 'traditional' or historical forms, and the houses' modest styling was only too vulnerable to the exigencies of the 'design-and-build' contract.

Cascades 1987–8   U44
2–4 Westferry Road E14
CZWG Architects (Campbell, Zogolovich, Wilkinson and Gough)
DLR Heron Quays

This heroic housing project interrupted a period in which there was a virtual moratorium on 'high rise' housing. Cascades recalls ideas in student housing projects from the late 1950s and early 1960s in which the inclined section was an almost obligatory ingredient. In this respect it is a nostalgic building incorporating various influences — the spirit of Le Corbusier's Unité d'Habitation in Marseille, the iconography of warehouses and ships and a character that is in a way curiously Swedish. If only the inclined shape had been generated by a funicular lift and not a stair.

Financial Times printing works   U45
1987–8
240 East India Dock Road, Blackwall Tunnel Approach E14
Nicholas Grimshaw & Partners
DLR Poplar

The *Daily Express* building L116 displayed to the pedestrian the machines on which the newspaper was printed. Grimshaw's building does the same for the *Financial Times*, but exhibits the appropriately huge shed to the passing motorist. Set between solid blocks of offices and services at each end, the window to the presses is constructed of frameless sheets of glass restrained by free-standing mullions of oval section.

Reuters 1987–8   U46
Richard Rogers Partnership
Aspen Way E14
DLR Brunswick

Built quickly for a company which deals in information, this very large building is sited over a dock at a bend in the River Thames. Plant, services and computers are at the lower levels, and above these are offices faced with a changeable system of either glass or opaque panels. The escape stairs are placed outside the main envelope. At roof level, an exposed steel structure cages a variable arrangement of plant and communication aerials.
Like many of Docklands' buildings, this one suffers from the almost complete lack of a rational, normal infrastructure. Consequently Reuters' site is entered past a bus stop through a small gate set in a substantial steel fence.

Housing 1987–9   U47
Roy Square, Narrow Street E14
Ian Ritchie Architects
DLR Limehouse

Much of the new housing in Docklands is silly in both arrangement and style. This scheme is an exception and is one of the best. Modelled on the generalized 'block', the 77 flats are arranged round and reached from a common landscaped courtyard which is raised above a garage. The style is assured, calm and timeless. The introspection of the scheme can be explained by its hostile and uncertain surroundings.

Finland Quays West 1989   U48
Onega Gate, Redriff Road SE16
Richard Reid Architects
⊖ Surrey Docks

This is one of the better housing developments in Docklands. The seven linked pavilions form an emphatic front to Greenland Dock, and unlike most recent housing in Docklands they address the large expanse of water with a robust and appropriate scale. The Paragon X5 in Blackheath is a reference acknowledged by the architect. The buildings give the impression externally of large urban villas in multiple occupancy. For the resident the interior gives a desirable variety of living conditions.

Canary Wharf Tower 1991   U49
1 Canada Square E14
Cesar Pelli and Associates with Adamson Associates (Toronto) and Frederick Gibberd, Coombes and Partners
DLR Canary Wharf, Heron Quays

The tower is 244m (800ft) high and is Britain's tallest building, Europe's second tallest and the jewel in the crown of Olympia and York's Canary Wharf development. It provides a landmark for the development and is now clearly visible from the hopfields of Kent in the south to the ridge of Hampstead Heath in the north. Unlike the fumbling pastiche of its immediate neighbours at Canary Wharf, Pelli's tower has a straightforward and abstract repetitiveness appropriate to very tall buildings. From a strictly proportional point of view it would have been enhanced by an additional twenty floors, and the crowning pyramid might have been more enjoyable as a public place.

Isle of Dogs Neighbourhood   U50
Centre 1991
Marsh Wall E14
Chassay Architects
DLR South Quay

This scheme was the result of a limited competition organized by the LDDC to provide community facilities for the London Borough of Tower Hamlets, and is one of the very few public commissions within Docklands. The separation of the rotunda from the supporting wall of council offices is now a familiar image of the town hall. But the project forms a convincing composition, and the cylindrical form of the council chamber announces the entry to March Wall.

Section V: Outer London, south-west

This section contains much good architecture, yet is dominated by its huge open spaces: the royal parks of Bushy, Hampton Court and Richmond, and the common lands of Wimbledon and Putney. The last three are on high ground to the east of the Thames which here is narrow and flows south to north. The tidal river meets its first weir at Teddington, near Richmond, which with Kingston is one of the two market towns on the Thames. Both have now been engulfed by twentieth-century London, but have their own histories outside the scope of this book.

Up to the eighteenth century the area consisted of open land: the royal palace at Hampton Court V1, manors, and court officials' houses were scattered between the Thames-side villages and market towns. Alexander Pope, Burlington's house-poet, set up house in Twickenham in 1719, quickly establishing it as the Hampstead of its day, and Walpole's Strawberry Hill V6, opposite Ham, continued the fashion. During the course of the eighteenth century, the towns and villages were peppered with middle-class and aristocratic houses (for example Montpelier Row V4 and Manresa House V7).

The nineteenth century brought the London and South Western Railway, running south of Kingston, and making the area suitable for city commuters' suburban houses. Twentieth-century development then joined the towns and villages together, closing round the open spaces. The heroic exceptions to the standard suburban pattern were the two LCC housing schemes at Alton V8 and V9, on high ground overlooking Putney Heath and Richmond Park. The latter is the most successful realization of Le Corbusier's theories in England: the view of the point blocks from Richmond Park remains a powerful reminder of a possible alternative to the existing city.

Roof of the Great Hall, Hampton Court

Great Gatehouse

Fountain Court

Hampton Court Palace VI

1514–1882

Sir Christopher Wren 1689–94; William Kent 1732

⇌ Hampton Court

Hampton Court is England's Tudor masterpiece, and although planned on a royal scale it was not originally a royal palace. The historical and physical development can be briefly summarized:

In 1514 Cardinal Wolsey bought a medieval manor from the Order of St John of Jerusalem; in the years that followed he was to make it the grandest house in England, and in 1529 he presented it to Henry VIII in an effort to retain royal favour. Wolsey's palace then consisted of the west front (without wings), the Base Court, the Clock Court (with different buildings on the north and south sides), buildings round the master carpenter's court, the Chapel and the cloisters to the west of it. Henry embarked on further building: the Great Hall is attributed to him, and he added a courtyard on the side of the present Fountain Court, and another north-east of the Chapel. He also remodelled Wolsey's structures around Clock Court and added wings to the west façade. Henry's successors used the palace as a royal retreat, and no further significant changes were made until Charles II ordered the construction of the long axial canal and the radiating avenues through Home Park from the 'French' formal gardens in front of the east block. These were the first moves in transforming Hampton Court from a very large medieval manor into a 'European' royal palace. William and Mary accomplished the final transformation when William decided to make Hampton Court his Versailles. In 1689 Wren started work with plans for the wholesale reconstruction of Wolsey's Tudor palace, and by William's death the structural work was complete on the new Fountain Court, the south range of Clock Court and the new Orangery. Luckily, Wren's comprehensive plans were not to be realized. Minor works continued for the next two centuries and the result is an extraordinary catalogue of English architecture.

The main approach to Hampton Court is from the south-west, crossing the Thames over Hampton Court Bridge (rebuilt in 1933 by Sir Edwin Lutyens in brick and Portland stone). The immediate impression is of the magnificent west façade's many twisted chimneys, turrets and castellations, all in red brick. The perpendicular Gothic façade is the grandest of its date in England. The **Great Gatehouse** leads into Wolsey's relatively modest **Base Court**, whose profile is broken by the west front of the **Great Hall**, in **Clock Court** beyond. The Base Court's brickwork is decorated with terracotta medallions by Giovanni da Majano, the earliest example of Italian Renaissance craftsmanship in England. Anne Boleyn's Gateway leads into Clock Court, which has the finest architecture in the Palace. To the north is Henry VIII's Great Hall, built over Wolsey's cellars and completed in 1536. To the south, Wolsey's range is unexpectedly concealed by Wren's grand Portland stone colonnade, which forms an entrance to the King's apartments. The new, white, classical architecture of this lofty arcade was as revolutionary in its time as the architecture of modernism was to the Edwardians at the beginning of this century. Between the colonnade and the Hall to the east are a range and doorway by William Kent, built in 1732, and one of the earliest examples of the Gothic Revival.

With Wren's 31 m × 36 m (101 ft × 117 ft) **Fountain Court** the classical transformation is complete. When it is compared with the court of the Louvre, 91 m (300 ft) square, which was Wren's model, it becomes clear that the standard bay of Fountain Court is a device for a much bigger idea. As Sir John Summerson has observed, 'the Fountain Court is a rather apologetic substitute for the Privy Court originally proposed, and the crowded fenestration gives an uncomfortably restricted sensation'. To the south are the King's apartments, to the north and east the Queen's, connected by the two-storey communication gallery. Fountain Court leads out to the east front of William and Mary's 'Versailles'. Wren was not to build his original designs at Hampton Court, with the grand central dome, end pavilions, and expressive detail, and as a result 'the mobile silhouette and the decorative intricacies have all disappeared ... the skyline is dead level and from an excess of variation Wren has passed over to something bordering on monotony' (Summerson). Despite Wren's lapses, however, Hampton Court shows marvellously the development from a Tudor manor house, built with defence in mind, to a mathematically-based, open and confident classical palace.

Roehampton House V2
1710–12
Roehampton Lane SW15
Thomas Archer, enlarged by Sir Edwin
Lutyens
⇌Barnes
Archer's first London work, built origin-
ally as a country house for Thomas Cary,
had a dignified brick façade, crowned
originally by a 'gargantuan broken pedi-
ment' (Pevsner). It was later extended by
Lutyens and converted into a hospital.

St Mary 1714–15 V3
Church Street, Twickenham
remodelled by John James
⇌Twickenham
James was the architect of St George,
Hanover Square J5, and his work in the
small riverside village of Twickenham was
clearly of metropolitan character. The
robust pedimented Tuscan decoration to
the sides is quite different from the
refinement of St George's, and more like
the work of James's contemporary,
Hawksmoor.

Montpelier Row 1722 V4
Twickenham
⇌St Margarets
Those visiting Twickenham's parish
church V3 or Marble Hill V5 should take in
this exquisite early Georgian terrace, the
best of the district's many surviving
houses of the period.

Marble Hill 1723–8 V5
Richmond Road, Twickenham
Henry Herbert, Roger Morris
⇌St Margarets
Herbert was a contemporary of Burlington, an amateur architect, and heir to
Inigo Jones's Wilton House, Salisbury.
After the publication of Campbell's
Vitruvius Britannicus in 1715 the house
became one of several models for the
eighteenth-century villa. Painstakingly
restored by the GLC, the interiors are
gaunt, giving the curious feeling (as at
Burlington's Chiswick House T6) that the
building has just been finished and the
owners have not yet moved in. The
exterior lacks edge and Palladio's exquisite sense of proportion; the outer
windows are placed firmly in the *centres* of
their bays, and the ground floor is clumsy.
The partnership of Herbert and Morris,
Master Carpenter to the Office of
Ordnance, went on to design the Palladian
bridge at Wilton.

Strawberry Hill 1749–76   V6
Waldegrave Road, Twickenham
Horace Walpole and his 'Committee of
Taste', including John Chute, Thomas
Gray, Richard Bentley, Thomas Pitt and
Robert Adam
⇄Strawberry Hill

As Lord Burlington is associated with the
birth of English Palladianism, so the name
of Horace Walpole (the younger son of
Prime Minister Sir Robert Walpole) is
synonymous with the advent of the
'Picturesque'. As an antidote to the
prevailing Palladian taste, Strawberry Hill
was the most influential Gothic Revival
building in England. But like Vanbrugh's
Castle U11 in Greenwich, it did not use
Gothic in the scholarly and medieval
fashion of Pugin or Ruskin in the following
century. This was a period of pluralism in
architecture (see Chambers' Pagoda T9 at
Kew), and the forms of Strawberry Hill
have as much to do with Chinese fretwork
as with Gothic tracery. In 1747 Walpole
bought a small riverside property,
and over the next thirty years made a
series of additions, each supervised by
his 'Committee of Taste'. Meanwhile
members of the committee scoured the
churches and abbeys of northern Europe
for inspiration – the tombs in Westminster Abbey were to reappear in
Strawberry Hill as mantelpieces.

The informal and asymmetrical disposition of the house is Walpole's principal
contribution. The entrance, reached from
the north past the little cloister, leads into
Bentley's Staircase Hall (1753) which rises
to an armoury. Beyond is the famous
Library (1754) by Chute (Bentley's design
was rejected by the committee). This is a
remarkable room: the fireplace is bor-

rowed from the tomb of John of Eltham in
Westminster Abbey, and the gilded bookcases derive from the screen in old St
Paul's Cathedral. The next room is the
Holbein Chamber (1759), also by Bentley,
with an imitation of the tripartite ogival
screen from Rouen Cathedral.

The Gallery, designed by Thomas Pitt, is
the most dramatic space of all. The
vaulting is borrowed from the aisles of
Henry VII's Chapel K8 at Westminster
Abbey, but the bays, recesses and mirrors
refer to the sensuous interiors of Robert
Adam. Walpole instructed Adam himself
(despite a declared antipathy to Adam's
'gingerbread and snippets of embroidery')
to design the Beauclerk Room (1766),
where the fireplace is borrowed from the
tomb of Edward the Confessor at Westminster. The Chapel (1763) and the Great
Bed Chamber (1772) should also be noted.
The house is now occupied (and excellently maintained) by St Mary's Roman
Catholic Training College.

Manresa House   V7
ex Bessborough House
1750–68
Roehampton Lane SW15
Sir William Chambers
⇄Barnes

Notwithstanding Burlington's work at
Chiswick T6, this is probably the most
authentically Palladian house in London:
the proportions of the Ionic portico are
copied faithfully from Palladio's work in
Vicenza. It is now a Jesuit college.

Housing, Alton East Estate   V8
1952–5
Portsmouth Road SW15
LCC Architects Department
⇄Barnes

Neutral and democratic Sweden was the
only European country with a significant
State housing achievement during the
Second World War. It is no coincidence
therefore that 'Swedish modern' should
be the style adopted by most architects
who worked for the Welfare State in the
immediate post-war era; apart from the
new towns (Harlow and Crawley, for
example) the Alton East Estate on the
edge of Richmond Park is the definitive
version of it. For its residents, the mixed
development of towers and terraced
houses, set among the mature trees of its
semi-rural 11 ha (28 acre) site (housing
2800 people), must have seemed a long
way from the memory of the war-time

city. For its socialist designers Alton East's
forms embodied the triumph of 'people's
detailing'. See also Alton West Estate V9.

Housing, Alton West Estate V9
1955–9
Roehampton Lane SW15
LCC Architects Department
⇌ Barnes

On one of the few sites appropriate to it, Le Corbusier's *Ville Radieuse* nearly found its London embodiment on 40 ha (100 acres) of rolling land overlooking Richmond Park. About 1850 dwellings are arranged in three building types: the eleven-storey slabs of maisonettes to the north, two clusters of twelve-storey point blocks, and rows of three-and four-storey maisonettes. Schools, shops, a library and old people's dwellings are scattered among these. All the buildings except the maisonettes are made of and clad in concrete, in a style as close to Le Corbusier's own as precise English workmanship would allow. Viewed from Richmond Park, the ensemble does look very like a city of separate big buildings set in parkland.

While the designs were the work of enthusiastic young architects anxious that the repetition of the Swedish-style mixed development of Alton East V8 should not occur, the layout lacks both a Corbusian geometrical order and a sensible circulation system. The copies of the *Unité* are nothing like social entities lifted off the ground: too small and without the new social order which the model required, they obstinately remain just blocks of flats – 'workers' housing'. The square point blocks derived from Swedish models are much more successful, and the group set among mature cedars suggests high-style high-rise. The appalling rows of maisonettes, which have weathered very badly, are best ignored.

Flats, Langham House 1958 V10
Langham House Gardens,
Ham Street, Richmond
James Stirling and James Gowan
⊖ Richmond

Built in the long, narrow back garden of Langham House (a Georgian mansion overlooking the common) these thirty flats hold an important position in the development of post-war English architecture. In opposition to the limp 'Swedish modern' of the Festival of Britain years, they show allegiance to the Dutch De Stijl movement of the 1920s and to Le Corbusier's Maisons Jaoul in Paris (1956). The careful, mannered, concrete and brick detailing (Jaoul is intentionally far less precise) both inside and out was later seen as evidence of the emerging 'Brutalist' sensibility.

The term 'Brutalism' has generally and inaccurately been applied just to buildings of exposed concrete. For the avant garde generation after the war the term reflected their frustration with the architectural establishment and their wish to get into better company. 'Mies is great but Corb communicates' was a maxim of Peter Smithson, the most vocal of this generation. James Stirling's essay entitled *From Garches to Jaoul* underlined a similar concern.

House and guest house 1970 V11
22 Parkside SW19
Richard and Su Rogers
⊖ Wimbledon

A fine example of suburban domestic architecture, these houses are a successful attempt to free the London house from its traditional masonry straitjacket. The programme was used as a vehicle for an exercise in possible serial production, but this is a one-off realization. It casually uses non-domestic building techniques – single-span steel frame, huge sliding panes of glass, sandwich wall panels – all of which are taken for granted in North America, especially round Chicago. The arrangement of the separate guest house facing the street, the larger house behind, and the delightful forecourt and lush planting, creates a small masterpiece of site planning.

Offices, shops and **flats** 1986–8   V12
Hill Street, Bridge Street, Richmond
Erith and Terry
⊖ Richmond
Next to the Thames, this redevelopment
of existing buildings and two ranges of
new ones roughly encloses three new
open spaces. The mostly ill-proportioned
façades of the new parts are in an assort-
ment of weary classical styles from a
variety of periods and places and in several
different materials. The resulting picturesque jumble has the newness of a poor
film set. Several of the pitched roofs which
were designed to last hundreds of years
were severely damaged in a storm in 1989.

Section W: Outer London, south

'South London' is a series of one-time villages and early eighteenth-century suburbs embedded since the mid-nineteenth century in the massive expansion of London. Those who live north of the river tend to see it as an incomprehensible obstacle to be negotiated *en route* for Gatwick airport or the south coast; but for south Londoners it has the advantages of being within easy reach of central London and not too far from open countryside.

Clapham was an early and rather grand suburb, with fine eighteenth-century terraces contemporary with Church Row in Hampstead. Mansions for wealthy bankers were built overlooking the Common, and from 1825 Thomas Cubitt laid out the elegant streets and imposing residences of Clapham Park; further south, Streatham was another well-endowed early suburb.

In the mid-eighteenth century Camberwell, Peckham and Dulwich to the east were villages, separated from each other by extensive fields, with hamlets such as Peckham Rye in between. These village nuclei are now hardly recognizable, but the commons at Clapham, Wandsworth and Tooting Bec, and the parks of Brockwell and Dulwich, are clues to a more agrarian past. Sir John Soane's Mausoleum and picture gallery of 1811–14 at Dulwich W3 are among the few significant buildings.

The development of the railways and arterial roads in the nineteenth century transformed the area. Ribbon development centred on Brixton Hill, Streatham Hill and Streatham High Road, which today have a character rather like the North American 'strip'. Decaying nineteenth-century semi-detached houses alternate with shopping parades, the spaces between and behind being occupied by large and mediocre twentieth-century local authority housing estates.

Between the wars the Northern Line underground was extended into Surrey: Colliers Wood, South Wimbledon and finally Morden (completed in 1926) were added to London's apparently endless suburbs, and Charles Holden built more excellent stations W11.

Clapham High Street

Bishop's Palace WI
cl410–20, 1510–20, 1765, 1867
Bishop's Avenue,
off Fulham Palace Road SW6
⊖ Putney Bridge

Fulham's principal historic monument is
more of a comfortable manor house than a
palace. The estate belonged to the Bishops
of London from the end of the seventh
century until 1868, when it was taken over
by the Church Commissioners. The Palace
has lost two of its chief external attract-
ions, as Pevsner has pointed out: the
direct connection with the river was
disrupted when the embankment was
built (cl775) and in 1921 the famous
Danish moat was filled in.

The courtyard (1510–20) is the principal
space, gentle and domestic in scale, and
built of brick with a black diaper pattern.
The bell tower is eighteenth-century, and

Butterfield's chapel (1866) is in stark
contrast: Gothic, with hard polychrome
brickwork.

The village

Pond cottages

Dulwich Village W2
SE21 18th century
⇄ North Dulwich

A pleasantly leafy outlying village, whose
remaining Georgian houses are now embedded in twentieth-century suburbia.

Walk south down College Road to the mill
pond, opposite Dulwich College W6, with
its minute and charmingly rural Pond
Cottages. Further still down this road are
the only remaining working toll-gate and
road in London.

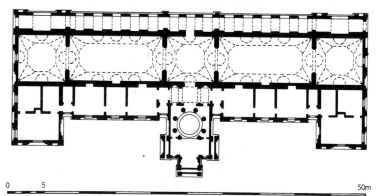

0   5   50m

Dulwich Mausoleum and W3
Picture Gallery 1811–14
College Road and Gallery Road
SE21
Sir John Soane
⇄ West Dulwich

London's earliest nineteenth-century
public art gallery, Soane's Picture Gallery
was built for Dulwich College W6 under
the bequest of Sir Francis Bourgeois, and
represents the most advanced stage of
Soane's personal abstraction of the classical. The gallery contains the collection of

paintings brought together by the art
dealer Noel Desenfans, intended for the
Empress of Russia but left to Bourgeois,
who in turn left them to the College. The
building also houses a small mausoleum
dedicated to both Desenfans and Bourgeois, and included almshouses – a touching commemorative ensemble. Badly
bombed in 1944, by 1953 it had been
renovated, with the almshouses converted to give extra gallery space (which is
not top-lit, and is therefore inconsistent
with the rest of the gallery).

Mausoleum

In 1980 it was redecorated in accordance with Soane's original colour scheme: burnt sienna, grey-green walls, and gilded edges to the arched apertures. Much has been written both about this complex building and about Soane's illusionist devices. The detachment of elements, the hovering planes of brickwork to the exterior and resultant slits of space, and the inventive decorative themes give this disarmingly modest building a pedigree well in advance of its time. The recent forms of Louis Kahn come to mind, as do the less recent ones of J N L Durand.

St Luke 1822 W4
Knight's Hill and
Norwood High Street SE27
F O Bedford
≷West Norwood

The general feeling of Bedford's many churches is that of correctness: here he manages to make even the usually sumptuous Corinthian look restrained. The order of the portico is an unusual variant of Corinthian, with fewer leaves and square ends to the flutes. The only decorative motif used in the design of the church is the acanthus. The interior was remodelled in 1878.

St Matthew, Brixton 1822   W5
Brixton Hill SW2
Charles F Porden
⊖ Brixton
Another Waterloo church, whose grand plain Doric portico is, since the destruction of Hardwick's propylaeum at Euston, perhaps the best in London. A century earlier, Gibbs had shown how to unite tower and portico at St Martin-in-the-Fields K40; Porden shows how to disunite them again, by placing his fine three-stage tower at the *east* end of his temple. Porden did for Doric what the Inwoods so splendidly did for Ionic in their St Pancras Church G21 of exactly the same date, the building of which he supervised.

Dulwich College 1866–70   W6
College Road SE21
Charles Barry Junior
⇌ West Dulwich
The College was founded in 1619, and the buildings from its foundation to the mid-nineteenth century stand on either side of Gallery Road facing the end of Dulwich Village. The newer buildings, to the south in College Road, are by Sir Charles's son and conform to the type of the Victorian institution: large, symmetrical and ornate, in Italian Renaissance rather than Gothic style. The central block contains the hall, but the northern block lacks the tower which was intended to make it symmetrical with the southern.

Shaftesbury Park Estate   W7
1872–7
Lavender Hill, Eversleigh Road
and Latchmere Road SW11
⇌ Clapham Junction
An early estate of 1135 two-storey cottages, thirty shops and a church built by the Artisans, Labourers and General Dwellings Company. Unlike the tenements of similar philanthropic enterprises, this estate of simple terraced houses remains pleasant to live in. The details are Gothic: the street-corners have turrets, and the houses have paired entrances under bracketed and steeply pitched porches. The streets are formally planted with plane trees.

Dixcote 1897   W8
North Drive SW16
C F A Voysey
⊖ Tooting Bec
All Voysey's familiar usages are evident in this big house overlooking Tooting Bec Common — the white pebble-dash, battered chimneys, horizontal windows with stone trim, wide low front door, and heart motifs on the garage doors' strap hinges. But only the design is his; it was built by another architect following Voysey's resignation from the job after a disagreement.

Brixton Town Hall 1908　　W9
Brixton Hill SW2
Septimus Warwick
≹Brixton
A spirited exercise in the Edwardian
mixed style. For Warwick's later, calmer
architecture see his Wellcome Building
G61.

Arding and Hobbs　　W10
Department Store 1910
Lavender Hill SW11
J Gibson
≹Clapham Junction
A fragment of Wigmore Street in
Clapham Junction (designed by the architects of Debenham and Freebody), Arding
and Hobbs represents similar Edwardian
aspirations towards urbanity. The grand
curved corner, topped by a cupola, and
the first-floor timber screen have more
affinity with Mountford's nearby Town
Hall than with the modest three-storey
commercial frontages of nineteenth-
century Lavender Hill.

Northern Line　　W11
Underground Stations 1926
Clapham South, Balham, Tooting Bec,
Tooting Broadway, Collier's Wood,
South Wimbledon and Morden
Charles Holden
The extension of the London Under-
ground in the 1920s was the initiative of
Frank Pick, the Managing Director of the
Underground Group of Companies. In
1923 Pick and Holden started a long
collaboration. Following his work on the
extension of the Northern Line to
Edgware in 1925, Holden tackled the
southern extension the following year.
The stations of Clapham South, Balham,
Tooting, Collier's Wood, South Wimbledon and Morden are remarkably consistent in design. The stone frontage on a
corner site, and the Doric columns supporting a triangular window over the
entrance were Holden's above-ground

expressions of the invisible but unifying
network of Frank Pick's Underground.
See also Holden's Piccadilly Line stations
R23 and T25.

Pullman Court 1935　　W12
Streatham Hill SW2
Frederick Gibberd
≹Streatham Hill
One of the most lively early modern (early
for England) designs in London, Pullman
Court confidently combines the best of
the lightness, picturesqueness and hygiene promised by modern architecture
for the progressive middle classes. The
three- and seven-storey blocks of flats are
arranged with studied asymmetry around
a green containing fine mature trees.
While the buildings seem rather close
together, the ensemble is a successful
pioneering design which brings the air of a
Mediterranean holiday resort to
Streatham.

Six Pillars 1935   W13
Crescent Wood Road SE26
Val Harding and Tecton
⇌Sydenham Hill
The high roof terrace, a wing of eccentric
shape (governed by the site) and the six
pillars at the entrance are the 'modernist'
attachments to this otherwise simple two-
storey house.

Children's Home 1960   W14
11–12 Frogmore SW18
James Stirling and James Gowan
⊖East Putney
With the old people's home in Blackheath
U29 (also 1961), these two houses for
abandoned children in Putney were the
last buildings of the Stirling and Gowan
partnership before it dissolved in 1963.
The buildings are in brick and are of a
domestic scale, and the outside play areas
are partially covered by the bedrooms at
the first-floor level. The scheme is
modest, but the stepped plan and the
development of the corner window anticipate work of both Stirling and Gowan in
their later independent practices –
Gowan's Trafalgar Road flats U31 in
Greenwich, and Stirling's Halls of
Residence at St Andrew's University,
Scotland (1964).

Pollard's Hill Housing 1971   W15
SW16
London Borough of Merton Architects
Department; P J Whittle, design by
P Bell, D Lea, R MacCormac,
N Alexander
⇌Norbury
During the 1960s Professor Leslie Martin
and Lionel March conducted research at
the Cambridge School of Architecture
into the Fresnel Square and its applic-
ability to housing. This was a significant
contribution to the low-rise high density
housing debate, later published in Lionel
March's *Urban Space and Structure*. The
resulting perimeter planning technique
(essentially a rationalization of the
eighteenth-century London square) was
first built at Pollard's Hill. The aim was to
combine a planning density of 250 people
per hectare (100 ppa) in three-storey
houses with a significant gain in public
open space. Its problems, however, derive
from the rigid and indivisible nature of the
plan, the 'double-fronted' effect of the
Radburn principle and the emptiness of
the central space.

Section X: Outer London, south-east

Eltham Palace X1 was established on the ridge overlooking the Thames in the fourteenth century, but it was not until the late eighteenth century that this section developed as a suburb. The village of Blackheath and the heath itself had been the setting for many important events in English history, but by the eighteenth century it was a fashionable suburb of the small town of Greenwich. Architectural respectability of a sort was bestowed by Vanbrugh's building of his own house U11, south of Greenwich Park. Sporadic additions were made to the village, but the grandest house and groups are from the end of the Georgian period: the very fine Paragon and Paragon House X5.

Blackheath was joined by Lewisham as the scene of early Victorian suburban experiments; their leafy, low-density, mildly Italianate housing now provides relief from the carpet of twentieth-century semis of the commuter suburbs, encouraged by the automation of the Southern Railway, and epitomized by Bromley.

Blackheath

Eltham Palace 1479   X1
King John's Walk SE9
⇌ Mottingham

High on the ridge which forms the southern edge of the Thames valley, Eltham was a royal palace in the four-teenth century, but the moated palace is of the fifteenth. The Hall is one of the four surviving examples in London – the others are at Westminster K6, Hampton Court V1 and Guildhall L7. It is 30 m (100 ft) long and 11 m (36 ft) wide, with a splendid hammerbeam roof. Unlike Westminster it has high windows, except at the dais end where they are much deeper. The rest of the Palace has disappeared, except for some fragments, and all the other build-ings on the site are later, but see the Courtyard for a pleasant accumulation of different styles and periods.

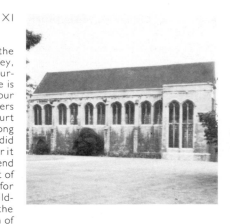

Morden College 1695   X2
Morden Road SE3
attributed to Sir Christopher Wren,
mason Edward Strong
⇌ Blackheath

A very beautiful almshouse group stand-ing in its own extensive grounds, Morden College was founded by Sir John Morden, a Turkey merchant, for less successful retired merchants. He and his wife are commemorated by statues set in a double arch in the pediment above the west door. The buildings have been attributed to Wren, and he was on the Greenwich Hospital Commission with Sir John. The central courtyard has low arcades sup-ported by Tuscan columns with small central pediments; opposite the entrance is the Chapel, aligned with a lamp standard in the form of a Roman Doric column in the centre of the quadrangle. Morden College and the Royal Hospital,

Chelsea, N2 are the best surviving examples of Wren's domestic, as opposed to his monumental, architecture.

Severndroog Castle 1784   X3
Castlewood,
off Shooters Hill Road SE18
W Jupp
⇌ Eltham Park

A triangular Gothic tower, secluded in the trees of Castlewood, commands the strategic high ground above Woolwich (Shooters Hill was a sixteenth-century beacon hill). Erected by Sir William James's widow to celebrate the capture of Severndroog Castle, Malabar, in 1755, the tower commands magnificent views over London but unfortunately is now closed to the public.

Colonnade House c1790   X4
South Row SE3
⇌ Blackheath

A fine detached house facing a small pond on the heath – the triangular composition of one, two and three storeys is held together by the long Tuscan colonnade.

The Paragon SE3 c1790   X5
Michael Searles
⮞Blackheath

An astonishingly grand group: fourteen very large semi-detached houses, linked by enclosed single-storey Tuscan colonnades, are set out in a shallow crescent overlooking the heath. The style is the summit of Georgian taste: spare Coade stone string-courses, arched heads to the ground-floor windows and, behind parapets, mansard slate roofs with thermal windows to the attics. Walk round the back, where the houses have pairs of curved bay windows with huge areas of glass. **Paragon House**, in South Row and Pond Road, is a grand, detached version of the Paragon's semis, with the same very large semicircular bay at the back, but with the elegant front door on the side.

Blackheath Park Estate SE3 c1825   X6
⮞Blackheath

An early suburb of tree-lined avenues, built on the grounds of Sir Gregory Page's estate following the demolition of the house in 1787. The open pattern of Victorian terraces and villas has now been filled in with more recent suburban housing.

Nunhead Cemetery 1840   X7
Linden Grove SE15
J B Bunning
⇌Nunhead

This cemetery is one of the series laid out in the 1830s and '40s, but unlike Highgate R9 or Kensal Green T14 it has no good architectural tombs, nor any famous architects buried there. The entrance has gateposts decorated with inverted torches in cast iron, and with its Soanian lodges is suitably severe. The derelict octagonal chapel at the top of the hill presides over the tombs, which are now hidden in a small forest.

Red House 1859   X8
Red House Lane, Bexleyheath
Philip Webb
⇌Bexleyheath

William Morris and Webb were co-workers for Street, and Morris asked the young Webb, who was then twenty-eight, to design a house in the country for him and his wife; this is the relaxed, comfortable (though large) red-brick result. The style is vague, with some medieval and some early eighteenth-century features, and overhanging barn-like tiled eaves. The interiors are bare, but with occasional crafted flourishes like the brick fireplace. It is an important design: a welcome relief from the contemporary overheated designs of the metropolis, and a reassertion of specifically English domestic values in which some architects today still find inspiration.

Horniman Museum   X9
1896–1901
100 London Road SE23
C H Townsend
⇌Forest Hill

C H Townsend was one of the most original of the Arts and Crafts architects. The Horniman Museum, contemporary with his design for the Whitechapel Gallery L96, is undoubtedly his masterpiece. It has a strong asymmetrical composition when seen from the street; the massive clock tower with its circular cornice is set to one side of the large blank façade. Behind this lie the top-lit galleries, which house the anthropological collection of the client, F J Horniman MP. The exterior shows the influence of the American architect H H Richardson in the almost exclusive use of smooth stone, an abundance of relief ornament, the battered walls and scarcity of openings. The large and central mosaic panel on the outside of the museum was executed by the painter Robert Anning Bell, a member of the Art Workers' Guild. Townsend believed interiors and exteriors could be treated quite separately: the Free Style expression of the exterior contrasts with the interiors, which are simple and functionally planned. Townsend added the lecture hall and library in 1910, using the same materials but a simplified language.

Pioneer Health Centre X10
1934–6
St Mary's Road SE15
Sir Owen Williams
⇌Queen's Road Peckham

Of all the home-grown contributors to modern architecture in England during the 1930s, Sir Owen Williams is one of the most impressive and enigmatic. His engineer's approach, coupled with a refusal to be part of the architectural coterie, encouraged the Williams enigma. His insistence on invention allowed him to pursue pioneering 'objectivity' without a residue of sentiment for previous styles.

Three of his London buildings have unfortunately already been demolished – Sainsbury's warehouse, Stamford Street SE1 (1934), Lilley and Skinner's warehouse, Pentonville Road N1 (1935), and the Provincial Newspapers Limited offices, Salisbury Square EC4 (1937). However, the Pioneer Health Centre, known as the Peckham experiment, remains as an example of Williams' inspiration to the new architecture.

Doctors I H Pearse and G S Williamson, founders of the Peckham Health Centre, believed that preventive action was the solution to society's ills: the Centre was to provide a place where families could meet to discuss their problems and trained staff could advise on treatment. The extensive sporting and recreational facilities could serve 2000 families at a

time, in a catchment area of 5–6000 families. Peckham has parallels with the city clubs of Russian constructivist utopias of the 1920s, but Williams, the practical man, was detached from such theory. His design follows the warehouse/industrial type of his other works, the central space being filled by the grand swimming pool and separated by glass screens from the other ancillary activities.

The exterior, with six gently curved bay windows, has always seemed a rather weak afterthought, and not typical of the Williams logic. The unsympathetic conversion by the LCC architects (c1954) has detracted from the structural clarity of the original design.

Housing 1957–9 X11
The Hall, The Keep and
Corner Row; South Row,
Blackheath SE3
Eric Lyons for Span
⇌Blackheath

These three middle-class housing schemes have been widely copied in form and style. Span was a development company which attempted to modify the standard house-builder's pattern – separate or semi-detached houses set well back from engineer-designed estate roads with over-generous sight-lines and turning circles. Lyons' designs provide two- and three-storey rows of houses or flats loosely arranged among densely planted common gardens, with car movement and parking firmly relegated to the edge of the site. While the layouts have been widely and successfully copied, Lyons' architectural style, with its attempt to extend the range of materials usable for houses (by such

means as tilehanging and weatherboarding), later degenerated, and was perhaps partly responsible for the present ubiquitous Pixie style.

Housing 1974–8 X12
Westmoreland Road, Bromley
Edward Cullinan
⇌Bromley South

This six-storey building of thirty-six flats for a South London housing association has two façades. The front to the quiet suburban street attempts to evoke the classical villa, having a plinth, a principal floor and an attic storey. The composition is symmetrical, with a large double-height central entrance. The back, facing the common garden, is 'democratic', and the individual units are clearly expressed. The front, a rendered wall with openings, has two access galleries connected by stairs, with ramps to the street either side of the entrance forecourt.

The Great Estates

1 Audley
2 Battlebridge
3 Bedford
4 Berkeley
5 Berners
6 Brett
7 Brompton Hospital
8 Burlington
9 Cadogan
10 Campbell Cole
11 Campden Charities
12 Chelsea Hospital

13 Church Commissioners
14 City
15 Crooke
16 Crown
17 Clothworkers' Company
18 Conduit-Mead
19 Cubitt
20 Curzon
21 Day
22 De Beauvoir
23 Duchy of Cornwall
24 Earl of Camden

25 Earl of Listowell
26 Edwards
27 Eton College
28 Eyre
29 Foundling Hospital
30 Gascoigne
31 Gibson
32 Grand Junction Canal Company
33 Gray's Inn
34 Grosvenor
35 Haberdashers' Company
36 Hall

The London square: chronological map

Four model squares

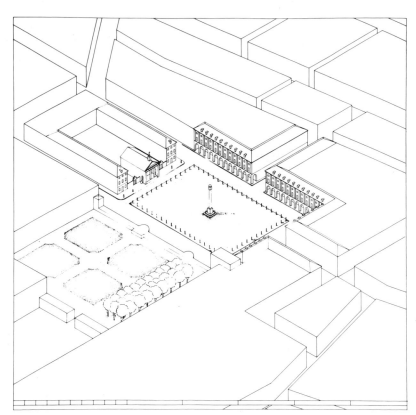

1631 Covent Garden Piazza K14 London's first real square, its arcades and name imported from Italy, was built by Inigo Jones under the patronage of the fourth Earl of Bedford. Jones's Etruscan temple K15, of 1631–8, forms the centrepiece on the west side.

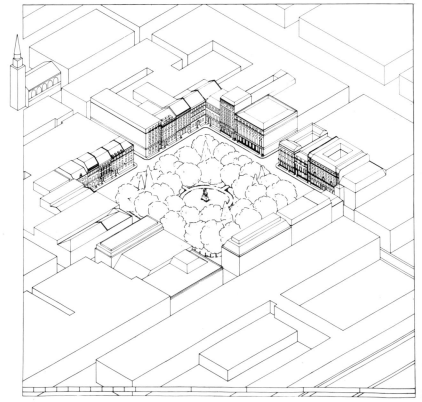

1665 St James's Square K18 The most regularly planned seventeenth-century square in London, entered through gated streets placed centrally on its sides. The vistas along these streets were later closed by monuments at their ends. The square was developed with individual houses of different designs.

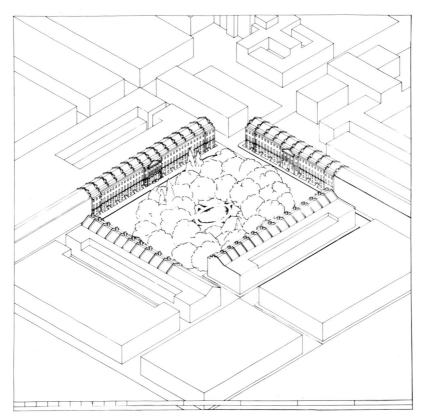

c1775 Bedford Square G12 The façades of the regular four-storey houses make a composition of four palaces facing each other across an oval garden, and the square is entered from its corners, rather than its sides, so connecting with the rest of Bloomsbury.

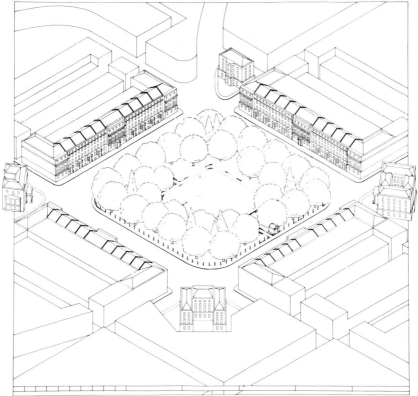

1825 Belgrave Square J23 Determined to break the mould of the Georgian square, Cubitt and Basevi introduced diagonally placed mansions, designed by individual architects, at the corners, and projecting porches to the varied elevations. The square was never gated.

Legal London
The Inns of Court: a continuous promenade from Theobald's Road to the Embankment

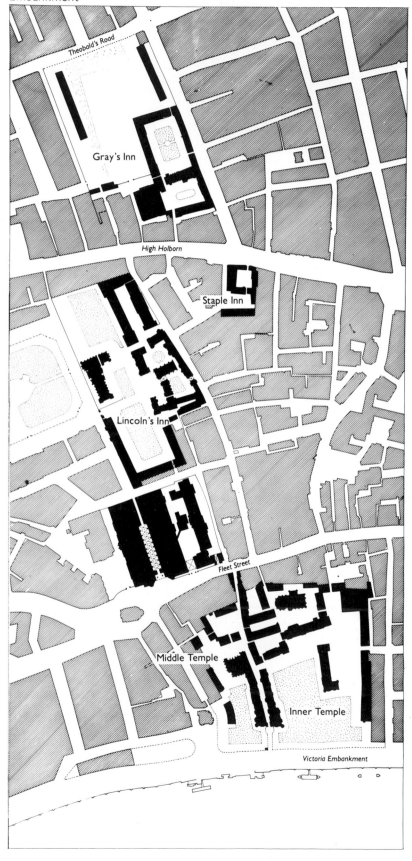

[handwritten:] ✗ Pevsner

Further Reading

The following books have been used as sources. Most of those in the first group are available in paperback, those in the second can be consulted in libraries.

Beattie, Susan *A Revolution in London Housing, LCC Architects and their Work 1893–1914* The Architectural Press, 1980
Cooke, Alistair and Robert Cameron *Above London* The Bodley Head, 1980
Cruickshank, Dan and Wyld, P *London: Art of Georgian Building* The Architectural Press, 1975
Downes, Kerry *Hawksmoor* Thames and Hudson, 1969
Fleming ed, *Penguin Dictionary of Architecture* new impression 1970
Frampton, Kenneth *Modern Architecture, a Critical History* Thames and Hudson, 1980
Hobhouse, Hermione *The History of Regent Street* McDonald & Janes, 1975
Olsen, Donald J *The Growth of Victorian London* Peregrine/Penguin, 1976
Pevsner, Sir Nikolaus *The Buildings of England: London* (2 vols) Penguin, 1957 and 1952 *[handwritten:] ✗*
Rasmussen, Steen Eiler *London, the Unique City* MIT Press, 1974
Service, Alastair *The Architects of London* Architectural Press, 1979
Service, Alastair *Edwardian Architecture* Thames and Hudson, 1977
Stamp, Gavin and Colin Amery *Victorian Buildings of London 1837–1887* Architectural Press, 1980
Stamp, Gavin ed. *Britain in the Thirties* Architectural Design Vol 149 no 10–11 1979
Stamp, Gavin ed. *London: 1900* Architectural Design Vol 48 no 5–6 1978
Summerson, John *Georgian London* Pelican, 1962 revised
Summerson, John *The Life and Work of John Nash: Architect* Allen & Unwin, 1980

Colvin, Howard *A Bibliographical Dictionary of British Architects 1660–1840* J Murray, 1978
Hitchcock, Henry-Russell *Early Victorian Architecture in Britain* (2 vols) The Architectural Press, 1954
LCC and the Survey of London Committee *The Survey of London* 40 vols, GLC ed Sir Francis Shepherd
Maxwell, Robert *New British Architecture* Thames & Hudson, 1952
Summerson, John *Sir John Soane* Art and Technics, 1952
Summerson, John *Architecture in Britain 1530 to 1830* Penguin, 1953

[handwritten:] For Pevsner See "Author's Acknowledgements" — at the very beginning of this book.

Acknowledgements

The authors would like to thank the following who have kindly supplied photographs and drawings (all other photographs by William Harrison and the authors):

Peter Bell C11, W15
Neave Brown R29
Richard Bryant K175, O17
London Borough of Camden A9, B36
Campbell Zogolovitch Wilkinson and Gough I30
Martin Charles A9, E12, O18, R29
David Chipperfield J79 (Jeremy Cockayne)
Colquhoun and Miller U30
Peter Cook I31, N37
Edward Cullinàn Architects C11, T34, X12
John Donat C10/1, U33
Erith and Terry V12
Evans and Shalev E10
Roy Fleetwood T3
Foster Associates C10/1, J79, T38, U33, U36, U37
François Gijzels G19, G25, J27, K2, K5, K12, K31, K34, K69, K93, K108, L96, N21, T6, T10, T11, T26, p18
Dennis Gilbert K176, U38, U39
Michael Gold S3
James Gowan U31/1, U31/2
Margot Griffin U2, U3, p14
Ben Haxworth G12, G38, R9, R26
Ron Herron G76
Michael Hopkins & Partners F59, L136
Tom Kay C10/2
Horst Kolo U50
Denys Lasdun, Peter Soffley & Associates K172
Desmond Lavery L132
Rolf Olsen B21
John Outram U41

Jo Reid and John Peck E13, F57, U42, U43, U44
Steve Reynolds H44
RIBA Drawings Collection G38, I9, K58, K90, L116, M4, T9, P20, P21, p24, p25, p31
Richard Rogers & Partners L111
Saatchi Collection E14
Jordi Sarra L134
Patrick Shanahan B6, F29, J44/1,2, J45, K67, K157/2, K157/3, L117/2, L117/3, N2, T16/3
By Courtesy of the Trustees of Sir John Soane's Museum K58, K67 (interior)
Michael Squire L138
James Stirling and Michael Wilford O5, P5, U29, p31
Weidenfeld and Nicolson Archives p9
YRM Architects and Planners H43, K166

Drawings were made by the following:

Roger Clarke, Christine Johnson, Ian Grant, Rachel Chidlow p6
Margot Griffin H6, J48, K2, K4, K6, K68, K69, L16, L18, L25, L29, L36, T6, W3, p9, p11, p15, p19, p23, p29
Di Hope and Kathy Kerr J23, K14, K18, pp420–26
Andreas Zannas G15

The photograph on page 403 is by Ian Graham and is reproduced by gracious permission of Her Majesty the Queen.

The maps on pages 9, 11, 15, 19, 23, 29 and 348–9 are based upon the Ordnance Survey maps, and the maps to sections A–P are reproduced at a scale of 1:12,500 from the Ordnance Survey's 1:10,000 series with the permission of the Controller of Her Majesty's Stationery Office, Crown Copyright reserved.

Index

Numbers alone refer to page numbers. References to entries consist of a letter and a number. Primary references are in **bold.**

434

Index of Building Types